Corwin on the
Constitution

Corwin on the Constitution

VOLUME THREE

On Liberty against Government

Edited with an Introduction
by RICHARD LOSS

 Cornell University Press, *Ithaca and London*

Copyright © 1988 by Cornell University

All rights reserved. Except for brief quotations in a review, this book, or parts thereof, must not be reproduced in any form without permission in writing from the publisher. For information, address Cornell University Press, 124 Roberts Place, Ithaca, New York 14850.

First published 1988 by Cornell University Press.

International Standard Book Number 0-8014-2176-4
Library of Congress Catalog Card Number 80-69823
Printed in the United States of America
*Librarians: Library of Congress cataloging information
appears on the last page of the book.*

*The paper in this book is acid-free and meets the guidelines for
permanence and durability of the Committee on Production Guidelines
for Book Longevity of the Council on Library Resources.*

For Kathy Loss

Contents

Preface

*Corwin on the Constitution Volume III: On Liberty against
Government* contains twelve essays on the limits of governmental power over
property and business, governmental action and personal and social rights, and a
nation and the states. My intention in editing *Corwin on the Constitution* has
been to include the essays that best delineate Corwin's argument in political
thought and constitutional law, and I have chosen these after carefully examining
his published work and the Corwin Papers at Princeton University.

I have excluded from this final volume three essays I had once planned to
include, two because they are of comparatively minor importance and one because Corwin's contribution could not be assessed independently of his co-
author's. For the sake of completeness I shall cite and briefly describe these
excluded essays. The first is "Constitutional Tax Exemption: The Power of
Congress to Tax Income from State and Municipal Bonds," 13 *National Civic
Review* 51–67 (1924). In this essay on tax reform Corwin concludes that "Congress should subject all future issues of national securities, as well as the incomes
therefrom, to the unimpeded operation of the general, non-discriminatory tax
laws of the states, and, on the other hand, claim a like operation for the national
income tax upon the incomes from all future state and municipal issues." The
second essay is "Sea Rights and Sea Power: The British Embargo," 204 *North
American Review* 515–30 (October, 1916), in which Corwin defined "the issue
which the British embargo presents our government at the present moment. . . .
Are we to resist it effectively and so preserve our trading rights and our neu-
trality, or are we passively to acquiesce in it and *pro tanto* surrender both these?"
The third essay, which Corwin co-authored with Mary Louise Ramsey, is "The
Constitutional Law of Constitutional Amendment," 26 *Notre Dame Lawyer*
185–213 (Winter, 1951). The essay's conclusion draws attention to the role of
Congress in determining the validity of ratification of constitutional amend-
ments: "To leave the way open for Congress to bury a proposed amendment

even after three-fourths of the states have approved it seems to be consonant with the purpose of the framers to permit changes in the fundamental law only when there is a strong preponderance of contemporaneous opinion in favor of it.''

For further understanding and appreciation of Corwin's thought, the reader is encouraged to consult the bibliography of Corwin's works and writings about him listed in Kenneth Crews, *Edward S. Corwin and the American Constitution: A Bibliographical Analysis* (1985).[1] A collection of Corwin's occasional writings which does not overlap with *Corwin on the Constitution* is *Corwin's Constitution: Essays and Insights of Edward S. Corwin* (Kenneth Crews ed. 1986).

I have made minor changes in the essays for consistency and ease of reading. I have standardized quotations from *The Federalist* according to Jacob Cooke's edition (1961), but semicolons replace dashes in the middle of a sentence, and ''Constitution'' (for the national Constitution) is always capitalized. I have used braces to distinguish my editorial comments in the text and notes from Corwin's brackets.

I am deeply grateful for permission to use the Regenstein Library and the Law School Library at the University of Chicago. Northwestern University Library also permitted me to use its collection. The National Endowment for the Humanities supported Volumes II and III of *Corwin on the Constitution* with a Fellowship for Independent Study and Research. Last but not least, the editors of the law reviews represented in these pages deserve special thanks for their cooperation.

RICHARD LOSS

Evanston, Illinois

1. For commentary on Corwin, see Richard G. Stevens, "The Constitution and What It Meant to Corwin," 10 *Political Science Reviewer* 1 (Fall, 1980); Gerald Garvey, "Edward S. Corwin in the Campaign of History: The Struggle for National Power in the 1930s," 34 *George Washington L. Rev.* 219 (December, 1965); Alfred S. Konefsky, "Men of Great and Little Faith: Generations of Constitutional Scholars," 30 *Buffalo L. Rev.* 365, 373–74 (Spring, 1981). For an alternative to Konefsky's economic interpretation of Corwin's thought, see by Richard Loss, "Introduction," *Presidential Power and the Constitution: Essays, by Edward S. Corwin* ix–xx (Richard Loss ed. 1976); "Edward S. Corwin: The Constitution of the Dominant Presidency," 7 *Presidential Studies Quarterly* 53–65 (Winter, 1977); "Alexander Hamilton and the Modern Presidency: Continuity or Discontinuity?" 12 *Presidential Studies Quarterly* 6–25 (Winter, 1982); and "Edward S. Corwin," in *Encyclopedia of the American Constitution* (Leonard Levy and Kenneth Karst eds. 1986).

Corwin on the
Constitution

Introduction

EDWARD S. CORWIN was born in 1878 near Plymouth, Michigan, and studied under Andrew C. McLaughlin, the distinguished constitutional historian, before graduating in 1900 from the University of Michigan. After study with the historian John Bach McMaster, Corwin received his doctorate in history in 1905 from the University of Pennsylvania. He was soon invited by Woodrow Wilson, then president of Princeton University, to become one of the original preceptors there. He continued to teach at Princeton until 1946. According to Alpheus T. Mason, Corwin's friend and successor as McCormick Professor of Jurisprudence at Princeton, as a teacher Corwin had the gift of "reaching within each person, of discovering something firm and worthwhile, of encouraging him to stand on it," and the skill "rare among teachers . . . to judge young men, not by what they are, but by what they may yet become."[1]

Corwin was president of the American Political Science Association, winner of the Benjamin Franklin Medal and the Henry M. Phillips Prize of the American Philosophical Society, and recipient of the Litt.D. degree from Harvard University in recognition of his scholarship. A prolific author, Corwin wrote eighteen books and numerous essays that appeared in legal and professional journals, in addition to editing the 1953 annotated *Constitution*. In 1935 he was constitutional adviser to the Public Works Administration, in 1936 special assistant, and in 1937 constitutional consultant to the attorney general. A biography of Corwin, which he reviewed before publication, stated that "in politics he is an independent." Corwin died in 1963.[2]

The essays in this volume are responsive to the theme of limitations on governmental power or, in Corwin's phrase, "liberty against government." They are organized into three parts: "The Limits of Governmental Power over Property

1. *A Princeton Companion* 119 (Alexander Leitch ed. 1978).
2. For a life of Corwin, see Kenneth Crews, *Edward S. Corwin and the American Constitution: A Bibliographical Analysis* 3–48 (1985).

13

and Business," "Governmental Action and Personal and Social Rights," and "A Nation and the States." The first essay in Part I is "The Basic Doctrine of American Constitutional Law" (1914), one of Corwin's most definitive essays. He teaches that the "main" purpose of constitutional law is "setting metes and bounds to legislative power." There are, Corwin tells us, two theories of the nature of the Constitution: rights limit governmental action; and the legislature has sovereign power. The "basic doctrine" of American constitutional law is the doctrine of vested rights, which assumes that "the property right is fundamental" and treats any law impairing vested rights as a bill of pains and penalties that is void. The doctrine of vested rights protected the right of someone who had already "acquired some title of control over some particular piece of property, in the physical sense, to continue in that control." Corwin distinguishes two forms of the doctrine of vested rights, the "milder and more flexible" and the "more abstract and rigorous."

The progress of the doctrine of vested rights was aided by the courts obscuring or obliterating essential distinctions such as between retrospective and prospective laws and between special and general acts. The doctrine of vested rights was also aided by the support it drew from other principles such as equality before the law. Of all principles that supported the doctrine of vested rights, the principle of separation of powers proved, at least before the Civil War, "of most varied and widest serviceability." The doctrine of vested rights, Corwin concludes, was "the first great achievement" of the courts after the establishment of judicial review. This doctrine "represented the essential spirit and point of view of the founders of American constitutional law, who saw before them the same problem that had confronted the Convention of 1787, namely, the problem of harmonizing majority rule with minority rights, or more specifically, republican institutions with the security of property, contracts, and commerce." Vested rights as a solution "met the needs and aspirations of a nation whose democracy was always tempered by the individualism of the free, prosperous Western world."

In "Social Insurance and Constitutional Limitations" (1917) Corwin challenges the indefeasibility of private rights. Social insurance means workmen's compensation and minimum wage laws. Corwin finds that the issue between the advocates of a rigorous and a lax interpretation of the Constitution is whether "legislation, which is otherwise well within the police power, is to be treated as invalid because of its incidental detriment to private rights." Corwin argues that the "judicial interpretation of the phrases 'liberty,' 'property,' and 'due process of law,' especially as these are used in the Fourteenth Amendment, leaves judicial control of state legislation with none but the vaguest limits." His essay illustrates "the triumph of 'laxism' in our constitutional law," but constitutional rigorism "still maintains certain outposts from which it must be dislodged, if our system of constitutional limitations is to be adapted to the needs of modern complex society." The constitutional validity of social insurance laws "depends . . . upon the existence of 'a real, a substantial' relation between a well considered measure embodying the idea and the public welfare, or rather, perhaps, upon the existence of a widespread public conviction that there is such a relation.'' Corwin relies upon ''an intelligent tribunal'' to uphold social insurance laws. Summing up the state of the law, Corwin says that ''constitutional 'rigorism' is at an end.''

''Social Planning under the Constitution—A Study in Perspectives'' (1932) is Corwin's presidential address to the 1931 meeting of the American Political Science Association. His essay responds to ''our present discontents'' or the Great Depression of the 1930s. His thesis is that ''there must be . . . in the long run a considerable measure'' of social planning—''either that or social dissolution, or a social order based on rather obvious force.'' He asks, ''What part is political science prepared to take in social planning?'' The answer depends ''to some extent'' on what is meant by social planning. Any defensible social plan must both consult the experience of businessmen and apply sanctions against the ''present structure of business.'' Any ''viable'' plan touching business in an important way must rely upon sanctions which only the national government can apply effectively. ''Planning means coercion for intransigent minorities—that at least—and if coercion is to be applied by the national government, it must usually be under the commerce clause.''

''What sanctions does the Constitution, that is to say, constitutional law, permit?'' Corwin argues that the ''present-day edifice of American constitutional law dates to an altogether unappreciated extent from this side of the year 1890.'' The October term of 1894 was one of the two terms of the Supreme Court that ''stand out above all others for the significance of their results to American constitutional law.'' In this term were decided the Sugar Trust case, the Income Tax cases and *In re* Debs. ''Nor would it be easy to conceive how three decisions could possibly have been more to the liking of business.'' By assimilating the interstate commerce of the sugar monopoly to the local process of manufacturing, the Sugar Trust decision paralyzed the Sherman Anti-Trust Act for a decade. In the Income Tax cases the Supreme Court ''seriously diminished'' the taxing powers of Congress, and *In re* Debs drastically expanded the power of the president and the courts to protect property.

Corwin chronicles the Supreme Court's laissez-faire decisions that established ''new restrictions on legislative power in control of business and property.'' Against this trend, Corwin argues that ''all businesses whose operations extend beyond the boundary lines of a single state should be regarded as subject through their interstate commercial activities to the control of Congress fairly and reasonably exercised.'' The state governments, Corwin holds, are unable in law and in fact to exercise effective control over interstate commerce. Corwin briefly notices the Supreme Court's work from 1905 to 1920. In the field of state legislation the ''outstanding achievement'' was workmen's compensation; in national legislation the outstanding achievement was the reconstitution of the Interstate Commerce Commission and the "immense" enlargement of its powers. The Court lent a "helpful hand" to both developments.

Judicial review and constitutional limitations "do not today assume the obstructive proportions that on first consideration might be expected." With the deadlock between the Supreme Court and President Franklin D. Roosevelt only years away, Corwin finds that constitutional law is "more flexible . . . than it has been at any time within forty years." The Supreme Court is more aware than "ever before" of the legislative character of its task, and a wider public is also aware of these facts. Corwin concludes that "political factors . . . are much more serious obstacles to 'social planning' than is our system of constitutional law." His examples of the political factors are the "ramshackle character" of Congress, the "imbecility" of the American party system, and the "entire lack of assurance of qualified political leadership which these conditions breed."

The thesis of "The New Deal in the Light of American Political and Constitutional Ideas," a previously unpublished 1936 address before an audience of lawyers, is that "criticism of the New Deal, well-grounded as it may be in other respects, fails in its endeavor to range it against American political ideas and ideals." Such criticism ignores "the fact that the very condition of survival is change and adaptation." Corwin sums up the creed of eighteenth- and nineteenth-century liberalism: "Man and his happiness are the fixed points of reference—all else is relative, and hence subject to alteration, amendment, or rejection, as circumstances may require." For Corwin liberalism understands both government and economic institutions as instrumental. Hence the proper relationship of government to business is simply a question of ways and means.

Corwin asks, what relationship of government to business is "best calculated to achieve the happiness in the long run of the American nation?" The American liberal tradition divides into the individualistic-localistic tradition of Jeffersonian democracy and the nationalistic–strong government policy of Hamiltonian federalism. Corwin finds that Hamilton and Jefferson sought the same end, the national good, but disagreed on the intermediate objective. Moreover, the Constitution was made by mercantilists, "by men who were entirely hospitable to the idea of governmental intervention in the realm of economics." Corwin gives examples of governmental intervention in the economic field throughout American history; these examples are intended to discredit laissez faire as an explanation of how government has behaved toward the economy. Corwin is "frank to declare that I regard it {the New Deal} as entirely defensible, even commendable from the point of view of the history of American political thought and action."

Corwin attributes the Great Depression to poor human judgment on the part of government and business and to the inherent limitations of business management in a nationalized economy. He looks favorably upon such comprehensive reforms as the Guffey Coal Conservation Act, the Social Security Act, and the

Wagner Labor Act. The New Deal proposals do not, he argues, represent a radical or revolutionary break from past public policy and constitutional interpretation. Corwin argues that although John Locke is the "philosopher *par excellence* of the American Revolution," his understanding of property is "for the most part irrelevant to any discussion of the political morality of the New Deal." Corwin concludes, however, that the purpose of the New Deal proposals "is much more fairly represented as an effort to realize the Lockean and early American conception of property, as individual possession of the comforts and decencies of life, than as an attempt to overthrow it."

The first essay under the topic "Governmental Action and Personal and Social Rights" is "Freedom of Speech and Press under the First Amendment: A Résumé" (1920). In this essay Corwin takes issue with the understanding of the First Amendment espoused by "our modern liberals," such as Zechariah Chafee, Jr. The "main purpose" of the essay is to examine the historical foundations of the understanding of the First Amendment that denies the common law doctrine of seditious libel, which marked as criminal all publications tending to bring church or state, or the officers of government, or the administration of the law, into contempt. Corwin's modestly titled "résumé" is in tune with the recent research of the well-known constitutional historian Leonard Levy, who writes in *Emergence of a Free Press*: "My principal thesis remains unchanged. I still aim to demolish the proposition formerly accepted in both law and history that it was the intent of the American Revolution or the Framers of the First Amendment to abolish the common law of seditious libel."[3]

Sir William Blackstone defined freedom of the press as freedom from restraint prior to publication, but his notion included the common law doctrine of seditious libel. Corwin finds that state constitutions asserting broad liberty of the press in the nineteenth-century still allowed prosecutions for seditious libel. He sums up his argument with the following propositions: first, Congress may forbid words that are intended to endanger national interests if a fair legislative discretion finds it "necessary and proper" to do so; second, the intent of the accused may be presumed from the reasonable consequences of his words; third, the Supreme Court will not review more strictly on appeal the jury findings in speech and press cases than in other penal cases. "In short, the cause of freedom of speech and press is largely in the custody of legislative majorities and juries, which, so far as there is evidence to show, is just where the framers of the Constitution intended it to be." In 1940 Corwin wrote of a citizen's freedom to express his opinions: "Yet even such rights, it is necessary to insist, must always depend for their most complete and beneficial realization much more upon the ordinary law as it comes from the legislature than upon the extraordinary inter-

---

3. Leonard Levy, *Emergence of a Free Press* xii (1985). This book is a revised and enlarged edition of Levy's *Legacy of Suppression* (1960). The bibliography cites Corwin's article, but the index fails to mention Corwin.

ventions of the Court."[4] Corwin, in his understanding of the Bill of Rights and the First Amendment, could agree with the late Herbert J. Storing: "The Bill of Rights provides a fitting close to the parenthesis around the Constitution that the preamble opens. But the substance is a design of government with powers to act and a structure arranged to make it act wisely and responsibly. It is in that design, not in its preamble or epilogue, that the security of American civil and political liberty lies."[5]

In "Bowing Out 'Clear and Present Danger' " (1952), Corwin finds that the origin of the clear and present danger test is a "dictum tossed off" by Justice Oliver Wendell Holmes, Jr., in an opinion upholding a conviction under the Espionage Act of 1917, Schenck v. United States (1919). Corwin asks, what is the future of the clear and present danger test after Dennis v. United States (1951)? The "outstanding result" of the Dennis holding is that of "a declaration of independence by the Court from the tyranny of a phrase." "It can be safely said that never again will the rule be successfully invoked in behalf of persons shown to have conspired to incite to a breach of federal law." Corwin concludes that the clear and present danger test may still be applicable in (1) trivial cases; (2) cases in which the speaker's intent is lawful but circumstances create a danger of substantive evils which government may prevent; and (3) cases in which the speech is ambiguous and "the evil purpose of the speaker can be reasonably inferred only from the 'clear and present danger' of evil which the utterance engenders."[6]

In "The Supreme Court as National School Board" (1949) Corwin criticizes the Supreme Court's decision in McCollum v. Board of Education, 333 U.S. 203 (1948). He first argues that the justification for the Court's intervention was "trivial" and contrary to previous restrictions on judicial review. The decision is based on a "figure of speech," the idea of a "wall of separation between Church and State." The McCollum decision stems from an unhistorical understanding of the meaning of establishment of religion in the First Amendment. The prohibition of the establishment of religion by Congress is not convertible into a similar prohibition on the states, under the Fourteenth Amendment, "unless the term 'establishment of religion' be given an application which carries with it invasion of somebody's freedom of religion, that is, of 'liberty.' " The McCollum decision, moreover, created "great uncertainty" in the school boards of forty-six states and twenty-two hundred communities. Finally, Corwin asks: "Is the decision favorable to democracy? Primarily democracy is a system of ethical values, and that this system of values so far as the American people are concerned is

4. Edward S. Corwin, "Liberty and Juridical Restraint," *Freedom: Its Meaning* 103 (Ruth N. Anshen ed. 1940).

5. Herbert J. Storing, "The Constitution and the Bill of Rights," *How Does the Constitution Secure Rights?* 35 (Robert Goldwin and William Schambra eds. 1985).

6. For a consideration of subversion and the Constitution, see Robert A. Horn, *Groups and the Constitution* (1971; 1956). This book was dedicated to Corwin.

grounded in religion will not be denied by anyone who knows the historical record." Corwin's phrase "a Constitution of powers in a secular state" adequately sums up the results of decisions such as McCollum.

The subject of "The Supreme Court's Construction of the Self-Incrimination Clause" (1930) is primarily the self-incrimination clause of the Fifth Amendment. This provision owes nothing to canon law. Rather, the maxim that nobody is bound to accuse himself appeared in England toward the end of the sixteenth century during the struggle between the common law courts and the Court of High Commission over the latter's claim to penal jurisdiction.[7] Corwin traces the gradual strengthening of the self-incrimination protection in English law before taking up the history of the clause in American constitutional law. He finds the first statement of protection against self-incrimination in America in the Virginia Declaration of Rights of 1776. In Boyd v. United States (1886) the Supreme Court unanimously held that the self-incrimination clause applied to the forced production in court by a person of his private papers to be used in evidence against himself. Corwin argues that "the precise holding in the Boyd case is today bad law" because the "invoice whose forced production gave rise to the Boyd case would today be subject to seizure under a proper search warrant." On the other hand, Corwin called Boyd v. United States "the great creative act of the Supreme Court" in its understanding of the self-incrimination clause because the Court linked the clause with the Fourth Amendment's provision against unreasonable searches and seizures.

The second Supreme Court decision of fundamental importance in understanding the self-incrimination clause is Counselman v. Hitchcock (1892). The case emerged out of a grand jury investigation instituted by the Interstate Commerce Commission into alleged violations by railroads of the statutes regulating interstate commerce. The Supreme Court upheld the witness Counselman's plea against self-incrimination: "No statute which leaves the party or witness subject to prosecution after he answers the incriminating question put to him can have the effect of supplanting the privilege conferred by the Constitution of the United States." Corwin argues that "the two least defensible features of the Court's system of doctrine in this field of constitutional law" are the rule in the Boyd decision forbidding search under a warrant of a person's premises for things solely of evidential value against such person, and the rule of the Counselman decision which classifies as incriminating evidence that which is likely to lead to the discovery of such evidence. The Counselman decision "adds a new resource to conscious guilt" and increases the difficulty of judicial supervision of the constitutional privilege of witnesses. Corwin concludes that "there are other features of our constitutional organization which hamper society in its war

7. See Leonard Levy, *Origins of the Fifth Amendment: The Right against Self-Incrimination* (1968). "The origins of the right against self-incrimination are English" (p. ix). See page 331 for the Court of High Commission. The bibliography omits reference to Corwin's article.

against crime more materially than does the Supreme Court's interpretation of the Fourth and Fifth Amendments, the 'federal system' itself being one of them."

The first essay in Part III, "A Nation and the States," is "National Power and State Interposition, 1787–1861" (1912). This essay lacks an explicit thesis, but Corwin is concerned to trace the theoretical source of President James Buchanan's doctrine that the national government, once expelled from a state, lacked the constitutional authority to subdue that state by force. Corwin argues that James Madison's doctrine of interposition in the Virginia Resolutions of 1798 was the origin of Buchanan's message of December 3, 1860. The doctrine that the Constitution was a compact of sovereign states was "the basic foundation of all theories upon which secession proceeded, as well as of that doctrine which initially paralyzed the national government in dealing with it." In "no sense" was this opinion shared by the founders of the Constitution, who believed that the Constitution was a compact among the people of the United States. Moreover, the founders furnished the Constitution and the national government with the means of self-preservation in the clause defining treason against the United States, in the clause authorizing the president to call out the militia to suppress "insurrection," and in the clause authorizing Congress to "pass all laws necessary and proper for carrying into execution the foregoing powers." Corwin concludes that it was the misfortune of President Buchanan and Attorney General Jeremiah Black that "instead of resorting to the true and authoritative sources of constitutional construction, they pinned their faith upon the unsuccessful views of a protesting minority,—views that had been framed largely for political effect under the brilliant but irresponsible direction of an opportunist doctrinaire." Corwin may have identified Thomas Jefferson as the guilty party because of his influence over James Madison.

The opening section of Article IV of the Constitution, also known as the "federal Article," reads as follows: "Full faith and credit shall be given in each state to the public acts, records, and judicial proceedings of every other state. And the Congress may by general laws prescribe the manner in which such acts, records and proceedings shall be proved, and the effect thereof." In "The 'Full Faith and Credit' Clause" (1933) Corwin concludes that it may be "seriously doubted" whether the application of this provision by the Supreme Court and Congress met the expectations of the founders, whose main concern was to render the judgments of state courts in civil cases effective throughout the Union. "Indeed," Corwin summarizes, "there are few clauses of the Constitution, the merely literal possibilities of which have been so little developed as the 'full faith and credit' clause."

The question raised in "National-State Cooperation—Its Present Possibilities" (1937) is "what species of national-state relationship do the . . . 'fixed data' of dual federalism admit of?" Except for the period immediately preceding the Civil War, Corwin finds that cooperative federalism has "generally prevailed" over competitive federalism. The Articles of Confederation held that the powers of the general government would be exercised through the state governments, a hope that was not realized in practice. The founders of the Constitution, on the other hand, anticipated a mixture of functional and dual federalism—"one which would permit the gradual transference of the greater part of the legislative power to the national government, while incorporating the judicial and executive organs of the states into the national administrative mechanism." In practice the relationship between the nation and the states, as in federal grants-in-aid, is one of "cooperation and reciprocal service." Corwin sees in the idea of national-state cooperation "a way of retreat in certain instances from the difficulties created by embarrassing precedents" of the Supreme Court.

"The Passing of Dual Federalism" (1950), the concluding essay in this volume, summarizes "the impact of a series of events and ideological forces of a very imperative nature." Corwin argues that "our system has lost resiliency and what was once vaunted as a Constitution of rights, both state and private, has been replaced by a Constitution of powers" lodged in the national government. "The Passing of Dual Federalism" deals with the shift of the federal system in the direction of "a consolidated national power." Corwin asks: "In just what fashion . . . has the shift . . . of our federal system toward consolidation registered itself in our constitutional law in response to the requirements of war, economic crisis and a fundamentally altered outlook upon the purpose of government?" The answer is found in the changed attitude of the Supreme Court toward certain axioms of constitutional interpretation touching the federal system that compose what Corwin means by dual federalism. These axioms are (1) the national government has only enumerated powers; (2) the national government may constitutionally promote only few purposes; (3) the nation and the states are sovereign and, hence, equal within their respective spheres; and (4) tension rather than collaboration characterizes the relations of the nation and the states.

Corwin finds that the doctrine of enumerated powers had become a "very shaky reliance" when applied to Chief Justice John Marshall's "great, substantive and independent powers," power over foreign policy, the power to levy taxes, the power to spend tax revenue, and the power over commercial relations. Moreover, the Supreme Court decided United States v. Butler (1939) in line with Hamilton's broad theory of the spending power. The germ of the notion of national-state equality was the theory of the Constitution's origin found in the Virginia and Kentucky Resolutions, which held that the Constitution was a compact of "sovereign" states instead of an ordinance of the people of America. In the period of laissez faire down to 1936, the Supreme Court held that certain subject matters—production, mining, agriculture, manufacturing, and the employer-employee relationship—could not be reached by national power. Today, Corwin argues, "this entire system of constitutional interpretation touching the federal system is . . . in ruins," thanks to the Supreme Court's decisions in the Social Security Act cases, N.L.R.B. v. Jones and Laughlin Steel Corporation, and United States v. Darby.

Today the competitive idea of federalism is "largely moribund" as a result of the rise of cooperative federalism, according to which the national and state governments are "mutually complementary parts of a single governmental mechanism all of whose powers are intended to realize the current purposes of government according to their applicability to the problem in hand." Corwin concludes that one objection to cooperative federalism is "more difficult to meet, if indeed it can be met." Cooperative federalism "unquestionably" means "further aggrandizement of national power." Corwin praises Justice Felix Frankfurter's protest against the "absorption of legislative power by the United States over every activity" as "brave words. Are they likely to determine the course of future history any more than Madison's similar utterance—130 years ago—has done to date?"

Volume III of *Corwin on the Constitution* follows the inquiry of Volume I into the foundations of American constitutional and political thought, the powers of Congress, and the president's removal power, and the inquiry of Volume II into the origins of judicial review, the development of judicial supremacy, the exercise of judicial review, and appraisals of judicial review. The essays on constitutional and political thought in Volume I address fundamental questions of the Constitution, democracy, and natural and higher law. The argument of my introduction to Volume I may be stated in brief. Corwin objected to "constitutional worship," by which he understood popular veneration of the Constitution's principles and the statesman's use of the founders' political science. Corwin argued in effect that President Lincoln ended constitutional worship and made opinion about the Constitution more democratic and realistic than the founders' political science.

For Corwin the problem of higher law was to a large extent whether unchangeable standards, superior to the will of human rulers, existed to guide legislators. His famous essay "The 'Higher Law' Background of American Constitutional Law" discouraged belief in the higher law by weakly defending it against the analytical school's separation of what is legal from what is just. Corwin also accepted the positive idea of law and historicism or the dependence of thought on its historical setting. In effect Corwin tried to show that higher law was an illusion because no unchangeable standards existed to guide human legislators. Together with his criticism of constitutional worship and his rejection of higher law, Corwin advocated popular sovereignty and an instrumental Constitution. Corwin deliberately replaced the founders' political science and higher law with the idea of progress, an instrumental Constitution, majority rule, and a dominant presidency. Corwin's late defense of natural law was limited and flawed because he defended natural law against Mr. Justice Holmes and the legal positivists without replying to the more important objections of historicism and egalitarianism.

The essays of Volume II have a natural unity in dealing with the judicial article of the Constitution, Article III. Volume II is a sequel to Volume I, which treated

Articles I and II of the Constitution, and to *Presidential Power and the Constitution: Essays by Edward S. Corwin* (Richard Loss ed. 1976), which collected most of Corwin's essays on the presidency. The essays of Volume II of *Corwin on the Constitution* show Corwin traveling full circle from his early rationalistic account of judicial review and complimentary attitude toward the founders' intention through his criticism of the founders' intention to end up criticizing the moral basis of the New Deal according to Chief Justice John Marshall's political thought.

The essays on the exercise of judicial review in Volume II are of more than routine interest. "Constitution v. Constitutional Theory" (1925), one of Corwin's most important essays, attacks the founders' intention in constitutional interpretation. He concludes that ideas of the founders' intention, "whatever their historical basis—and that is frequently most precarious—have no application to the main business of constitutional interpretation, which is to keep the Constitution adjusted to the advancing needs of the time." Corwin concedes that his criticism departs from the opinion of the average Supreme Court justice, who takes the founders' intention "very seriously." One might accept his criticism of the Supreme Court's historical scholarship without being compelled totally to reject the founders' intention.

Corwin's alternative to the founders' intention is the popular will explanation of the Constitution's supremacy and authority. He understands the Constitution as a law deriving "all" of its force "from the people of the United States of this day and hour." Corwin's alternative to both the founders' intention and higher law was an almost wholly popular and majoritarian Constitution. His defense of the New Deal, however, conceded that "it is a good point—. . . a written Constitution was devised with the idea of putting certain limits on the power of the legislature." The essays of Volume II unintentionally demonstrate the difficulty of finding an alternative to the founders' intention as a guide to what Thomas Reed Powell, a scholar near Corwin's rank, called the "way of wisdom in making an indefinite series of practical judgments." The Corwin of Volume II failed to replace the founders' intention with anything more solid than what Powell termed "Mr. Corwin's chaotic conception of the scope of national power."[8] One of the delights of studying Corwin's essays, Volumes I to III, is that he scouts the alternative to the living Constitution he defended in the 1920s and 1930s. In many respects Corwin is his own most cogent critic.

8. Thomas Reed Powell, "Comment on Mr. Corwin's Paper," 19 *APSR* 305, at 300 (May, 1925).

I.

THE LIMITS OF GOVERNMENTAL POWER OVER PROPERTY AND BUSINESS

1. The Basic Doctrine of American Constitutional Law

THE two leading doctrines of American constitutional law before the Civil War, affecting state legislative power, were the doctrine of vested rights and the doctrine of the police power. The two doctrines are in a way complementary concepts, inasmuch as they represent the reaction upon each other of the earlier conflicting theories of natural rights and legislative sovereignty. But the older doctrine is the doctrine of vested rights, which may be said to have flourished before the rise of the Jacksonian Democracy. Furthermore, if constitutional law be regarded from the point of view of its main purpose, namely, that of setting metes and bounds to legislative power, it is the more fundamental doctrine.

Judicial review, we are told repeatedly, rests only upon the written constitution. We shall find ample reason presently to impugn the accuracy of this assertion, particularly for that most important formative period when the tree of constitutional law was receiving its initial bent. But letting it for the moment pass unchallenged, the question still remains, what is a constitution for—does it exist to grant power or to organize it? The former of these views is undoubtedly the older one, not only of the national Constitution, but of the state constitutions as well. For the written constitution, wherever found, was at first regarded as a species of social compact, entered into by sovereign individuals in a state of nature. From this point of view, however, governmental authority, wherever centered, is a trust which, save for the grant of it effected by the written constitution, were nonexistent, and private rights, since they precede the constitution, gain nothing of authoritativeness from being enumerated in it, though possibly something of security. These rights are not, in other words, fundamental because they find mention in the written instrument; they find mention there because {they are} fundamental. Suppose then the enumeration of such rights to have

From 12 *Michigan Law Review* 247–76 (1914). Reprinted by permission.

been but partial and incomplete, does that fact derogate from the rights not so enumerated? Article IX of the amendments to the United States Constitution answers this question. The written Constitution is, in short, but a nucleus or core of a much wider region of private rights, which, though not reduced to black and white, are as fully entitled to the protection of government as if defined in the minutest detail.

And by the other view of the written Constitution, whether the so-called "natural rights" were enumerated or not was also a matter of indifference, but for precisely the opposite reason. By this view too the Constitution was in a certain sense a grant of power, since government always rests upon the consent of the governed. The power granted, however, was not simply this or that item of specifically designated power but the sum total of that unrestrained sovereignty which in the state of nature was each man's dower. By the very act of calling government into existence, or more accurately, the legislative branch of government, this vast donation of power was conferred upon it, and irretrievably too, save for the right of revolution. Thus, whereas by the first view a constitution is wrapped about, so to say, by an ocean of rights, by this view it is enclosed in an enveloping principle of sovereign power. It thus follows first, that the mere coexistence of three departments within a written constitution leaves the legislature absolute, and secondly, that a mere enumeration of rights in the written constitution leaves them subject to legislative definition. Only by pretty specific provision of the written constitution is the legislative power, by this view, to be held in leash, even with judicial review a recognized institution, and the maxim that all doubts are to be resolved in its favor is to be taken for all that it seems to mean.

But let us consider the effect of these two theories of the nature of the Constitution upon the question of the scope of judicial review more directly. The two theories were brought into juxtaposition in the classic case of Calder v. Bull,[1] which was decided by the Supreme Court in 1798. In that case an act of the Connecticut legislature setting aside a decree of a probate court and granting a new hearing for the benefit of those claiming under a will was denounced by the heirs at law as *ex post facto* and so void under Art. I, section 10 of the United States Constitution. The Court rejected this view, holding partly upon the authority of Blackstone, partly upon the *usus loquendi* of the state constitutions, and partly on that of the United States Constitution, that the prohibition in question did not extend to all "retrospective" legislation, but only to enactments making what were innocent acts when they were done criminal or aggravating the legal character and penalty of past acts. The prohibition was intended, said Justice Chase, "to secure the *person* of the subject from injury or *punishment,* in consequence of such a law." It was not intended to secure the citizen in his "*personal rights,*" i.e., "his *private rights,* of either *property* or *contracts.*"

Whether this construction of the *ex post facto* clause of Art. I, section 10 met

---

1. 3 Dall. 386 (1798).

the intentions of the framers of the Constitution is an open question.[2] But it is certain that it did not entirely satisfy the Court that made it. Said Justice Paterson: "I had an ardent desire to have extended the provision in the Constitution to retrospective laws in general. There is neither policy nor safety in such laws." Justice Chase's condemnation was hardly less sweeping. He admitted that there were "cases in which laws may justly and for the benefit of the community, and also of individuals, relate to a time antecedent to their commencement, as statutes of oblivion, or of pardon," but statutes taking away or impairing "*rights vested,* agreeably to existing laws," were also "retrospective," "generally unjust," and "oppressive." Nor was it at all his intention to throw open the doors to such legislation. True the *ex post facto* clause bore a narrow technical meaning, but other clauses of the same section were of broader application: the clause prohibiting states from making laws impairing the obligation of contracts and that prohibiting them from making anything but gold or silver a legal tender. Furthermore there were certain fundamental principles of the social compact and republican government.

"I cannot subscribe," wrote Justice Chase in a passage which must be regarded as furnishing American constitutional law with its leavening principle, "to the *omnipotence* of a *state legislature,* or that it is *absolute* and *without* control, although its authority should not be *expressly* restrained by the *constitution or fundamental law* of the state. The people of the United States erected their constitutions . . . to establish justice, to promote the general welfare, to secure the blessing of liberty, and to protect persons and property from violence. The purposes for which men enter into society will determine the nature and terms of the social compact; and as they are the foundation of the legislative power, they will decide the proper objects of it. The *nature* and *ends* of *legislative* power will limit the *exercise* of it. . . . There are acts which the federal or state legislatures cannot do without exceeding their authority. There are certain vital principles in our free republican governments which will determine and overrule an apparent and flagrant abuse of legislative power. . . . An *Act* of the legislature (for I cannot call it a *law*) contrary to the great principles of the social compact cannot be considered a rightful exercise of legislative authority. . . . A law that punishes an innocent action . . .; a law that destroys, or impairs the lawful private contracts of citizens; a law that makes a man a judge in his own cause; or a law that takes *property* from A and gives it to B: it is against all reason and justice for a people to entrust a legislature with *such* powers; and therefore it cannot be presumed that they have done it. The *genius,* the *nature,* and the *spirit* of our state governments amount to a prohibition of such acts of legislation; and the *general principles of law and reason* forbid them." To hold otherwise were a "political heresy" "altogether inadmissible."

This appeal from the strict letter of the Constitution to general principles Chase's associate Iredell, on the other hand, flatly pronounced invalid. True,

2. See 2 Farrand, *Records of the Federal Convention* 368, 375, 378, 448, 571, 596, 610, 617, 656 {title hereinafter *Records*}; 3 *Records* 165. See also note by Johnson, J., in 2 Pet. 681 (1829).

"some speculative jurists" had held "that a legislative act against the natural justice must, in itself, be void," but the correct view was that if "a government composed of legislative, executive and judicial departments were established by a constitution which imposed no limits on the legislative power . . . whatever the legislative power chose to enact would be lawfully enacted, and the judicial power could never interpose to pronounce it void. . . . Sir William Blackstone, having put the strong case of an act of Parliament which should explicitly authorize a man to try his own cause, explicitly adds that even in that case 'there is no court that has the power to defeat the intent of the legislature' " when couched in unmistakable terms.[3] Besides, "the ideas of natural justice are regulated by no fixed standard: the ablest and purest men have differed upon the subject; and all that the court could properly say in such an event, would be that the legislature (possessed of an equal right of opinion) had passed an act which, in the opinion of the judges, was inconsistent with the abstract principles of justice."

Now which of these two views of the range of judicial power under the Constitution has finally prevailed? In appearance, Iredell's has, but in substance, as I have already hinted, it is Chase's theory that his triumphed. The evidence for both these propositions is to be found in Cooley's *Constitutional Limitations*.[4] Dealing with the subject "of the circumstances under which a legislative enactment may be declared unconstitutional," Cooley writes: "If the courts are not at liberty to declare statutes void because of their apparent injustice or impolicy, neither can they do so because they appear to the minds of the judges to violate fundamental principles of republican government, *unless it shall be found that those principles are placed beyond the legislative encroachment by the Constitution*. . . . Nor are the courts at liberty to declare an act void, because in their opinion it is opposed to a *spirit* supposed to pervade the Constitution, *but not expressed in words*." Farther along but still dealing with the same topic, he continues: "It is to be borne in mind . . . that there is a broad difference between the Constitution of the United States and the constitutions of the states as regards the power which may be exercised under them. The government of the United States is one of *enumerated* powers; the governments of the states are possessed of all the general powers of legislation. . . . We look in the Constitution of the United States for *grants* of legislative power, but in the constitution of the state to ascertain if any limitations have been imposed upon the complete power with which the legislative department of the state was vested in its creation."

And thus far the victory seems to rest with Iredell's view,—but it is in appearance only, as we immediately discover. For whatever terms he may use at times, it is as far as possible from Cooley's intention to admit in any real sense

3. 1 *Comm.* 91.
4. Cooley, *Constitutional Limitations* (1st ed.) 169–73; (7th ed.) 237–42.

the principle of legislative sovereignty. Thus he proceeds: *"It does not follow however, that in every case the courts, before they can set aside a law as invalid, must be able to find in the constitution some specific inhibition which has been disregarded, or some express command which has been disobeyed. Prohibitions are only important when they are in the nature of exceptions to a general grant of powers; and if the authority to do an act has not been granted by the sovereign to its representative, it cannot be necessary to prohibit its being done."* But he has just said that a state constitution exists to limit the *otherwise plenary* power of the legislature. How explain this apparent contradiction? An explanation has already been supplied by a quotation from the New York decision of Sill v. Corning.[5] The object of the constitution, runs the passage quoted, "is not to grant legislative power, but to confine and restrain it. Without constitutional limitations, the power to make laws would be absolute. These limitations are created and imposed by the express words, *or, arise by necessary implication. The leading feature of the constitution is the separation and distinction of the powers of the government. It takes care to separate the executive, legislative and judicial powers and to define their limits."* In a word the power which is conferred upon the legislature is the *legislative* power, and no other. This single phrase tells the tale. It is no longer good form, because it is no longer necessary, for a court to invoke natural rights and the social compact in a constitutional decision. But the same result is achieved by construing the very term by which "legislative power" is conferred upon the legislature. Such doctrine plainly has nothing in common with that of Iredell. His theory was that in a constitution which should stop short with creating the three departments of government, the legislative power would be absolute. The doctrine espoused by Cooley, on the other hand, reposes the main structure of constitutional law upon the simple fact of the coexistence of the three departments in the same Constitution. Natural rights, expelled from the front door of the Constitution are readmitted through the doctrine of the separation of powers. And what does this fact signify for judicial review? The answer is self-evident. Once it was recognized that to define "legislative power" finally and authoritatively lay with the courts, the power of judicial review became limited only by the discretion of the judges and the operation of the doctrine of *stare decisis*. The history of judicial review is, in other words, the history of constitutional limitations.

Preliminary, however, to entering upon this story, it is necessary for us to turn back a little way to supply a phase of the topic just under discussion. The date of the decision in Sill v. Corning was 1857 and Cooley's great work did not appear until 1868. Such recognition moreover as is accorded the principle of legislative sovereignty in these places, slight and banal as upon investigation it is seen to be, was due to developments lying this side the formative period of American constitutional law, in fact to developments that brought that period to a close.

5. 15 N.Y. 297, 303 (1857). See also Weister v. Hade, 52 Pa. St. 474, 477 (1866).

Despite therefore his tone of disparagement for the views of "speculative jurists," if we are to judge of views from their comparative success in establishing themselves in practice, it was Iredell himself who was "speculative." The fact of the matter is that Iredell's tenet that courts were not to appeal to natural rights and the social compact as furnishing a basis for constitutional decisions was disregarded by all the leading judges and advocates of the early period of our constitutional history. Marshall, it is true, had imbibed from Blackstone's pages much the same point of view as had Iredell. But on the crucial occasion of his decision in Fletcher v. Peck,[6] he freely appealed to "the nature of society and government" as setting "limits to the legislative power," and putting the significant query, "How far the power of giving the law may involve every other power," proceeded to answer it in a way that he could not possibly have done had he not, for the once, at least, abandoned Blackstone. The record of others has not even this degree of ambiguity. Justices Wilson, Paterson, Story, and Johnson, Chancellors Kent and Walworth, Chief Justices Grimke, Parsons, Parker, Hosmer, Ruffin, and Buchanan all appealed to natural rights and the social compact as limiting legislative powers. They and other judges based decisions on this ground. The same doctrine was urged by the greatest lawyers of the period, without reproach. How dominant indeed were Justice Chase's "speculative" views with both bench and bar throughout the period when the foundation precedents of constitutional interpretation were being established is shown well by what occurred in connection with the case of Wilkinson v. Leland,[7] decided by the Supreme Court of the United States in 1829, at the very close of this epoch. The attorney of defendants in error was Daniel Webster. "If," said he, "at this period, there is not a general restraint on legislatures, in favor of private rights, there is an end to private property. Though there may be no prohibition in the constitution, the legislature is restrained from acts subverting the great principles of republican liberty and of the social compact." To this contention his opponent, William Wirt, responded thus: "Who is the sovereign? Is it not the legislature of the state and are not its acts effectual, *unless they come in contact with the great principles of the social compact?*" The act of the Rhode Island legislature under review was upheld, but said Justice Story speaking for the Court: "That government can scarcely be deemed to be free where the rights of property are left solely dependent upon the will of a legislative body without any restraint. The fundamental maxims of a free government seem to require that the rights of personal liberty and private property should be held sacred." Forty-five years later, Justice Miller, speaking for an all but unanimous bench in Loan Association v. Topeka,[8] makes the same doctrine the basis of a decision overturning a state enactment, while Iredell's view receives reiteration in the lone dissent of Justice Clifford.

6. 6 Cranch 87 (1810).
7. 2 Pet. 627, 646–47, 652, 657 (1829).
8. 20 Wall. 655 (1874).

But now was it the intention of these men to leave it with the courts to draw the line between legislative power and *all* rights which might be designated "natural rights"? We speedily discover that it was not, and in so doing discover at last Iredell's vindication. *A priori,* it is difficult to see how our judges, having set out to be defenders of "natural rights," were in a position to decline to defend, and therefore to define, all such rights whether mentioned in the Constitution or not. The difficulty is disposed of, however, the moment we recollect that our judges envisaged their problem not as moral philosophers but as lawyers, and especially as students of the common law. "Natural rights," in short, were to be defined in light of common law precedents.

But there was also a second consideration limiting and easing the task of the judges. In his chapter on "The Absolute Rights of Individuals" Blackstone had written thus: "These may be reduced to three principal or primary articles . . . I. The right of personal security" consisting "in a person's legal and uninterrupted enjoyment of his life, his limbs, his body, his health, and his reputation. . . . II. . . . the personal liberty of individuals . . ." consisting "in the power of locomotion, of changing situation, or moving one's person to whatsoever place one's own inclination may direct, without imprisonment or restraint, *unless by due course of law.* . . . III . . . The absolute right, inherent in every Englishman . . . of property: which consists in the free use, enjoyment and disposal of all his acquisitions, without any control or diminution, *save only by the laws of the land.*"[9] As we have already seen Blackstone regarded Parliament's power as legally unlimited. His subordination of the "Absolute Rights of Individuals" in each case to the law signifies therefore their plenary control by the legislature and so for our purpose must be ignored. What *is* to our purpose is the definition given in the above quotation of the rights pronounced "absolute." For these are the rights precisely which, with judicial review based upon the social compact and directed to keeping legislative power within its inherent limitations, the courts were called upon to protect against legislative attack.

But were all these rights in fact exposed to legislative attack? The right of *personal security* certainly was not. On the contrary, from the very beginning we find the courts characterizing the legislative power as calculated to safeguard that right by assuring the prevalence of the maxim of the common law: "*Sic utere tuo ut alienum non laedas.*" Again it was little likely that the right of *personal liberty* would be infringed under a republican form of government. This was a right that all were capable of enjoying equally merely by virtue of their being persons. Furthermore, the rights of accused persons were safeguarded in both the federal Constitution and, for the most part, the state constitutions by elaborate and detailed specification; and the decision in Calder v. Bull had not weakened these safeguards. The right meant to be safeguarded by the appeal to the social compact and natural rights was therefore the property right. This was the right

9. 1 Black., *Comm.* 129–37.

which, the old *Dialogue of Doctor and Student* informs us, was protected by the "law of reason," by which term those "learned in the law of England" were wont to designate the "law of nature."[10] More than that, it was the right precisely which, in the estimation of the fathers, representative institutions had left insecure.

We are now prepared to consider the underlying doctrine of American constitutional law, a doctrine without which indeed it is inconceivable that there would have been any constitutional law. This is the doctrine of vested rights, which—to state it in its most rigorous form—setting out with the assumption that the property right is fundamental, treats any law impairing *vested rights,* whatever its intention, as a bill of pains and penalties, and so, void.

The fundamental character of the property right was asserted repeatedly on the floor of the Convention of 1787.[11] It is therefore no accident that the same doctrine was first brought within the purview of constitutional law by a member of that Convention, namely, Justice Paterson in his charge to the jury in Van Horne's Lessee v. Dorrance,[12] the date of which is 1795. "The right of acquiring and possessing property and *having it protected* is one of the natural, inherent and unalienable rights of man. Men have a sense of property: property is necessary to their subsistence, and correspondent to their natural wants and desires; its security was one of the objects that induced them to unite in society. No man would become a member of a community in which he could not enjoy the fruits of his honest labor and industry. The preservation of property, then, is a primary object of the social compact and by the late constitution of Pennsylvania was made a fundamental law. . . . The legislature therefore had no authority to make an act divesting one citizen of his freehold and vesting it in another, without a just compensation. It is inconsistent with the principles of reason, justice, and moral rectitude; it is incompatible with the comfort, peace and happiness of mankind; it is contrary to the principles of social alliance, in every free government; and lastly, it is contrary both to the letter and spirit of the constitution." On the basis of this reasoning an act of 1789 is pronounced "void, . . . a dead letter and of no more virtue or avail than if it never had been made."

A full decade earlier, however, than Van Horne's Lessee v. Dorrance, the doctrine of vested rights is simply assumed by the Supreme Court of Connecticut in the Symbury Case.[13] Again in 1789 in the case of Ham v. McClaws and wife,[14] the Supreme Court of South Carolina had invoked similar principles to give to a particular statute such construction as would "be consistent with justice, and the dictates of natural reason, though contrary to the strict letter of the law." Three years later, the same court pronounced invalid an act of the

10. C. H. McIlwain, *The High Court of Parliament and Its Supremacy,* 105–6.
11. 1 Farrand, *Records,* 424, 533–34, 541–42; 2 Farrand, *Records,* 123; cf. 1 Farrand, *Records,* 605. See also *Federalist* 10.
12. 2 Dall. 304, 310 (1795).
13. Kirby 444 (1785).
14. 1 Bay 93, 98 (1789).

assembly passed in 1712, transferring a freehold from the heir at law to another individual. The court announced itself as "clearly of the opinion that the plaintiffs could claim no title under the act in question, as it was against common right, as well as against the Magna Carta to take away the freehold of one man and vest it in another, . . . without any compensation, or even a trial by the jury of the country, to determine the right in question; that the act was therefore *ipso facto* void; and that no length of time could give it validity, being originally founded on erroneous principles."[15] It is a striking fact that in at least half of the original fourteen states, to include Vermont in the reckoning, the doctrine of judicial review was first recognized in connection with cases involving also an acceptance of the doctrine of vested rights.[16] We are able therefore to comprehend the significance of a remark by Justice Chase in 1800 to the effect that the Court ought to accord different treatment to laws passed by the states during the Revolution and those passed since the Constitution of the United States had gone into effect, since "few of the revolutionary acts would stand the rigorous tests now applied."[17]

This assertion soon received striking confirmation. In 1802 the Virginia Court of Appeals, after having in 1797 given the most sweeping possible interpretation to the law forbidding entails,[18] proceeded to the very verge of overturning laws disposing of the church's lands, which was saved by the mere accident of Justice Pendleton's death the night before the decision, leaving the court equally divided. And even the judges who affirmed the constitutionality of the statute under review took pains not to traverse the doctrine of vested rights, one of them, Judge Roane, going so far as to say that the constitution itself could not validly impair such rights.[19]

But the acceptance of this doctrine by the courts one after the other is but the beginning of the story. We must see how the progress of the doctrine was aided by the obscuration on the part of the courts of essential distinctions, or even their deliberate obliteration; how the doctrine attracted to its support other congenial principles; how it vitalized certain clauses of the written constitution; how in short it gradually operated to give legal reality to the notion of governmental power as *limited power*.

Of the distinctions above referred to the one whose disappearance we should first note is that between "retrospective laws," in the strict sense of laws designed "to take effect from a time anterior to their passage," and laws "which

---

15. Bowman v. Middleton, 1 Bay 252 (1792).

16. Besides the cases just mentioned, see the case described by Jeremiah Mason in his *Memories* {*Memoir*?}, pp. 26–27, in which the New Hampshire court pronounced an act unconstitutional, in 1784. The same case is referred to by William Plumer's *Life of William Plumer*, p. 59. See also Proprietors, etc. v. Laboree, 2 Greenl. (Me.) 275, 294 (1823); Emerick v. Harris, 1 Binn. (Pa.) 416 (1808); Whittington v. Polk, 1 Harr. & J. (Md.) 236 (1802).

17. Cooper v. Telfair, 4 Dall. 14, 19 (1800).

18. Carter v. Tyler, 1 Call 165 (1797).

19. Turpin v. Locket, 6 Call 113 (1804).

though operating only from their passage affect vested rights and past transactions.'' The distinction is recognized by Story in Society v. Wheeler,[20] but only to be thrust aside. "Upon principle," he declares, "every statute which takes away or impairs vested rights acquired under existing laws, or creates a new obligation, imposes a new duty, or attaches a new disability in respect to transactions or considerations already past, must be deemed retrospective." In support of his argument he cites Calder v. Bull, and warrantably. The distinction in fact was not so much obscured as entirely ignored from the first. Of more vital necessity, however, to the doctrine of vested rights, was the elimination of the distinction underlying the decision in Calder v. Bull between legislative enactments designed to punish individuals for their past acts and enactments which in giving effect to the legislature's view of public policy incidentally affected private rights detrimentally. Doubtless, this result was facilitated by the oft-expressed reluctance of the courts to enter into the question of the motives of the legislature, i.e., of its members. And this question and that of the intention underlying the legislature's acts, though two quite different matters, it was easy to confuse. Hence it became doctrine in many quarters that the validity of statutes must depend upon external tests, particularly upon their actual operation upon private rights. The matter is one that will receive further attention later on.

But if the obliteration of one distinction is thus sufficiently explained, that of another is by the same line of reasoning made the more difficult of palliation. This is the very obvious distinction between *special* acts and *general* acts. The mischief of what has been called "prerogative legislation," that is, legislation modifying the position of named parties before the law, was one of the most potent causes of the general disrepute into which state legislatures had fallen before 1787.[21] For such measures, furthermore, rarely or never could the justification be pleaded of an imperative public interest. When accordingly such measures bore heavily upon the vested rights of particular, selected persons it was not strange that the courts should have treated them as equivalent to bills of pains and penalties. But the case of general statutes is obviously different. To enact these is of the very essence of legislative power. Their generality indeed furnishes the standard of legislation from which special acts are condemned. It is true that such measures will often bear more particularly upon some members of the community than others, but this fact is perhaps but the obverse of the necessity for their enactment. Notwithstanding these considerations the courts, building upon the common law maxim that statutes ought not in doubtful cases be given a retrospective operation, laid down from the first the doctrine as one of constitutional obligation, that in no case was a statute to receive an interpretation which brought it into conflict with vested rights.[22] So far as a statute did not impair

20. 2 Gall. C. C. 105, 139 (1814), Fed. Cas. 13, 156.
21. See, e.g., *Federalist* 48 (Lodge ed.).
22. Cf. Elliott v. Lyell, 3 Call 268, 286 (1802) and Turpin v. Locket, 6 Call 113 (1804). See also Dash v. Van Kleeck, 7 Johns. (N.Y.), 477, 498 (1811).

vested rights, it was good, but so far as it did, it was a bill of pains and penalties and void, not under Art. I, section 10 of the United States Constitution,—for the actual precedent of Calder v. Bull still held, despite protests from eminent judges,—but under the general principles of constitutional law held to underlie all constitutions.

We turn next to consider the support which the doctrine of vested rights drew from other principles. In this connection our attention is first drawn to the decision of the Massachusetts Supreme Court in Holden v. James,[23] in which the sentiment of equality before the law, given its classic expression in the Declaration of Independence, is forged into a maxim of constitutional law. More specifically it was held in this case that, notwithstanding the fact that the twentieth article of the Massachusetts constitution expressly recognized the power of the legislature to suspend laws, such suspensions must be general and not for the benefit of a particular individual or individuals, it being "manifestly contrary to the first principles of civic liberty, natural justice, and the spirit of our constitution and laws that any one citizen should enjoy privileges or advantages which are denied to all others under like circumstances." The converse of this doctrine was stated by Chief Justice Catron of the Tennessee Supreme Court fifteen years later in the much cited case of Vanzant v. Waddell.[24] There it was declared that the kind of legislation which the legislature was created to enact was "general, public law equally binding upon every member of the community . . . under similar circumstances." The final clause of the first section of the Fourteenth Amendment takes its rise thence.

But of all principles brought to the support of the doctrine of vested rights, the one destined to prove, at least before the Civil War, of most varied and widest serviceability was the principle of the separation of powers. I have already touched upon the matter a few pages back. At this point I wish to review briefly some historical phases of the subject. Our starting point is the case of Cooper v. Telfair,[25] decided by the Supreme Court of the United States in 1800 on appeal from the United States Circuit Court for the District of Georgia. The measure under review was the act of the Georgia legislature of May 4, 1782, inflicting penalties on, and confiscating the estates of, certain persons declared guilty of treason. In opposition to the statute it was urged especially that it transgressed Art. I of the Georgia constitution of 1777, which provided that "the legislative, executive and judiciary departments shall be separate and distinct, so that neither exercise the powers properly belonging to the other." The act was nevertheless upheld as valid. Said Justice Cushing: "The right to confiscate and banish, in the case of an offending citizen, must belong to every government. It is not within the judicial power, as created and regulated by the constitution of Georgia: and it

23. 11 Mass. 396 (1814). See also Lewis v. Webb, 3 Greenl. (Me.) 326 (1825).
24. 2 Yerg. (10 Tenn.) 259 (1829). See also Wally's Heirs v. Kennedy, 2 Yerg. (10 Tenn.) 554 (1831) and Jones' Heirs v. Perry, 10 Yerg. (18 Tenn.) 59 (1836).
25. 4 Dall. 14 (1800).

naturally, as well as tacitly, belongs to the legislature." Said Justice Paterson: "The legislative power of Georgia, though it is in some respects restricted and qualified, *is not defined* by the constitution of the state." To the same effect were the words of Justice Chase: "The general principles contained in the constitution are not to be regarded as rules to fetter and control, but as *matter merely declaratory and directory.*"

At first, in other words, the doctrine of the separation of powers, even when formulated in the written constitution, was not deemed precise enough to admit of its being applied by courts as a constitutional limitation. The other point of view, however, was not long in making its appearance. In Ogden v. Blackledge,[26] which was certified to the Supreme Court from the United States Circuit Court for the District of North Carolina in 1804, the question to be determined was whether the state statute of limitations of 1715 had been repealed in 1789, the North Carolina legislature having declared in 1799 that it had not been. Said attorneys for plaintiff: "To declare what the law is, or has been, is a judicial power; to declare what it shall be, is legislative. One of the fundamental principles of all our governments is that the legislative power shall be separated from the judicial." "The Court," runs the report, "stopped counsel, observing that it was unnecessary to argue that point." Without recurring to the constitutional question, the court held that "under all the circumstances stated," the act in question had been repealed in 1789. Fifteen years later, the New Hampshire Supreme Court, in the leading case of Merrill v. Sherburne,[27] brought the principle of the separation of powers squarely to the support of the doctrine of vested rights. There was henceforth no apology or evasion on the part of judges in the manipulation of this principle.

The doctrine of vested rights was at last within reach of the haven of the written constitution; in fact it had already found anchorage there, in certain jurisdictions. The reflex effect upon it of its new security was what might have been anticipated: it became a yet more exacting and rigorous test of legislation than ever before. Henceforth, accordingly, it becomes necessary to recognize two varieties of the doctrine of vested rights, the milder and more flexible, the more abstract and rigorous. Courts which continued to appeal to natural rights were compelled by their own logic to consider constitutional questions not simply in their legal aspects but in their moral aspects as well. We thus find Chief Justice Parker in Foster v. Essex Bank[28] declaring, with reference to the immunity claimed by the defendant corporation under its charter, from action for debt, that "there is no vested right to do wrong." A little later, Chief Justice Hosmer in Goshen v. Stonington[29] sustained on the ground of its reasonableness and

26. Cranch 272 (1804); see also Ogden v. Witherspoon, 2 Haywood 227, 3 N.C. 404 (1802).
27. 1 N.H. 199, 204 (1819).
28. 16 Mass. 245, 273 (1819); see also State v. Newark, 3 Dutcher (27 N.J.L.) 185, 197 (1858).
29. 4 Conn. 209, 221 (1822). See also Booth v. Booth, 7 Conn. 350 (1829) and Welch v. Wadsworth, 30 Conn. 149 (1861).

justice a statute the retrospective operation of which he admitted to be "indisputable" and "equally so its purpose to change the legal rights of the litigating parties." The decision of the United States Supreme Court in Livingston v. Moore[30] was to like effect. Those courts, on the other hand, which sought to effect an absolute separation of legislative and judicial powers regarded any enactment disturbing vested rights, whatever the justification of it, as representing an attempt by the legislature to exercise powers not belonging to it and *ipso facto* void. This attitude is well represented by the New Hamphsire Supreme Court in Opinions of the Judges,[31] but it also became in time the attitude embodied in the conservative doctrine of New York.

This differentiation of two varieties of the doctrine of vested rights brings us to a highly important branch of our subject: namely, the effect of this doctrine upon the acknowledged prerogatives and functions of government. As we have already seen, the doctrine of vested rights takes its origin from a certain theory of the nature and purpose of government. But political theory is not constitutional law, though often the source of it. The doctrine of vested rights, however, is constitutional law; indeed in one disguise and another it is a great part of it. Its protean faculty of appearing ever in new forms and formulations is, however, to be of later concern. What we need to do now is to see it at work in the forms which it assumed from the first, shaping the great uncontroverted powers of the American state, the power of taxation, the power of eminent domain, and what is today designated "the police power."

Mention has been made of the conservative New York doctrine. The founder of this doctrine and so to no small extent the founder of American constitutional law was the great Chancellor Kent, whose *Commentaries* were and remain not only a marvel of legal learning but also of literary expression, and altogether one of the greatest intellectual achievements to the credit of any American. The work is divided into "Parts," which in turn fall into "Lectures." The opening Lecture of Part V, the 34th of the work, deals with "The History, Progress and Absolute Rights of Property" and to this Lecture, which was composed about the year 1825, we now turn.

Kent sets out by disparaging the idea of "a state of man prior to the existence of any notion of separate property." "No such state," he contends, "was intended for man in the benevolent dispensations of Providence. . . . The sense of property is inherent in the human breast and the gradual enlargement and cultivation of that sense from its feeble force in the savage state to its full vigor and maturity among polished nations forms a very instructive portion of the history of civil society. Man was fitted and intended by the author of his being for society and government and for the acquisition and enjoyment of property. It is, to speak correctly, the law of his nature: and by obedience to this law, he

---

30. 7 Pet. 469, 551 (1833).
31. 4 N.H. 565, 572 (1827).

brings all his faculties into exercise and is enabled to display the various and exalted powers of the human mind." Nevertheless, "there have been modern theorists," Kent marvels, "who have considered separate and exclusive property and inequalities of property as the cause of injustice and the unhappy result of government and artificial institutions. But," he rejoins to such theorists, "human society would be in a most unnatural and miserable condition if it were possible to be instituted or reorganized upon the basis of such speculations. The sense of property is bestowed on mankind for the purpose of rousing them from sloth and stimulating them to action. . . . The natural and active sense of property pervades the foundations of social improvement. It leads to the cultivation of the earth, the institution of government, the establishment of justice, the acquisition of the comforts of life, the growth of the useful arts, the spirit of commerce, the productions of taste, the erections of charity, and the display of the benevolent affections." "The legislature," therefore, "has no right to limit the extent of the acquisition of property. . . . A state of equality as to property is impossible to be maintained, for it is against the laws of our own nature; and if it could be reduced to practice, it would place the human race in a state of tasteless enjoyment and stupid inactivity, which would degrade the mind and destroy the happiness of social life." And by the same token, "civil government is not entitled, in ordinary cases, . . . to regulate the uses of property in the hands of the owners by sumptuary laws or any other visionary schemes of frugality and equality. . . . No such fatal union (as some have supposed) necessarily exists between prosperity and tyranny or between wealth and national corruption in the harmonious arrangements of Providence." Liberty *"depends essentially upon the structure of government, the administration of justice and the intelligence of the people and it has very little concern with equality of property and frugality of living. . . ."*

The interest and importance of these words of Kent arise from no novelty of doctrine advanced in them, but on the contrary, from their explicit formulation of a point of view that is so far from novel that it is ordinarily simply assumed. And so it would have remained with Kent, very likely, had he not deemed it necessary to meet and refute the levelling doctrines of Harrington, Condorcet, and Rousseau. But the matter of especial importance at this stage is to find out how this point of view manifested itself when brought into contact with those prerogatives which Kent freely accorded government.

As to taxation, Kent's theory is obviously the *quid pro quo* theory and this has remained the theory of American courts from that day to this. From it follows the maxim that taxation must be "equal in proportion to the value of property."[32]

With reference to the power of eminent domain, Kent but reiterates in his *Commentaries* the views which as chancellor he had earlier developed in the leading case of Gardner v. Newburgh,[33] to which therefore we turn directly. In

32. 2 Kent, *Comm.* 332.
33. 2 Johns. Ch. 162, 166–67 (1816).

this case, which was decided in 1816, the statute under review was one authorizing the trustees of the village of Newburgh to supply its inhabitants with water by means of conduits. As stated by the chancellor, the statute made "adequate provision for the party injured by the laying of the conduits through his land" and also "to the owners of the spring or springs from whence the water" was to be taken. But no compensation was provided the plaintiff Gardner, "through whose land the water issuing from the spring" had been accustomed to flow. At this date there was no provision in the New York constitution with reference to the power of eminent domain. Nevertheless upon the authority of Grotius, Puffendorf, Bynkershoeck, and Blackstone, Kent developed the following propositions: 1st, that the legislature might "take private property for necessary or useful *public* [sic] purposes"; 2ndly, that such taking, however, did not involve the absolute "stripping of the subject of his property," but, in the language of Blackstone, "the giving him a full indemnification," since "the public is now considered as an individual treating with an individual for an exchange"; 3rdly, that such indemnification was due not merely those whose property was actually appropriated by the state but also those whose property should be injured in consequence of the use made by the state of the property appropriated; 4thly, that the legislature itself was not the final judge of what sum was "a full indemnification" of owners whose property was taken or injured. The court thereupon issued an injunction against the trustees, "to see whether the merits of the case will be varied," it being a nuisance at the common law to divert a watercourse and an injunction being necessary to prevent an impending injury. In his *Commentaries* ten years later Kent reaffirms all these propositions. His exposition of them furthermore makes it plain that he regards the requirement of a public purpose a true constitutional limitation, susceptible of judicial enforcement. In other words, not every purpose for which the legislature may elect to exercise the power of eminent domain is for that reason a *public* purpose. The legislature cannot even by the power of eminent domain transfer the property of A to B without A's consent.[34]

The third power of government touching property rights Kent describes in the following terms: "But though property be thus protected, it is still to be understood, that the law-giver has a right to prescribe the mode and manner of using it, so far as may be necessary to prevent the abuse of the right to the injury or annoyance of others or of the public. The government may by general regulations interdict such uses of property as would create nuisances and become dangerous to the lives and health or peace or comfort of the citizens. Unwholesome trades, slaughter houses, operations offensive to the senses, the deposit of gunpowder, the building with combustible materials, and the burial of the dead, may all be interdicted by law, in the midst of dense masses of population, on the general and rational principle that every person ought so to use his property as not to injure

34. 2 Kent, *Comm.* 340, and notes. Cf. Paterson, J., in Van Horne's Lessee v. Dorrance, 2 Dall. 304, 310 (1795).

his neighbors, and that private interests must be made subservient to the general interest of the community."[35]

But is the power thus described unlimited, that is, limited only by the discretion of the lawgiver? In the first place, be it noted, the power in question is described as a power of *regulation,* which, at least so it came eventually to be urged, is distinguishable from a power of *prohibition.* True Kent himself admits that there are uses of property which constitute *nuisances* in certain cases, and he says in another place, that there are "cases of urgent necessity" in which property may be destroyed, as for instance when houses are razed to prevent the spread of a conflagration.[36] But it is apparent from his citations that he regards such cases as already provided for in common law precedent, that he has no intention of recognizing in the legislature a power to define cases of nuisance and urgency, unrestrained by precedent. Again his doctrine of consequential damages must not be forgotten in this connection. For if it was incumbent upon the state to render compensation for damages resulting from its use of the power of eminent domain, why should it not also be the state's duty to pay private owners for damages resultant from the use of its police powers? Lastly, it is entirely apparent that Kent had not the least idea in the world of abandoning the doctrine which had received his repeated sanction, that a legislative enactment must never be so interpreted as to impair vested rights.[37]

For further instruction in the New York doctrine we turn to some New York decisions following Kent's *Commentaries.* The very year of the publication of the second volume of this work occurred the cases of Vanderbilt v. Adams and Coates v. Mayor of the City of New York, both to be found in the seventh volume of Cowen's reports.[38] In the former, plaintiff in error contended that a statute authorizing harbor masters to regulate and station vessels in the East and North rivers did not extend to owners of private wharves; or that if it did so extend, it assumed to authorize an interference with private property in a way that was beyond the power of the legislature. The argument was founded upon Gardner v. Newburgh, Dash v. Van Kleeck, Fletcher v. Peck, and derivative cases. The court upheld the statute but in language significantly cautious. Said Justice Woodworth: "It seems to me that the power exercised in this case is essentially necessary for the purpose of protecting the rights of all concerned. It is not in the legitimate sense of the term a violation of any right, but the exercise of a power indispensably necessary where an extensive commerce is carried on. . . . The right assumed under the law would not be upheld if exerted beyond what may *be considered* a necessary police regulation. The line between what would *be a clear invasion of the right, on the one hand, and regulations not lessening the value of the right and calculated for the benefit of all must be*

35. 2 Kent, *Comm.* 340 and notes.
36. *Id.,* 338–39 and notes.
37. Dash v. Van Kleeck, 7 Johns. 477, 498 (1811); see also 1 Kent, *Comm.* 455–56 and notes.
38. Vanderbilt v. Adams, 7 Cow. 349 (1827) and Coates et. al. v. Mayor etc., 7 Cow. 585 (1827).

distinctly marked. . . . Police regulations are legal and binding because for the general benefit and *do not proceed to the length of impairing any right in the proper sense of the term.* The sovereign power in a community, therefore, may and ought to prescribe the manner of exercising individual rights over property. It is for the better protection and enjoyment of that absolute dominion which the individual claims. . . .'' The individual himself, as well as others, is benefitted by legitimate regulation.

But what is *legitimate regulation?* In Coates v. Mayor, the statute under review authorized the City of New York to make by-laws ''for regulating, or if they found it necessary, preventing, the interment of the dead'' within the city. In pursuance of this statute the city had passed a prohibitory ordinance, which plaintiffs in error claimed to be inoperative in their cases on account of certain grants of land held in trust by them for the sole purpose of interment. The argument against the legislative power in the premises again rested upon Gardner v. Newburgh, Fletcher v. Peck, and like precedents. ''The public good,'' it was conceded, ''is paramount. This is admitted in taking land for roads and canals. But land thus taken must be paid for. Is it not the same thing,'' it was asked, ''whether the public good is to be promoted by taking the use of property for public benefit or destroying the property for the same purpose?'' ''The legislature cannot take away a single attribute of private property without remuneration.'' To meet these contentions the attorneys for the municipality were forced to resort to doctrine from an alien jurisdiction, doctrine which moreover bore in its origin no reference to the question before the New York court. Thus in his opinion in Gibbons v. Ogden,[39] Chief Justice Marshall had described the field of legislation left to the states *by the Constitution of the United States* in very broad terms. This description was now utilized to show the scope of legislative power *under the state constitution* in relation to the property right. Again, in McCulloch v. Maryland,[40] Marshall had construed the words ''necessary and proper'' of Art. I, section 8, of the United States Constitution as meaning ''expedient,'' and it was now urged that the term ''necessary'' in the legislative grant of power to the municipality must be similarly defined. Finally, in Martin v. Mott,[41] the Supreme Court of the United States had held that where a discretionary authority was vested by the Constitution in the president, its use was not subject to judicial review. The same line of argument was now contended to be applicable to a state legislature in the exercise of its powers. ''The power in question,'' declared defendant's attorney, ''is a legislative power, which must, on the subject of regulation, be transcendent. The legislators are the judges and their decision must be conclusive. Even a general law to prevent the growing of grain throughout the state, however despotic, could not be disobeyed as wanting constitutional validity.''

39. 9 Wheat. 1 (1824).
40. 4 Wheat. 316 (1819).
41. 12 Wheat. 19 (1827).

The by-law, and the statute upon which it was based, were both sustained. Speaking of the question of the necessity of the former, the court said: "This necessity is not absolute. It is nearly synonymous with *expediency* or *what is necessary for the public good.*" To judge of that matter, however, is the function of the legislature; it being "of the nature of legislative bodies to judge of the exigency upon which their laws are founded." And the law itself is "equivalent to an averment that the exigency has arisen, been adjudicated and acted upon." The duty of the court is merely to see "that the law operates upon the subject of the power."

It would be easy to interpret this language in a way to release the legislature from all constitutional restraints. To do this, however, was as far as possible from the intention of the court. "We are of opinion," its decision proceeds, "that this by-law is not void, either as being unconstitutional, or as conflicting with what we acknowledge as a *fundamental principle of civilized society, that private property shall not be taken even for public use without just compensation.* No property has in this instance been entered upon or taken. None are benefitted by the destruction, or rather the suspension, of the rights in question in any other way than citizens always are when one of their number is forbidden to continue a nuisance."

Coates v. Mayor therefore seems to furnish authority for the following propositions: (1) The legislature is the exclusive judge of the expediency of exercising its powers; (2) Property can be appropriated by the state only for a public use and upon the making of just compensation; (3) The legislative power of regulation extends to the abatement of nuisances, existing or impending; (4) If in such cases, property rights are destroyed, no compensation is due their owner. The power of eminent domain and that of regulation are distinct and the doctrine of consequential damages does not apply in the case of the latter.

One question remains, however: Who is to say finally whether there *is* a nuisance? The plain inference from the whole line of argument taken by the court in this case is that, what is a nuisance is a question of fact to be judged of in the last analysis by the courts in accordance with common law standards. And this inference becomes certainty when we turn to a line of decisions, extending from 1837 to 1845, in which a statute authorizing municipal officers to destroy buildings to prevent the spread of fire, is reviewed and applied by the court of errors and appeals.[42] The language of some of the lay members of the court is especially significant. By Senator Edwards the statute is treated as merely defining and limiting a common law right of even private persons in such an exigency. By Senator Verplanck, the right assumed by the statute is described as "a natural

42. The ensuing quotations are from Stone v. Mayor, 25 Wend. 157 (1840) at 161 and 174. See also Hart v. Mayor, 9 Wend. 571 (1832); Van Wormer v. Mayor, 15 Wend. 262 (1836); Meeker v. Van Rensselaer, 15 Wend. 397 (1836); and Mayor v. Lord, 17 Wend. 285 (1837). In Van Wormer v. Mayor the court held that the finding of a board of health, that certain premises were a nuisance, could not be traversed in court. The citation of Mouse's case is 12 Coke 62.

right, arising from inevitable and pressing necessity, when [of] two immediate evils, one must be chosen and the less is voluntarily inflicted in order to avoid the greater.'' In support of this definition is cited Coke's language in Mouse's case, where it was said, with reference to baggage thrown overboard in time of storm, that ''if the danger accrued by the act of God . . . everyone ought to bear his loss for safeguard of the life of man.'' In other words, since no right of action would lie for private trespass in such a case, neither could compensation be claimed against the state. The same course of reasoning is pursued by Senators Sherman and Porter in Russell v. Mayor.[43] The occasions, in short, when the state might legitimately press its power of regulation to the extent of actually destroying property rights were relatively few and were plainly indicated in the common law.

The New York doctrine invites comparison with that of Massachusetts. In the latter commonwealth the rejection of the doctrine of consequential damages and the resultant differentiation of the power of eminent domain from that of police regulation preceded, though it does not seem to have aided, the like development in the former. And once again, the starting point was furnished by the law of private trespass. In the case of Thurston v. Hancock,[44] decided in 1815, it was concluded, from an exhaustive review of the precedents by Chief Justice Parker, that where one dug so deep into his own land as to endanger a house on land adjoining, the owner of the latter had no right of action for the damage done the house, but only for the damage arising from the falling of the natural soil into the pit so dug. In Callender v. Marsh,[45] decided eight years later, it was held, on the basis of this precedent, that the tenth article of the Massachusetts Declaration of Rights gave ''no right to compensation for an indirect or consequential damage or expense resulting from the right use of property already belonging to the public.'' Finally, in Baker v. Boston,[46] which was an action to prevent the municipality from filling up a creek which had become injurious to the public health, it was ruled that ''police regulations to direct the use of private property so as to prevent its being pernicious to the citizens at large are not void though they may in some measure interfere with private rights without providing for compensation.'' Kent in his *Commentaries* stigmatizes the doctrine of Callender v. Marsh as ''erroneous'' and in contravention of ''a palpably clear and just doctrine,'' for which he cites his own decision in the Newburgh case.[47] At the same time he apparently approves of the New York decision in the Coates case. The explanation of the apparent contradiction is to be found in his recognition that the property right infringed in the New York case was a nuisance by common law standards.

43. 2 Denio 461 (1844).
44. 12 Mass. 220 (1815).
45. 1 Pick. 417 (1823).
46. 12 Pick. 184 (1831). See also Com. v. Breed, 4 Pick. 460 (1827); Com. v. Tewksbury, 11 Metc. 55 (1846); and Com. v. Alger, 7 Cush. 53 (1851).
47. 2 Kent, *Comm.* 340, footnote (p. 526 of 14th edition).

This, however, is not to say that common law standards did not obtain in Massachusetts, in interpreting the Constitution, but only that they were applied in a rather more flexible fashion than in New York. To illustrate this point is therefore the second object of our comparison of the two doctrines. The relative flexibility of the Massachusetts doctrine was due in part, as we have already seen, to the retention of the natural rights theory as the foundation of the doctrine of vested rights. But a further reason for it is to be found in the very words in which legislative power is vested by the Massachusetts constitution in the General Court. This is described as the power "to make, ordain, and establish all manner of *wholesome and reasonable* orders, laws, statutes, and ordinances . . . as they shall judge to be for the government and welfare of the commonwealth."[48] Quoting this passage in the case of Rice v. Parkman,[49] Chief Justice Parker ruled, in 1820, that the General Court must be deemed to have a parental or tutorial power over persons not *sui juris,* that is "minors, persons *non compos mentis,* and others," and upon that basis upheld a legislative act licensing the sale of the real estate of certain minors. In New Hampshire, where vested rights had been brought under the protection of the doctrine of the separation of powers, similar legislative acts were overturned. The New York court in Cochran v. Van Surley,[50] accepted the Massachusetts doctrine, but at that date the doctrine of natural rights had not yet been decisively expelled from New York. Also the broader basis for the Massachusetts decision was not adverted to.

But another avenue for the entry of the doctrine that legislation must be "reasonable," in some sense or other, was afforded by the terms in which power is usually conferred by the state legislature upon municipal corporations. A case in point, in which the doctrine in question was turned against the legislation under review, is that of Austin v. Murray,[51] decided by the Massachusetts Supreme Court in 1834. The question at issue was the validity of a by-law interdicting the bringing of the dead into the town from abroad for purposes of burial, a prohibition which touched chiefly or exclusively Catholic parishioners. The court overturned the by-law as being "wholly unauthorized" by the act of the legislature, and as "an unreasonable infringement on private rights." Elaborating the latter point it said: "The illegality of a by-law is the same whether it may deprive an individual of the use of a part or of the whole of his property; no one can be so deprived unless the public good requires it. And the law will not allow the right of property to be invaded under the guise of a police regulation for the preservation of health when it is manifest that such is not the object and purpose of the regulation. . . . [This by-law] is a clear and direct *infringement of the right of property without any compensating advantages, and not a police regulation, made in good faith for the preservation of health.*" In other words

48. Part the Second, Chapter 1, Section 1, Article 4. 3 Thorpe 1894.
49. 16 Mass. 326, 331 (1820).
50. 20 Wend. 365, 373 (1838).
51. 16 Pick. 121 (1834).

the ordinance is overturned, not simply because it impaired vested rights but because it did so without any good public reason. Had such reason been present, the measure would have been upheld. For then the individual whose rights were infringed would himself have benefitted as a member of the public. The police power, like the power of taxation, is controlled by the principle of a *quid pro quo*. The line of reasoning is the same as had been taken by the New York court in Vanderbilt v. Adams.[52]

But the question of the flexibility of the doctrine of vested rights involves yet another question. This doctrine, to restate it as compendiously as possible, is that the legislature cannot, at least except for reasons of public policy, enact laws impairing vested rights. The doctrine has therefore two dimensions, so to say, the term "impair" and the term "vested rights." But the general significance of the former term we have already learned in our investigation of the operation of the doctrine upon the powers of government. And even of the second term we have supplied most of the materials for a definition, which only awaits our more circumstantial formulation.

Vested rights are rights vested in specific individuals in accordance with the law in what the law recognizes as *property*. But what, for the purposes of the doctrine of vested rights, did the law recognize as property? What, in other words, was the objective of the rights which this doctrine treated as vestable?

In his Essay on Property, composed in 1792, Madison had written thus: "This term in its particular application means 'that dominion which one man claims and exercises over the external things of the world, in exclusion of every other individual.' But in its larger and juster meaning, it embraces everything to which a man may attach a value and have a right; and which leaves to every *one else the like advantage*. In the former sense, a man's land, or merchandise, or money is called his property. In the latter sense, a man has property in his opinions and a free communication of them. He has a property of peculiar value in his religious opinions, and in the profession and practice dictated by them. He has property very dear to him in the safety and liberty of his person. He has an equal property in the free use of his faculties and free choice of the objects on which to employ them. In a word, as a man is said to have a right to his property, he may be equally said to have a property in his rights. . . . If there be a government then which prides itself on maintaining the inviolability of property, which provides that none shall be taken directly even for public use without indemnification to the owner, and yet directly violates the property which individuals have in their opinions, their religion, their person, and their faculties, nay more which indirectly violates their property in their actual possessions, in the labor that acquires their daily subsistence, and in the hallowed remnant of time which ought to

52. 7 Cow. 349 (1827). For further illustrations of the Massachusetts doctrine, see Com. v. Tewksbury, 11 Metc. 55 (1846), and Com. v. Alger, 7 Cush. 53 (1851). See also Stoughton v. Baker, 4 Mass. 522 (1808); Vinton v. Welsh, 9 Pick. 87 (1829); and Com v. Badlam, 9 Pick. 361 (1830).

relieve their fatigues and soothe their cares, the inference will have been antici-pated that such a government is not a pattern for the United States. If the United States mean to obtain or deserve the full praise due to wise and just governments they will equally respect the rights of property and the property in rights."[53]

These words are important as showing the elasticity attaching to the term "property," as used by American statesmen, from the beginning. Such lati-tudinarian views, however, found little or no support from the common law, and had in consequence before the Civil War little influence upon judges. So far as the courts liberalized the legal notion of the property right it was chiefly by analyzing it into its constituent elements, the right of use, the right of sale, the right of control, and so on, which were sometimes recognized as property rights even when inhering in another than the legal owner.[54] But the objective of these rights remained, for the most part, tangible property, property which could be taken by the power of eminent domain, hence especially real property.[55] Still there were some exceptions to this rule. Art. I, section 10, of the United States Constitution was regarded from the outset as placing the legal fruits of one's lawful contracts in the category of vested rights. By the same token, the Dartmouth College decision extended the concept to charter rights, a result which, however, had been antici-pated at least in Massachusetts independently of the contract clause.[56] Finally in Dash v. Van Kleeck, Chancellor Kent, by treating the right to prosecute an action at law, already begun, as a vested right, entered a more controversial field. In a much stronger case some years later, Chief Justice Parker declared the more usual view that "there is no such a thing as a vested right to a particular remedy."[57]

And doubtless attorneys and suitors would fain have extended the application of the term still further. Said Justice Nelson in People v. Morris:[58] "Vested rights are indefinite terms, and of extensive signification; not unfrequently re-sorted to when no better argument exists, in cases neither within the reason or spirit of the principle." Despite this tendency, however, the concept is soon seen, when we bring it into comparison with ideas that have become current since the Fourteenth Amendment was added to the Constitution, to have been kept, first and last, well within bounds. Certainly no one would have thought of suggesting before the Civil War that the right to engage in trade, the right to contract, the right—to employ Madison's phrase—of the individual "in the use of his faculties," were "vested rights." To this fact Madison's own antithesis between "rights to property" and "property in rights" is indirect testimony, but most direct evidence is by no means lacking. Especially pertinent are some of the

53. 6 Madison, *Writings* 101ff. (Hunt ed.).
54. See some New York cases: Holmes v. Holmes, 4 Barb. 295 (1848); White v. White, 5 Barb. 474 (1849); Perkins v. Cottrell, 15 Barb. 446 (1851); Westervelt v. Gregg, 12 N.Y. 202 (1854).
55. See McLean, J., in West River Bridge Co. v. Dix, 6 How. 507 (1848) at 536–37.
56. Trustees of Dartmouth College v. Woodward, 4 Wheat. 518 (1819). The Massachusetts case referred to is Wales v. Stetson, 2 Mass. 143 (1806). Cf. Austin v. Trustees, 1 Yeates (Pa.) 260 (1793).
57. Com. v. Commissioners of Hampden, 6 Pick. 501 (1828). See also Yeaton v. United States, 5 Cranch 281 (1809).
58. 13 Wend. 325, 329 (1835).

utterances of Chief Justice Parker in deciding the case of Portland Bank v. Apthorp,[59] in which the question at issue was the validity of a tax on the stock of an incorporated bank. Said the court: "The privilege of using particular branches of business or employment, as the business of an auctioneer, of an attorney, of a tavern-keeper . . . etc." have been subjected to taxation "from the earliest practice," and this notwithstanding the fact that "every man has a natural right to exercise either of these employments free of tribute, as much as a husbandman or mechanic to use his personal calling. . . . Every man has the implied permission of the government to carry on any lawful business, and there is no difference in the right between those which require a license and those which do not, *except in the prohibition, either express or implied,* where a license is required."[60]

Nor is the logical implication of this language weakened when we turn to consider legislative measures designed not to tax but to regulate business. Many such measures were municipal ordinances, and while their validity was challenged again and again, it was never on grounds furnished by the doctrine of vested rights or any collateral doctrine. In Massachusetts the favorite argument against such by-laws was that they were in restraint of trade and that therefore the authority to enact them had not been conferred by the legislature. This was the argument in the case of Commonwealth v. Worcester,[61] where the ordinance under review forbade persons in charge of wagons, carts, etc., from driving their horses through the streets at a trot. The court rejected the contention, as also it did the like argument in Nightingale's case,[62] where the by-law before the court provided that no one not offering the produce of his own farm for sale should occupy any stand for the vending of commodities except by the permission of the clerk of the market. Vandine's case[63] was argued and decided on like grounds.

But of course when the objectionable legislation came from the legislature itself, other principles had to be resorted to. Yet even in such cases, with a simple exception so plainly anomalous as not to merit comment in this connection,[64] fundamental principles were conspicuously not appealed to. Two cases especially to the point are a Massachusetts case of 1835, Hewitt v. Charier,[65] and an Ohio case of 1831, Jordan v. Overseers of Dayton.[66] In these cases the statutes drawn into question confined the practice of medicine to members of certain medical societies and to persons qualified in other stipulated ways. In the

59. 12 Mass. 252 (1815). See also Shaw, C. J., in Com. v. Blackington, 24 Pick. 352 (1837).
60. The point of view of Marshall, C. J., in Ogden v. Saunders is the same. The obligation of contracts, which arose from the moral law, was protected by Article I, section 10 of the Constitution, but the right to contract was subject absolutely to legislative control. 12 Wheat. 213, 346–49.
61. 3 Pick. 462 (1826).
62. 11 Pick. 168 (1831).
63. 6 Pick. 187 (1828).
64. The reference is to Ex parte Dorsey, 7 Porter (Ala.) 293 (1838). The line of reasoning there employed was rejected by the same court and same judges in Mobile v. Yuille, 3 Ala. 137 (1841), where a municipal ordinance prescribed the price of bread.
65. 16 Pick. 353 (1835).
66. 4 Ohio 295 (1831). Some other citations of like import may be added: Furman v. Knapp, 19 Johns. (N.Y.) 248 (1821); People v. Jenkins, 1 Hill (N.Y.) 469 (1841); Com. v. Ober, 12 Cush. (Mass.) 493 (1853).

Massachusetts case the protestant, who had continued in practice in defiance of the statute, based his case, not upon the ground that would seem most available today, that the statute operated to deprive him of his livelihood and chosen profession, but upon art. 6 of the Massachusetts Declaration of Rights, which forbids, in essence, special privileges to favored indidividuals. The court over-ruled the argument. Said Chief Justice Shaw: "Taking the whole article together, we think it manifest that it was especially pointed to the prevention of hereditary rank." But even in applying it according to its literal meaning, "it is necessary to consider whether it was the *intent or one of the leading and substantive purposes of the legislature* to confer an exclusive privilege on any man or class of men," or whether "this is indirect and incidental, . . . not one of the purposes of the act," and therefore not "a violation of this article of the Bill of Rights." His conclusion was that the act under review was not "a violation of any principle of the constitution."

In the Ohio case, the argument of plaintiff in error was even more far-fetched, being based upon a patent which he held from the national government for certain drugs and concoctions. Said the court in response: "The sole purpose of a patent is to enable the patentee to prevent others from using the products of his labor except with his consent. But his own right of using is not enlarged or affected. There remains in him . . . the power to manage his property or give direction to his labors at his pleasure, subject only to the paramount claims of society, which require that his enjoyment may be . . .regulated by laws which render it subservient to the general welfare." The court concluded with a long list of trades which were at that time regulated by statute in the state of Ohio.

Our conclusion then from these and similar cases must be that the doctrine of vested rights was interposed to shield only the property right, in the strict sense of the term, from legislative attack. When that broader range of rights which is today connoted by the terms "liberty" and "property" of the Fourteenth Amendment were in discussion other phraseology was employed, as for example the term "privileges and immunities" of Art. IV, section 2, of the Constitution. In his famous decision in Corfield v. Coryell,[67] rendered in 1823, Justice Washington defined this phrase to signify, as to "citizens in the several states," "those privileges and immunities which are in their nature, *fundamental,* which belong of right to the citizens of all free governments; and which have, at all times, been enjoyed by the citizens of the several states which compose this union." "What these fundamental principles are," he continued, "it would perhaps be more tedious than difficult to enumerate. They may, however, be all comprehended under the following heads; protection by the government: the enjoyment of life and liberty, with the right to acquire and possess property of every kind, and to pursue and obtain happiness and safety; subject nevertheless to such restraints as the government may justly prescribe for the good of the whole."

67. 4 Wash. C. C., 371, 380–81 (1823), Fed. Cas. 3230.

But now of all the rights included in this comprehensive schedule, one only, and that in but a limited sense, was protected by the doctrine of vested rights, the right namely of one who had *already* acquired some title of control over some particular piece of property, in the physical sense, to continue in that control. All other rights, however fundamental, were subject to limitation by the legislature, whose discretion as that of a representative body in a democratic country, was little likely to transgress the few, rather specific, provisions of the written constitution.

To conclude:—The doctrine of vested rights represents the first great achievement of the courts after the establishment of judicial review. In fact, in not a few instances, judicial review and the doctrine of vested rights appeared synchronously and the former was subordinate, in the sense of being auxiliary, to the latter. But always, before the Fourteenth Amendment, judicial review, save as a method of national control upon the states, would have been ineffective and lifeless enough, but for the *raison d'etre* supplied it by the doctrine of vested rights, in one guise or other.[68] Furthermore, the doctrine represented the essential spirit and point of view of the founders of American constitutional law, who saw before them the same problem that had confronted the Convention of 1787, namely, the problem of harmonizing majority rule with minority rights, or more specifically, republican institutions with the security of property, contracts, and commerce. In the solution of this problem the best minds of the period were enlisted, Wilson, Marshall, Kent, Story, and a galaxy of lesser lights. But their solution, grounded though it was upon theory that underlay the whole American constitutional system, would yet hardly have survived them had it not met the needs and aspirations of a nation whose democracy was always tempered by the individualism of the free, prosperous Western world. That distrust of legislative majorities in which constitutional limitations were conceived, from being the obsession of a superior class, became, with advancing prosperity, the prepossession of a nation, and the doctrine of vested rights was secure.[69]

---

68. For the most important guise which the doctrine assumed in state courts, particularly the New York Courts, see the writer's article on "The Doctrine of Due Process of Law before the Civil War" in 24 *Harvard L. Rev.* 366, 460 (1911). The most important guise which the doctrine developed in the federal courts is to be seen in their interpretation of Article I, section 10. See Fletcher v. Peck, 6 Cranch 87 (1810), and Trustees of Dartmouth College v. Woodward, 4 Wheat. 518 (1819).

69. See the discussion of the relation of government to the property right, in the Massachusetts Convention of 1820, *Journal* (Boston, 1853), pp. 247, 254, 275–76, 278, 280, 284–86, 304ff. The speakers are Webster, Story, John Adams, et al. Webster's Oration on the Completion of Bunker Hill Monument is a splendid statement of the theory that a democracy in which men are equal will inevitably want to protect private rights against governmental excesses. 1 *Writings and Speeches* 259 ff. (National ed. 1903). On March 21, 1864, Lincoln addressed a committee from the Workingmen's Association of New York. He closed with the following words: "Property is the fruit of labor; property is desirable; is a positive good in the world. That some should become rich shows that others may become rich, and hence is just encouragement to industry and enterprise. Let not him who is houseless pull down the house of another, but let him work diligently and build one for himself, thus by example assuring that his own shall be safe from violence when built." *Complete Works* 54 (Ed. of 1905). See also 5 *Complete Works* 330, 361.

2. Social Insurance and Constitutional Limitations

STUDENTS of the development of constitutional limitations upon legislative power in the United States will find an interesting parallel in the history of the Roman confessional. Confronted with the alternative of adhering rigorously to the primitive standards of Christian conduct and of "contrition" for misconduct, or of relaxing these standards in the interest of broadening its supervision of the lives of its communicants, the church has generally chosen the latter course. Similarly, it is the "laxists" rather than the "rigorists" who have determined the final character of our constitutional law.

Forty years ago constitutional law still rested in great part upon the foundations originally supplied it by eighteenth-century political philosophy, upon the reciprocally implied yet reciprocally contradicted notions of the "sovereignty" of the state and the "natural rights" of the citizen. It thus resulted that, within a very broad field, the authority of the state legislature was treated as legally illimitable, at least in the absence of specific provision to the contrary, while in a much narrower field, comprising especially what were called "vested rights," private rights were treated as indefeasible. Today constitutional law, both on its negative and on its positive side, is much more flexible. On the one hand, judicial interpretation of the phrases "liberty," "property," and "due process of law," especially as these are used in the Fourteenth Amendment, leaves judicial control of state legislation with none but the vaguest limits. On the other hand, judicial definition of "the police power" as the power of the state to promote "the general welfare" by legislation "reasonably adapted" to that end, renders this widely extended supervision highly elastic.

But while this is true enough as a general statement of the matter, certain recent events make it clear that constitutional "rigorism" still maintains certain

Reprinted by permission of the Yale Law Journal Company and Fred B. Rothman & Company from the *Yale Law Journal*, Vol. 26, pp. 431–43 (1917).

outposts from which it must be dislodged, if our system of constitutional limitations is to be adapted to the needs of modern complex society. The recent judicial utterance most to the point in this connection is the much debated decision of the New York Court of Appeals in the Ives case,[1] in which a workmen's compensation act was overturned. The court admitted that the statute involved dealt with appreciable evils, that it had been drawn up with great care and only after diligent investigation, and that it met the best opinion on the subject. Yet in the face of these admissions, the act was pronounced void on two grounds: first, because it imposed "liability without fault" upon certain classes of employers and so, in effect, confiscated property of A and gave it to B; secondly, because it comprised "an unreasonable regulation of the status of employment," and so deprived both employers and employees of their "freedom of contract." The obstacles interposed by this type of doctrine to workmen's compensation acts have since been overcome in a measure by what is known as the "elective" statute—but only in a measure[2]—and the menace of it to minimum wage legislation and other social insurance projects is apparent. And the general issue raised is even farther reaching. It is whether legislation, which is otherwise well within the police power, is to be treated as invalid because of its incidental detriment to private rights. This, in a word, is the issue between "rigorism" and "laxism" today.

The maxim that property cannot be transferred by act of government from one private owner to another is a landmark of our constitutional law. Indeed, it antedates our constitutional law, for it is stated by Coke, while on Coke's authority a Massachusetts magistrate of the seventeenth century pronounced void, on this ground, a town vote which was meant to provide the local minister with a dwelling-house at public expense.[3] Though not explicitly recognized even to this day in any state constitution, so fundamental a principle of public morality soon found embodiment in judicially enforced limitations on legislative power. In early days the most obnoxious species of legislation from the point of view of vested rights was to be found in so-called "prerogative" acts, whereby legislatures frequently undertook to adjudicate private controversies. In combating this evil, the courts found the principle of the separation of powers and the maxim against confiscation for private benefit their most potent weapons. Thereafter the maxim was adduced in support of the principle that the power of eminent domain may be exercised for public purposes only; that is, for purposes deemed by the *courts* to be public. Later still, and on the same basis, a similar dogma was erected against the taxing power.[4]

Like most constitutional doctrines protective of private rights, this maxim has today been assimilated into the judicial theory of "due process of law." The form in which it confronts projects of social insurance is illustrated by a passage from

1. Ives v. So. Buffalo Ry. Co. (1911) 201 N.Y. 271.
2. See Ashton v. Boston and Maine Ry. Co. (1915) 222 Mass. 65.
3. Giddings v. Brown, *Select Essays in Anglo-American Legal History*, Vol. 1, p. 376.
4. Loan Association v. Topeka (1874) 20 Wall. (U.S.) 655.

Mr. Justice Holmes' opinion in the Oklahoma Bank Guarantee case which runs as
follows:

> It is well established by a series of cases that an ulterior public advantage may justify a
> comparatively insignificant taking of private property for what, in its immediate pur-
> pose, is a private use.[5]

This utterance, taken in its context, is not without its reassuring features. If the
state may assess all banks to provide a fund from which to recoup depositors in
banks which fail, why may it not assess employers to provide funds from which to
recoup employees for losses growing out of their employment? No doubt if the
Court were bent on avoiding this conclusion, it could seek refuge behind the
phrase "comparatively insignificant"; yet hardly securely. For if this phrase
implies a limitation on the taxing power, it would seem that Mr. Justice Holmes's
characteristic caution in expression had this time betrayed him into inaccuracy,
since it does not appear that the *insignificance* of the taking has ever been a
criterion with the courts in passing upon legislation challenged as confiscatory,
when such legislation was referable to the taxing power; the sole question with the
judges in such cases has always been whether an ulterior public interest was
served. And with reference to this question, it seems to me that the entire
implication of Mr. Justice Holmes's opinion is that the concept of "public
purpose," as a limitation on the taxing power, is to be defined in light of the
concept of "general welfare," as a dimension of the police power; that all the
powers of the state march abreast and are of mutual serviceability.

Yet, it is just at this point that constitutional "rigorism" will enter a *caveat*.
This will consist in drawing a sharp line between the powers of taxation and
eminent domain, on the one hand, and the police power, on the other; and it will
be argued that, whereas the former comprise, by very definition, the power to
take property, the latter is a power of *regulation* merely, which does not and
cannot extend to the *taking* of property, or to what is its equivalent, the compelling of its transfer from one person to another. Accordingly, it will be insisted
that while the police power is a power to promote the public welfare, its ends
must be achieved by the methods inherent to it. Otherwise, the settled boundaries
between the great fields of governmental power will speedily become obliterated, and all powers will assume the guise of the one least susceptible of legal
control, with the inevitable result that private rights, in any valuable sense, will
soon be at an end.

This argument directs its appeal to that way of thinking which sets public
policy and the security of private rights in sharpest antithesis, whereas the history
of law proves that the recognition and protection of private rights by the state has
always been a phase, though but *one* phase, of public policy. Furthermore, when
we turn to the more readily accessible verdict of the history of constitutional
limitations, we find that the line so insisted upon, as demarking *regulation* from

5. Noble Bank v. Haskell (1911) 219 U.S. 104, 110.

taking, has been by no means a stationary one, and we accordingly feel warranted in questioning whether its present placement is necessarily so definite, after all. Thus, shortly before the Civil War, the New York Court of Appeals, in the famous Wynehamer case,[6] set aside an anti-liquor law on the ground that, as to existing stocks of liquor, it constituted an act not of regulation but of *destruction*, and so of *taking* without just compensation. Thirty years later, in Mugler v. Kansas,[7] the United States Supreme Court sustained precisely the same kind of law as within the police power, to which, it said, all property is at all times held subject.

In other words, the state may, in the exercise of its police power, absolutely outlaw what was good property when it was acquired. But even as to property remaining under the protection of the law it may, by the same power, limit the owner's use and control thereof for the public benefit,[8] and frequently for what, in its immediate aspect, is a private benefit. Thus the right of alienation may be restricted in the interest of creditors, dependents, and heirs-at-law;[9] while in directing the use of property held in common or in trust, and even of property held in severalty which without regulation could not be beneficially used, the state has large powers.[10] Finally, the state may cast special obligations upon property which may be met only by expenditures for prescribed purposes. So the expenses of mine inspection may be charged against the owners of mines;[11] of sanitary improvements, against the owners of tenements;[12] of constructing and maintaining grade crossings and suitable trackage connections, against railroad companies;[13] of laying and cleaning street sidewalks, against the owners of abutting premises.[14] In none of these cases is there a *taking* in the sense of the term which is today established.

The problem may be approached from yet another angle. Consider for instance the decision of the United States Supreme Court in Hawker v. New York. The appellant in this case had been convicted of the crime of abortion in New York, in 1878, and sentenced to ten years imprisonment. An act of the legislature, passed in 1893 and amended in 1895, made it a misdemeanor for any person to practice medicine in the state after conviction of a felony. Hawker violated this statute, and appealed from his conviction under it on the ground that it violated the prohibition against *ex post facto* laws.

"On the one hand," said Mr. Justice Brewer, speaking for the Court, "it is said that defendant was tried, convicted, and sentenced for a criminal offense. He suffered

6. Wynehamer v. People (1856) 13 N.Y. 378.
7. (1887) 123 U.S. 623.
8. Hudson County Water Co. v. McCarter (1908) 209 U.S. 349.
9. Lemieux v. Young (1909) 211 U.S. 489.
10. Head v. Amoskeag Mfg. Co. (1885) 113 U.S. 9; Wurtz v. Hoagland (1885) 114 U.S. 606.
11. Charlotte, etc., R. R. Co. v. Gibbes (1892) 142 U.S. 386.
12. Health Department v. Trinity Church (1895) 145 N.Y. 32.
13. See C.B. & Q.R.R. v. Nebraska (1898) 170 U.S. 57; Wis., etc., R.R. Co. v. Jacobson (1900) 179 U.S. 287; C.B. & Q.R.R. Co. v. Illinois ex rel. Drainage Commissioners (1905) 200 U.S. 561.
14. Norwood v. Baker (1898) 172 U.S. 269.

the punishment pronounced. The legislature has no power to thereafter add to that punishment. . . . On the other hand, it is insisted that within the acknowledged reach of the police power, a state may prescribe the qualifications of one engaged in any business so directly affecting the lives and health of the people as the practice of medicine. . . . We are of opinion that this argument is the more applicable and must control [the case]. . . . That the form in which this legislation is cast suggests the idea of the imposition of an additional punishment for past offenses is not conclusive. We must look at the substance, and not the form; and the statute should be regarded as though it in terms declared that one who had violated the criminal laws of the state should be deemed of such bad character as to be unfit to practice medicine, and that the record of a trial and conviction should be conclusive evidence of such violation."[15]

Could a better illustration be demanded of the triumph of "laxism" in our constitutional law, as I have earlier defined this tendency? Looked at from the point of view of its operation upon defendant's rights—which, as Mr. Justice Harlan's dissenting opinion shows was the better established point of view—the statute before the Court was unquestionably an *ex post facto* law; but looked at from the point of view of its tendency to promote the ends of good government, it was within the police power; and despite the weight of precedent, the latter point of view prevailed. Why, then, should not the maxim against confiscation meet with the like fate, if confronted with a well-considered minimum wage or other social insurance scheme? Granted that in its immediate operation on private property, such a scheme would, by certain standards, be confiscatory; yet can it be denied that such a scheme would be calculated to further a widespread public interest? At least, it would seem that the constitutional issue must turn on this question, rather than on the question of alleged confiscation; and the more so since, as I have already indicated, the maxim against confiscation is today grounded on the "due process" clause, which, however, we have been repeatedly assured, does not override the power of the state to provide for the public health, safety, morals, and welfare.[16]

But the applicability of the maxim forbidding confiscation to social insurance projects may be challenged from yet another point of view. This maxim prohibits the *taking* of *private* property save on certain conditions, which implies that the property whose taking is thus forbidden has become definitely vested, in accordance with the law, in some private owner. Thus the question arises, in accordance with *what* law *is* property so vested? No one, I take it, would deny that all businesses are subject, to a greater or less extent, to public regulation for the public good, notwithstanding the fact that profits may be thus more or less curtailed. Yet what is this but to admit that the owner of a business has no indefeasible right to the profits thereof until the obligations legally chargeable against these have been met? Undoubtedly a system of social insurance would

15. Hawker v. New York (1898) 170 U.S. 189, 191.
16. See, especially, Atlantic Coast Line Co. v. Goldsboro (1914) 232 U.S. 548, and cases there cited.

comprise a lien upon business profits but, from what has already appeared, that fact would be far from classifying such a system as an invasion of vested rights.

We are thus brought to consider the second objection to social insurance legislation: the objection that the police power does not extend to the regulation of the status of employment, at least in the case of persons *sui juris*. In the Ives case the decision of the United States Supreme Court in Lochner v. The People of New York[17] was cited for this proposition, but, I think quite unwarrantably. The Lochner decision is undoubtedly open to criticism for the assumption which it makes that the welfare of the public is not affected by the hours of work of able-bodied laborers engaged in ordinary employments, but it clearly admits that the "freedom of contract," whether of employer or employee, is subject to the state in the reasonable exercise of its police power. And the more recent decision in Coppage v. Kansas,[18] which is also frequently cited in this connection, repeats the admission, albeit the Court fails to take the "judicial cognizance" which it has in other cases, of the actual disadvantage of employees in entering into contracts with large employers.[19] Moreover, if the concept of "freedom of contract" amounts to anything, it ought to secure an owner at least as great liberty of action in making contracts of sale as in making contracts of employment. Yet it is established doctrine that if a business is so widespread as to be of really public concern, the state may regulate its charges, and that independently of any right in the public to claim the service of the business.[20]

The question of the constitutional validity of social insurance depends, therefore, it seems to me, upon the existence of "a real, a substantial" relation[21] between a well-considered measure embodying the idea and the public welfare, or rather, perhaps, upon the existence of a widespread public conviction that there is such a relation.[22] Granted this much, and all other questions become impertinent. Nor does this signify, by any means, the negation of constitutional limitations: on the contrary, it signifies the affirmation of that species of constitutional limitations which already control in the great majority of cases touching the relation of legislative power and private rights.

Thus for one thing, it must be the *public* welfare which is to be promoted by legislation demanding vindication by this sort of test, not simply the welfare of an individual or a class. The recent Adamson Act may be considered as a case in point. Its immediate benefits are to go to a comparatively restricted group of

17. (1905) 198 U.S. 45.
18. (1915) 236 U.S. 1.
19. Holden v. Hardy (1898) 169 U.S. 366; Knoxville Iron & Coal Co. v. Harbison (1901) 183 U.S. 13; McLean v. Arkansas (1909) 211 U.S. 539.
20. Munn v. Illinois (1876) 94 U.S. 113; German Alliance Insurance Co. v. Lewis (1914) 233 U.S. 389.
21. Powell v. Pennsylvania (1888) 127 U.S. 678.
22. C.B. & Q.R.R. Co. v. McGuire (1911) 219 U.S. 549; Otis v. Parker (1903) 187 U.S. 606; Noble Bank v. Haskell, above; Price v. Illinois (1915) 238 U.S. 446; Laurel Hill Cemetery v. San Francisco (1910) 216 U.S. 358.

workmen while the claims of other groups better entitled by equity to legislative intervention in their behalf are ignored. It is true that the *enactment* of the measure may be reasonably thought to have averted a crisis, but in such a way as to invite its recurrence at any time, while the precise *provisions* of the act bear only the remotest relation to the public welfare. Also, far from springing from a widespread public conviction of its necessity, it is notorious that this statute came as a complete and most unpleasant surprise to almost everybody, while the ambiguity of its provisions attests in the most striking fashion their entire lack of constitutional *bona fides*. Nevertheless, I think that the purport of these provisions, expressed unambiguously, and embodied in a general scheme betokening the intention of Congress to put the relations of the great carriers and their employees on a stable and equitable basis, would stand on a far different footing legally—that they would, in fact, be constitutional.[23]

In the second place, however, the word "welfare" itself has certain implications that are not to be disregarded in determining the scope of legislative authority. From time immemorial the concept of public welfare and that of justice between man and man have existed side by side, taking color each from the other. So far, therefore, as such decisions as those in the Ives and Coppage cases imply that the "public welfare" is not to be defined regardless of what is rightly due from one man to another in a given situation, they are entitled to all respect. But this is far from conceding that the legal standards of justice that have come down to us from the past are today always adequate. Take for instance the rule against "liability without fault." As expressed in the common law doctrine of the "assumption of the risks of the trade" and as applied to the facts of modern machine industry, the rule is the merest solecism—a contradiction in terms. Again, consider Mr. Justice Pitney's suggestion in the Coppage case, that the Constitution does not permit a legislative distribution of the natural and inevitable advantages of wealth. Of course not; but neither does it forbid the elimination of many of the inequities that disparity of wealth and economic power produce. For the purpose of the Constitution in protecting wealth was to "establish justice" and "promote the general welfare," and such presumably is its purpose still.

23. The recent decision of the Supreme Court, Wilson v. New and Ferris, Receivers (March 19, 1917) October Term, 1916 No. 115, sustaining the Adamson Act seems to be based on the proposition that the act was an allowable measure in meeting an extraordinary emergency which threatened the total interruption of interstate commerce. The Court takes very broad cognizance of the circumstances constituting the emergency. Feeling as I do that the emergency was largely the result of the means employed by the government in meeting it, I must express my sympathy with the views of the minority of the Court. The words of Mr. Justice Day seem especially appropriate:

Inherently, such legislation requires that investigation and deliberation shall precede action. Nevertheless, Congress has in this act itself declared the lack of sufficient information and knowledge to warrant the action taken, and has directed an experiment to determine what it should do.

Such legislation, it seems to me, amounts to the taking of the property of one and giving it to another in violation of the spirit of fair play and the due process clause.

The phrase "social justice" is one that has fallen into some disrepute of late on account of the abuse of it by enthusiasts, and so circumspect folk generally give it wide berth. It has nonetheless real meaning, and especially does it call attention to the fact that the community as a whole ought to shoulder the burdens of modern community life, rather than those classes which are often made to do so precisely because they are least capable of doing it. In the simple economy of a frontier society, it was at once equitable and expedient to leave to the determination of accident, or private contract, many relationships which the more closely interwrought industrialized society of today must, both in justice to its weaker members and in support of the defensive powers of society, undertake to control directly. Hence the movement for a rational system of social insurance. The old time direct personal contact between master and servant has long since largely vanished from the world of production, but it is coming to be appreciated that the newer impersonal relationship of capital and labor is not devoid of moral responsibilities on both sides which the state is frequently warranted in attempting to elevate to legal responsibilities. Moreover, while the economic burden of social insurance must fall primarily upon investment capital, ultimately it will come to rest, as part and parcel of the whole cost of production, upon society at large. Nor is this to say that the courts must take cognizance of the speculations of political economists; for they can and do take cognizance of the practices of industry and commerce;[24] and at any rate it must be presumed that they may do whatever is necessary to a beneficial exercise of their powers.

It is, therefore, incredible that an intelligent tribunal would today endeavor to classify a well-considered minimum wage law, workmen's compensation law, or social insurance law with bills of pains and penalties, legislative forfeitures, or acts of confiscation, or as an attempt to limit "freedom of contract" unreasonably and arbitrarily. "Jurisprudence," the Court itself has informed us, "is a progressive science."[25] No doubt the admission may be unfairly stressed, since the normal function of the law is conservative, and not even the reformer would have it otherwise, once he has attained his objective. Still the fact remains that constitutional principles, which interpreted very adequately the needs of a prosperity resting upon individual thrift and exertion, today leave a great part of the industrial organism sprawling outside the legal shell. Such a situation, clearly, cannot endure nor be endured indefinitely. This would be the fact even though we could be confident henceforth of the immunity we have so long enjoyed from troublesome international relationships; the appreciation that we cannot enjoy such immunity only makes the problem the more imperious. And this is to say that the great effort toward national reorganization which is today just getting under way and the goal of which we have labelled "preparedness" has its constitutional phase, the solution of which will, necessarily, fall in considerable

---

24. Robbins v. Shelby County Taxing District (1887) 120 U.S. 489.
25. Holden v. Hardy, above.

part to the courts. In endeavoring their task, the judges cannot do better than to hark back to the view of our Constitution with which Chief Justice Marshall essayed so successfully a similar work—the view of it as an instrument "intended to endure for ages and consequently to be adapted to the various crises of human affairs."[26]

Since the foregoing was written the Supreme Court has rendered two decisions of much significance in connection with the matters herein discussed. In the New York Central Railroad Co. v. White[27] it sustained the recent New York Workmen's Compensation Act, and in the Mountain Timber Co. v. Washington[28] it upheld the Washington statute. Both these acts are of the "compulsory" type and govern hazardous employments, but there is this important difference between them. Whereas the New York act leaves the employer free to insure himself against the risks which it creates and accordingly puts it in his power to lessen these and the consequent expense by careful management, employers under the Washington statute must make an annual contribution to a state fund which is proportioned to the number of their employees entirely regardless of the extent to which injury has befallen such employees.

In the New York case Chief Justice White, speaking for a unanimous court, had little difficulty in disposing of the "liability without fault" argument. The idea, said he, "is not a novelty in the law," citing the common law liability of innkeepers, the rule as to dangerous things, and the principle of *respondeat superior*. "In excluding the question of fault as a cause of injury," he continued, "the act in effect disregards the proximate cause and looks to one more remote— the primary cause, as it may be deemed—and that is the employment itself." Also, he shrewdly pointed out that, "just as the employee's assumption of ordinary risks at the common law presumably was taken into account in fixing the rate of wages, so the fixed responsibility of the employer [under the new system] presumably will be reflected in the wage scale."

The Washington case was decided by a closely divided Court, Justice Pitney speaking for the majority. "The crucial inquiry under the Fourteenth Amendment," said he, "is whether it [the act] appears to be not a fair and reasonable exertion of governmental power, but so extravagant or arbitrary as to constitute an abuse of power." The following passage from the Court's answer to this question is of such importance from the point of view of social insurance projects that it deserves extensive quotation:

> Special burdens are often necessary for general benefits—for supplying water, preventing fires, lighting districts, cleaning streets. . . . Regulations for these purposes may press with more or less weight upon one than another, but they are designed, not to impose unequal or unnecessary restrictions on anyone, but to promote, with as little individual inconvenience as possible, the general good. . . . Certainly,

26. McCulloch v. Maryland (1819) 4 Wheat. (U.S.) 316, 415.
27. (March 6, 1917) U.S. Sup. Ct., October Term, 1916 No. 320.
28. (March 6, 1917) U.S. Sup. Ct., October Term, 1916 No. 13.

the operation of industrial establishments that in the ordinary course of things frequently and inevitably produce disabling or mortal injuries to the human beings employed is not a matter of wholly private concern. It hardly can be questioned that the state might expend public moneys to provide hospital treatment, artificial limbs, or like aid to persons injured in industry, and home or support for the widows or orphans of those killed. Does direct compensation stand on less secure ground? A familiar exercise of state power is the grant of pensions to disabled soldiers and to the widows and dependents of those killed in war. Such legislation usually is justified as fulfilling a moral obligation or as tending to encourage a public duty of defense. But is the state powerless to compensate with pensions or otherwise those who are disabled, or the dependents of those whose lives are lost, in the industrial occupations that are so necessary to develop the resources and add to the wealth and prosperity of the state? A machine as well as a bullet may produce a wound . . . , "the workman is the soldier of organized industry accepting a kind of pension in exchange for absolute insurance on his master's premises." Stertz v. Industrial Insurance Commission, 158 Pac. Rep., 256, 263. It is said that the compensation or pension under this law is not confined to those who are left without means of support. This is true. But is the state powerless to succor the wounded except they be reduced to the last extremity? Is it debarred from compensating an injured man until his own resources are first exhausted? This would be to discriminate against the thrifty in favor of the improvident. The power and discretion of the state are not thus circumscribed by the Fourteenth Amendment.

It seems to me that this utterance by the justice who spoke for the Court in the Coppage case goes very far indeed to dispense with the notion of an indefeasible right of either property or contract as against the reasonable exercise by the state of its police powers. In other words, constitutional "rigorism" is at an end.

3. Social Planning under the Constitution— A Study in Perspectives

I

OUR present discontents have evoked many earnest words on the subject of "social planning." We are told that "capital can be defended only by constructive programs based on the consideration of social responsibility"; that we are headed for "a frightful cataclysm" unless we adopt "a national plan that will control and guide the basic industries, govern the investment of capital, and keep purchasing power in step with production"; that if we are to avoid revolution, "we dare not sit indefinitely in contemplative inaction"; that "we require a leadership that will help us think less about the theories of individualism and more about the tragedies to individuals," inasmuch as "men cannot eat words . . . cannot wear words . . . cannot trust their old age to words."[1] In brief, if we are to avoid something worse, we must take some thought for the morrow.

There have, to be sure, been dissident voices too. One of these was raised at the recent Episcopal Convention at Denver. In a report submitted to this body occurred the following passage:

And yet, side by side with such misery and idleness, there are warehouses bursting with goods which cannot be bought; elevators full of wheat, while bread lines haunt our cities; carefully protected machinery lying idle, while jobless men throng our streets; money in abundance in the banks available at low rates. It is becoming increasingly evident that the conception of society as made up of autonomous independent individuals is as faulty from the point of view of economic realism as it is from the

Presidential address delivered before the American Political Science Association at its twenty-seventh annual meeting, Washington, D.C., December 28–30, 1931. From 26 *American Political Science Review* 1–27 (1932). Reprinted by permission.

1. For the above sentiments, see, in order, Dean Donham's *Business Adrift*, p. 101; *New York Times*, July 20, 1931, Professor Stuart Chase speaking; *id.*, June 3, President Butler speaking; *id.*, June 22, President Frank speaking.

standpoint of Christian idealism. Our traditional philosophy of rugged individualism must be modified to meet the needs of a cooperative age.[2]

When this was read, that wise and good man who is best known to the world as the principal author of the Great Wickersham Mystery arose and made solemn protest. "I think," said he, "this is an expression of social philosophy that is expressed by the Soviet government of Russia. It is a negation of the whole concept of American civilization." It was thereupon explained to Mr. Wickersham that the sentences to which he objected had been culled largely from recent addresses by Mr. Gerard Swope and Mr. Owen D. Young.

Mr. Wickersham's objection to social planning is in substance the same as Mr. Hoover's: "The American way of life must be preserved." Others have urged the inherent difficulties of the task. "What folly!" exclaims former Secretary of the Treasury David F. Houston:

> What man or group of men in this country would know how to direct all, or many, of the leading activities of this great nation; and who is so innocent as to assume that, if they were to make a plan, our people would follow it, unless they could be made slaves? Certainly the federal government could not formulate or direct such a plan. It is none too successful in discharging its constitutional functions. It cannot even run a routine business like the Post-Office without a huge deficit.

Mr. Newton D. Baker is of the same persuasion. He doubts "whether there can be wisdom enough to plan an economic future for the United States," and adds, "progress is a function of freedom"—that is, presumably, freedom from social planning.[3]

Moreover, difficulty is a matter which is relative to character. So it is important to take into account Mr. J. T. Adams's suggestion that we Americans are not a planning race, having always taken the easier way of running away from our troubles. Hence he ventures to question whether it was the really capable Puritans who braved the Atlantic for New England's rockbound coast, hinting on the contrary that the best of the breed stayed at home, cut off King Charles's head, and eventually remade the English constitution to their liking. And ever since then, Mr. Adams continues, instead of facing the difficulties and at the same time appropriating the richer cultural possibilities of a stabilized life at home, we have, as population became denser and social arrangements more intricate, raced off toward the frontier, with the result that now when the frontier has vanished we are at a loss what to do.[4]

The easy and obvious answer to all which is that plans *have been* offered. No less a personage than the president of the United States, despite his faith in "the American way of life," has offered two plans at different times. The earlier one, antedating the catastrophe of October, 1929, called "with the help of God" for

2. *New York Times,* September 29, 1931.
3. Quoted by Professor Beard in his article in the *Forum,* July, 1931.
4. This, I take it, is the general purport of views advanced by Mr. Adams in his recent *Epic of America.*

the early abolition of poverty; the other, elaborated after that event and with outside assistance no longer available, demanded in its first item a twenty million increase in population during the next twenty years—the idea being no doubt to relieve the Federal Farm Board of some of its anxieties.

Nor have our business leaders failed us in this crisis. Their program is that buying should be stimulated, to which end wages should come down and railway rates go up; also the Sherman Act should be repealed or modified, and at the same time "government should get out of business"—this is to say, out of the business of trying to govern; furthermore, in order that social planning may have a certain idealistic cast, the American taxpayer should be permitted to manifest his natural humanitarianism by agreeing to cancel Europe's war debts to the United States, thereby putting speculative banking loans to Germany on a sounder basis; and that this display of altruism may be truly national, the income tax must not be increased as to the upper brackets. Lastly, but by no means least, that most un-American contrivance, the "dole," must at all costs be avoided—except of course in its American form of the protective tariff. Provided with such a program, we have only to mount the business cycle, and before we know it we shall be whisked back to the golden days of 1929, but with this difference—forwarned by what happened then, we shall all sell out at the peak of the market this time and be able to retire millionaires!

And with business thus alert to its opportunity, the question necessarily arises, What part is political science prepared to take in social planning? The answer depends to some extent on what is meant by "social planning." When Charlie Chaplin met Mahatma Gandhi in London, he told him that he did not understand the reason for using such a crude device as Mr. Gandhi's hand spinning wheel when modern machinery seemed better for the purpose. Mr. Gandhi explained that it was necessary to provide occupation for India's millions and that modern machinery would leave them with too much leisure. "We might install modern looms like they have in Lancashire," he said, "but then we would produce more than we need and enforce idleness upon some other part of the world as a result of our overproduction."[5]

Of course, anything like social planning on the scale suggested by the Mahatma's words may be dismissed at the outset in the presence of "the American way of life." Despite Professor Einstein's warning that "anyone who thinks science is trying to make human life easier or more pleasant is utterly mistaken," that is just what we do think, especially when science assumes the guise of technology, in other words, enters the service of business and profit-taking. So we remain blithe while the trucks and buses shove us off the highways and bankrupt the railways; we permit "the N.B.C. and associated stations" to turn over a major invention like the radio to crooning troubadours and purveyors of toothpaste,

5. *New York Times*, September 23, 1931.

thanking God the meanwhile that it has been kept free of "political control"; and we greet always with renewed enthusiasm any triumph of inventive genius whereby, we are assured, thousands of fresh recruits will be made available to the ranks of the unemployed.

No; with us social planning—in the probable absence from the scene of some miraculous combination of Confucius, Aristotle, Mussolini, Lenin, and a few others—must take place in the frame—or the "frame-up"—provided by technology as above defined. It will, therefore, develop no grand strategy, nor reveal any considered theory of social arrangement and individual happiness. It will consist rather in desultory attacks upon what the pragmatists delight to term "situations" and "predicaments." At that, its eventual role may not be unimportant if the habit be permitted to grow.

And in this work the part of political scientists should also be important; provided they choose their tools and techniques for the task in hand rather than *vice versa,* and provided also they continue to talk intelligibly. Some recent articles in the *Review* are hardly reassuring on the latter score.[6] They remind one of the plight of small Genevieve. "Yes," said the proud mother, "Genevieve is now in school and is studying French and algebra. Come and say good morning to the lady in algebra, Genevieve." When political science begins talking algebra, it will make no great practical difference whether the people who understand it do so or not.

II

It is a maxim approved of cooks that if you would make an omelet you must break some eggs. Mr. Owen D. Young has recently voiced his endorsement of this maxim in his remarks on Mr. Gerard Swope's plan:[7]

> May I say, Mr. President, that economic planning will contribute to a standardized and so more stable prosperity, but in the same breath may I remind you that, like all other things in this world, it demands its price. A plan written on paper is of no service. A plan proposed for education is of some service, but it is likely to become obsolete before it becomes effective. A plan to be productive of quick results must be executed promptly. No one concern can make it effective. Cooperation is required by the great majority of the participants and the coercion of the rest may ultimately be necessary. I hate not only the term but the idea of coercion, and yet we are forced to recognize that every advance in social organization requires the voluntary surrender of a certain amount of individual freedom by the majority and the ultimate coercion of the minority. It is not the coercion of the recalcitrant minority but the voluntary submission by the large majority which should impress us. Anyhow, the question is whether the people who are calling for economic planning really mean what they say. Are they willing to surrender their individual freedom to the extent necessary to execute a plan?

6. I refer to my friend Professor Charles H. Titus's articles in the February and August, 1931, issues of this *Review*.
7. *New York Times,* September 17, 1931.

And again:

> We can retain in this country unorganized individual planning and operation, but if
> we do its action will necessarily be at times chaotic, and we shall, as a result, pay the
> economic penalty of that disorder, such as we are paying now. We can in this country
> have organized economic planning with some curtailment of individual freedom
> which, if the plan be wise and properly executed, will tend to diminish economic
> disorder and the penalties which we pay. Then too, the question is to whom this
> individual freedom is to be surrendered? If the government is to undertake the great
> obligations which Mr. Swope's plan visualizes, then the price must be in the form of a
> surrender to political government. If industry itself is to perform those obligations, as
> is here contemplated, then the surrender of the individual units is to be made to the
> organized group, of which the unit is a part. If results are to be obtained, they call for
> surrender somewhere. The question for the public is to say whether they wish the
> results, and if so, by what agency they are to be accomplished.

While Mr. Young here holds out the possibility of business setting its own house in order, he at the same time admits that there will always be recalcitrant minorities to be coerced. What is more, his expectation of the major part of business seems a trifle optimistic, to say the least. The present depression is the fifteenth major depression of the past century, and no other—in the absence of that fillip to creative thinking which bears the label "Moscow"—seems to have suggested to either business or government anything more than hand to mouth expedients. What is more, no single important measure of the past forty years meant to correct business practices in the interest of a wider public can be pointed to which had the support of business. The Interstate Commerce Act did not, the Sherman Act did not, the Federal Trade Commission did not, the Clayton Act did not, the Federal Reserve Act did not. On the contrary, business presented in every one of these instances an almost solid front of opposition.

Any viable plan affecting business in an important way must unquestionably consult business experience, in other words, the experience of businessmen. With equal certainty, it must rely in part upon sanctions which only government can supply; and that means ordinarily, in view of the present structure of business, sanctions which only the national government can apply effectively. And so the question presents itself, What sanctions does the Constitution, that is to say, constitutional law, permit?

The present-day edifice of American constitutional law dates to an altogether unappreciated extent from this side of the year 1890, and so is fully a century younger than the Constitution itself; and especially is this true of those doctrines and principles concerning which the social planner needs feel special concern. These are not, in the main, the outgrowth of earlier precedents; more often they are the repudiation of them. They derive from a point of view which became dominant with the Court about 1890 and remained so for somewhat more than a decade and a half.

Never had "the American way of life" been in such peril as in the decade which is divided by the year 1890. The Federation of Labor, the Haymarket riots, the Chicago stockyards strike, the Homestead strike, the panic of 1893, "Coxey's army," the Pullman strike, "Free Silver," "Coin" Harvey, "Crown of Thorns and Cross of Gold," Altgeld, Pennoyer, "Bloody-Bridles" Wait, and so on and so forth; why continue? The country was in a state of riot, and, in the phraseology of the common law, "men of firm mind, with property in the neighborhood and women and children to protect," were alarmed.

To compensate, on the other hand, for this most distressing situation of fact, what may be termed the ideological situation was most reassuring to those to whom, in the contemporary words of the president of the Reading Railway, "God in His Wisdom had confided the destinies of this great nation."[8] There was not a teacher of political economy of any reputation in the country who did not teach that economic activity was governed by laws of its own which, so long as government did not interfere with their operation, worked inevitably for human betterment. Then to back the teachings of the classical political economy was the lesson drawn from the current Darwinian biology. Evolution was a universal process which had all nature, including human nature, in its grip, and was tugging it along to some far off divine event willy-nilly. For evolution meant "the survival of the *fittest*"; only it must be *evolution,* that is, improvement by the slow accumulation of minute differences, not *revolution,* of which indeed the century had earlier had rather more than its fill.

So when Mr. Gladstone uttered his well-intentioned eulogy of the Constitution of the United States as "the greatest work ever struck off at a given time by the brain and purpose of man," the pundits assailed him from every side. "Brain and purpose of man"—a gross heresy! The American Constitution was only a copy of the British constitution "with the monarchy left out," and the British constitution was the superlative embodiment of political wisdom which it was because in sooth it embodied no wisdom at all, being "a growth," "an accumulation." To consider the Constitution of 1789 as an instance of social planning was an utterly abhorrent notion to the generation of 1890.

But the mind which compacted the laissez-faire political economy and biological evolutionism into a systematic philosophy was that of Herbert Spencer, whose *Social Statics* Mr. Justice Holmes once informed the Court, though unavailingly at the time, the Fourteenth Amendment was not intended to enact. There are few less humorous books in the language than Spencer's *Autobiography,* although this does not signify that it is entirely unamusing. Spencer's foible, along with omniscience, was originality, and indeed his claims on the latter score may usually be conceded. Educated in a haphazard fashion, he had developed something like genius for picking up information wherever he went and with whomever he conversed, and an equal genius, if so it should be termed, for

8. See W. J. Ghent's contemporary *Our Benevolent Feudalism.*

combining facts and ideas into systems; whence Huxley's gibe that "Spencer's idea of a tragedy was a beautiful theory killed by an ugly fact." Had he been a mechanic, Spencer would have spent his days tinkering at perpetual motion; had he been a mathematician, he would have squared the circle, at least to his own satisfaction. Having, however, given his interest to social theory, or "sociology," he did what was equivalent, reconciled—to his own satisfaction—the doctrine of natural rights, which he had imbibed in youth from the discourses of dissenting preachers, with the notion of society as an organism, an adoption and adaptation from the current Darwinism.

Society, being an organism, is, of course, subject to the evolutionary process, albeit in a manner somewhat peculiar. For the social organism, on examination, possesses two "organizations," the "nervous," which is the state or government, and the "alimentary," or industry. The former is "inferior," and therefore destined eventually to disappear through the operation of evolution on its constituent cells, that is, human beings, thus leading to increasing "individuation" and ultimately political anarchy. The evolution of the latter, on the other hand, is attended by progressive "integration of function" or "sympathy" among its cells, that is, these same human beings. So in the end the human family, pleasantly relieved of its nervous system, is absorbed into the social stomach, and along with this apotheosis universal peace and goodwill hold sway. In short, while political subordination is utterly antagonistic to the nature of man, economic subordination is not.[9]

Mr. Ernest Barker opines that Spencer is just the kind of political philosopher that England deserved, a statement which is not intended apparently to be especially complimentary to either of the parties mentioned. The apostle of Spencer to the American people—and a very fervent one—was John Fiske. Of Fiske, his rival, the historian Winsor, maliciously, and perhaps a bit enviously, declared that he was "the greatest of historians among philosophers and the greatest of philosophers among historians." And through Fiske or more directly, American judges and lawyers became indoctrinated with the Spencerian concept of "equal freedom," that is, "such measure of freedom for each as is compatible with the like freedom for all"—a conception which Mr. Al Capone would undoubtedly applaud, implying as it does, the right of anybody to become a gunman or racketeer so long as he refrains from "elbowing in" tactics.

At any rate, furnished with this endorsement of the "American way of life" as part and parcel of a universal, ineluctable, and all-beneficent process, "the naïf, simple-minded men" (the phrase is Justice Holmes's) who composed the Supreme Court of the years 1890 and following set to work, with the resolution which only consciousness of a righteous cause can lend, to remake our constitutional law, and within a decade and a half had succeeded in doing so with astonishing completeness.

9. See Ernest Barker's *Political Thought from Spencer to the Present Day* and Francis W. Coker's *Organismic Theories of the State*.

III

In the history of the Supreme Court, two terms of Court stand out above all others for the significance of their results to American constitutional law, the February term of 1819, when McCulloch v. Maryland, Sturges v. Crowninshield, and Dartmouth College v. Woodward were decided; and the October term of 1984 when the Sugar Trust case, the Income Tax cases, and *In re* Debs were passed upon.[10] Nor would it be easy to conceive how three decisions could possibly have been more to the liking of business than the three decisions last mentioned. In the Sugar Trust case, the recently enacted Sherman Anti-Trust Act was put to rest for a decade, during which period capital, fulfilling the Pauline injunction of "diligence in business, serving the Lord," made the most of its opportunities. In the Income Tax cases, the Court, undertaking to correct what it termed a "century of error," ruled that the wealth of the country was to be no longer subject to national taxation. At the same time, when the said wealth was menaced with physical violence, it was entitled, by the decision in the Debs case, to have every resource of the national executive and judicial power brought to its protection.

The so-called Sugar Trust was a combination of manufacturers which, the Court admitted, controlled a vast portion of the sugar market of the United States; and, as the government pointed out, a manufacturer manufactures in order to sell his product, and in the case of a necessary of life like sugar the overwhelming proportion of the product will be sold outside the state where it is produced, and, if the concern is a monopoly, on terms dictated by it. The Court answered, nevertheless, that "this was no more than to say that trade and commerce served manufacture to fulfill its function!" Thus the very process which the Anti-Trust Act was designed to govern, namely, commerce in the etymological sense of "buying and selling," was assimilated to the local process of manufacturing—in short, was held not to exist. The result is the more striking in view of the fact that in the first case to arise under the commerce clause, Gibbons v. Ogden, the question at issue was whether "commerce" ever meant anything but buying and selling.

And so the law stood until the Swift case of 1905,[11] when the Court announced that it would no longer permit "a course of business" which was essentially interstate to be characterized by its intrastate incidents for the purpose of rendering national control of it ineffective. This holding, in which Justice Holmes spoke for the Court, injected new life into the Anti-Trust Act just as the second Roosevelt administration was getting under way. But meantime most of the damage had been done, and the Court so realized. In the Standard Oil and Tobacco cases[12] of 1912, Chief Justice White announced the famous "rule of

10. 156 U.S. 1; 157 U.S. 429 and 158 U.S. 601; 158 U.S. 564.
11. 196 U.S. 375.
12. 221 U.S. 1 and 106.

reason," which is properly to be interpreted as an attempt on the part of the Court to effect a *modus vivendi* between the resuscitated Sherman Act and the existing structure of American big business for which the Court itself was so largely responsible. The act had been restored to the statute books, to be sure, but there must be no "running amuck" with it.

Even more remarkable was the Court's correction of a "century of error" in the Income Tax cases. An error so venerable ought, one would think, to have become entitled long since to be regarded as truth, not to mention the fact that the trail of this particular error led to the very doors of the body which framed the Constitution. This was the idea that the term "direct taxes" comprehended only land and poll taxes, having been inserted in the Constitution, not for the purpose of reducing materially the complete power of taxation which elsewhere in the Constitution had been conferred on the national government, but for the very limited purpose of reassuring the southern slaveholders that their broad acres and slaves would not be subjected to land and poll taxes. And the Court was equally dashing in its encounters with the precepts of the Aristotelian logic. The chief justice's opinion for the Court comprised the contention that a tax on income which is derived from property must be regarded as a tax on said property, and *so as a direct tax on it,* although if words be given their "ordinary meaning," as the chief justice was scrupulous to insist, it would seem clearly evident that a tax burden which reaches property in consequence of being imposed upon income derived from it reaches the property *indirectly.*

But the decision has also its "inarticulate major premise," save that, thanks to Justice Field, it did not remain inarticulate. In the words of his concurring opinion, the income tax was "but a beginning" of "an assault upon capital" which was bound to spread until "our political contests will become a war of the poor upon the rich"; and while Justice Gray, the other of the two Nestors of the bench, kept silent—indeed very much so—he reversed the opinions of a lifetime—"over night," as Mr. Bryan would have it—to help resist the assault *in principiis.* The schoolboy who defined "property" as "what socialists attack" had, it may be surmised, been reading the Income Tax decision.

And, while the regulatory and taxing powers centered in Congress were being thus seriously diminished, the protective powers centered in the president and the courts were undergoing a contrary process in the Debs case. Correcting another "century of error," the Court held in that case that the executive has the prerogative right to enter the national courts independently of statutory authorization, and obtain an injunction to protect any widespread public interest of a proprietary nature, and to support the injunction with all requisite force. Should "the man on horseback" ever put in an appearance, he might well baptize his Bucephalus "In Re Debs."

Meantime, beginning with the first Minnesota Rate case, decided in 1890, our laissez-faire Court had been struggling with the question of railway rate regulation, but did not achieve final results until Smyth v. Ames, seven years later.[13]

13. 134 U.S. 418; 169 U.S. 466.

The original theory of rate regulation was stated in 1876 in the great case of Munn v. Illinois,[14] while the Court was under the liberal presidency of Chief Justice Waite. It is to the effect that property embarked in a business which is "affected with a public interest"—a point subject ordinarily to legislative determination—is property which from the moment of its investment is "dedicated to a public use," and is therefore subject to the risk of regulation by and for the public. The theory underlying Smyth v. Ames is almost the exact antithesis of this. It is that a public regulation of charges is *pro tanto* an appropriation of property which up to that moment was *juris privati* only, a premise from which ensues almost mathematically the rule that rates which are set by public authority must yield a fair return on "the present value" of the property undergoing regulation. As is well known, this rule is the rock upon which, outside the jurisdiction of the Interstate Commerce Commission, all programs of public utility regulation have come to grief, and the only reason why it has not been a source of disaster in the national field is that there it has been largely ignored. The inability of the railroads, without the consent of the Interstate Commerce Commission, to boost rates in a situation in which rates, as today, are not yielding a "fair return" on railroad property can be reconciled with the doctrine of Smyth v. Ames only with the greatest difficulty, if at all.

But if Smyth v. Ames set up new restrictions on legislative power in control of business and property, by the same token it also enlarged judicial review in safeguard of those interests, and the decision in Holden v. Hardy[15] in the same term of Court did so even more strikingly. In this case the Court, following some earlier backing and filling with respect to the matter, finally discarded the rule laid down in Munn v. Illinois for the determination of cases arising under the due process clause, that "if a state of facts could exist justifying legislation, it must be presumed that they did exist," and gave unmistakable warning that it intended henceforth to require the state to show special justification in support of measures restrictive of the right of employers to make such terms as their economic advantage enabled them to in dealing with employees and those seeking employment, that is, so-called "freedom of contract." This time, it is true, the special justification was found in the special dangers of underground mining, and so an eight-hour law for such employments was sustained as "reasonable" and therefore due process of law. The implications of the case became explicit, however, when, seven years later, such special justification not being found to exist as regards the baking business, a ten-hour law for such employments was held void in the famous Lochner case.[16]

The truly miraculous effect of Smyth v. Ames and Holden v. Hardy upon the Court's power of judicial review is not open to question. Anterior to that time, thirty years under the Fourteenth Amendment had given rise to one hundred and thirty-four cases under all clauses of the amendment. In the course of the next

14. 94 U.S. 113.
15. 169 U.S. 366.
16. 198 U.S. 45.

fifteen years, more than three times as many cases were decided under the due process of law and equal protection clauses alone. The Court had become a third house of every legislature in the country, or, as Justice Brandeis has expressed it, a "super-legislature."

Two other closely related lines of doctrine in this period may be dismissed more briefly, although they are of great importance for the protection which in combination they afford "the American way of life." The first is illustrated by the "Liquor cases,"[17] in which the Court for the first time projected the commerce clause sharply into the field of the states' police power. In these cases it was held that, liquor being "a good article of commerce," the states could not forbid interstate traffic in it, a doctrine which put the solution of the liquor question on a local basis out of the bounds of constitutional possibility, and so led finally to the Eighteenth Amendment, in somewhat the same way that the Dred Scott decision, by rendering a legislative solution of the slavery question constitutionally impossible, contributed to bring on the Civil War.

The other line of cases referred to was headed by the "Lottery case," Champion v. Ames.[18] In that case the Court, after three arguments, sustained, by a vote of five to four, an act of Congress excluding lottery tickets from interstate transportation, but did so on grounds which strongly implied that all efforts on the part of Congress to control concerns engaged in interstate business by the threat of stopping their interstate trade would be likely to be frustrated by the Court. The culmination of the course of reasoning adopted by the Court in Champion v. Ames is to be seen in the first Child Labor case, Hammer v. Dagenhart.[19] There Congress was informed that it could not prohibit the interstate transportation of child-made goods, since to do so would be to invade the police powers of the states; although by the Liquor cases just referred to any attempt by a state to do the same thing would amount to an invasion of the power of Congress to regulate interstate commerce.

Once again the Court was correcting a "century of error." That the power to regulate commerce comprises the power to prohibit it appears to the point of demonstration from the simple consideration that when prohibition is for any reason essential, it is the regulatory power which must provide it. And so it was assumed by the Federal Convention; otherwise, why the provision that the slave trade was not to be prohibited until 1808? As Judge Davis pointed out in the early case of the *William*,[20] growing out of Jefferson's embargo, this provision shows that "the national sovereignty" was thought to be authorized to abridge commerce "in favor of the great principles of humanity and justice," and for "other purposes of general policy and interest." Indeed, Hamilton in the *Federalist* had listed the commercial power as one of the powers which are vested in Congress

17. 125 U.S. 465; 135 U.S. 100.
18. 188 U.S. 321.
19. 247 U.S. 251.
20. 28 Fed. Cas. No. 16,700.

"without any limitation whatsoever"; and Marshall's later consideration of the same subject in Gibbons v. Ogden[21] is to like effect: "The wisdom and discretion of Congress, their identity with the people, and the influence which their constituents possess at elections, are, in this, as in many other instances, as that, for example, of declaring war, the sole restraints on which they have relied to secure them from its abuse."

The issue raised by the confrontation of these words with those of the Court in Champion v. Ames and Hammer v. Dagenhart is of the utmost importance from the point of view of any considerable program of social planning. As we have seen, planning means coercion for intransigent minorities—that at least—and if coercion is to be applied by the national government, it must usually be under the commerce clause.

I do not mean to suggest, however, that to Congress should be attributed an unconditional power over everybody's privilege of engaging in interstate commerce in all situations and for all purposes—that, for instance, of controlling marriage and divorce. What I do mean is that *all businesses whose operations extend beyond the boundary lines of a single state should be regarded as subject through their interstate commercial activities to the control of Congress fairly and reasonably exercised.* Commerce is business, and today business is dominated by its interstate characteristics—buying and selling across state lines, transportation across state lines, communication across state lines. So, in "the typical and actual course of events," even manufacturing becomes but a stage in the flow of the raw product to the mill and the outflow of the finished product from the mill to the market; and while checking momentarily the current of interstate commerce, is at the same time, to adapt the words of Chief Justice Taft in Stafford v. Wallace,[22] "indispensable to its continuity." In short—to reverse the expression of the Court in the Sugar Trust case—manufacturing today serves trade and commerce to fulfil *their* function.

Over business thus organized the states are unable, in point both of law and of fact, to exert any effective control; nor would interstate compacts assist them materially in the attempt to do so if unaccompanied by extensive delegations of power from Congress. By Congress alone can the public interest which modern business purports to serve be safeguarded ordinarily, for it is the interest of the country as a whole.

IV

"What proximate test of excellence can be found," asks Justice Holmes in his essay on Montesquieu, "except correspondence to the actual equilibrium of forces in the community—that is, conformity to the wishes of the dominant

21. 9 Wheat. 1.
22. 258 U.S. 495. See also 262 U.S. 1.

power?'' ''Of course,'' he adds, ''such conformity may lead to destruction, and it is desirable that the dominant power be wise. But, wise or not, the proximate test of good government is that the dominant power have its way.'' Hence, ''the true science of the law,'' as he elsewhere remarks, ''consists in the establishment of its postulates from within upon accurately measured social desires''—a point for our statisticians.[23]

Justice Holmes brought his pragmatic outlook—perhaps it should be spelled with a capital ''P''—to the bench in December, 1902, although it was some years before its leaven began to affect perceptibly the heavy theological Spencerianism of that tribunal. Indeed, his opinion in the Swift case is the first clear assertion of the new point of view. And to his pragmatism—wherein he was the teacher rather than the disciple of his fellow Cantabrigian, William James— Holmes the legal philosopher added the contribution of Holmes the historian of the common law—the discovery, revolutionary at the time, that the judges are not the mere automata of established rules of law, but are lawmakers, whether they would be or not, and so must accept responsibility for the kind of law they make.

And yet—and this is the third point in the Holmesian credo—the traditions of their office should inspire judges with a certain aloofness toward the issues of the day. They should endeavor to look at things *sub specie quasi aeternitatis,* so to speak, and not be in a bustle to align themselves with either ''the dominant forces of society'' or the contrary forces. They should, indeed, let such forces have a fair field, and only come in at the end when their craftsmanship is needed to record the terms of settlement.

> ''It is a misfortune,'' he once asserted, with both our constitutional law and our common law in mind, ''if a judge reads his conscious or unconscious sympathy with one side or the other prematurely into the law, and forgets that what seem to him to be first principles are believed by half his countrymen to be wrong. . . . When twenty years ago a vague terror went over the earth and the word Socialism began to be heard, I thought and still think that fear was translated into doctrines that had no place in the Constitution or the common law. Judges are apt to be naïf, simple-minded men, and they need something of Mephistopheles.''[24]

Thus Justice Holmes became the mouthpiece on the bench of a new gospel of laissez faire, namely, of laissez faire for legislative power, because legislative power is, or under the democratic dispensation ought to be, the voice of ''the dominant power'' of society.

At about the same time, moreover, the Court was also introduced to a new technique in the weighing of constitutional issues. This occurred when Mr. Louis D. Brandeis handed the Court, in defense of an Oregon statute limiting the working hours of women,[25] his famous brief, three pages of which were devoted

23. *Collected Legal Papers,* pp. 224–26 and 258.
24. *Id.,* p. 295.
25. Muller v. Oregon, 208 U.S. 412.

to a statement of the constitutional principles involved and 113 pages of which were devoted to the presentation of facts and statistics, backed by scientific authorities, to show the evil effects of too long hours on women, "the mothers of the race." The act was sustained, Justice Brewer, the arch-conservative of the Court, delivering the opinion. And the work thus begun by Attorney Brandeis has been continued by Justice Brandeis. The Court's function, under the due process of law clause, he has defined as that of determining the reasonableness of legislation "in the light of all facts which may enrich our knowledge and enlarge our understanding."[26] Indeed, this technique has imparted a new flexibility to the concepts of constitutional law in almost every one of its more important departments, and to have given it scope is the really valuable aspect of the modern doctrine of due process of law.

For our purposes, no detailed consideration of the work of the Court from 1905 to 1920 is essential. In the field of state legislation, the outstanding achievement was workmen's compensation; in that of national legislation, it was the reconstitution of the Interstate Commerce Commission and the immense augmentation of its powers, and in both instances the Court lent a helpful hand. A few dicta of the period are, however, so much to our purpose as to warrant quotation, notwithstanding limitations of time and space.

Speaking for the Court in the workmen's compensation cases, Justice Pitney hinted the premise of a much more comprehensive scheme of social insurance, characterizing the worker as "the soldier of industry" and industry as "the joint enterprise" of capital and labor.[27] Voicing the Court's approval of an act of Kansas regulating insurance rates, Justice McKenna protested "against that conservatism of the mind which puts to question every new act of regulating legislation and regards the legislation as invalid or dangerous until it has become familiar." In the face of this, said he, "government—state and national—has pressed on in the general welfare and our reports are full of cases where in instance after instance the exercise of regulation was resisted and yet sustained against attacks asserted to be justified by the Constitution of the United States. The dread of the moment having passed, no one is now heard to say that rights were restrained or their constitutional guarantees impaired."[28]

To the same justice must also be credited a notable statement, in support of the White Slave Act, of the concept of cooperative federalism: "Our dual form of government has its perplexities, state and nation having different spheres of jurisdiction . . .but it must be kept in mind that we are one people; and the powers preserved to the states and those conferred on the nation are adapted to be exercised, whether independently or concurrently, to promote the general welfare, material and moral"[29]—a sentiment which, unfortunately, precisely one-

26. 264 U.S. 504, 534.
27. 243 U.S. 188 and 219.
28. 233 U.S. 389.
29. 227 U.S. 308.

half of one justice too many was to forget or ignore when it came to deciding the first Child Labor case.

To the same period also belong the memorable words of Justice Holmes in sustaining the migratory game treaty with Canada:

> When we are dealing with words that are also a constituent act like the Constitution of the United States, we must realize that they have called into life a being the development of which could not have been forseen completely by the most gifted of its begettors. It was enough for them to realize or to hope that they had created an organism. . . . The case before us must be considered in the light of our whole experience and not merely in the light of what was said a hundred years ago.[30]

Such statements evidence an inclination of mind, and one never can tell of what value they may be in imparting to a puzzled Court the same favorable inclination again.

V

Chief Justice White's presidency of the Court was, therefore, in the main, one of the expansive views of governmental power, although not always; Chief Justice Taft's period, on the other hand, was one, frequently, of reaction toward earlier concepts, sometimes indeed of their exaggeration. Yet even when the more advanced positions of the earlier period were later relinquished, they were not therefore obliterated. In the corporate memory of bench and bar and jurists— to say nothing of the dissents of Justices Holmes and Brandeis, reinforced later on by Justice Stone—they still survive as *points d' appui* for the Court of today and tomorrow.

The *chef d' oeuvre* of the Taft Court was its decision in the minimum wage case, to which the chief justice himself dissented.[31] In the course of the war with Germany, the Court had sustained several measures, both state and national, on the ground that they met an existing emergency. From this circumstance the new membership of the Court proceeded to draw the rather questionable conclusion that an emergency must be forthcoming to justify even legislation designed to remedy long-standing conditions; and naturally in an era of "return to normalcy" a justifying emergency was often hard to produce.

For the rest, the Court's disposition of the minimum wage case reduces to this: that whatever might be urged on behalf of the statute on the score of the public interest involved or of widespread popular approval, inasmuch as it invaded fundamental property rights, it was null and void. Incontestably this is a position for which much may be said on historical grounds. The doctrine of vested rights, as applied in a number of the state courts before the Civil War, was to the general effect that the property right was subject to regulation primarily for the purpose

30. 252 U.S. 416.
31. 261 U.S. 525.

of making the subject matter of the right more secure in the hands of the owner and more useful to him in the long run; if the state wished to venture beyond this, it must employ the power of eminent domain. But the property right then thought of was, for the most part, a right of direct control over definite, tangible *things* and belonged to natural *persons,* parties to the social contract and endowed with the inalienable rights of man. Today the ownership of the vast proportion of the wealth of the country, probably of all of it of which the social planner would have to take account, is vested in corporations; and a corporation, in the language of that notable conservative, Justice Brewer, "while by fiction of law recognized for some purposes as a person . . . is not endowed with the inalienable rights of a natural person."[32]

Ownership, in a word, has become *depersonalized;* and this signifies, so far as the individual owner is concerned, a transference of control over his property which, were it to government, would amount to outright confiscation. When this association was in session in Cleveland last year, we all had the opportunity of reading in the Cleveland papers of the outcome of a suit between the Bethlehem Steel Corporation and the Youngstown Sheet and Tube Company. From testimony taken in this litigation it transpired that the Bethlehem Steel directors had presented its executives, including several of said directors, nearly thirty-two millions of dollars during a period when dividends to the holders of common stock totalled less than forty-one millions; that indeed during the years 1925 to 1928 inclusive, when not a dollar was paid to the common stock holders, nearly seven millions of dollars had been paid to ten or a dozen favored executives and directors. A few months later a suit was brought in the New Jersey chancery court by certain stockholders to force an accounting from the bonus-grabbing directors and executives, and in passing on a preliminary phase of the suit the vice-chancellor said: "The administration of the bonus system has been sedulously suppressed from the stockholders, the result only coming to their notice recently." The defense of the bonus system was undertaken by Mr. Schwab, who assumed full responsibility for it. With his customary *suavity,* he declared: "I had the feeling that this damn company belonged to me, you know, and I went ahead and did the best I could." In point of fact, the books of the company showed that Mr. Schwab owned no common stock at all, but that his sole stock interest comprised forty-three thousand eight hundred sixty-six shares of preferred stock. The bonus system continues, nevertheless, although on a reduced scale. Nor is the principle which this parable illustrates at all obscure or recondite. It is phrased in a recent Supreme Court opinion in the following words: "The corporation is a person and its ownership is a non-conductor that makes it impossible to attribute an interest in its property to its members."[33]

But not only has ownership become depersonalized through absorption of its

32. 193 U.S. 197, 362.
33. 282 U.S. 19.

active elements into the rapidly expanding prerogatives of corporation management; property of all kinds has, as it were, become *dematerialized,* by which I mean merely that economic value is today a function of social arrangement as never before, so that when social process falters, value simply takes to itself wings. Within the last twenty-seven months, it has been estimated, anywhere between one-half and two-thirds of the "property," so-called, in this country has simply evaporated. The circumstance is of too impressive dimensions to leave constitutional theory respecting the property right unaffected. Nor should we overlook the concessions which the Court itself has made in recent years to governmental power in times of emergency—emergency being just what life nowadays "ain't nothing but."[34]

The truth is that even judicial conservatism is not always obdurate to ideas of social planning. The same Court which decided the Minimum Wage case, speaking through the same justice, upheld, in Euclid v. Ambler Realty Company,[35] a zoning ordinance which the company asserted would reduce the market value of land owned by it from ten thousand to twenty-five hundred dollars per acre. "A belief, no matter how fervently or widely entertained, that municipal authorities can assert some sort of communal control over privately owned land," said counsel "is at variance with the fundamental nature of private ownership"; to which the Court responded: "The constantly increasing density of our urban populations, the multiplying forms of industry and the growing complexity of our civilization make it necessary for the state . . . to limit individual activities to a greater extent than formerly." Ownership, then, is not something static but an *activity,* and one that must be adjusted to other activities.

And in the meantime the same Court had endorsed a definition of "liberty" under the Fifth and Fourteenth Amendments the logical possibilities of which are at least challenging. In Holden v. Hardy and the Lochner case, "liberty" was defined as "liberty of contract"—a necessary adjunct, to the mind of a laissez faire Court, of the property right. Recent cases, however, bring within its protection freedom of speech and of the press; and if these, why not other comparable interests?[36] *The day may come, in other words, when the Court will treat the term "liberty" as itself embodying constitutional recognition of the entire range of those personal and humane values which enlightened social legislation is designed to promote.*

The Child Labor Tax case,[37] also decided by the Taft Court, merits a briefer word. Like the earlier Child Labor case, it proceeds on the assumption that the Court has a special mandate from the Constitution to refrigerate the distribution of power between the states and the national government as it exists at any

---

34. 243 U.S. 332; 252 U.S. 135 and 170.
35. 272 U.S. 365. See also 254 U.S. 300, sustaining a "conservation" statute; also 260 U.S. 393, both opinions.
36. 283 U.S. 697, and cases there cited.
37. 259 U.S. 20.

particular time—in other words, a mandate to stereotype the so-called "federal equilibrium." Obfuscated by its sense of mission, the Court adopted in both these cases the very procedure against which Marshall protests in Gibbons v. Ogden. "In support of a theory not to be found in the Constitution," they denied "the government powers which the words of the grant, as usually understood, import."

Such a procedure indicates a serious misapprehension on the part of the Court of certain realities. It is by no means the case that any extension of national power into fields which were once occupied solely by the states necessarily spells a weakening of state power. One of the most evident extensions of national power within recent years is that which takes the form of so-called "federal grants-in-aid," and far from having proved annihilative of state power, these have generally proved stimulative of it—rather too much so in some instances. Indeed, it may be said broadly that under modern conditions more power to the national government means more actually effective power to the states, the cause of effective government being confronted by the same hostile interests in both fields. Nor have our administrators overlooked this fact, with the result that a man can hardly commit murder in either Chicago or New York these days without having his income tax record ransacked by the federal authorities. There may still be cases, no doubt, in which the aggrandizement of national power may be justifiably regarded as taking place at the expense of the states; but even in such cases the question remains whether, with industry and crime both organized on the national scale that they are, the state can make efficacious use of its theoretical powers. If the answer is no, then such powers are to all honest intents and purposes nonexistent, and a realistic jurisprudence will so adjudge them.

VI

What is the Court's outlook today—its cosmology? Fortunately, the preachments of our present-day scientific pontiffs are quite incapable of impelling the thought even of "naïf, simple-minded" men along a single track as did laissez faireism backed by evolutionism, backed in turn by belief in a benevolent unknown. Today, the biologist and sociologist have had to yield place to the physicist and mathematician, and while these gentlemen are generally in agreement that God too is a mathematician, at that point consensus ceases. "Eddington deduces religion," Lord Russell points out, "from the fact that atoms do not obey the laws of mathematics; Jeans deduces it from the fact that they do."[38] On another point, however, Jeans and Eddington find themselves in alliance once more, namely, in assertion of the second law of thermodynamics, which says that the universe is running down, whereupon Professor Millikan protests that they have evidently overlooked the restorative properties of cosmic rays.

38. *The Scientific Outlook* (1931).

Then there is the interesting question whether the universe is a sort of four dimensional (at latest reports, five dimensional) bird cage or a species of toy balloon in process of rapid inflation; also, assuming it is the latter, just how long it will be until the final inevitable catastrophe? Six hundred thousand millions of years, avers Professor Jeans; ten thousand millions of years, asserts Professor Eddington. In either event, there ought to be time to try out some sort of social plan—even perhaps to give the "experiment noble in intention" a fair chance!

Nor must the lesson of "relativity" be overlooked in this connection. Suppose a judge to learn that by "the Fitzgerald principle of contraction" he is actually a smaller man when he is driving sixty miles an hour than when he is standing still, instead of being a bigger one as he had felt himself to be—is such a one likely henceforth to hold that doctrines laid down by the Court even so long ago as 1900 were laid down for all time? Nor could he fail to be edified by what has happened to Professor Einstein's one absolute, the speed of light. Queries a critic, at what speed then would two rays of light proceeding in opposite directions pass each other?—a question still unanswered.[39]

The truth of the matter seems to be that modern science throws man back on his own resources once more. Law, even in the scientific sense, is held to be a creation of the human mind, rather than a datum conferred by a benevolent Providence; it is an instrument of human power and control, as is the human mind itself. To be sure, the idea is one which might easily be misapplied. For instance, I should hesitate to advise anyone that either Einstein or Planck has so far repealed Newton that one can step off a roof into midair with complete impunity. But the point remains, nevertheless, that what measure of utopia we are destined for—and it is probably a very modest measure—must be of our own contrivance. We are no longer headed for heaven in a perambulator labeled evolution, laissez faire, or any other uncomprehended force. If we get there, it will be on our own power.[40]

Although only passing notice requires to be given to the recently constituted Court, a necessary preface thereto is a further word of acknowledgment of that

39. James Mackaye, in *The Dynamic Universe*.

40. "Nature does not obey definite physical laws and physical laws are not sufficient to determine the future of any object, living or not living. This question is vital to mankind for the reason, first urged strongly by Socrates, that if man's actions are determined by physical law, his motives and purposes are ineffective and life becomes meaningless. . . . It thus becomes possible, in light of modern science, to see once more the vision that Plato saw, of man as master of his own destiny." Professor Arthur H. Compton, Address before the National Academy of Sciences, *New York Times*, November 22, 1931. On the other hand, both Einstein and Planck continue to assert the mechanical nature of the universe. Says the latter in his *Universe in the Light of Modern Science*, recently translated from the German, "All studies dealing with the behavior of the human mind are equally [that is, with physics] compelled to assume the existence of strict causality." Professor C. G. Darwin, of the University of Edinburgh, a grandson of Charles Darwin, also offers "a most strenuous opposition" to the idea that "the new outlook will remove the well-known philosophical conflict between the doctrines of free-will and determinism. . . . The question is a philosophic one outside the region of thought of physics, and I cannot see that physical theory provides any new loophole." *New York Times*, December 14, 1931.

series of dissenting opinions, often brilliant, in which between the years 1920 and 1930 Justices Holmes and Brandeis, and more recently Justice Stone, kept the spark of life in the *Corpus Juris* of the decade preceding. Nor was this the only result of their inspired obstinacy. The public—or that portion of it which counts in such matters—was at last advised of the necessity of scrutinizing the philosophy of life no less than the professional attainments of a nominee to the Supreme Bench. The Senate debates over the nomination of Judge Parker and of Chief Justice Hughes demonstrated that.

Already the Court, under the able leadership of Chief Justice Hughes—who was also, it should be recalled, a member of the Court in the fruitful years immediately following 1910—has recovered an important segment of lost territory. In the Indiana Chain Stores case, the autonomy of state legislative power under the Fourteenth Amendment was asserted in what, from some angles, was a rather extreme case. In the New Jersey Insurance Commission case, the Court returned once more to the general outlook of Munn v. Illinois regarding price regulation. In other cases a check was at last given to the vastly exaggerated principle of tax exemption and hints thrown out that may lead eventually to a radical revision of the entire doctrine.[41]

The present "liberal" majority of the Court is, to be sure, a narrow and precarious one. But this very fact should serve to drive home the lesson of the importance of having judges of broad experience and outlook, and so to emphasize the responsibility of the president for proposing such men and of the Senate for seeing to it that only such men are finally approved.

Pertinent in this connection are the words of Mr. Justice Brandeis, then plain Mr. Brandeis:

> I see no need to amend our Constitution. It has not lost its capacity for expansion to meet new conditions, unless it be interpreted by rigid minds which have no such capacity. Instead of amending the Constitution, I would amend men's economic and social ideas. . . . Law has always been a narrowing, conservatising profession. . . . What we must do in America is not to attack our judges but to educate them.[42]

Or, harking back some two hundred and fifty years, we may recall the words of Lord Halifax, spoken with reference to the English constitution: "The Constitution cannot make itself; somebody made it, not at once but at several times. It is alterable; and by that draweth nearer Perfection; and without suiting itself to differing Times and Circumstances, it could not live. Its Life is prolonged by changing seasonably the several Parts of it at several Times."[43] Whereto it needs only be added that the body whose task it is to keep the Constitution of the United States adjusted to time and circumstance, that is to say, *alive,* is ordinarily the Supreme Court.

41. 283 U.S. 527; 282 U.S. 251; 282 U.S. 216 and 379.
42. A. T. Mason, in 79 *Penn. L. Rev.,* at p. 693.
43. *Works of George Saville, First Marquess of Halifax* (Raleigh ed.), 211, quoted by Professor Frankfurter in 45 *Harv. L. Rev.,* at p. 85.

Are we at the beginning of an epoch or in the midst of an episode? Hardly the latter merely. The forces which brought about the present crisis will still remain after it has passed away—assuming it ever does pass away—and will be potent, if not curbed, to produce similar crises again. Individual initiative may be, as my old teacher Charles Horton Cooley was wont to assert, "the life-giving principle of institutions." Unfortunately, that form of individual initiative which is called forth by the profit-taking motive—"the American way of life"—does not invariably work for the good of society as a whole; although if democracy means anything, it is precisely that the good of society as a whole should supply the forces which act upon and within society with their rational objective. So there must be, I venture to suggest, a measure of "social planning," and in the long run a considerable measure of it—either that or social dissolution, or a social order based on rather obvious force.

As to the difficulties which face the social planner, the peculiarly American institutions of judicial review and constitutional limitations do not today assume the obstructive proportions that on first consideration might be expected. This is so for three reasons: first, because constitutional law is today more flexible, more free from autonomous concepts, than it has been at any time within forty years; secondly, because the Court itself is more realistically aware than ever before of the essentially legislative character of its task—more aware of its real freedom of choice in the presence of the vast variety of juristic materials which a century and a half of discussion and decision have made available to it; thirdly, because a wider public is also aware of these things, and so not disposed to be unduly impressed by mystifying talk about the nature of the "judicial process."

For all which reasons, once the idea of "social planning" comes to be seriously entertained, the interest of political science will, I predict, turn less to questions of governmental power than to questions of governmental function and arrangement. What ought government try to do? And is our government a well-constructed government to undertake such tasks? And if not, how ought it be amended? The ramshackle character of the national legislative machine, the imbecility of the American party system, the entire lack of assurance of qualified political leadership which these conditions breed—these, to speak only of political factors, are much more serious obstacles to "social planning" than is our system of constitutional law.

4. The New Deal in the Light of American Political and Constitutional Ideas

MORE than 2,000 years have elapsed since the Greek philosopher Heracleitus burst into tears as the thought occurred to him that he would never be able to step into the same stream twice. A like lugubrious habit seems to have fastened itself upon some of our modern politicians when confronted with the eternal spectacle of change. Yet it was a politician, and a great one,—as well as being a great lawyer—who remarked 300 years ago: "He that will not apply new remedies must expect new evils, for time is the greatest innovator. . . . A froward retention of custom is as turbulent a thing as innovation." And since Bacon's day our biologists have taught in vain if we have not learned that change and adaptation are the very condition of survival.

I am not one of those who believe that we are called upon to discard the fundamental ideas which have thus far guided and directed our development as a nation. I decline to take a defeatist attitude as to their adequacy for the solution of obvious problems. For although, as Justice Holmes pointed out, "historic continuity with the past is not a duty," but "only a necessity," yet a part of that necessity arises from the need of mankind for symbols. The characteristic assumption of the conservative that he alone can understand and properly value the past is assumption merely; and when the past in question sprang, as ours did, from the womb of revolution, the assumption becomes presumption. Nothing could do a greater disservice to conservatism itself than to persuade the American people that their political tradition had become crystallized and hence incapable of responding to the actualities that press in upon us from all sides.

What are these fundamental ideas to which I have referred? With the national holiday a week away, it seems appropriate to turn to the great Declaration for instruction:

Address to the Federation of Bar Associations, Western New York, June 27, 1936, Category 6, Carton 2, Edward S. Corwin Papers, Princeton University Library. Printed with the permission of Princeton University. I have added Corwin's final revisions to the text.

We hold these truths to be self-evident—that all men are created equal; that they are endowed by their Creator with certain unalienable rights; that among these are life, liberty and the pursuit of happiness. That, to secure these rights, governments are instituted among men, depriving their just powers from the consent of the governed; that, whenever any form of government becomes destructive of these ends, it is the right of the people to alter or to abolish it, and to institute a new government, laying its foundations on such principles, and organizing its powers in such form, as to them shall seem most likely to effect their safety and happiness.

What are the ideas which here stand forth? One is that man was "created," suggesting his unique significance in the universal order; and that in this aspect all men are equal. And they are also equal in that all are endowed with certain "unalienable rights"—those to life, liberty, and the pursuit of happiness—property is not mentioned. Finally, we learn that government does not exist for its own sake, or for the sake of the governors of mankind, but for the sake of the governed—it is the instrument of human rights and human happiness. As the same thought is put in an early case:

Man, fearfully and wonderfully made, is the workmanship of his all perfect *Creator*: a *State*, useful and valuable as the contrivance is, is the *inferior* contrivance of *man*; and from his *native* dignity derives all its *acquired* importance.

Nor may this idea be confined to government. All institutions are instrumental and to be evaluated for their serviceability to the dominant objective of human welfare. "Man was not made for the Sabbath, the Sabbath was made for man;" or as the philosopher Kant phrased it, "Man may never be treated as merely a means."

Such, as I interpret it, is the liberal philosophy of {the} state, the creed of eighteenth- and nineteenth-century liberalism. Man and his happiness are the fixed points of reference—all else is relative, and hence subject to alteration, amendment, or rejection, as circumstances may require. Furthermore, such change or adjustment is thought of as *possible* and *feasible*, as a *task not beyond the scope of human judgment.* And existing institutions may be utilized to effect it to the extent of their inherent capabilities for such a task. One such institution is *government.*

Indeed, the initial achievement of liberalism was to place the powers of government at the disposal of the people. By feudal ideas government was an adjunct of proprietorship of the soil—a species of property. Eventually there emerged from the vast horde of competing proprietors, endowed with the right of corvée, justice, the pit and the gallows, a few powerful magnates, the founders of the great European dynasties. Government thereupon became over wide areas a *monopoly.* The next step was the taking over of this monopoly by the governed. And the last inches of this step were accomplished on our own soil. By a historical accident, its completion involved the overthrow of a prefeudal proprietarian institution—human slavery. By November, 1863, the consummation was in sight—"A government of the people, by the people, for the people."

Nor is it essential today to debate the question of the purpose of *economic institutions*—they, too, are instrumental, are meant to advance human happiness, that is to say, the happiness of society at large, and not peculiarly that of a special section or class thereof. Even Mr. Baer assumed this to be the case when, forty years ago, he suggested that the American people should give thanks that "God in his wisdom, had entrusted the destinies of this nation" to a certain few of whom Mr. Baer was one.

The question of the proper relation of government to business is therefore, nowadays simply a question of *ways and means*. What relationship of the former to the latter is best calculated to achieve the happiness in the long run of the American nation? In answer to this question, we find that the American liberal tradition divides, although less radically than some people would make out. On the one hand we have the individualistic-localistic tradition of Jeffersonian Democracy—on the other hand the nationalistic-strong government policy of Hamiltonian federalism, from which the Republican creed was formerly supposed to stem; and today we are witnessing an interesting exchange of viewpoints by the two historic parties. The exchange may after all, however, be one more of appearance than of reality. Nor am I, in saying this, referring to the extensive endorsement which is given the New Deal—behind a screen of denunciatory language—in the Cleveland Platform. The substantial difference between Jefferson and Hamilton was one of *intermediate objective*. Both sought the same ultimate end, *the national good*; but whereas Hamilton, being a mercantilist, believed national prosperity to be the outcome of commerce, and so was driven to identify it as the by-product of the prosperity of a relatively small class; Jefferson, a physiocrat, identified it with the immediate prosperity of the small farmers of the nation, "the masses" of those days. And this difference of *intermediate objective* remains today, although it has to be translated into different terms if it is to be understandable in the presence of modern conditions.

So undertaking this task of translation, I should say that the substantial question between supporters and opponents of the New Deal is this: To what extent should the prosperity of the country be deemed the by-product of the prosperity of big business, to what extent should the prosperity of big business be deemed the by-product of the prosperity of the people generally? For if emphasis is put on the former relationship then great deference will be paid to the views of business management; but if emphasis is placed on the latter relationship, then the policies of business management will be subjected to political criticism and curtailment at many turns, with the end in view of securing a larger share in the current product of industry to the numbers who have the votes.

Turning first to the policy of deference to business management, we may term this the policy of laissez faire—or hands-off—the general thought being that the less government has to do with business, the better for all concerned. This policy, or theory, has a certain rootage in earlier frontier conditions. It has been able in the past to urge in its favor the great truth that all the energies of society are at bottom the energies of specific individuals, specific talents. With much less justification it urges in its favor the theory that economic activities are governed by certain laws which can be violated only to the detriment of the transgressor and, through him, to that of society at large. Most of the alleged laws amount only to more or less plausible generalizations from what has taken place in certain circumstances, and afford no safe basis for prediction of what will occur in different circumstances. What is more, so far as these generalizations can be counted on, they may be and are very frequently "overridden," and with much profit to the transgressor, as in the case of monopoly and in that of the tariff, both of which "override" the "law of supply and demand."

Finally, once we leave the frontier, we find that laissez faire receives little support, indeed, from the facts of American history. The Constitution itself was framed by men who were quite unacquainted with this theory. It was framed by mercantilists, by men who were entirely hospitable to the idea of governmental intervention in the realm of economics. Adam Smith's *Wealth of Nations* had, it is true, been published some years earlier, but it was to be 70 years before its teachings were to influence public policy even in England; and outside the Supreme Court their influence in this country on public policy has always been slight.

For centuries before the Constitution, government in England, as in Europe generally, interfered constantly in economic affairs, and one of those interferences remains to this day to furnish the most important title of private law—I mean judicial enforcement of private contracts. This was given substantially its present scope during the reign of Elizabeth, when the Court of Common Pleas recognized that a promise can be consideration for a promise.

Other examples of governmental intervention in the economic field which have been constant throughout our own history are these: (1) the protective tariff, already mentioned; (2) the conferring on business enterprisers of the advantages of corporate organization; (3) the creation of public utility monopolies, and endowing them with the power of eminent domain; (4) the bestowal of immense grants and subsidies, particularly on railroad companies; (5) the national "free land" policy, by which the settlement of the West was immensely facilitated, while at the same time industrial wages were maintained at a high level in the older parts of the country.

Every one of these policies, most of them policies of the national government, has contributed materially to the rapid—perhaps too rapid—development of the country and to the creation of American capitalism. All of these policies, moreover, seem to have been in time accepted both by the courts and by public opinion as harmonious with the Constitution, though in the case of the tariff the question was long the subject of acrimonious debate. Indeed, it is not a little instructive even today to read Justice Story's summary in his *Commentaries* of the constitutional argument against the tariff and compare it with the argument which was recently levelled against the A.A.A:

The constitution is one of limited and enumerated powers; and none of them can be rightfully exercised beyond the scope of the objects specified in those powers. It is not disputed that when the power is given, all the appropriate means to carry it into effect are included. Neither is it disputed, that the laying of duties is, or may be, an appropriate means of regulating commerce. But the question is a very different one, whether under pretence of an exercise of the power to regulate commerce, congress may in fact impose duties for objects wholly distinct from commerce. The question comes to this, whether a power exclusively for the regulation of commerce, is a power for the regulation of manufactures. The statement of such a question would seem to involve its own answer. Can a power granted for one purpose be transferred to another? If it can, where is the limitation in the constitution? Are not commerce and manufactures as distinct as commerce and agriculture? If they are, how can a power to regulate one arise from a power to regulate the other? It is true, that commerce and manufactures are, or may be, intimately connected with each other. A regulation of one may injuriously or beneficially affect the other. But that is not the point in controversy. It is, whether congress has a right to regulate that which is not committed to it, under a power which is committed to it, simply because there is or may be, an intimate connection between the powers. If this were admitted, the enumeration of the powers of congress would be wholly unnecessary and nugatory. Agriculture, colonies, capital, machinery, the wages of labor, the profits of stock, the rents of land, the punctual performance of contracts, and the diffusion of knowledge would all be within the scope of the power; for all of them bear an intimate relation to commerce. The result would be, that the powers of congress would embrace the widest extent of legislative functions, to the utter demolition of all constitutional boundaries between the state and national government.

What, then, is the duty of government in the presence of a situation for which it is as much responsible as is business management, perhaps more so? Certainly the formula, "hands-off" is no sufficient answer. The true answer on recognized American principles clearly is this: The government—by which I mean primarily the national government—is bound to use its own best judgment as to what the public interest requires, and act accordingly. Which, of course, does not mean at all that government should not consult business judgment and experience—but rather the contrary. Still the final responsibility for judging and acting must rest with the government and not with business management, except so far as constitutional limitations may vest the latter with the final say, of which more presently. And evaluating the New Deal with these considerations in mind, I am frank to declare that I regard it as entirely defensible, even commendable from the point of view of the history of American political thought and action.

I do not, I may say, subscribe to the theory that the collapse of 1929 was due exclusively to the bad judgment of business management; but neither do I subscribe to the idea that the collapse and succeeding depression were inevitable— the inescapable result of those economic "laws" of whose beneficence we hear so much when prosperity holds sway. The collapse and ensuing depression were due first, to bad human judgment—partly governmental, partly business—and secondly, to the inherent limitations of business management in the presence of an economy which has become nationalized.

Certain policies of the Coolidge and Hoover administrations clearly invited the collapse, the discontinuance of the policy of paying off the public debt in order to lower the income tax in the midst of prosperity; and the insensate Smoot-Hawley Tariff—to itemize no further. On the other hand, and dovetailing with these policies, were those policies of business management which all sum up in its failure to spread its market fast enough and far enough while Ford cars, for instance, were being turned out at the rate of one every forty-seven seconds, its failure to raise wages proportionately to profits, its loans abroad to foster a mythical foreign market, its super-salesmanship to induce people to want what they had not the money to buy, its encouragement of installment buying, with its guaranty that if and when bankruptcy came it would be universal.

There is, however, no need to dwell on these painful facts, all of which were readily admitted by business leaders in the days when prosperity was "just around the corner," but appear now to have been forgotten when this elusive corner seems at last to have been turned. From the end of 1929 to the end of 1933 business management was bowed in sack-cloth and ashes in the purlieus of R.F.C. or in the less cheerful precincts of the bankruptcy court.

And this brings us to the second point: the inherent limitations of private action with respect to an economy which has become nationalized. Concentrated as it is in many lines, business management is still dispersed, and competition or the possibility of it is still a factor determining business policies, and frequently an unfavorable factor for the public good. To put the same thought more concretely—in its struggle for markets a particular business must meet the prices set by its competitors. It results that its labor policies will be determined in part by its competitors, and more particularly by its less scrupulous competitors. On the other hand, a concern or combination of concerns which dominates the market will be in a position to determine prices on a monopoly basis. If American principles require the elimination of unfair business practices, justice to labor and its security, as well as fair prices to consumers, then it is obvious that these same principles require such degree of governmental intervention in business management as is essential to bring these about.

Such, indeed, was the theory of the N.I.R.A. and of the Guffey Coal Conservation Act, as it is of the Social Security Act and of the Wagner Labor Act. None of these reforms was, or is, within the ability of even the best-intentioned business management to achieve, acting by itself. They must be generally applied, or not at all; and by the same token they must be sanctioned by the powers of the national government. For with business able to shift from state to state to avoid regulation, the states too are economic rivals. It is emphatically a field in which—as the Court said in the T.V.A. Case with regard to the development of water-power—"There can be no divided empire."

The charge still remains nonetheless that the New Deal has violated fundamental American principles, if not in its aims, then at any rate by its methods. Is this so? The question should be treated in the first instance as a question of constitutional law and theory, for while these do not exhaust the resources of American political thought by any means, they represent an important section of it, and that section of it in which the terminology of discussion is most definite.

The main reliance of the supporters of the New Deal legislative program has been upon the power of Congress to regulate commerce among the states; the main reliance of opponents of this program has been upon the principle of "dual federalism" and the reservation of powers to the states by the Tenth Amendment.

As to the former reliance, the chief objection must be to its vagueness. In the words of Assistant Attorney General Dickinson, in his brilliant argument before the Court in Carter v. Carter Coal Co., in which the Coal Conservation Act was set aside:

> No one would deny that dualism is a fundamental principle of the Constitution. There can be no doubt that ours is a dual system of government, certain powers being conferred upon the Federal Government and others reserved to the States. But I submit that the question of what that dualism means, in respect of any particular power, and whether, under the dual system, a particular power belongs to the Federal Government, on the one hand, or to the States, on the other hand, is not to be determined by resorting from the obscure to the more obscure, and by appealing to a vague general descriptive abstract word like dualism, but is to be determined rather by the express language of the Constitution itself, and that it does not justify an appeal from the specific language of the Constitution to an extraneous and descriptive abstraction which is nothing more than a generalized and therefore incomplete statement about what the instrument is supposed to contain. . . .
>
> Our Government is a dual government only because the Constitution makes it so, and it is a dual government only to the extent and in the way in which the Constitution makes it so; and if we look to the Constitution we find that it has conferred on the Federal Government—subject, of course, to other express provisions of the Constitution—the power to regulate interstate commerce with all that that implies.

The Tenth Amendment cannot be so briefly disposed of. It reads:

> The powers not delegated to the United States by the Constitution, nor prohibited by it to the States, are reserved to the States, respectively, or to the people.

Now the doctrine of the majority of the Court in the case of Carter v. Carter Coal Co., as well as in United States v. Butler—though that involved the spending power primarily—seems to be this: that the above language is sufficient to reserve to the states exclusively certain "subjects," "concerns," "interests," which therefore the national government may not validly attempt to regulate even indirectly through its control over commerce; and that one of these "subjects" or "concerns" is production, and especially the *employer-employee relationship in connection with production*. It is difficult to see, nevertheless, how this proposition can be maintained logically, even on the basis of the above quoted language alone. The Tenth Amendment speaks only of *powers*; it says nothing of "subjects" or "concerns" on which the powers referred to may be exercised; nor does it reserve even *powers* to the states except conditionally upon their not having been delegated to the United States.

What is more important still, however, is the fact that along with the Tenth Amendment goes the supremacy clause of the Constitution, which ordains that all laws of the United States made in pursuance of the Constitution shall have the right of way over any conflicting state laws or constitutions whatsoever, and which makes no exception in favor of state laws which have been enacted to govern certain "subjects," or "concerns"—production, for instance.

Besides, as Justice Holmes once said, "A page of history is worth a volume of logic"—at least that is so sometimes, and this may be one of them. The page of history in question is the following item from the Journal of the Philadelphia Convention for July 17th:

> It was moved and seconded to postpone the considn of the second clause of the Sixth resolution reported from the Committee of the whole House in order to take up the following
>
> "To make laws binding on the People of the United States in all cases which may concern the common interests of the Union: but not to interfere with the government of the individual States in any matters of internal police which respect the government of such States only, and wherein the general welfare of the United States is not concerned." which passed in the negative (Ayes-2; noes-8.) It was moved and seconded to alter the second clause of the 6th resolution so as to read as follows, namely
>
> "and moreover to legislate in all cases for the general interests of the Union, and also in those to which the States are separately incompetent, or in which the harmony of the United States may be interrupted by the exercise of individual legislation
>
> which passed in the affirmative (Ayes-6; noes-4.) . . .

And having rejected the suggestion that the national government should not interfere in the internal concerns of the states, the Convention proceeded to adopt the supremacy clause in its original form unanimously.

Construing the Supremacy clause, Madison remarked in 1791: "The powers of the States are no criterion of the powers of Congress," and in Gibbons v. Ogden, Marshall asserted that no matter by what "uncontroverted power" a state law may have been enacted, it could not oppose or limit a constitutional act of Congress.

The idea that the reserved powers of the state afford a constructive principle of and limitation upon otherwise constitutional powers of the national government has, moreover, been rejected by the Court again and again. It has been rejected within recent years, indeed, as to the treaty-making power, the power to regulate foreign commerce, and the power to regulate railway rates—a branch of the power to regulate commerce among the states. Thus, meeting the argument in the Minnesota Rate Cases that Congress's power over interstate carriers could not extend to their local rates because these fell within the reserved powers of the states, Justice Hughes said:

> This reservation to the States manifestly is only of that authority which is consistent with and not opposed to the grant to Congress. There is no room in our scheme of government for the assertion of state power in hostility to the authorized exercise of Federal power. . . .

Or as he later put the same idea:

> Within its sphere as recognized by the Constitution, the Nation is supreme. The question is simply of the Federal power as granted, where there is authorized exercise of that power, there is no reserved power to nullify it—a principle obviously essential to our national integrity, yet continually calling for new applications.

The sole question, therefore, is this: What *is* the power to *regulate* commerce; and this may be answered in Justice Johnson's words in Gibbons v. Ogden: "The power of a sovereign state over commerce amounts to nothing more than a power to limit and restrain it at pleasure." Nor can there be any doubt that Congress was deemed in 1789 to have the same power over commerce among the states as over that with foreign nations, the same right to restrain or prohibit the one as the other for what Congress thought to be promotive of the good of the country; nor had judicial interpretation of the Constitution altered respecting this matter a hundred years later. The Court's present doctrine is of recent origin, being traceable in the main no further back than the five-to-four decision in the first Child Labor case of 1918. Furthermore, it is confined, as I pointed out above, to a single field and to a single purpose—the insulation of the employer-employee relationship in productive industry from national regulation.

Nor is that sort of inconsistency to be found in the decisions alone. Thus it would be interesting to know how many of those who are at present urging the national government, in the furtherance of safer betting, to prevent the passage of "doped" racing steeds from one state to another, belong to the American Liberty League. And how many members of that organization would care to have the national government repeal the laws under which it today cooperates with the states in combating crime, or to lower its tariff walls to the products of foreign "cheap labor"? Yet when, on the other hand, it is suggested that Congress has power to prohibit interstate commerce in goods produced by concerns whose unsocial methods enable them to undersell their competitors in the interstate market, then we are informed that the federal system and states rights are in imminent peril!

But it will be urged, and justifiably, that private rights as well as states rights are involved in the question of the constitutional validity of the New Deal legislative program, and of its harmony with American ideas. This time, however, it is the theoretical rather than the legal aspect of the question which should be stressed. So far as constitutional limitations are concerned, they are those which have come to be associated with the modern derived conception of due process of law as "reasonable law," that is *reasonable* to the mind of the Court. The difficulty of distinguishing the judicial from the legislative function in this field of so-called "constitutional law" is confessed by the Justices themselves. Indeed, in his dissent in the New York Milk case two years ago, Justice McReynolds frankly claimed for the Court the right to pass upon the "wisdom" of legislation; and in his dissent in the recent New York Minimum Wage case, in which the Court refused to follow the Nebbia case, Justice Stone, dissenting for himself and Justices Brandeis and Cardozo, accused his majority brethren of basing their decision on their "own economic predilections." This assertion provoked from a defender of the Court the retort in the columns of the *New York Times* that Justice Stone was following his economic predilections too. That may very well be—but at least, he was not overturning a state statute in so doing.

So transferring the discussion to a somewhat different terrain, the question before us takes this form: Do the New Deal proposals represent a radical, nay "revolutionary," departure, from the course of public policy and constitutional interpretation in this country? It seems to me that clearly they do not. Such degree of revolution as they represent is in response to a revolution which had already occurred in the facts of everyday living—the kind of revolution which Madison had in mind when he wrote in the *Federalist*: "A system of government, meant for duration, ought to contemplate these revolutions, and be able to accommodate itself to them." The "revolution" Madison had here in mind was that which would come when manufacturing displaced agriculture in importance in the national economy.

Certainly it cannot be said that any of the outstanding New Deal proposals taken by itself is unprecedented. The parallel between the A.A.A. and the protective tariff amounted to coincidence so far as private rights were concerned. The precedent afforded for Social Security insurance by Workmen's Compensation acts is excellent, and is enhanced when we turn to the constitutional justification of the latter in such opinions as that of Justice Pitney in the Mountain Timber Co. v. Washington. The lack of substantial difference between hour legislation and wage legislation has been asserted by the highest legal talent many times; and we are warranted by equal weight of authority in denying that price regulation involves any special or peculiar invasion of private rights.

A homily once delivered by Justice McKenna in an opinion for the Court is pertinent in this connection. Sustaining the power of a state to regulate insurance rates he said:

> Against that conservatism of mind which puts to question every new act of regulating legislation and regards the legislation invalid or dangerous until it has become familiar, government—state and national—has pressed on in the general welfare, and our reports are full of cases where in instance after instance the exercise of regulation was resisted and yet sustained against attacks asserted to be justified by the Constitution of the United States. The dread of the moment having passed, no one is now heard to say that rights were restrained or their constitutional guarantees impaired.

As a matter of fact, political power has rarely achieved any result of first-rate importance in this country, without somebody raising the cry of "unconstitutionality." The Constitution itself was "unconstitutional" by an argument which Madison felt it necessary to answer in the *Federalist*. Most of Hamilton's legislative program was unconstitutional in the opinion of half of Washington's cabinet. The Louisiana Purchase was unconstitutional in the opinion of the president who accomplished it. The most important measure by which the slavery issue was kept in abeyance for years was unconstitutional in the opinion of large numbers of people and finally of the Supreme Court itself. The Civil War was brought to a successful issue by resort to measures that at least two out of every three Americans alive at the time would have voted to be unconstitutional; and according to the Democratic Platform of 1868, the Thirteenth Amendment was unconstitutional,—and so on and so forth!

But let us move the discussion still further away from technical ground, and view the question of the relation of the New Deal to private rights as one of political ethics. We start, necessarily, with the thought that except for the protection afforded them by government, there are no effective rights. But against this recognition, we must at once set the assertion in the Declaration of Independence of "unalienable rights" which no just government will transgress. As we saw, the Declaration does not list the property right among these; but others have, both before and since, including Locke, who was the philosopher *par excellence* of the American Revolution. On the other hand, Locke regards *all* rights in society as relative only—that indeed is the great difference between political society and the state of nature; and for the most part he leaves the definition of rights to the supreme legislative power. Furthermore, Locke's idea of property is very concrete and definite—"property" means *things,* especially the things that make life comfortable. In short, it is individual possessions which he has foremost in mind, and the origin of these, as well as of the right to them, he traces to *labor* and to individual *thrift.*

That such notions of property are for the most part irrelevant to any discussion of the political morality of the New Deal seems to me obvious. In the words of Professor Dewey, "From the stand-point of modern economic theory, the most surprising thing about modern industry is the small number of persons who have any effective interest in the acquisition of wealth." On the other hand, with what has happened in this country since 1929 still fresh in mind, few can have the hardihood to question that the outstanding characteristic of wealth today is that it is a function of social process, so that when social process falters, wealth simply vanishes into thin air, leaving an impoverished society. Nor is that large share of the country's wealth which is today held in concentrated ownership primarily a source of individual security—it is a source of power over other people's lives, and power of a kind that has never hesitated to thwart or corrupt the processes of political democracy in order to secure its own purposes.

Giving such considerations their due weight, it seems to me that the general purpose of the New Deal legislation is much more fairly represented as an effort to realize the Lockean and early American conception of property, as individual possession of the comforts and decencies of life, than as an attempt to overthrow it.

But, it will be asked, how about "liberty," the right to which is *explicitly* asserted by the Declaration of Independence to be "unalienable"? The liberty thought of is primarily political, and its greatest potential enemy is thought to be the state. The liberty, on the other hand, with which the New Deal is concerned is economic liberty, the liberty conferred by economic security.

But this transmutation of the word is not an original or exclusive contribution of the New Deal by any means, as we speedily discover when we turn, for example, to Mr. Hoover's *Challenge to Liberty.* American liberalism, the distinguished author of this work asserts, "holds that there should be a just diffusion of national income which will give protection and security to those who have the will to work. . . . It holds that other freedom cannot be maintained if economic freedom be impaired," whether by "monopoly, group or class advantage, economic domination, Regimentation, Fascism, Socialism, Communism, or any other form of tyranny, small or great."

To be sure, Mr. Hoover contends that the New Deal spells regimentation, and so is hostile to liberty. But in the same breath, he also concedes that liberty connotes something more than political liberty and that it may be endangered by economic domination as well as by government. These concessions seem to me to answer the question with which we are concerned. The New Deal program may have been ill-conceived, it may have done more harm than good to economic liberty, but at any rate one is not entitled *a priori* to set it down as transcending the sphere of government according to American ideas thereof.

But it is contended, the powers which are today wielded by the president are especially menacing to liberty. I confess, this seems to me about the least substantial of any of the apprehensions of those who contend that "America is in peril." Certainly presidential leadership, especially in times of stress, is no new phenomenon. It has existed from the first under the Constitution and the founders of our government intended that it should exist. Neither on the other hand is fear of the presidency or professed fear of it, anything new. Hamilton, in the *Federalist,* ridiculed the exaggeration of opponents of the Constitution on this point. The enemies of Washington's administration were sure that it was headed for monarchy. In Jackson's time the shoe was on the other foot, and the anomalous Whig party sprang into existence to save American institutions—and gather some of the spoils of party warfare to themselves. Lincoln, inevitably, was a despot. Said a leading northern paper, in the second year of his administration, and before he had hardly got into his stride:

> We saw the executive power grasp in one hand the sword and the purse of the nation and in the other the legislative and the judicial authority, and hold them in relentless grip to the complete annihilation of our constitutional rights. . . . We saw trade disordered, government finances ruined, an enormous debt piled incalculably high, intolerable taxes. . . . We saw the superb Constitution, under which our country has grown great and respected, torn in shreds.

There is no need to continue the recital. The country is not yet Mexicanized, nor is it likely to be by any one whom the American people put in the presidential chair. Toward those who outside the government would "gang up" against it,

Black Legions, Ku Kluxes, and the like, perhaps we should take a less complacent attitude. The present dictatorships of Europe recruited their strength *outside* the governments they later captured and made their tools, not within them.

The argument for the New Deal sums it up as an effort to broaden the basis of national prosperity. This effort, the argument further maintains, was dictated for the most part by two ideas: (1) the avoidance of future economic depression; and the grave threat to our political structure which these present; (2) considerations of social justice. The effort may have been badly executed, but that is not the question. The question is whether such an effort was in harmony with American political and constitutional ideas and whether the measures by which it was implemented were harmonious with those ideas; and to this question, I submit, the answer is, on the whole, affirmative, and this notwithstanding the upsets which New Deal legislation has experienced in the Court—usually by closely divided decisions.

Two more arguments in favor of the New Deal need only be touched upon inasmuch as they are only indirectly connected with the above question. The first is this: We are under the compulsion of recognizing that the New Deal is an expression of powerful political forces, and that it is the very purpose of democratic institutions to afford a vent to such forces in terms of public policy. The failure, indeed, to do so may easily lead to fascism, if we can judge from what happened in Italy and Germany.

The second thought is this: The case for social justice is not solely sentimental—it is also biological. All history proves that societies die at the top and are recruited from the bottom; and when the bottom ceases to be a suitable recruiting ground, the society dies entirely. This is one explanation at least of the fall of Rome—its fall would have been irretrievable but for the invasion of the Barbarians. It is certainly one justification of the New Deal that its intention looks to maintaining among our resident barbarians a recruiting ground for social renewal, rather than for social decay.

In a word, I say that criticism of the New Deal, well-grounded as it may be in other respects, fails in its endeavor to range against it American political ideas and ideals. In trying to do so, such criticism overlooks, as I said at the outset, the fact that the very condition of survival is change and adaptation. In the words of a distinguished modern philosopher: "Those societies which cannot combine reverence to their symbols with freedom of revision must ultimately decay either from anarchy, or from the slow atrophy of a life stifled by useless shadows."

II.

GOVERNMENTAL ACTION AND
PERSONAL AND SOCIAL RIGHTS

5. Freedom of Speech and Press under the First Amendment: A Résumé

> Congress shall make no law respecting an establishment of
> religion or prohibiting the free exercise thereof; or abridging
> the freedom of speech or of the press; or the right of the
> people peaceably to assemble and to petition the Government
> for a redress of grievances.
>
> —Federal Constitution, First Amendment

THE opponents of the Sedition Act of 1798 denied that the national government had the right to enact any law whatever limiting freedom of the press. The critics of the Espionage Act[1] do not in theory go so far—though actually they arrive at much the same result as did their predecessors. In brief their view of the matter may be stated thus: It was the purpose of the First Amendment of the Constitution to relieve the press in the United States of the restraints imposed by the common law doctrine of seditious libel, which condemned as criminal all publications having a tendency to bring church or state, or the officers of the government, or the administration of the law into contempt. It follows, therefore, that the legal condemnation of a writing because of the bad "intent" of the author or publisher thereof would also be contrary to the First Amendment, since this intent is ordinarily determined simply from the tendency of the writing. In fact, it is urged, there can be, under the Constitution, no such thing as seditious libel, however determined, but only the power to punish incitements to crime, when there is imminent danger that the incitement will prove successful; and if this doctrine is not embodied in the First Amendment, at least it is implied in our theory of government, which makes government the property of the people and not vice versa.[2]

Reprinted by permission of the Yale Law Journal Company and Fred B. Rothman & Company from the *Yale Law Journal*, Vol. 30, pp. 48–55 (1920).

1. For a detailed discussion of the Espionage Act and its amendments and of the cases arising under it, see Carroll, "Freedom of Speech and of the Press in War Time: The Espionage Act," 17 *Mich. L. Rev.* 621 (1919). See also Hart, "Power of Government over Speech and Press," 29 *Yale Law Journal* 410 (1920).

2. This, in general, seems to be the position taken by Zechariah Chafee, Jr., in his article, "Freedom of Speech in War Time," 32 *Harv. L. Rev.* 932 (1919).

This part of the argument is not impressive. It may very well be that just because the people feel the government to be theirs, they also feel that they may concede it power to protect itself and other social interests without too great danger to liberty. The question is, who are the people? The real basis of the interpretation of the First Amendment just given is the belief that the people are a moral unit, that the social contract still holds among all men, that there are no irreconcilables in our midst—and this belief may be questionable.

The main purpose of this article, however, is to examine the historical foundations of this interpretation of the First Amendment. This amendment was written into the Constitution by students of Blackstone, in the pages of whose *Commentaries* the notion of the freedom of the press, from being a literary and political watchword, is first raised to the position of an accepted legal concept. But Blackstone's notion of freedom of the press, while it records the final result of an important historical struggle, is a somewhat modest one. Briefly, Blackstone defined freedom of the press as on the one hand freedom from restraint previous to publication, and on the other hand, subjection to the law for abuse of this freedom. Of course, the law which he has in mind is the common law of his day and includes, therefore, the common law of seditious libel.[3]

It is urged against Blackstone's right to be regarded as an expositor of the First Amendment, that he was a Tory and defended Parliament's right to tax the American colonies, that he wrote before the enactment of Fox's Libel Act, and that his view overlooks, therefore, the grievance felt in England itself on account of certain trials for sedition which took place there in the course of the eighteenth century.[4] These objections to a great extent answer one another. For if Blackstone was a Tory, Fox at least was a Whig, who resisted vehemently Parliament's right to tax America; and yet Fox felt it sufficient in order to meet English public sentiment on the subject of seditious libel, not to alter the substance of the common law, but merely the procedure by which it had come to be enforced, which had been to reserve the question of the tendency of the writing to the court, and so to leave to the jury the right only of passing upon the fact of publication and what was called "the truth of the innuendoes," that is to say, their meaning. The Libel Act of 1792, however, by authorizing the jury to bring in a general verdict of "guilty" or "not guilty" in prosecutions for seditious libel, as for other crimes, virtually transferred the question of tendency also to the jury. This act, it should be noted, came after both the First Amendment and the *Commentaries*.

But the real question, of course, is not as to Blackstone's authority in relation to the First Amendment, but that of the common law. The First Amendment was preceded by provisions of a more sweeping character on the same subject in several of the early state constitutions. The "liberty of the press" is "inviolate," it is "not to be restrained," it is "to be inviolably preserved." Yet in exactly

3. See 4 Blackstone, *Commentaries* 151 (Cooley ed. 1871).
4. See Chafee, *op. cit.* 938–39.

contemporaneous documents in neighboring states, the "responsibility" of those who enjoy this liberty for its "abuse" is pronounced and the occurrence of trials for "libel both criminal and civil" is prevised. It seems, indeed, very improbable that there was any idea in the minds of those who framed these provisions that they were repealing the ordinary standards of the common law; and as a matter of fact, prosecutions for seditious libel occurred even in the 19th century in states whose constitutions asserted "liberty of the press" in the broadest terms.[5]

But perhaps it will be rejoined that the fate of the Sedition Act at any rate proves that the First Amendment was regarded as having swept away the common law of seditious libel.[6] In the words of Justice Holmes, in his dissent in the recent case of Abrams v. United States,[7] "I had conceived that the United States through many years had shown its repentance for the Sedition Act of July 14, 1798, by repaying fines that it had imposed." To begin with, this argument cannot refer to the first section of the Sedition Act, which penalized conspiracy to oppose the measures of the government and "counselling" or "advising" riot or insurrection. Even opponents of the act—though inconsistently with their main argument—refrained from demanding its repeal, and its provisions still remain in substance on the statute book, nearly one hundred and twenty years after the demise of the act.

The reference is, therefore, to the second section of the act, which provided that if any person should write, print, or publish any "false, scandalous, and malicious writing" against the government of the United States, or either house of Congress, or the president, "with intent to defame" the same "or to bring them into contempt . . . or to stir up sedition within the United States," such persons should be liable to the penalties of the act. It is true, as Justice Holmes points out, that the United States subsequently remitted fines paid under this section; but why? On account of the definition which it gave to "freedom of the press"? To some extent perhaps, but principally because the act was deemed to represent an intrusion of the national government into a field entirely closed to it and so reserved exclusively to the states. The other phase of the question was sometimes touched upon tentatively, but it involved too many pitfalls to be entered upon with assurance. Thus Nicholas of Virginia, who made the best argument delivered in Congress against the act, was forced to defend an act passed by Virginia herself during the Revolution, the opening section of which penalized "any word, open deed, or act" defending the jurisdiction of the British king or Parliament in Virginia. Asked how he reconciled such a measure with "liberty of the press," he answered:

5. See Respublica v. Dennie (1805, Pa. N.P.) 4 Yeates, 267; see People v. Croswell (1804, N.Y. Sup. Ct.) 3 Johns. Cas. 337, discussed below note 12.

6. For a thorough and accurate discussion of the Sedition Act and the contemporary debate over it, see Carroll, "Freedom of Speech and of the Press in the Federalist Period," 18 *Mich. L. Rev.* 615 (1920).

7. 250 U.S. 616, 40 S. Ct. 17 (1919). For comment on this case see "Comments," 29 *Yale L. J.* 337 (1920); Wigmore, 14 *Ill. L. Rev.* 539 (1920); Chafee 33 *Harv. L. Rev.* 747; (1920); D.K., *id.,* 442; and a note, 14 *Ill. L. Rev.* 601 (1920).

> This section passed at the beginning of the most awful contest in which ever man was engaged . . . was to establish what? Not the inviolability of the Governor of the State, nor the majority of either House of the Legislature, but to punish men who should promote resistance to the right of the people to govern themselves, to the principle of the Constitution, to the Republican principle.[8]

Here, however, is the whole doctrine of "tendency" which underlies the common law of seditious libel, though the benefit of it is denied to persons. And of like import is the letter in which Jefferson, while the Sedition Act was still fresh in the minds of everybody, gave the signal for the impeachment of Justice Samuel Chase on account of the latter's "seditious attack" before a grand jury at Baltimore "on the principles of our Government."[9]

In the long run the protest against the Sedition Act accomplished two results: It laid to rest the idea of a national common law of seditious libel of which the act was merely declaratory; while within the states it rendered prosecution for political libels less and less frequent until they ceased altogether, leaving officials dependent for their protection on the ordinary law of slander and libel. On the other hand, the opponents of the act were forced to make two important concessions, at least inferentially: first, that the national government could regulate freedom of speech and of the press to the extent of forbidding the counselling of disorder and breach of the law; and secondly, that the state constitutions had left the common law of seditious libel operative so far as was necessary to protect the fundamental principles of government in the United States. For the rest, the Sedition Act itself is notable as an effort to mitigate the rigors of the common law which spread its influence to the states and so became the starting point of a new formulation of "liberty of the press."

The second section of the Sedition Act, quoted above, marked two departures from the common law: The "scandalous and malicious" publications which it banned must also be "false," and further they must be uttered "with the intent" to bring about the results discountenanced by the act. The third section of the act took a farther step and provided that defendants under it should be permitted "to give in evidence, in their defense, the truth of the matter" charged to be libellous, and that the jury should have the right "to determine the law and the fact, under the direction of the court, as in other cases,"—a development which had indeed been foreshadowed by a decision of the Supreme Court in 1794.[10] The test of intent which was thus brought into the law of libel for the first time was a reecho on this side the water of some of Erskine's famous pleas; the test of truth harks back, it may be surmised, to the famous Zenger case,[11] which, though it had no value as a precedent, had left behind a widespread though badly confused tradition as to its import.

8. *Annals* (5th Cong.) col. 3005ff. See also *id.* col. 2149ff.

9. See also Jefferson's letter to Mrs. Adams, September 11, 1804, 4 *Writings of Thomas Jefferson* (Washington ed.) 560.

10. Brailsford v. Georgia 3 Dall. 1 (1794 U.S.).

11. 17 How. St. Tr. 675 (1735, N.Y.).

The later importance of the Sedition Act becomes evident as we turn for a moment to the case of State v. Croswell which came before the New York Supreme Court in 1804.[12] Croswell had been convicted of having published "a scandalous, malicious, and seditious libel" traducing Thomas Jefferson, president of the United States, and intending to bring him "into the great contempt" of the people of the United States and of the state of New York. At the close of the trial the chief justice had charged the jury that it was not part of their province to decide on the intent of the defendant "or whether the publication in question was true or false or malicious," but only "whether the defendant was the publisher of the piece charged in the indictment" and "as to the truth of the innuendoes." On appeal Alexander Hamilton, for Croswell, attacked this ruling on the ground that the Sedition Act of 1798 had declared the common law for the United States. He then laid down a definition of liberty of the press which has been since repeated hundreds of times.

> The liberty of the press consists in the right to publish with impunity, truth, with good motives, for justifiable ends, though reflecting on government, magistracy, or individuals.

Hamilton's argument was accepted by Kent, who furthermore pointed out the place that the defense of truth ought to have in the entire defense, as follows:

> As a libel is a defamatory publication, made with a malicious intent, the truth or falsehood of the charge may, in many cases, be a very material and pertinent consideration. There can be no doubt that it is competent for the defendant to rebut the presumption of malice drawn from the fact of publication; and it is consonant to the general theory of evidence and the dictates of justice, that the defendant should be allowed to avail himself of every fact and circumstance that may serve to repel that presumption. And what can be a more important circumstance than the truth of the charge to determine the goodness of the motive in making it?

Hamilton's view, supplemented by Kent's, did not, it is true, prevail with the court, which rejected the contention that the Sedition Act established the common law for New York, and grounded their decision on Lord Mansfield's exposition of the common law in the Dean of St. Asaph's Case.[13] But Hamilton's triumph was not long postponed. The same year a bill was introduced into the state legislature which embodied his definition of freedom of the press, linked up with the provisions of Fox's Libel Act, and twelve months later this bill was enacted into law by the unanimous vote of both houses. A few years later the same formula was introduced into the New York constitution and today it finds place in nearly a third of our state constitutions.

Our modern liberals, however, object to this most widely prevalent definition of liberty of the press on the ground, as we have seen, that to the extent that the intent of the writer is judged from the tendency of his writing, the test of intent

12. Above, note 5, at p. 101.
13. 4 Doug. 73 (1784, K.B.).

leaves the common law of seditious libel in effect. It is therefore argued that in order to render congressional legislation invoking the test of intent constitutional—since the First Amendment cannot be deemed to have presupposed the common law of seditious libel as definitive of freedom of the press—this test must be given redefinition. Such, at least, I take it, is the purport of Justice Holmes's dissent in the recent Abrams case.[14]

The facts of this case, which already promises to become a notable one, were as follows: Abrams and others had printed and distributed circulars denouncing "the hypocrisy of the United States and her allies" and summoning the "workers" to "a general strike."

> Workers in the ammunition factories you are producing bullets, bayonets, cannon, to murder not only the Germans, but also your dearest, best, who are in Russia and are fighting for freedom. . . . Workers, up to fight.

On the strength of this and similar passages the defendants were convicted under the Espionage Act, one of the counts being that they had urged a curtailment of products essential to the prosecution of the war, "with intent by such curtailment to cripple or injure the United States in the prosecution of the war." From this verdict they appealed to the Supreme Court on the ground that there was no substantial evidence in the record to support it.

In the portion of his dissent above referred to, Justice Holmes admits that the defendants had urged a curtailment in the production of things necessary for the prosecution of the war, but he denies that there was evidence to show that this was done with the *intent* penalized by the act.

> I am aware that the word "intent" as vaguely used in ordinary legal discussion means no more than the knowledge at the time of the act that the consequences said to be intended will ensue. . . . But when words are used exactly, a deed is not done with intent to produce a consequence unless that consequence is the aim of the deed. . . .
>
> It seems to me that this statute must be taken to use its words in a strict and accurate sense. They would be absurd in any other. A patriot might think that we were wasting money on aeroplanes . . . and might advocate curtailment with success; yet, even if it turned out that the curtailment hindered . . . the United States in the prosecution of the war, no one could hold that conduct a crime.

The clear implication of Justice Holmes's language is that the legal test of intent establishes a conclusive presumption, and that is not so. I have not the charge in the Abrams case before me, but another charge under the same act reads thus:

> If you find beyond a reasonable doubt that the defendant did in fact utter the words imputed to him in the indictment or words in substance and effect like them, in determining what their purpose and intent was in so doing, you will have a right to consider what would be the natural, usual, and necessary consequences of uttering such words *at the time and place and in the presence and hearing of the people referred to in the indictment.*[15]

14. For comment on this case, see note 7 above.
15. Italics mine.

Then the charge proceeds a little further on as follows:

> There is no presumption which is conclusive, either in law or in fact, that he actually intended what may appear to you to be the natural, usual, and necessary consequences of uttering such words, and you will consider this matter in connection with all the other evidence in the case for the purpose of determining what was in fact the defendant's actual purpose and intent.[16]

There would be, I suspect, little difficulty in clearing Justice Holmes's advocate of curtailment in aeroplane production under such a charge, especially if that person were discreet enough to refrain from applying the term "murder" to the war which he was ostensibly promoting. But even as to Abrams and his associates, it cannot be admitted that the application of the legal doctrine of intent to their case did injustice. As Justice Clarke points out in his opinion for the Court, these men were entirely willing to cripple the prosecution of the war with Germany if only by so doing they might also cripple action against Russia. In law, as in ethics and in common sense, men must be held to intend, if not the usual consequences of their acts, certainly the necessary means to their objectives.

The issue raised by Justice Holmes is at basis the historical issue. He is at one with those who urge that Congress must stop short, in its regulation of speech and the press, with punishing words which "directly incite to acts in violation of law" and which "bring the speaker's [or writer's] unlawful intention reasonably near to success."[17] His own words are:

> The United States constitutionally may punish speech that produces or is intended to produce" (the sense in which the word "intended" is used in this passage is left uncertain) "a clear and imminent danger that it will bring about forthwith certain substantive evils that the United States constitutionally may seek to prevent.[18]

There is no doubt that the United States has this power—that was admitted in effect even by opponents of the Alien and Sedition Acts. But is this the limit of its power? The foregoing historical sketch does not support an affirmative answer to this question, nor do general principles. The elbow-room accorded Congress by the "necessary and proper" clause is admittedly broad, and it is a sound maxim of constitutional interpretation that the Constitution does not grant power in one place to withdraw it in another.[19] The majority in the Abrams case stand on secure ground.[20]

There is another aspect to this subject. For the most part those who are

16. "Interpretation of War Statutes," Bull. 191 (1918). See also to the same effect Bulls. 4, 49, 52, 79, 83, 112, 116, 123, 131, 133, 142, 143, 148, 149, 156, etc. *Cf.* also Kent's language quoted above.

17. Chafee, *op. cit.* note 3, at pp. 947–48.

18. This seems to imply that the Court may hold as a matter of law that the probability of harm resulting from an utterance is so remote that a conviction under the law for such utterance is unwarrantable. See also his words in Frohwerk v. United States 249 U.S. 204, 39 S.Ct. 249 (1919).

19. See Billings v. United States 232 U.S. 261, 34 S. Ct. 421 (1914); Brushaber v. Union Pacific R. Co. 240 U.S. 1, 36 S. Ct. 236 (1915).

20. They continue, moreover, to hold their ground in the subsequent cases of Pierce v. United States 40 S. Ct. 205 (1920 U.S.), and Schaefer v. United States 40 S. Ct. 259 (1920 U.S.).

endeavoring today to elaborate constitutional restrictions upon Congress's power over the press have shown themselves in the past distinctly opposed to the curtailment of legislative discretion by definite, unbending constitutional limitations. Personally, I am disposed to agree with their earlier rather than their later position. Amid the uncomplicated conditions of frontier life it was entirely feasible to assure each individual a certain quantum of "inalienable rights," but today the pursuit of happiness has become a joint-stock enterprise in which the welfare of all is embarked. In this situation it is much more to the point to insist upon the responsibility of legislators than their lack of power. Besides, is there anyone who seriously supposes that fair discussion of men and measures looking to the realization of public ends by lawful means is, or is likely to be, in any peril in this country from government? The real peril is quite a different one—but that is another story.

To sum up, the following propositions seem to be established with respect to constitutional freedom of speech and press: first, Congress is not limited to forbidding words which are of a nature "to create a clear and present danger" to national interests, but it may forbid words which are intended to endanger those interests if in the exercise of a fair legislative discretion it finds it "necessary and proper" to do so;[21] second, the intent of the accused in uttering the alleged forbidden words may be presumed from the reasonable consequences of such words, though the presumption is a rebuttable one; third, the Court will not scrutinize on appeal the findings of juries in this class of cases more strictly than in other penal cases. In short, the cause of freedom of speech and press is largely in the custody of legislative majorities and of juries, which, so far as there is evidence to show, is just where the framers of the Constitution intended it to be.

21. The party platforms and recent utterances of Attorney General Palmer make it clear that the good sense of the country is coming to the conclusion that to ban utterances advocating or threatening violence is all that is required at present.

6. Bowing Out "Clear and Present Danger"

"Every institution," wrote Emerson, "is the lengthened shadow of one man." The observation is nowhere borne out more strikingly than in judicial doctrines, which often exert an influence truly institutional in scope. An outstanding example in the field of American public law is Chief Justice Marshall's famous dictum that "the power to tax is the power to destroy."[1] Reflecting the lesson that Marshall drew from his experience as a young soldier under a government whose activities were repeatedly balked by local selfishness, this dictum came ultimately, through his dominant agency, to furnish the core of an important chapter of our constitutional law. A comparable instance in recent times is afforded by Justice Holmes's personal responsibility for the "clear and present danger" formula, a formula which illustrates a facet of its distinguished author's education and habit of mind.

Mr. Biddle tells in his little book on Holmes how, when the justice was a lad, his father, the once celebrated "Autocrat of the Breakfast Table," was accustomed to reward "Wendell" with an extra dab of marmalade "for saying what the Governor [the Autocrat] thought was worth saying. . . ."[2] The result of this matutinal drill in the making of bright remarks was a pronounced turn for epigram, which sometimes indeed took on the more portentous tone of oracle. Was the "clear and present danger" formula, we may ask, one of Holmes's more fortunate or one of his less fortunate ventures in epigram-making? As we shall see, the justice himself appeared at first to take his brain-child very casually, until, as we may surmise, somebody alerted him to its possibilities, thereby converting a biographical detail into constitutional history.

From 27 *Notre Dame Lawyer* 325–59 (1952). Reprinted with permission. © by the *Notre Dame Lawyer*, University of Notre Dame. The publisher is responsible for any errors that have occurred in reprinting or editing.
   1. McCulloch v. Maryland, 4 Wheat. 316, 431, 4 L. Ed. 579 (U.S. 1819).
   2. Biddle, *Mr. Justice Holmes* 27 (1942).

I

As it finally matured into a doctrine of constitutional law, the "clear and present danger" formula became a measure of legislative power in the choice of values which may be protected against unrestricted speech and publication. Before an utterance could be punished by government, it must have occurred in such circumstances or have been of such a nature as (1) to create a "clear and present danger" that (2) it would bring about "substantive evils" within the constitutional power of government in the United States to combat; and on both these points the Supreme Court of the United States was, by virtue of the protection which is today thrown about freedom of speech and press by the First and Fourteenth Amendments, the final judge.

The phrase "clear and present danger" first appeared in Holmes's opinion for a unanimous Court in Schenck v. United States,[3] which was decided March 3, 1919. Four years prior the same justice had written the opinion, also for a unanimous Court, in Fox v. Washington,[4] where the question at issue was the constitutionality of a Washington statute which made it unlawful to publish or circulate any matter "advocating, encouraging or inciting, or having a tendency to encourage or incite the commission of any crime. . . ."[5] The defendant had been convicted of publishing an article which was sharply critical of those who opposed nudism. According to Justice Holmes, this article "by indirection but unmistakably . . . encourages and incites a persistence in what we must assume would be a breach of the state laws against indecent exposure; and the jury so found."[6] Stating further that "We understand the state court by implication at least to have read the statute as confined to encouraging an actual breach of the law,"[7] he brushed aside the argument that it infringed the constitutional guarantee of freedom of speech. Nothing was said about the degree of danger that breach of the law would result from the publication; nor was the question raised whether appearance in public in a decent minimum of clothing is a "substantive" value which government in the United States is entitled to protect. The plain implication is that incitement to crime or encouragement thereof is sufficient, without reference to its actual consequences.[8]

Did the Court, or did Justice Holmes himself, intend to depart from these Fox

3. 249 U.S. 47, 39 S. Ct. 247, 63 L. Ed. 470 (1919).
4. 236 U.S. 273, 35 S. Ct. 383, 59 L. Ed. 573 (1915).
5. As quoted in *id.*, 236 U.S. at 275.
6. *Id.*, 236 U.S. at 277.
7. *Id.*
8. In Davis v. Beason, 133 U.S. 333, 10 S. Ct. 299, 33 L. Ed. 637 (1890), the question at issue was the constitutionality of a statute of the Territory of Idaho, providing that "no person who is a bigamist or polygamist, or who teaches, advises, counsels or encourages any person or persons to become bigamists or polygamists or to commit any other crime defined by law, or to enter into what is known as plural or celestial marriage, or who is a member of any order, organization or association which teaches, advises, counsels or encourages its members or devotees or any other person to commit the crime of bigamy or polygamy, or any other crime defined by law, either as a rite or

views in the Schenck case? Read out of context, the following passage,[9] in which the words "clear and present danger" were first used, suggests an affirmative answer:

We admit that in many places and in ordinary times the defendants in saying all that was said in the circular would have been within their constitutional rights. But the character of every act depends upon the circumstances in which it is done. . . . The most stringent protection of free speech would not protect a man in falsely shouting fire in a theatre and causing a panic. It does not even protect a man from an injunction against uttering words that may have all the effect of force. Gompers v. Buck's Stove & Range Co., 221 U.S. 418, 439. . . . The question in every case is whether the words used are used in such circumstances and are of such a nature as to create a clear and present danger that they will bring about the substantive evils that Congress has a right to prevent. It is a question of proximity and degree. When a nation is at war many things that might be said in time of peace are such a hindrance to its effort that their utterance will not be endured so long as men fight and that no Court could regard them as protected by any constitutional right.

Reading these sentences, however, in light of the facts of the case and of other portions of the same opinion, we reach a different conclusion, as did the overwhelming majority of the Court itself as soon as its doing so became determinative. Defendants in Schenck had been convicted of a conspiracy to violate the Espionage Act of 1917[10] by attempting to cause insubordination in the armed forces and to obstruct recruiting. Pursuant to that conspiracy they had mailed to

---

ceremony of such order, organization or association, or otherwise, is permitted to vote at any election, or to hold any position or office of honor, trust or profit within this Territory."

A unanimous Court held this enactment to be within the legislative powers which Congress had conferred on the territory and not to be open to any constitutional objection. Said Justice Field for the Court:

"Bigamy and polygamy are crimes by the laws of all civilized and Christian countries. They are crimes by the laws of the United States, and they are crimes by the laws of Idaho. They tend to destroy the purity of the marriage relation, to disturb the peace of families, to degrade woman and to debase man. Few crimes are more pernicious to the best interests of society and receive more general or more deserved punishment. To extend exemption from punishment for such crimes would be to shock the moral judgment of the community. To call their advocacy a tenet of religion is to offend the common sense of mankind. If they are crimes, then to teach, advise and counsel their practice is to aid in their commission, and such teaching and counseling are themselves criminal and proper subjects of punishment, as aiding and abetting crime are in all other cases." 133 U.S. at 341–42.

There was no talk about the necessity for showing that the prohibited teaching, counseling, advising, etc., must be shown to have occurred in circumstances creating a "clear and present danger" of its being followed; or of monogamy being a value which government in the United States is authorized to protect.

9. 249 U.S. 47, 52, 39 S. Ct. 247, 63 L. Ed. 470 (1919). It should be observed in passing that advocates of "clear and present danger" always quote the part about "shouting fire in a theatre," but usually omit the reference to the Gompers case where speech was held restrainable in enforcement of an anti-labor injunction.

10. 40 Stat. 217 (1917). This statute is now substantially embodied in 18 U.S.C. section 793 (Supp. 1951).

members of the armed forces circulars which criticized conscription in strong language and exhorted readers to assert and support their rights. Apparently these circulars did not in express terms counsel insubordination or obstruction to recruiting, nor was that result proved. Indeed, so far as the opinion discloses, no evidence was presented as to their possible or probable effect apart from their contents and the fact of their publication. This circumstance, however, did not trouble Justice Holmes who disposed of the point by saying:[11]

> Of course the document would not have been sent unless it had been intended to have some effect, and we do not see what effect it could be expected to have upon persons subject to the draft except to influence them to obstruct the carrying of it out.

And he later added:[12] "If the act, (speaking, or circulating a paper,) its tendency and the intent with which it is done are the same, we perceive no ground for saying that success alone warrants making the act a crime." In the final analysis the doctrine announced in the Schenck case is indistinguishable from that presented in Fox.

Within the next two weeks, two more convictions under the Espionage Act were also unanimously upheld in opinions written by Justice Holmes. These two pronouncements went far to dispel whatever impression may have been created by the earlier opinion that there is a constitutional requirement that "clear and present danger" of some "substantive evil" be proved where intent to incite a crime is found to exist. In Frohwerk v. United States,[13] the defendant was convicted of conspiring to violate the Espionage Act and of attempting to cause disloyalty, mutiny, and refusal of duty in the armed forces by the publication of twelve newspaper articles criticizing this country's entry into the war and the conscription of men for service overseas. The claim of privilege under the First Amendment Justice Holmes brusquely rejected:[14]

> With regard to that argument we think it necessary to add to what has been said in Schenck v. United States . . . only that the First Amendment while prohibiting legislation against free speech as such cannot have been, and obviously was not, intended to give immunity for every possible use of language. . . . We venture to believe that neither Hamilton nor Madison, nor any other competent person then or later, ever supposed that to make criminal the counselling of a murder within the jurisdiction of Congress would be an unconstitutional interference with free speech.

Of significance, too, in view of some things said later in the Dennis case,[15] is the following passage from the same opinion:[16]

> It is said that the first count is bad because it does not allege the means by which the conspiracy was to be carried out. But a conspiracy to obstruct recruiting would be

11. 249 U.S. 47, 51, 39 S. Ct. 247, 63 L. Ed. 470 (1919).
12. *Id.*, 249 U.S. at 52.
13. 249 U.S. 204, 39 S. Ct. 249, 63 L. Ed. 561 (1919).
14. *Id.*, 249 U.S. at 206.
15. Dennis v. United States, 341 U.S. 494, 71 S. Ct. 857, 95 L. Ed. 1137 (1951).
16. Frohwerk v. United States, 249 U.S. 204, 209, 39 S. Ct. 249, 63 L. Ed. 561 (1919).

criminal even if no means were agreed upon specifically by which to accomplish the intent. It is enough if the parties agreed to set to work for that common purpose. That purpose could be accomplished or aided by persuasion as well as by false statements, and there was no need to allege that false reports were intended to be made, or made. It is argued that there is no sufficient allegation of intent, but intent to accomplish an object cannot be alleged more clearly than by stating that parties conspired to accomplish it.

On the same day Justice Holmes also delivered the opinion in Debs v. United States,[17] sustaining a conviction for the same kind of offense. The charge arose out of a speech delivered by the defendant in which he extolled socialism and criticized the participation of the United States in World War I. As in the preceding cases there was no explicit exhortation to any criminal offense. The principal points at issue concerned the weight and admissibility of evidence bearing upon the unlawful intent of Debs's address. The Court held[18] that the jury was warranted

> . . .in finding that one purpose of the speech, whether incidental or not does not matter, was to oppose not only war in general but this war, and that the opposition was so expressed that its natural and intended effect would be to obstruct recruiting. If that was intended and if, in all the circumstances, that would be its probable effect, it would not be protected by reason of its being part of a general program and expressions of a general and conscientious belief.

In short, we find three cases, decided within a period of two weeks, in which convictions for violation of the Espionage Act were unanimously sustained for utterances of such general nature that they might all have borne innocent interpretations if made in other circumstances, but which were deemed to be unlawful because the circumstances warranted the finding that their probable and intended effect would be to obstruct the war effort. Furthermore, in the last two of these three cases we hear not a word about "clear and present danger."

Eight months later, however, the apparently forgotten phrase leaps suddenly into prominence in the dissenting opinion of Justice Holmes for himself and Justice Brandeis in Abrams v. United States.[19] The defendants were Russian sympathizers who called upon workers to stop producing munitions which, they asserted, were being used against Russia as well as Germany. The majority held that even though defendants' primary purpose was to prevent injury to the Russian cause, they were accountable for the easily foreseeable effects which their utterances were likely to produce in the way of obstructing the war effort against Germany.

The intention of Justice Holmes's dissent is ambiguous. At first he seemed to be basing his case on the statute alone. Thus he said:[20]

---

17. 249 U.S. 211, 39 S. Ct. 252, 63 L. Ed. 566 (1919).
18. *Id.*, 249 U.S. at 214–15.
19. 250 U.S. 616, 40 S. Ct. 17, 63 L. Ed. 1173 (1919).
20. *Id.*, 250 U.S. at 626–27.

I am aware of course that the word "intent" as vaguely used in ordinary legal discussion means no more than knowledge at the time of the act that the consequences said to be intended will ensue. . . . But, when words are used exactly, a deed is not done with intent to produce a consequence unless that consequence is the aim of the deed. . . . It seems to me that this statute must be taken to use its words in a strict and accurate sense.

But he soon transferred the discussion to the First Amendment, as to the bearing of which on the case he wrote:[21]

I do not doubt for a moment that by the same reasoning that would justify punishing persuasion to murder, the United States constitutionally may punish speech that produces or is intended to produce a clear and imminent danger that it will bring about forthwith certain substantive evils that the United States constitutionally may seek to prevent. . . . It is only the present danger of immediate evil or an intent to bring it about that warrants Congress in setting a limit to the expression of opinion where private rights are not concerned. Congress certainly cannot forbid all effort to change the mind of the country. Now nobody can suppose that the surreptitious publishing of a silly leaflet by an unknown man, without more, would present any immediate danger that its opinions would hinder the success of the government arms or have any appreciable tendency to do so. Publishing those opinions for the very purpose of obstructing, however, might indicate a greater danger and at any rate would have the quality of an attempt. So I assume that the second leaflet if published for the purposes alleged in the fourth count might be punishable.

And being now in the full flood of composition, the justice concluded his opinion with an appeal to history, as follows:[22]

Persecution for the expression of opinions seems to me perfectly logical. . . . But when men have realized that time has upset many fighting faiths, they may come to believe even more than they believe the very foundations of their own conduct that the ultimate good desired is better reached by free trade in ideas—that the best test of truth is the power of the thought to get itself accepted in the competition of the market, and that truth is the only ground upon which their wishes safely can be carried out. That at any rate is the theory of our Constitution. It is an experiment, as all life is an experiment.

Certain questions arise: Did Justice Holmes, when he spoke of "persuasion to murder," mean successful persuasion? This is obviously something quite different from the "counselling of murder" which he said, in his Frohwerk opinion, that Hamilton and Madison never supposed could not be constitutionally punished. And was it his intention to assert it as a rule of constitutional law that the Court should disallow any act of Congress which is interpretable as punishing utterances that do not in its opinion produce a "clear and present danger" to an interest which it thinks of sufficient importance to deserve such protection? If so, how could he have said the Frohwerk and Debs cases were in his opinion correctly decided? And what did he mean by his suggestion that utterances which

21. *Id.*, 250 U.S. at 627–28.
22. *Id.*, 250 U.S. at 630.

have "the quality of an attempt," to wit, of acts done for the purpose of committing a crime, but falling short of it, may be constitutionally punished? Was the suggestion intended to narrow still further the category of constitutionally restrainable utterances?

Coming then to the hortatory portion of the opinion—that concerning "fighting faiths"—did Justice Holmes mean that faiths are entitled to survive only so long as they don't fight, and that "the ultimate good desired" has always prevailed of its own inherent qualities without anybody fighting for it? And if so, how does this teaching square with the belief expressed by its author elsewhere that the "proximate test of excellence" is "correspondence to the actual equilibrium of forces in the community—that is, conformity to the wishes of the dominant power"?[23] The answer is perhaps supplied in the following passage from the same justice's dissent in the Gitlow case,[24] five years later: "If in the long run the beliefs expressed in proletarian dictatorship are destined to be accepted by the dominant forces of the community, the only meaning of free speech is that they should be given their chance and have their way."

In short, the "ultimate good desired" and the triumph of destiny are one and the same thing, and the function of freedom of speech is to forward this triumph, not to block it, although just why destiny needs an assist does not quite appear. That the Constitution is an "experiment" need not be questioned; unquestionable too is the fact that its maintenance has not been achieved without a certain amount of fighting at times, in some of which the youthful Holmes himself bore a gallant part.

It should be noted that in his correspondence with Sir Frederick Pollock about Abrams, Holmes justified his dissent solely by reference to his reading of the word "intent" as used in the statute.[25] As to the "clear and present danger" formula he said not a word.

Between Abrams and Justice Holmes's retirement from the bench, twelve years elapsed. In this interval he succeeded in enrolling only one other justice under his banner, his fellow Bostonian and fellow graduate from Harvard Law School, Justice Brandeis, whose initial contribution to the discussion occurs in 1920 in connection with Schaefer v. United States.[26] Sustaining here a conviction based upon the publication of a series of newspaper articles which criticized the government in its conduct of the war, the majority used language quite similar to that employed by Holmes in the Schenck case. With respect to the contents of the articles, the Court, speaking by Justice McKenna, chanted the following answer:[27]

23. Holmes, *Collected Legal Papers* 258 (1920).
24. Gitlow v. New York, 268 U.S. 652, 673, 45 S. Ct. 625, 69 L. Ed. 1138 (1925).
25. 2 *Holmes-Pollock Letters* 29–45 (Howe ed. 1941).
26. 251 U.S. 466, 40 S. Ct. 259, 64 L. Ed. 360 (1920).
27. *Id.*, 251 U.S. at 478–79.

Coarse indeed, this was, and vulgar to us; but it was expected to produce, and it may be did produce, a different effect upon its readers. To them its derisive contempt may have been truly descriptive of American feebleness and inability to combat Germany's prowess, and thereby chill and check the ardency of patriotism and make it despair of success, and in hopelessness relax energy both in preparation and action. If it and the other articles . . . had not that purpose, what purpose had they? . . . Their effect or the persons affected could not be shown, nor was it necessary. The tendency of the articles and their efficacy were enough for offense—their "intent" and "attempt," for those are the words of the law—and to have required more would have made the law useless. It was passed in precaution. The incidence of its violation might not be immediately seen, evil appearing only in disaster, the result of the disloyalty engendered and the spirit of mutiny.

Justice Brandeis's *riposte* for himself and Holmes is launched from the latter's dictum in Schenck. This is asserted to be a "rule of reason" and the measure, as "declared by a unanimous Court," of the power of Congress to "interfere with free speech." The opinion continues:[28]

Correctly applied, it will preserve the right of free speech both from suppression by tyrannous, well-meaning majorities, and from abuse by irresponsible, fanatical minorities. Like many other rules for human conduct, it can be applied correctly only by the exercise of good judgment; and to the exercise of good judgment calmness is, in times of deep feeling and on subjects which excite passion, as essential as fearlessness and honesty. The question whether in a particular instance the words spoken or written fall within the permissible curtailment of free speech is, under the rule enunciated by this court, one of degree; and because it is a question of degree the field in which the jury may exercise its judgment is necessarily a wide one. But its field is not unlimited. The trial provided for is one by judge *and* jury, and the judge may not abdicate his function. If the words were of such a nature and were used under such circumstances that men, judging in calmness, could not reasonably say that they created a clear and present danger that they would bring about the evil which Congress sought and had a right to prevent, then it is the duty of the trial judge to withdraw the case from the consideration of the jury; and, if he fails to do so, it is the duty of the appellate court to correct the error. In my opinion, no jury acting in calmness could reasonably say that any of the publications set forth in the indictment was of such a character or was made under such circumstances as to create a clear and present danger, either that they would obstruct recruiting or that they would promote the success of the enemies of the United States.

What follows is a critical examination of the incriminating documents which seems to prove their gross misuse by the prosecution, effected with the aid and consent of the trial court. The necessity of invoking the "clear and present danger" formula to meet this situation is, however, left obscure. Justice Clarke also dissented, but on the ground that the proceedings constituted "a case of flagrant mistrial." He refused to concede that "the disposition of this case involves a great peril either to the maintenance of law and order and governmental authority on one hand, or to the freedom of the press on the other."[29]

28. *Id.*, 251 U.S. at 482–83.
29. *Id.*, 251 U.S. at 501.

II

In 1925 occurred Gitlow v. New York,[30] a pivotal case for two reasons. In the first place, the Court adopted, as it had in the Fox case, the assumption that the Fourteenth Amendment was intended to render the restraints imposed by the First Amendment on Congress available also against the states so far as freedom of speech and press are concerned. In the second place, the case involved the first peacetime prosecution for criminal anarchy. The New York criminal anarchy statute made it a felony for any person to advise or teach the duty, necessity, or propriety of overthrowing or overturning organized government by force and violence. The defendant had participated in the publication of a left-wing manifesto advocating "revolutionary mass action" for the purpose of conquering and destroying the parliamentary state and establishing Communism in its place. Since, according to the majority opinion, there was no evidence of any effect resulting from the publication and circulation of the manifesto, the jury's verdict of guilty imported a finding that the defendant had acted with unlawful intent in teaching and advocating unlawful acts for the purpose of overthrowing the government. So interpreted and applied, the statute was sustained by the Court, seven to two. Said Justice Sanford for the majority:[31]

It is a fundamental principle, long established, that the freedom of speech and of the press which is secured by the Constitution, does not confer an absolute right to speak or publish, without responsibility, whatever one may choose, or an unrestricted and unbridled license that gives immunity for every possible use of language and prevents the punishment of those who abuse this freedom.

The Court accepted the soundness of the rule that a state, in the exercise of its police power, may punish one who abuses the freedom of speech by utterances tending to corrupt public morals, incite to crime, or disturb the peace.[32] All the more then may it punish utterances endangering the foundations of organized government:[33]

It [freedom of speech and press] does not protect publications prompting the overthrow of government by force; the punishment of those who publish articles which tend to destroy organized society being essential to the security of freedom and the stability of the State. . . . And a State may penalize utterances which openly advocate the overthrow of the representative and constitutional form of government of the United States and the several States, by violence or other unlawful means. . . . In short this freedom does not deprive a State of the primary and essential right of self preservation; which, so long as human governments endure, they cannot be denied.

Justice Sanford pointed out that the state, by enacting the statute, had determined that utterances advocating the overthrow of organized government by

30. 268 U.S. 652, 45 S. Ct. 625, 69 L. Ed. 1138 (1925).
31. *Id.*, 268 U.S. 666.
32. Patterson v. Colorado, 205 U.S. 454, 27 S. Ct. 556, 51 L. Ed. 879 (1907); Robertson v. Baldwin, 165 U.S. 275, 17 S. Ct. 326, 41 L. Ed. 715 (1897).
33. Gitlow v. New York, 268 U.S. 652, 668, 45 S. Ct. 625, 69 L. Ed. 1138 (1925).

force and violence are so inimical to the general welfare and involve such danger of substantive evil that they may be penalized under the police power. That determination, he added, "must be given great weight. Every presumption is to be indulged in favor of the validity of the statute."[34] He then continued:[35]

> That utterances inciting to the overthrow of organized government by unlawful means, present a sufficient danger of substantive evil to bring their punishment within the range of legislative discretion, is clear. Such utterances, by their very nature, involve danger to the public peace and to the security of the State. They threaten breaches of the peace and ultimate revolution. And the immediate danger is none the less real and substantial, because the effect of a given utterance cannot be accurately foreseen. The State cannot reasonably be required to measure the danger from every such utterance in the nice balance of a jeweler's scale. A single revolutionary spark may kindle a fire that, smouldering for a time, may burst into a sweeping and destructive conflagration. It cannot be said that the State is acting arbitrarily or unreasonably when in the exercise of its judgment as to the measures necessary to protect the public peace and safety, it seeks to extinguish the spark without waiting until it has enkindled the flame or blazed into the conflagration. It cannot reasonably be required to defer the adoption of measures for its own peace and safety until the revolutionary utterances lead to actual disturbances of the public peace or imminent and immediate danger of its own destruction; but it may, in the exercise of its judgment, suppress the threatened danger in its incipiency.

Moreover, the statute's validity being settled,[36]

> . . . it may be applied to every utterance—not too trivial to be beneath the notice of the law—which is of such a character and used with such intent and purpose as to bring it within the prohibition of the statute. . . . In other words, when the legislative body has determined generally, in the constitutional exercise of its discretion, that utterances of a certain kind involve such danger of substantive evil that they may be punished, the question whether any specific utterance coming within the prohibited class is likely, in and of itself, to bring about the substantive evil, is not open to consideration. It is sufficient that the statute itself be constitutional and that the use of the language comes within its prohibition.

The Schenck case Justice Sanford distinguished with the assertion that its "general statement" concerning "clear and present danger" had been intended to apply only to cases where the statute merely prohibits certain acts involving the danger of substantive evil, without any reference to language itself, and had no application where the legislative body itself had "previously determined the danger of substantive evil arising from utterances of a specified character."[37]

Speaking for himself and Justice Brandeis, Justice Holmes dissented in an opinion of which the following passage is the material one:[38]

---

34. *Id.* The Court also cited as authority Mugler v. Kansas, 123 U.S. 623, 8 S. Ct. 273, 31 L. Ed. 205 (1887).

35. 268 U.S. 652, 669, 45 S. Ct. 625, 69 L. Ed. 1138 (1925).

36. *Id.,* 268 U.S. at 670.

37. *Id.,* 268 U.S. at 671.

38. *Id.,* 268 U.S. at 673.

If what I think the correct test is applied, it is manifest that there was no present danger of an attempt to overthrow the government by force on the part of the admittedly small minority who shared the defendant's views. It is said that this manifesto was more than a theory, that it was an incitement. Every idea is an incitement. It offers itself for belief and if believed it is acted on unless some other belief outweighs it or some failure of energy stifles the movement at its birth. The only difference between the expression of an opinion and an incitement in the narrower sense is the speaker's enthusiasm for the result. Eloquence may set fire to reason. But whatever may be thought of the redundant discourse before us it had no chance of starting a present conflagration.

One comment is quite inevitable. The assertion that "every idea is an incitement" is manifestly irrelevant to the question whether incitement in the sense of an utterance counselling or encouraging the commission of a crime may be punished by the state. It is in fact no better than a pun, which another master of oracular discourse, the late Dr. Samuel Johnson, pronounced "the lowest form of wit." Certainly it is not impressive when appearing in the context of a judicial opinion, even as exhortation.

And again we find Justice Holmes singularly reticent on the subject of "clear and present danger" when discussing the case with Sir Frederick Pollock. In a letter written a week before the opinion was announced Holmes confessed:[39]

> I am bothered by a case in which conscience and judgment are a little in doubt concerning the constitutionality under the 14th amendment of a State law punishing the publication of a manifesto advocating the forcible overthrow of government. . . . Such is the effect of putting a doubt into words that I turned aside from this letter and wrote my views which are now waiting to go to the printer. The theme is one on which I have written majority and minority opinions heretofore and to which I thought I could add about ten words to what I have said before.

His next letter to Pollock underscored the fact that his dissent was prompted largely by the impression that the publication was utterly futile. "My last performance during the term," he wrote, "was a dissent (in which Brandeis joined) in favor of the rights of an anarchist (so-called) to talk drool in favor of the proletarian dictatorship."[40] "Drool"—the publication was intrinsically contemptible, and beneath the notice of the law. Evidently "*de minimis,*" not "clear and present danger," was the root-stem of this dissent. Justice Stone, consistent champion of personal liberty, joined in the judgment of the Court.

Two years later occurred Whitney v. California.[41] Here the defendant had been found guilty of violating the California Criminal Syndicalism Act by wilfully assisting in organizing and becoming a member of a group organized to "advocate, teach or aid and abet criminal syndicalism."[42] It was not denied that

---

39. 2 *Holmes-Pollock Letters* 162 (Howe ed. 1941).
40. *Id.*, at 163.
41. 274 U.S. 357, 47 S. Ct. 641, 71 L. Ed. 1095 (1927).
42. As quoted in *id.*, 274 U.S. at 360.

the evidence warranted the jury in finding that the accused assisted in organizing the Communist Labor party of California and that this party was organized to advocate and abet criminal syndicalism. She insisted, however, that the conviction was invalid because there was no showing of a specific intent on her part to join in the forbidden purpose. Holding that this was a question of fact foreclosed by the verdict of the jury, and consequently not open to review, the Supreme Court sustained the conviction. Its decision was unanimous, but Justice Brandeis wrote a separate concurring opinion in which Justice Holmes joined. A material passage reads as follows:[43]

> Every denunciation of existing law tends in some measure to increase the probability that there will be violation of it. Condonation of a breach enhances the probability. Expressions of approval add to the probability. Propagation of the criminal state of mind by teaching syndicalism increases it. Advocacy of law-breaking heightens it still further. But even advocacy of violation, however reprehensible morally, is not a justification for denying free speech where the advocacy falls short of incitement and there is nothing to indicate that the advocacy would be immediately acted on. The wide difference between advocacy and incitement, between preparation and attempt, between assembling and conspiracy, must be borne in mind. In order to support a finding of clear and present danger it must be shown either that immediate serious violence was to be expected or was advocated, or that the past conduct furnished reason to believe that such advocacy was then contemplated.

It is somewhat hazardous to assess this collocation of sentences for its bearing on the topic here under discussion, but apparently there are two ideas present: First, that there is a "wide difference between advocacy and incitement"—that is, of or to illegal action—a proposition for which not one iota of supporting authority is offered and which is refuted again and again by the *usus loquendi* of the Court in the entire line of decisions reviewed above; secondly, that no utterance which the Court chooses to label "advocacy" may be constitutionally punished unless it was of immediate serious violence or unless the utterer was known to have a predilection for violence.

The opinion then proceeds:[44]

> To courageous, self-reliant men, with confidence in the power of free and fearless reasoning applied through the processes of popular government, no danger flowing from speech can be deemed clear and present, unless the incidence of the evil apprehended is so imminent that it may befall before there is opportunity for full discussion. If there be time to expose through discussion the falsehood and fallacies, to avert the evil by the processes of education, the remedy to be applied is more speech, not enforced silence.

Indulging the assumption that this passage was not written merely as exhortation, but with the serious intention of proposing a rule of constitutional law, we may well ask what it means? Apparently, it means that the ultimate test of the constitutionality of legislation restricting freedom of utterance is whether there is

43. *Id.*, 274 U.S. at 376.
44. *Id.*, 274 U.S. at 377.

still sufficient time to educate the utterers out of their mistaken frame of mind, and the final say on this necessarily recondite matter rests with the Supreme Court!

Four years later, in Stromberg v. California,[45] both Justices Holmes and Brandeis joined in a decision which held the California Red Flag Law unconstitutional in so far as it prohibited display of such a flag as a symbol of peaceful and orderly opposition to government by legal means and within constitutional limitations, but expressly found the statute valid in prohibiting display of a red flag as a stimulus to anarchistic action or as an aid to propaganda which amounted to advocacy of force or violence in overthrowing the government of a state. During the same period two other state court convictions for subversive utterances were reversed for lack of evidence proving that the defendant had actually advocated criminal conduct to effect industrial or political change.[46] But after the Whitney case, no talk about "clear and present danger" was heard for a full decade.

III

The formula achieved a second resurrection in 1937, in Herndon v. Lowry,[47] and at last in a majority opinion! The role which it played on this occasion was, however, a minor and quite dispensable one. Here a conviction under a state statute for an attempt to "incite insurrection" was reversed by a closely divided Court, on the ground that as construed by the state courts the act set up an unascertainable standard of guilt and thereby offended the due process clause of the Fourteenth Amendment. Said Justice Roberts:[48]

> The Act does not prohibit incitement to violent interference with any given activity or operation of the state. By force of it, as construed, the judge and jury trying an alleged offender cannot appraise the circumstances and character of the defendant's utterances or activities as begetting a clear and present danger of forcible obstruction of a particular state function.

Nor was any specified conduct or utterance of the accused made an offense. In short, the "clear and present danger" formula is one of several elements which, independently of each other, will satisfy the constitutional requirement of certainty in defining an offense. In his 1951 Oliver Wendell Holmes Lectures at Harvard Law School,[49] former Justice Roberts does not mention Herndon v. Lowry.

Nevertheless, beginning with Thornhill v. Alabama,[50] decided in 1940, a majority of the Court frequently invoked the "clear and present danger" formula in nullifying state action, in fields unrelated to the advocacy of forbidden con-

45. 283 U.S. 359, 51 S. Ct. 532, 75 L. Ed. 1117 (1931).
46. De Jonge v. Oregon, 299 U.S. 353, 57 S. Ct. 255, 81 L. Ed. 278 (1937); Fiske v. Kansas, 274 U.S. 380, 47 S. Ct. 655, 71 L. Ed. 1108 (1927).
47. 301 U.S. 242, 57 S. Ct. 732, 81 L. Ed. 1066 (1937).
48. *Id.,* 301 U.S. at 261.
49. Roberts, *The Court and the Constitution* (1951).
50. 310 U.S. 88, 60 S. Ct. 736, 84 L. Ed. 1093 (1940).

duct; e.g., laws prohibiting picketing, restricting the use of public places for propagating religious beliefs,[51] or requiring registration of labor organizers,[52] and judgments imposing sentences for contempt of court for criticism of judicial action.[53] The interest of these cases in the present connection is twofold: first, in many of them the Court reversed convictions on the ground that the interest which the state was endeavoring to protect was "too insubstantial to warrant restriction of speech,"[54] thus suggesting the converse tactic employed by the chief justice in his opinions in American Communications Assn. v. Douds[55] and in the Dennis case;[56] and secondly, they show a widening rift among the justices touching the scope and constitutional basis of the "clear and present danger" doctrine prior to the case of the Eleven Communists.

This diversity of opinion among the justices concerned the following three closely related topics: first, the restrictive force of the test; second, the constitutional status of freedom of speech and press; third, the kind of speech which the Constitution is concerned to protect. On the first point the following passage from Justice Black's opinion in Bridges v. California is pertinent:[57]

> What finally emerges from the "clear and present danger" cases is a working principle that the substantive evil must be extremely serious and the degree of imminence extremely high before utterances can be punished. Those cases do not purport to mark the furthermost constitutional boundaries of protected expression, nor do we here. They do no more than recognize a minimum compulsion of the Bill of Rights. For the First Amendment does not speak equivocally. It prohibits any law "abridging the freedom of speech, or of the press." It must be taken as a command of the broadest scope that explicit language, read in the context of a liberty-loving society, will allow.

With this should be compared the following words from Justice Frankfurter's concurring opinion in Pennekamp v. Florida,[58] which involved an issue closely related to the one dealt with in the Bridges case:[59]

> "Clear and present danger" was never used by Mr. Justice Holmes to express a technical legal doctrine or to convey a formula for adjudicating cases. It was a literary phrase not to be distorted by being taken from its context. In its setting it served to indicate the importance of freedom of speech to a free society but also to emphasize that its exercise must be compatible with the preservation of other freedoms essential to a democracy and guaranteed by our Constitution. When those other attributes of a democracy are threatened by speech, the Constitution does not deny power to the States to curb it.

51. Cantwell v. Connecticut, 310 U.S. 296, 60 S. Ct. 900, 84 L. Ed. 1213 (1940).
52. Thomas v. Collins, 323 U.S. 516, 65 S. Ct. 315, 89 L. Ed. 430 (1945).
53. Craig v. Harney, 331 U.S. 367, 67 S. Ct. 1249, 91 L. Ed. 1546 (1947); Pennekamp v. Florida 328 U.S. 331, 66 S. Ct. 1029, 90 L. Ed. 1295 (1946); Bridges v. California, 314 U.S. 252, 62 S. Ct. 190, 86 L. Ed. 192 (1941).
54. Dennis v. United States, 341 U.S. 494, 508, 71 S. Ct. 857, 95 L. Ed. 1137 (1951).
55. 339 U.S. 382, 70 S. Ct. 674, 94 L. Ed. 925 (1950).
56. Dennis v. United States, 341 U.S. 494, 71 S. Ct. 857, 95 L. Ed. 1137 (1951).
57. 314 U.S. 252, 263, 62 S. Ct. 190, 86 L. Ed. 192 (1941).
58. 328 U.S. 331, 66 S. Ct. 1029, 90 L. Ed. 1295 (1946).
59. Id., 328 U.S. at 353.

The second question, in more definite terms, is whether freedom of speech and press occupies a "preferred position" in the constitutional hierarchy of values so that legislation restrictive of it is presumptively unconstitutional. An important contribution to the affirmative view on this point is the following dictum written by Justice Cardozo in 1937:[60]

> . . . one may say that it is the matrix, the indispensable condition, of nearly every other form of freedom. . . . So it has come about that the domain of liberty, withdrawn by the Fourteenth Amendment from encroachment by the states, has been enlarged by latter-day judgments to include liberty of the mind as well as liberty of action. The extension became, indeed, a logical imperative when once it was recognized, as long ago it was, that liberty is something more than exemption from physical restraint, ..nd that even in the field of substantive rights and duties the legislative judgment, if oppressive and arbitrary, may be overriden by the courts.

Touching on the same subject a few months later, Chief Justice Stone suggested a narrow scope for the operation of the presumption of constitutionality when legislation appears to be within a specific prohibition of the Constitution, "such as those of the first ten amendments, which are deemed equally specific when held to be embraced within the Fourteenth."[61] Developing this theme, the chief justice continued:[62]

> It is unnecessary to consider now whether legislation which restricts those political processes which can ordinarily be expected to bring about repeal of undesirable legislation, is to be subjected to more exacting judicial scrutiny under the general prohibitions of the Fourteenth Amendment than are most other types of legislation.

But the most confident assertion of this position occurs in Justice Rutledge's opinion for a sharply divided Court in Thomas v. Collins, where it is said:[63]

> The case confronts us again with the duty our system places on this Court to say where the individual's freedom ends and the State's power begins. Choice on that border, now as always delicate, is perhaps more so where the usual presumption supporting legislation is balanced by the preferred place given in our scheme to the great, the indispensable democratic freedoms secured by the First Amendment. . . . That priority gives these liberties a sanctity and a sanction not permitting dubious intrusions. And it is the character of the right, not of the limitation, which determines what standard governs the choice. . . .
> For these reasons any attempt to restrict those liberties must be justified by clear public interest, threatened not doubtfully or remotely, but by clear and present danger. The rational connection between the remedy provided and the evil to be curbed, which in other contexts might support legislation against attack on due process grounds, will not suffice. These rights rest on firmer foundation. Accordingly, whatever occasion would restrain orderly discussion and persuasion at appropriate time and place, must have clear support in public danger, actual or impending. Only the gravest abuses, endangering paramount interests, give occasion for permissible limitation.

60. Palko v. Connecticut, 302 U.S. 319, 327, 58 S. Ct. 149, 82 L. Ed. 288 (1937).
61. United States v. Carolene Products Co., 304 U.S. 144, 152 n. 4, 58 S. Ct. 778, 82 L. Ed. 1234 (1938).
62. *Id.*
63. 323 U.S. 516, 529–30, 65 S. Ct. 315, 89 L. Ed. 430 (1945).

This was 1945. Four years later a majority of the Court, in sustaining a local ordinance, endorsed a considerably less latitudinarian appraisal of freedom of speech and press.[64] Thus while alluding to "the preferred position of freedom of speech in a society that cherishes liberty for all," Justice Reed went on to say that this "does not require legislators to be insensible to claims by citizens to comfort and convenience. To enforce freedom of speech in disregard of the rights of others would be harsh and arbitrary in itself."[65] And Justice Frankfurter flatly denied the propriety of the phrase "preferred position," saying:[66]

> This is a phrase that has uncritically crept into some recent opinions of this Court. I deem it a mischievous phrase, if it carries the thought, which it may subtly imply, that any law touching communication is infected with presumptive invalidity. It is not the first time in the history of constitutional adjudication that such a doctrinaire attitude has disregarded the admonition most to be observed in exercising the Court's reviewing power over legislation, "that it is *a constitution* we are expounding," M'Culloch v. Maryland, 4 Wheat. 316, 407. I say the phrase is mischievous because it radiates a constitutional doctrine without avowing it. Clarity and candor in these matters, so as to avoid gliding unwittingly into error, make it appropriate to trace the history of the phrase "preferred position."

—which Justice Frankfurter then proceeded to do.

The third question concerns the quality and purpose of the speech which the Constitution aims to protect. In 1949 Justice Douglas, speaking for a sharply divided Court, returned the following robustious answer to this question:[67]

> . . . a function of free speech under our system of government is to invite dispute. It may indeed best serve its high purpose when it induces a condition of unrest, creates dissatisfaction with conditions as they are, or even stirs people to anger. Speech is often provocative and challenging. It may strike at prejudices and preconceptions and have profound unsettling effects as it presses for acceptance of an idea. That is why freedom of speech though not absolute . . . is nevertheless protected against censorship or punishment, unless shown likely to produce a clear and present danger of a serious substantive evil that arises far above public inconvenience, annoyance, or unrest.

But early in 1951 Justice Jackson, in a dissenting opinion, urged the Court to review its entire position in the light of the proposition that "the purpose of constitutional protection of freedom of speech is to foster peaceful interchange of all manner of thoughts, information and ideas," and that "its policy is rooted in faith in the force of reason."[68] He considered that the Court had been striking blindly at permit systems which indirectly may affect First Amendment freedoms. He said:[69]

64. Kovacs v. Cooper, 336 U.S. 77, 69 S. Ct. 448, 93 L. Ed. 513 (1949).
65. *Id.*, 336 U.S. at 88.
66. *Id.*, 336 U.S. at 90.
67. Terminiello v. Chicago, 337 U.S. 1, 4, 69 S. Ct. 894, 93 L. Ed. 1131 (1949).
68. Kunz v. New York, 340 U.S. 290, 295, 302, 71 S. Ct. 312, 95 L. Ed. 280 (1951).
69. *Id.*, 340 U.S. at 305–6.

Cities throughout the country have adopted permit requirements to control private activities on public streets and for other purposes. The universality of this type of regulation demonstrates a need and indicates widespread opinion in the profession that it is not necessarily incompatible with our constitutional freedoms. Is everybody out of step but this Court?

He was of the opinion that the Court was assuming a hypercritical position in invalidating local laws for want of standards when the Court itself had set down no particular standard. He would leave a large measure of discretion to the local community or state in dealing with speech which is outside the immunity of the Constitution. He also "venture[d] to predict" that the Court "will not apply, to federal statutes the standard that they are unconstitutional if it is possible that they may be unconstitutionally applied,"[70]—a prophecy soon verified by event.

IV

The immediate precursors of the Dennis case are two cases decided under the Taft-Hartley Act[71] a year earlier. That law requires, as a condition of a union's utilizing the opportunities afforded by the act, each of its officers to file an affidavit with the National Labor Relations Board (1) that he is not a member of the Communist party or affiliated with such party, and (2) that he does not believe in, and is not a member of any organization that believes in or teaches the overthrow of the United States government by force or by any illegal or unconstitutional methods. In American Communications Association v. Douds,[72] five of the six justices participating sustained the first requirement and an evenly divided Court sustained the second against the objection that the act exceeded the power of Congress over interstate commerce and infringed freedom of speech and the rights of petition and assembly. And in Osman v. Douds[73] the same result was reached by a Court in which only Justice Clark did not participate. In the end only Justice Black condemned the first requirement while the Court was evenly divided as to the second. In the course of his opinion for the controlling wing of the Court in the American Communications case, Chief Justice Vinson said:[74]

. . . the attempt to apply the term, "clear and present danger," as a mechanical test in every case touching First Amendment freedoms, without regard to the context of its application, mistakes the form in which an idea was cast for the substance of the idea.

The question with which the Court was dealing, he asserted, was not the same one that Justices Holmes and Brandeis had considered in terms of "clear and

70. *Id.*, 340 U.S. at 304.
71. 61 Stat. 146 (1947), 29 U.S.C. section 159(h) (Supp. 1951).
72. 339 U.S. 382, 70 S. Ct. 674, 94 L. Ed. 925 (1950).
73. 339 U.S. 846, 70 S. Ct. 901, 94 L. Ed. 1328 (1950).
74. American Communications Assn. v. Douds, 339 U.S. 382, 394, 70 S. Ct. 674, 94 L. Ed. 925 (1950).

present danger,'' since the government's interest in American Communications was in protecting the free flow of commerce from what Congress considered to be substantial evils of conduct rather than in preventing dissemination of Communist doctrine or the holding of particular beliefs because of a fear that unlawful conduct might result therefrom.[75] Applying that distinction, the chief justice recited:[76]

> The contention of petitioner . . . that this Court must find that political strikes create a clear and present danger to the security of the Nation or of widespread industrial strife in order to sustain § 9(h) similarly misconceives the purpose that phrase was intended to serve. In that view, not the relative certainty that evil conduct will result from speech in the immediate future, but the extent and gravity of the substantive evil must be measured by the ''test'' laid down in the Schenck case.

In thus balancing the gravity of the interest protected by legislation from harmful speech against the demands of the ''clear and present danger'' rule, the Court paved a feasible way for its decision a year later in Dennis v. United States.[77]

And undoubtedly it was Chief Justice Vinson's initial inclination, in his opinion for himself and Justices Reed, Burton, and Minton, to rest decision in Dennis on a like calculation. Thus emphasizing the substantial character of the government's interest in preventing its own overthrow by force, he said this was the ultimate value of any society, for if a society cannot protect itself from internal attack, ''it must follow that no subordinate value can be protected.''[78] The opinion continues:[79]

> If, then, this interest may be protected, the literal problem which is presented is what has been meant by the use of the phrase ''clear and present danger'' of the utterances bringing about the evil within the power of Congress to punish.
>
> Obviously, the words cannot mean that before the Government may act, it must wait until the *putsch* is about to be executed, the plans have been laid and the signal is awaited. If Government is aware that a group aiming at its overthrow is attempting to indoctrinate its members and to commit them to a course whereby they will strike when the leaders feel the circumstances permit, action by the Government is required. The argument that there is no need for Government to concern itself, for Government is strong, it possesses ample powers to put down a rebellion, it may defeat the revolution with ease needs no answer. For that is not the question. Certainly an attempt to overthrow the Government by force, even though doomed from the outset because of inadequate numbers or power of the revolutionists, is a sufficient evil for Congress to prevent. The damage which such attempts create both physically and politically to a nation makes it impossible to measure the validity in terms of the probability of success, or the immediacy of a successful attempt.

The chief justice concluded this part of his opinion by quoting from Chief Judge Learned Hand's opinion for the circuit court of appeals in the same case,

75. *Id.*, 339 U.S. at 396.
76. *Id.*, 339 U.S. at 397.
77. 341 U.S. 494, 71 S. Ct. 857, 95 L. Ed. 1137 (1951).
78. *Id.*, 341 U.S. at 509.
79. *Id.*

as follows:[80] "'In each case [courts] must ask whether the gravity of the 'evil,' discounted by its improbability, justifies such invasion of free speech as is necessary to avoid the danger.'" On this he commented:[81]

> We adopt this statement of the rule. As articulated by Chief Justice Hand, it is as succinct and inclusive as any other we might devise at this time. It takes into consideration those factors which we deem relevant, and relates their significance. More we cannot expect from words.

That is to say, if the evil legislated against is serious enough, advocacy of it does not, in order to be punishable, have to be attended by a "clear and present danger" of success.

But at this point the chief justice, as if recoiling from this abrupt dismissal of the "clear and present danger" formula, makes a last-moment effort to rescue the babe that he has so incontinently tossed out with the bath, stating that the Court was in accord with the circuit court, which affirmed a finding by the trial court that the requisite danger actually existed, and noting particularly that the "highly organized conspiracy . . . coupled with the inflammable nature of world conditions . . . convince us that their convictions were justified on this score."[82]

His final position seems to be that the question is one for judicial discretion, unbound by formulas, for he recites:[83]

> When facts are found that establish the violation of a statute, the protection against conviction afforded by the First Amendment is a matter of law. The doctrine that there must be a clear and present danger of a substantive evil that Congress has a right to prevent is a judicial rule to be applied as a matter of law by the courts.

In short, "clear and present danger" is informed that *the Court, not it, is on top.*

Justice Frankfurter's lengthy concurring opinion premises the "right of a government to maintain its existence—self-preservation . . . [as] the most pervasive aspect of sovereignty."[84] At the same time he admitted that there are competing interests to be assessed, but asked which agency of government is to do the job:[85]

> Full responsibility for the choice cannot be given to the courts. Courts are not representative bodies. They are not designed to be a good reflex of a democratic society. Their judgment is best informed, and therefore most dependable, within narrow limits. Their essential quality is detachment, founded on independence. History teaches that the independence of the judiciary is jeopardized when courts become embroiled in the passions of the day and assume primary responsibility in choosing between competing political, economic and social pressures.
>
> Primary responsibility for adjusting the interests which compete in the situation

80. *Id.*, 341 U.S. at 510.
81. *Id.*
82. *Id.*, 341 U.S. at 511.
83. *Id.*, 341 U.S. at 513.
84. *Id.*, 341 U.S. at 519.
85. *Id.*, 341 U.S. at 525.

before us of necessity belongs to the Congress. The nature of the power to be exercised by this Court has been delineated in decisions not charged with the emotional appeal of situations such as that now before us. We are to set aside the judgment of those whose duty it is to legislate only if there is no reasonable basis for it.

But a difficulty seems to exist in the "clear and present danger" doctrine, for Justice Frankfurter admitted that defendants' argument could not be met by reinterpreting the phrase. He also was of the opinion that defendants' argument could not be met by citing isolated cases, but that their convictions should "be tested against the entire body of our relevant decisions."[86]

Turning then to an examination of the cases he exclaims at last: "I must leave to others the ungrateful task of trying to reconcile all these decisions."[87] The nearest precedent was the Gitlow case. Here "we put our respect for the legislative judgment in terms which, if they were accepted here, would make decision easy. . . . But it would be disingenuous to deny that the dissent in Gitlow has been treated with the respect usually accorded to a decision."[88] He concludes with a homily on the limitations which the nature of judicial power imposes on the power of judicial review:[89]

> To make validity of legislation depend on judicial reading of events still in the womb of time—a forecast, that is, of the outcome of forces at best appreciated only with knowledge of the topmost secrets of nations—is to charge the judiciary with duties beyond its equipment. We do not expect courts to pronounce historic verdicts on bygone events. Even historians have conflicting views to this day on the origins and conduct of the French Revolution. . . . It is as absurd to be confident that we can measure the present clash of forces and their outcome as to ask us to read history still enveloped in clouds of controversy.

Not without some justification has Justice Frankfurter's opinion been called "an interesting study in ambivalence."[90]

Justice Jackson's opinion underscores the conspiratorial element of the case, and is flat-footed in rejecting the "clear and present danger" formula for this type of case. He writes:[91]

> The test applies and has meaning where a conviction is sought to be based on a speech or writing which does not directly or explicitly advocate a crime but to which such tendency is sought to be attributed by construction or by implication from external circumstances. The formula in such cases favors freedoms that are vital to our society, and, even if sometimes applied too generously, the consequences cannot be grave. But its recent expansion has extended, in particular to Communists, unprecedented immunities. Unless we are to hold our Government captive in a judge-made verbal trap, we must approach the problem of a well-organized, nationwide conspiracy, such as I have described, as realistically as our predecessors faced the trivialities that were being prosecuted until they were checked with a rule of reason.

86. *Id.*, 341 U.S. at 528.
87. *Id.*, 341 U.S. at 539.
88. *Id.*, 341 U.S. at 541.
89. *Id.*, 341 U.S. at 551–52.
90. Woolsey, "The Supreme Court: 1951–52," *Fortune*, October, 1951, pp. 119, 162.
91. Dennis v. United States, 341 U.S. 494, 568, 71 S. Ct. 857, 95 L. Ed. 1137 (1951).

He emphasizes that the Constitution does not make conspiracy a civil right and that the Court has consistently refused to do so on previous occasions and should so continue, whether the conspiracy be one to disturb interstate commerce or to undermine the government. He disposes of the dissenters' contention that some overt act was necessary to support the convictions in the following words:[92]

> . . . no overt act is or need be required. The Court, in anti-trust cases, early upheld the power of Congress to adopt the ancient common law that makes conspiracy itself a crime. Through Mr. Justice Holmes, it said: "Coming next to the objection that no overt act is laid, the answer is that the Sherman Act punishes the conspiracies at which it is aimed on the common law footing—that is to say, it does not make the doing of any act other than the act of conspiring a condition of liability." . . . It is not to be supposed that the power of Congress to protect the Nation's existence is more limited than its power to protect interstate commerce.
>
> I do not suggest that Congress could punish conspiracy to advocate something, the doing of which it may not punish. Advocacy or exposition of the doctrine of communal property ownership, or any political philosophy unassociated with advocacy of its imposition by force or seizure of government by unlawful means could not be reached through conspiracy prosecution. But it is not forbidden to put down force or violence, it is not forbidden to punish its teaching or advocacy, and the end being punishable, there is no doubt of the power to punish conspiracy for the purpose.

It would be "weird legal reasoning," he opined, for the Court to hold that conspiracy is one crime and its consummation another and then further hold that "Congress could punish the one only if there was 'clear and present danger' of the second."[93]

The dissenting opinions of Justices Black and Douglas indicate that they would not only apply the "clear and present danger" test to this type of case, but that they would give it the same broad reach which they had claimed for it in cases where the speech involved was not intended to induce violation of law. Justice Black reiterates his previously expressed opinion that:[94]

> At least as to speech in the realm of public matters, I believe that the "clear and present danger" test does not "mark the furthermost constitutional boundaries of protected expression" but does "no more than recognize a minimum compulsion of the Bill of Rights." *Bridges v. California*, 314 U.S. 252, 263. [Justice Black is here quoting Justice Black.]

And Justice Douglas italicized Justice Brandeis's dictum in the Whitney case: "'*If there be time to expose through discussion the falsehood and fallacies, to avert the evil by the processes of education, the remedy to be applied is more speech, not enforced silence.*' "[95] The answer is that education had not in fact prevented the formation of the conspiracy for which the eleven defendants were convicted. If that be deemed a danger at all, it was certainly a "clear and

92. *Id.*, 341 U.S. at 574–75.
93. *Id.*, 341 U.S. at 576.
94. *Id.*, 341 U.S. at 580.
95. *Id.*, 341 U.S. at 586.

present'' one. Both dissenters, in fact, ignore the conspiracy element, although Justice Holmes had not done so in Frohwerk, nor had Justice Brandeis in Whitney.

Conclusion

"It is one of the misfortunes of the law," wrote Justice Holmes in 1912, "that ideas become encysted in phrases and thereafter for a long time cease to provoke further analysis."[96] No better confirmation of this observation could be asked than that which is afforded by the remarkable extension of the influence of the "clear and present danger" formula both with courts and commentators in the decade just ended. To sum up the history reviewed above: The phrase had its origin in 1919 in a dictum tossed off by Holmes himself in an opinion sustaining a conviction under the Espionage Act of 1917,[97] but was soon thereafter invoked by its author and by Justice Brandeis in opinions dissenting from similar judgments. Not till nearly twenty years later, and after Holmes's death, did the formula find its way into a majority opinion of the Court[98] which reversed a judgment of conviction, and here it was invoked against the application of the statute to the facts of the case, not directly against the statute itself. Frequent repetition since 1940 in cases presenting problems entirely different from those raised by espionage and criminal anarchy statutes, or by incitements to breach of the law, had, however, by 1951, established the authority of this cliché so firmly that in Dennis v. United States five justices of the Court wrote separate opinions variously construing it, three conceding its application in some sense or other. What effect does the judgment in Dennis, considered in the light shed by these opinions, have on the formula? How far does Dennis go in supplying the analysis that Justice Holmes would presumably have welcomed, or otherwise?

The writer of this article is inclined to the opinion that the Court would have done quite as well to have based its holding in Dennis on the Gitlow case, as the solicitor general invited it to do. As the preceding pages amply demonstrate, not a single precedent would have had to be overturned to reach such a result. Furthermore, the chief justice's acceptance[99] of the explanation given by the Court in Gitlow of the reason why the "clear and present danger" formula had appeared in the Schenck case, smoothed the way to an unqualified reiteration of the Gitlow decision, which had had the support of seven of the nine justices. That this course was not adopted was due in part, no doubt, to the fact that "the Case of the Eleven Communists" had been inflated by propaganda far beyond its strictly legal significance, and to the feeling of the Court, in consequence, that it must deal with the case at respectful length, and of course "significantly." But

96. Hyde v. United States, 225 U.S. 347, 390, 32 S. Ct. 793, 56 L. Ed. 1114 (1912).
97. 40 Stat. 217 (1917).
98. Herndon v. Lowry, 301 U.S. 242, 57 S. Ct. 732, 81 L. Ed. 1066 (1937).
99. Dennis v. United States, 341 U.S. 494, 505–6, 71 S. Ct. 857, 95 L. Ed. 1137 (1951).

an even more important factor may have been the Court's habitual reluctance to cast aside at one fell swoop any formula or doctrine which lends its umpirage support and promises it an available "out" against undesired legislation—i.e., undesired by the Court. It prefers the tactics of the rear-guard action to those of outright retreat.

Taken, then, in the context of the opinions which support it, what conclusions does the decision suggest as to the future of "clear and present danger"? The outstanding result of the holding, undoubtedly, is that of *a declaration of independence by the Court from the tyranny of a phrase.* As expounded in the dissenting opinions of Justices Black and Douglas, the "clear and present danger" formula is a kind of slide rule whereby all cases involving the issue of free speech simply decide themselves automatically. By treating the formula as authorizing it to weigh the substantive good protected by a statute against the "clear and present danger" requirement, the Court rids itself of this absurd "heads-off" automatism and converts the rule, for the first time, into a real "rule of reason."

At the same time, the range of the rule's applicability has undoubtedly been curtailed, though just how greatly is not at present altogether apparent. It can be safely said that never again will the rule be successfully invoked in behalf of persons shown to have conspired to incite to a breach of federal law. On the other hand, as Justice Jackson suggests in effect, the "clear and present danger" test may still be applicable: (1) in cases essentially trivial; (2) in cases where the intent of the speaker is lawful, but circumstances create a danger of violence or other substantive evils which government has a right to prevent; (3) in cases where the speech is ambiguous and the evil purpose of the speaker can be reasonably inferred only from the "clear and present danger" of evil which the utterance engenders. But the common law, properly charged, would probably do just as well in such cases without any assistance from the formula.

Moreover, the vast majority of such cases arise under state and municipal legislation. Indeed, since the Court is apt to favor easily discernible boundaries, "clear and present danger" may "just fade away" in the field of congressional power. Such a result could be justified both on logical and on practical grounds. Thus it would take account of the well-recognized rule of legal interpretation that the general yields to the specific. From this point of view it may well be held that freedom of speech and press stand in a different relation to enumerated powers of Congress than they do to the vague, undefined residual powers of the states. And that the protection of the larger interests of our ever more closely integrated society gravitates more and more to the national government is a proposition that nobody is apt to contest.

7. The Supreme Court as National School Board

As a student at the University of Michigan a half century ago I had frequent occasion to attend convocations, lectures, and concerts in University Hall. Each time my eyes were confronted with the words, emblazoned on the wall over the great organ, "Religion, morality, and knowledge, being necessary to good government and the happiness of mankind, schools and the means of education shall forever be encouraged." These words are from the famous Northwest Ordinance which was enacted in 1787 by the last Congress of the Confederation,[1] and which from the provision it makes for the establishment of public schools is the matrix of the public school system of a great part of the United States. Two years later many of the same men, representatives of the same people, sitting as the first Congress under the Constitution, proposed the following amendment to the Constitution: "Congress shall make no law respecting an establishment of religion, or prohibiting the free exercise thereof. . . ." Do these words represent a fundamental change in attitude on the part of the American people on the question of what relation should subsist between public education and the teaching of religion? Prima facie it seems doubtful,[2] but that it is so, nevertheless, is the implication of the decision on March 8, 1948, of the United States Supreme Court in Illinois ex rel. Vashti McCollum v. Board of Education of Champaign County.[3]

The facts and holding in the case may be set forth as follows:

A local board of education in Illinois agreed to the giving of religious instruction in the schools under a "released time" arrangement whereby pupils, whose parents

From 14 *Law and Contemporary Problems* 3–22 (1949). Reprinted by permission. This is a revision of an article published in 43 *Thought* 665 (1948).

1. July 13, 1787, 1 Stat. 51, n., Art. III.
2. This doubt becomes doubly doubtful when we recall that Congress reenacted the Northwest Ordinance in 1791!
3. 333 U.S. 203 (1948).

signed "request cards," were permitted to attend religious-instruction classes conducted during regular school hours in the school building by outside teachers furnished by a religious council representing the various faiths, subject to the approval and supervision of the superintendent of schools. Attendance records were kept and reported to the school authorities in the same way as for other classes; and pupils not attending the religious instruction classes were required to continue their regular secular studies.

The Court held, in an opinion by Black, J., that this arrangement was in violation of the constitutional principle of separation of Church and State, as expressed in the First Amendment and made applicable to the states by the Fourteenth Amendment, and accordingly that the state courts below had acted erroneously in refusing relief to the complainant, parent and taxpayer, against the continued use of school buildings for such religious instruction.

This conclusion was supported further in a separate concurring opinion by Frankfurter, J., in which the historical backgrounds of the principle of separation of church and state, and of "released time" arrangements, are considered at length. Justices Jackson, Rutledge, and Burton joined in this opinion; and Justices Rutledge and Burton also concurred in the opinion written by Justice Black.

Jackson, J., in an additional opinion, although concurring in the result, expressed doubt as to the standing of the complainant to raise the question at issue, and also felt that the relief granted, prohibiting all religious instruction in the schools, was too broad and indefinite.

Reed, J., dissented on the ground that the co-operative "released time" arrangement did not involve either an "establishment of religion" or "aid" to religion by the state, sufficient to justify the Supreme Court in interfering with local legislation and customs.[4]

The holding and the opinions accompanying it raise all sorts of questions. "Released-time" programs prior to the decision operated in some 2,200 communities spread over forty-six states.[5] Are all of these programs rendered unconstitutional by the ruling in the McCollum case, or only those which are conducted in public school buildings? Justice Frankfurter, after characterizing the Champaign plan as "a conscientious attempt to accommodate the allowable functions of Government and the special concerns of the Church within the framework of our Constitution,"[6] says that some released-time programs may be constitutional, others unconstitutional, and which are the one or the other must await "close judicial scrutiny"[7] as cases arise. From the point of view of persons vested with the responsibility of administering the public school system of the country, this is not exactly a consoling utterance. And positively disturbing to all public educational authorities, both those at the school level and those at the college and university level, is Justice Jackson's[8] suggestion that the holding may contain a threat to courses on religion and religious history, or even to

4. 92 L. Ed. 451 (1948).
5. McCollum v. Board of Education, 333 U.S. 203, 224–25 n. 16 (1948).
6. *Id.* at 213.
7. *Id.* at 225.
8. *Id.* at 236.

courses in art, philosophy, and literature, which can hardly be taught without reference to religion, the seed-bed of them all.[9]

In fact, the decision seems to have fully satisfied very few people. Even Mrs. McCollum is disappointed in the final outcome, to date, of her efforts. What she asked for was a judicial mandate that

> would ban all teaching of the Scriptures. She especially mentions as an example of invasion of her rights "having pupils learn and recite such statements, "The Lord is my Shepherd, I shall not want.'" And she objects to teaching that the King James version of the Bible "is called the Christian's Guide Book, the Holy Writ and the Word of God," and many other similar matters.[10]

She also avows a distaste for the word "sin." Yet all that the Court did was to remand the cause {case?} to the state supreme court "for proceedings not inconsistent with this opinion,"[11] a directive with which the latter court complied by banning the Champaign system. Comments the lady, according to the Champaign *News-Gazette:*

> I am right back where I started from three years ago. I have wasted all this time and money without an order prohibiting the schools from aiding and abetting in carrying on these classes. The schools should be definitely ordered against corralling students for religious classes. I told Mr. Dodd [her attorney] that I was dissatisfied and wanted to appeal. I believe we will take any further action that is open to us.[12]

My interest in this case is, however, not in the question of its practical soundness, but in that of its constitutional soundness; in the question, in brief, whether the Constitution *does* require that all public-supported education be kept strictly secular. Some comparatively recent decisions suggest the contrary. In the New Jersey Bus case,[13] which was decided thirteen months prior to the Champaign case, it was held that the state is not inhibited from aiding religious instruction incidentally to the exercise by it of the police power for the protection of the health and safety of school children on the way to school; while in 1930, in Cochran v. Louisiana,[14] it was held that children attending parochial schools could be made beneficiaries of that state's free textbook law without offense to the Constitution. The interest of the statute, said the Court, "is education, broadly; its method comprehensive. Individual interests are aided only as the common interest is safeguarded."[15] Federal appropriations in support of free lunches for school children embrace parochial schools, presumably on the same

---

9. A great many state constitutional provisions seem likely to undergo Supreme Court scrutiny under the McCollum decision. See 3 Frederic J. Stimson, *The Law of the Federal and State Constitutions of the United States,* sections 2–48 (1908).

10. McCollum v. Board of Education, above note 5, at 234–35.

11. *Id.* at 212.

12. Speech delivered before National Council of Catholic Women, Convention in New Orleans, September 11, 1948, by George E. Reed of Washington, member of the Council's legal department.

13. Everson v. Board of Education, 330 U.S. 1 (1947).

14. 281 U.S. 370 (1930).

15. *Id.* at 375.

justification. The parochial school is regarded as a distributing agency of social benefit, including education. Are these holdings invalidated by the McCollum decision?

I

We encounter the characteristic almost at the outset of Justice Black's "Opinion of the Court" in his brusque dismissal of the question whether Mrs. McCollum's own interest in the constitutional issue raised by her was sufficient to entitle the Supreme Court, under the rules governing judicial review, to decide it.[16] The basic principle involved was stated by Justice Sutherland for the Court a quarter of a century ago, in these words:

> We have no power *per se* to review and annul acts of Congress on the ground that they are unconstitutional. That question may be considered only when the justification for some direct injury suffered or threatened, presenting a justiciable issue, is made to rest upon such an act. Then the power exercised is that of ascertaining and declaring the law applicable to the controversy. It amounts to little more than the negative power to disregard an unconstitutional enactment, which otherwise would stand in the way of the enforcement of a legal right. *The party who invokes the power must be able to show not only that the statute is invalid but that he has sustained or is immediately in danger of sustaining some direct injury as the result of its enforcement, and not merely that he suffers in some indefinite way in common with people generally.*[17]

The McCollum case originated, to be sure, in the courts of Illinois and was decided by them prior to its appeal to the Supreme Court, on writ of certiorari; but that fact does not alter the situation so far as the question above posed is concerned. In the words of Justice Frankfurter, dealing in 1939 in the case of Coleman v. Miller[18] with a situation which was on all fours with the one before us:

> To whom and for what causes the courts of Kansas [*sc.* Illinois] are open are matters for Kansas to determine. But Kansas can not define the contours of the authority of the federal courts, and more particularly of this Court. It is our ultimate responsibility to determine who may invoke our judgment and under what circumstances. . . .
>
> It is not our function, and it is beyond our power, to write legal essays or to give legal opinions, however solemnly requested and however great the national emergency . . . our exclusive business is litigation. The requisites of litigation are not satisfied when questions of constitutionality though conveyed through the outward forms of a

---

16. McCollum v. Board of Education, above note 5, at 206–7.

17. Frothingham v. Mellon, 262 U.S. 447, 488 (1923). (Italics supplied.) It should be noted that formerly the vast majority of constitutional cases arose out of the effort of some official agency or of some private individual to enforce legislation which the defendant in the case attacked as unconstitutional. There can be no doubt as to the *special* interest of such a defendant in having the constitutional question passed upon. The practice which has developed within the last half century of raising the question of constitutionality in suits for injunctions alters the picture somewhat. But it is as to taxpayers' suits that the doctrine of direct or special injury is most evidently relevant. See 16 C. J. S. *Constitutional Law*, sections 76, 80–82 (1939).

18. 307 U.S. 433 (1939).

conventional court proceeding do not bear special relation to a particular litigant. The scope and consequences of our doctrine of judicial review over executive and legislative action should make us observe fastidiously the bounds of the litigious process within which we are confined. *No matter how seriously infringement of the Constitution may be called into question, this is not the tribunal for its challenge except by those who have some specialized interest of their own to vindicate, apart from a political concern which belongs to all.*[19]

While these words are from a dissenting opinion, they voice on this particular issue the views of the Court as a whole, as is shown by its explicit ruling that Coleman had a sufficient interest to entitle him to prosecute the case before it. In the McCollum case, nevertheless, Justice Black brushes aside the question of the materiality of Mrs. McCollum's interest in these curt words: ''A second ground for the motion to dismiss is that the appellant lacks standing to maintain the action, a ground which is also without merit. Coleman v. Miller, 307 U.S. 433, 443, 445, 464.''[20] The passages thus cited in no wise challenge Justice Sutherland's position; to the contrary, they assume its correctness. It is clear that the learned justice had as much, and as little, right to cite Coleman v. Miller in support of his ruling as he would have had to invoke the Book of Revelations.

Of the remaining members of the Court sitting in the McCollum case, Justice Jackson alone expresses any qualms as to the right of the Court to exercise its jurisdiction. Comparing the case with the New Jersey School Bus case mentioned earlier, he says:

. . . in the Everson Case there was a direct, substantial and measurable burden on the complainant as a taxpayer to raise funds that were used to subsidize transportation to parochial schools. Hence, we had jurisdiction to examine the constitutionality of the levy and to protect against it if a majority had agreed that the subsidy for transportation was unconstitutional.

In this case, however, any cost of this plan to the taxpayers is incalculable and negligible. It can be argued, perhaps, that religious classes add some wear and tear on public buildings and that they should be charged with some expense for heat and light, even though the sessions devoted to religious instruction do not add to the length of the school day. But the cost is neither substantial nor measurable, and no one seriously can say that the complainant's tax bill has been proved to be increased because of this plan. I think it is doubtful whether the taxpayer in this case has shown any substantial property injury.[21]

''Incalculable and negligible'' sums up with substantial accuracy the purport of the extensive finding of facts by the Circuit Court of Champaign County, in which Mrs. McCollum instituted her action. Besides, what of the opposed public interest—why should not that have been considered by the Court? In fact, it always has been considered in cases in which taxpayers have sought to challenge

19. *Id.* at 462–64. (Italics supplied.)
20. McCollum v. Board of Education, above note 5, at 206.
21. *Id.* at 233–34. See also Transcript of Record, p. 69. The state Supreme Court agreed. *Id.* at 274–75.

the constitutional validity of expenditures from the national fisc, with the result that no such challenge has succeeded thus far.[22] Why the same rule should not be observed in the case of local expenditures is hard to see; and especially disappointing is the indifference shown on this occasion by those two or three members of the Court who have so frequently in recent years protested their love for the federal system and deplored its impairment.

I should like to point out, moreover, that a strange difference appears to exist today between public school buildings and public parks in respect to their availability for religious uses. In the Lockport case,[23] which was decided three months after the McCollum case, it was held by a vote of five justices to four that an ordinance of the city of Lockport, New York, which forbids the use of sound amplification devices except with the permission of the chief of police was unconstitutional as applied in the case of a Jehovah's Witness who used sound equipment to amplify lectures in a public park on Sunday, on religious subjects. The proposition for which the case seems to stand is that when a municipality establishes a public park it thereby renders the park a potential forum for any blatherskite politician or whirling deverish who wishes to peddle his doctrinal wares over a public address system, and that a park for quiet uses, to serve the amenities of civilized living, is unconstitutional.[24]

At any rate, the discrepancy between the two holdings is apparent. In one it is held that a school board may not constitutionally permit religious groups to use on an equal footing any part of a school building for the purpose of religious instruction to *those who wish to receive it*. By the other the public authorities are under a *constitutional obligation* to turn over public parks for religious propaganda to be hurled at all and sundry whether they wish to receive it or not. The Court seems to cherish a strange tenderness for *outré* religious manifestations which contrasts sharply with its attitude toward organized religion.

But it appears that Mrs. McCollum had a second string to her bow, and that her appeal for the Court's protection was based also on her right and duty as *parent*. This ground for the Court's intervention is, if possible, even flimsier than

22. See note 17 above.
23. Saia v. New York, 334 U.S. 558 (1948).
24. In Kovacs v. Cooper, 336 U.S. 77, decided January 31, 1949, the Court sustained a Trenton ordinance which banned from that city's streets all loudspeakers and other devices which emit "loud and raucous noises." The decision is asserted by three of the four dissenters to it to amount to a flat overruling of the decision in the Saia case, and I am inclined to agree with them. So much the better, say I. Justice Frankfurter's concurring opinion in the Kovacs case deserves special attention for its criticism of Justice Reed's reference, in his opinion for the Court, to "the preferred position of freedom of speech." *Id*. at 88. Justice Frankfurter follows a review of other similar dicta in recent opinions with the observation that the claim that any legislation which restrains "liberty" in the sense of the First and Fourteenth Amendments considered together, is "presumptively unconstitutional," "has never commended itself to a majority of this Court." *Id*. at 94–95. I wish to add that, even were it otherwise, still the Court would not be warranted in taking jurisdiction of a case which involved such a restraint, on the mere application of a person who had not shown sufficient direct injury because of the restraint in question.

the one just considered. What it simmers down to is the contention that plaintiff's son James Terry was subjected, in consequence of his nonparticipation in the program, to "embarrassment" and "humiliation." These allegations too, like those regarding the expense of the program, the court of first instance found to be unsubstantiated by "the great preponderance of evidence," a circumstance to which Justice Black makes no allusion.[25] But even had the weight of testimony been otherwise, still the problem raised would seem to have been one of school discipline, to be settled in the principal's office, rather than one of constitutional interpretation for the Supreme Court at Washington. Besides, so far as anything to the contrary appears, had James Terry and his parent made proper application, the school authorities would have willingly assigned accommodations where the two of them might have foregathered during the released-time period to confer with regard to their common faith—or lack of it.[26]

To conclude this phase of the McCollum case—which may in the long run prove to be its most important phase—I wish to make two observations. The first is that Justice Black's brusque disposal of the question of Mrs. McCollum's *locus standi* in court to maintain her action reduces—or elevates—the doctrine of "special interest" to a jurisdictional fiction. All that anyone has to do to get the Court to pass on the constitutionality of a state statute or administrative order, under the First Amendment at any rate, is to allege that its enforcement will involve expense and that he is a taxpayer; neither of which allegations appears to be traversable, otherwise the Court must have paid some heed to the Illinois court's findings of fact. Whether the Court is wise in thus enlarging its jurisdiction in an area in which its performance has been in the past so obviously at the mercy of the individual prepossessions of its members, and is consequently so spotted with self-contradictions and inconsistencies, prompts a doubt—one which its holding in the case at bar is not calculated to dispel.

My second observation is advanced more diffidently. It is that under the principles governing award of mandamus, if the Champaign School Board had peremptorily refused the use of public school rooms for the released-time program, the backers of the plan would have had a far stronger case against the board than Mrs. McCollum had. Their combined interest in compelling a fuller use of public property to the creation and maintenance of which they contributed as taxpayers would have been impressive. Moreover, it would have been an *affirmative* interest. Mrs. McCollum, it seems to me, ought to have asked for an *injunction,* not *mandamus.*

---

25. McCollum v. Board of Education, above note 5, at 232. Transcript of Record, p. 68. It appears that Mrs. McCollum herself considers James Terry to be something of a "problem child," unable to get along with other children.

26. This question occurs to me: Suppose that Jehovah's Witnesses' children should complain that they were "embarrassed," etc., in consequence of their not participating along with other school children in saluting the flag, would that render the salute requirement invalid for all school children? At least, their grievance would seem to be fully as substantial as James Terry's.

II

People of the State of Illinois ex rel. Vashti McCollum, Appellant v. Board of Education of School District No. 71, Champaign County was welcomed by the Court with open arms, as affording it a grand opportunity to break a lance—or several of them—in behalf of the "constitutional principle"—as it is asserted to be—of separation of church and state. Actually, the Constitution does not mention this principle. In fact, it does not contain the word "church," nor yet the word "state" in the generic sense except in the Second Amendment, in which a "well regulated militia" is asserted to be "necessary to the security of a free state"; even the word "separation" fails to put in an appearance. These singular omissions—singular, if what the framers wanted was "separation of church and state" in the Court's understanding of it—are now supplied by the Court by the interpretation which it affixes to the "establishment of religion" clause of the First Amendment. The Court's theory, which was stated in the first instance by Justice Black in his opinion for the Court in the New Jersey Bus case, is that, under this clause, supplemented by the word "liberty" of the Fourteenth Amendment, "Neither a state nor the Federal Government can [1] set up a church"; [2] "pass laws which aid one religion, [3] aid all religions, or [4] prefer one religion over another."[27] For this reading of the clause the Court relies primarily on historical data. *Do historical data, on the whole, sustain it?* The answer is, not in such a way or such a sense as to vindicate the McCollum decision.

So far as the *national government* is concerned, the first of the above four propositions is true; originally, indeed, it came near being the whole truth; as to the *states* it is not, as we shall see, *necessarily* true even today. Of the remaining assertions, the second may be ignored as ambiguous; the third is untrue historically; the fourth is true. In a word, what the "establishment of religion" clause of the First Amendment does, and *all that it does, is to forbid Congress to give any religious faith, sect, or denomination a preferred status;* and the Fourteenth Amendment, in making the clause applicable to the states, does not add to it, but *logically* curtails it.

Where, then, did Justice Black get his confident reading of the "establishment of religion" clause? He got it from Justice Rutledge's dissenting opinion in the New Jersey Bus case, which in turn is based largely on James Madison's *Memorial and Remonstrance Against Religious Assessments* of 1785.[28] At that time—four years *before* the First Amendment was framed—a proposal was pending in the Virginia Assembly to levy a tax for the benefit of "teachers of the Christian religion." The father of the measure was Patrick Henry, but it was also supported outside the Assembly by Washington, Marshall, and other great names. Madison, on the other hand, with the recent successful fight for the disestablish-

27. Everson v. Board of Education, above note 13, at 15.
28. *Id.* at 63ff., quoting 2 *The Writings of James Madison* 183–91 (Hunt ed. 1901).

ment of the Episcopal church in mind, fought the measure tooth and nail, fearing that if it was enacted that body would have its foot in the stirrup for a fresh leap into the saddle. The keynote of the *Remonstrance,* which summed up his opposition, is sounded in the following passage:

> Who does not see that the same authority which can establish Christianity, in exclusion of all other Religions, may establish with the same ease any particular sect of Christians, in exclusion of all other Sects? That the same authority which can force a citizen to contribute three pence only of his property for the support of any one establishment, may force him to conform to any other establishment in all cases whatsover?[29]

As those very words show, however, Madison's conception of an "establishment of religion" in 1785 was precisely that which I have set forth above—*a religion enjoying a preferred status.* The same conception, moreover, underlies the state constitutions of the day, when they deal with the subject.[30] It also underlies all but one of the proposals from the states which led to the framing of the First Amendment in the first Congress. Thus Virginia proposed that "no particular religious sect or society ought to be favored or established, by law, in preference to others"—a formula which North Carolina reiterated word for word, and which New York reiterated save for the word "particular." Only New Hampshire, concerned for her own "establishment," wanted a broader prohibition, one that would keep Congress out of the field of religion entirely.[31]

But, it may well be asked, what bearing do the views which Madison advanced in 1785 in a local political fight regarding the subject of religious liberty in Virginia have on the question of the meaning of the First Amendment? Justice Rutledge's theory is (1) that Madison was the author of the First Amendment, and (2) that he must have intended by the ban which is there imposed on Congress's legislating "respecting an establishment of religion" to rule out the kind of legislation which he had opposed in Virginia four years earlier. Neither of these positions is correct.

As originally introduced into the House of Representatives by Madison, the proposal from which the religion clauses of the First Amendment finally issued read as follows:

> The civil rights of none shall be abridged on account of religious belief or worship, nor shall any national religion be established, nor shall the full and equal rights of conscience be in any manner, or on any pretext, infringed.[32]

These words Madison later elucidated thus:

29. Justice Rutledge's dissenting opinion in Everson v. Board of Education, above note 13, at 65–66, quoting 2 *The Writings of James Madison* 183, 186 (Hunt ed. 1901).

30. See 1 Francis Newton Thorpe, *The Federal and State Constitutions, Colonial Charters, and Other Organic Laws of the States, Territories, and Colonies Now or Hereafter Forming the United States of America* 567 (Dela.); 3 *id.* 1890 (Mass.); 4 *id.* 2454 (N.H.); 5 *id.* 2597 (N.J.), 2636 (N.Y.), 2793 (N.C.); 6 *id.* 3255 (S.C.).

31. 3 *The Debates in the Several State Conventions on the Adoption of the Federal Constitution* 659 (Elliott ed. 1836); 1 *id.* 326; 4 *id.* 244, 251. See also 2 *id.* 553.

32. 1 Annals of Congress 434 (1789–91).

. . . he apprehended the meaning of the words to be, that Congress should not establish a religion, and enforce the legal observation of it by law, nor compel men to worship God in any manner contrary to their conscience . . . if the word "national" was inserted before religion, it would satisfy the minds of honorable gentlemen. He believed that the people feared one sect might obtain a pre-eminence, or two combine together, and establish a religion to which they would compel others to conform. He thought if the word "national" was introduced, it would point the amendment directly to the object it was intended to prevent.[33]

In short, "to establish" a religion was to give it a preferred status, a preeminence, carrying with it even the right to compel others to conform. But in fact, before Madison's proposal was passed by the House and went to the Senate it had been changed to read: "Congress shall make no law establishing religion, or to prevent the free exercise thereof, or to infringe the rights of conscience"; and in the Senate this proposal was replaced by the following formula: "Congress shall make no law establishing articles of faith or a mode of worship or prohibiting the free exercise of religion."[34] That is, Congress should not prescribe a national faith, a possibility which those states with establishments of their own—Massachusetts, New Hampshire, Connecticut, Maryland, and South Carolina— probably regarded with fully as much concern as those which had gotten rid of their establishments. And the final form of the First Amendment, which came from a committee of conference between the two houses, appears to reflect this concern. The point turns on the significance to be attached to the word "respecting," a two-edged word, which bans any law *disfavoring* as well as any law *favoring* an establishment of religion. As will be seen in a moment, Story's reading of the First Amendment makes "respecting" the pivotal word of the "no establishment" clause.

To come back for a moment to Madison. Thanks to his exertions, Henry's bill was defeated, and unquestionably his *Remonstrance* should be given considerable credit for this result. But political management also played a role, and no unimportant one. The great problem was to overcome the tremendous influence which Henry's oratory exerted in the Virginia Assembly. Writing Madison at this

33. *Id.* at 730–31.
34. Records of the United States Senate, September 9, 1789, United States National Archives, cited in Appellees' Brief (Messrs. Franklin, Peterson, Rall, and Fisk) in the McCollum case, above note 5. Here attention is drawn to the fact that the Virginia legislature postponed ratification of the third proposed amendment (Amendment 1 of the first ten amendments) until December 15, 1791 (3 Annals of Congress 54), by which time they had already received the approval of the required three-fourths of the state legislatures. The leaders in opposition to the First Amendment voiced their objections in the following terms: ". . . although it goes to restrain Congress from passing laws establishing any national religion, they might, notwithstanding, levy taxes to any amount for the support of religion or its preachers; and any particular denomination of Christians might be so favored and supported by the general government, as to give it a decided advantage over the others, and in the process of time render it powerful and dangerous as if it was established as the national religion of the country." Evidently, as Appellees' Brief remarks, Virginians, who, after all, were the ones most familiar with the Virginia concept of religious freedom, did not interpret the First Amendment as living up to the spirit or the letter of the Virginia Bill for Establishing Religious Freedom. Brief, pp. 53–54.

time from Paris, Jefferson said: "What we have to do, I think, is devotedly to pray for his death." Madison, however, had a better scheme. Relying on Henry's vanity, he concocted a movement to make him governor, and Henry took the bait, hook, line, and sinker, thus automatically removing himself from the Assembly and destroying his brain-child.[35]

Yet it is probably due to his part in this fight that in his later years Madison carried the principle of separation of church and state to pedantic lengths, just as he did the principle of the separation of powers. In his essay on *Monopolies*, which was written after he left the presidency (probably long after), he put himself on record as opposed to the exemption of houses of worship from taxation, against the incorporation of ecclesiastical bodies with the faculty of acquiring property, against the houses of Congress having the right to choose chaplains to be paid out of national taxes, which, said he, "is a palpable violation of equal rights, as well as of Constitutional principles,"[36] and also against chaplains in the army and the navy. He states, indeed, that as president he was averse to issuing proclamations calling for days of thanksgiving or prayer, but was in some instances prevailed upon to affix his name to proclamations of this character at the request of the houses of Congress.[37] In all these respects, of course, Madison has been steadily overruled by the verdict of practice under the Constitution, as the data assembled by Justice Reed in his dissenting opinion show.[38]

To conclude this—the Madisonian—phase of our subject: the importance attached by Justice Rutledge in the School Bus case to Madison's *Memorial and Remonstrance* of 1785 as interpretive of the First Amendment is obviously excessive. First, the *Remonstrance* antedated the framing of the amendment by four years; second, Madison himself never offered it as an interpretation of the amendment; third, he was not the author of the amendment in the form in which it was proposed to the state legislatures for ratification; fourth, even had he been, the *Remonstrance* itself is excellent evidence that "an establishment of religion" meant in 1785 a religion, sect, or denomination enjoying a privileged legal position; finally, Madison himself asserted repeatedly as to the Constitution as a whole that "the legitimate meaning of the Instrument must be derived from the text itself."[39] Rejecting in a recent case the proposition that the Fourteenth Amendment, but more particularly the "due process" clause thereof, was intended to impose upon the states all of "the various explicit provisions of the first eight Amendments," Justice Frankfurter said: "Remarks of a particular proponent of the Amendment no matter how influential are not to be deemed part of the Amendment. What was submitted for ratification was his proposal, not his

35. Irving Brant, *James Madison, The Nationalist* 345–46 (1948).
36. Fleet, "Madison's 'Detached [*sic*] Memoranda,' " 3 *William and Mary Q.* 534, 558 (3d Ser.) (1946).
37. *Id.* at 551–62.
38. McCollum v. Board of Education, above note 5, at 253–55.
39. 3 *The Works of James Madison* 228, 552 (Phila. 1867).

speech.''[40] And Madison was not even the proponent of the First Amendment in its final form!

But Justice Rutledge, and the Court also, urge the authority of Jefferson as an interpreter of the First Amendment, although, being in Paris at the time, Jefferson had no hand in framing it. The reason for the Court's deference to the third president is that in 1802 he wrote a letter to a group of Baptists in Danbury, Connecticut, in which he declared that it was the purpose of the First Amendment to build ''a wall of separation between church and state.''[41] What, then, was Jefferson's idea of such a wall? So far as it bears on the question of religion in the schools, it certainly does not support the position of the Court in the McCollum case. Dealing with the subject with respect to his own recently established University of Virginia, Jefferson wrote in 1822:

> It was not, however, to be understood that instruction in religious opinion and duties was meant to be precluded by the public authorities, as indifferent to the interests of society. On the contrary, the relations which exist between man and his Maker, and the duties resulting from those relations, are the most interesting and important to every human being, and most incumbent on his study and investigation. The want of instruction in the various creeds of religious faith existing among our citizens presents, therefore, a chasm in a general institution of the useful sciences. . . . A remedy, however, has been suggested of promising aspect, which, while it excludes the public authorities from the domain of religious freedom, will give to the sectarian schools of divinity the full benefit the public provisions made for instruction in the other branches of science. . . . It has, therefore, been in contemplation, and suggested by some pious individuals, who perceive the advantages of associating other studies with those of religion, to establish their religious schools on the confines of the University, so as to give to their students ready and convenient access and attendance on the scientific lectures of the University; and to maintain, by that means, those destined for the religious professions on as high a standing of science, and of personal weight and respectability, as may be obtained by others from the benefits of the University. . . . Such an arrangement would complete the circle of the useful sciences embraced by this institution, and would fill the chasm now existing, on principles which would leave inviolate the constitutional freedom of religion, the most inalienable and sacred of all human rights, over which the people and authorities of this state, individually and publicly, have ever manifested the most watchful jealousy; and could this jealousy be now alarmed, in the opinion of the legislature, by what is here suggested, the idea will be relinquished on any surmise of disapprobation which they might think proper to express.[42]

And again:

> . . . by bringing the sects together, and mixing them with the mass of other students, we shall soften their asperities, liberalize and neutralize their prejudices, and make the general religion a religion of peace, reason, and morality.[43]

40. Adamson v. California, 332 U.S. 46, 64 (1947).
41. Saul K. Padover, *The Complete Jefferson* 518–19 (1943).
42. *Id.* at 957–58.
43. 12 *The Works of Thomas Jefferson* 272 (Ford ed. 1905). These passages are both quoted by Justice Reed in a footnote, 333 U.S. 203, 245, 246 n. 11.

The eager crusaders on the Court make too much of Jefferson's Danbury letter, which was not improbably motivated by an impish desire to heave a brick at the Congregationalist-Federalist hierarchy of Connecticut, whose leading members had denounced him two years before as an "infidel" and "atheist." A more deliberate, more carefully considered evaluation by Jefferson of the religious clauses of the First Amendment is that which occurs in his Second Inaugural: "In matters of religion, I have considered that its free exercise is placed by the constitution independent of the powers of the general government."[44] In short, the principal importance of the amendment lay in the separation which it effected between the respective jurisdictions of state and nation regarding religion, rather than in its bearing on the question of the separation of church and state. For the rest, it is not irrelevant to the major subject opened up by the Court's decision to note that Jefferson regarded religion as "a supplement to law in the government of men," as "the alpha and omega of the moral law"—an attitude closely akin to that voiced in the Northwest Ordinance.[45]

Finally, I wish to adduce the evidence afforded by some important systematic works on the subject of constitutional interpretation, as to the meaning of the term "an establishment of religion." The first of these, although the Court seems to have overlooked it entirely in its researches on the present occasion, carried vast authority a century ago, especially north of the Potomac. I refer to Story's *Commentaries on the Constitution*. Interestingly enough, with one important exception, Story's hard-bitten New England views are quite in line in this instance with those of the Virginians. The exception is that according to Story, while the "no establishment" clause inhibited Congress from giving preference to any sect or denomination of the Christian faith, it was not intended thus to withdraw the Christian religion as a whole from the protection of Congress. Thus he wrote:

> Probably at the time of the adoption of the Constitution, and of the amendment to it, now under consideration, the general, if not the universal sentiment in America was, that christianity ought to receive encouragement from the state, so far as was not incompatible with the private rights of conscience, and the freedom of religious worship. An attempt to level all religions, and to make it a matter of state policy to hold all in utter indifference, would have created universal disapprobation if not universal indignation.[46]

Nor was it the purpose of the amendment to discredit state establishments of religion, but simply "to exclude from the National Government all power to act on the subject."

44. 1 *Messages and Papers of the Presidents* 379 (Richardson ed. 1896).
45. 7 *The Writings of Thomas Jefferson* 339 (H. A. Washington ed. 1854); 1 *id.* at 545. For the latter reference, I am indebted to J. M. O'Neill, *Religion and Education under the Constitution*. This work, now in press, is a devastating assault upon the McCollum decision from several angles.
46. Joseph Story, *Commentaries on the Constitution*, section 1874 (1833).

The situation . . . of the different states equally proclaimed the policy, as well as the necessity of such an exclusion. In some of the states, episcopalians constituted the predominant sect; in others, presbyterians; in others, congregationalists; in others, quakers; and in others again, there was a close numerical rivalry among contending sects. It was impossible, that there should not arise perpetual strife and perpetual jealousy on the subject of ecclesiastical ascendency, if the national government were left free to create a religious establishment. The only security was in extirpating the power. But this alone would have been an imperfect security, if it had not been followed up by a declaration of the right of the free exercise of religion, and a prohibition (as we have seen) of all religious tests. Thus, the whole power over the subject of religion is left exclusively to the state governments, to be acted upon according to their own sense of justice, and the state constitutions; and the Catholic and the Protestant, the Calvinist and the Arminian, the Jew and the Infidel, may sit down at the common table of the national councils, without any inquisition into their faith, or mode of worship.[47]

A generation later Cooley's famous work on *Constitutional Limitations* appeared, the province of which is the constitutional restraints imposed by the state constitutions of that date on the state legislatures. In striking contrast to the passage just quoted from Story, Cooley's work records the disappearance of religious establishments from the state constitutions. His conception of "an establishment of religion" is, however, still the same as that of Story, Madison, and Jefferson, viz., "a sect . . . favored by the State and given an advantage by law over other sects."[48] And in his later *Principles of Constitutional Law,* Cooley is more explicit: "By establishment of religion is meant the setting up or recognition of a state church, or at least the conferring upon one church of special favors and advantages which are denied to others [citing 1 Tuck. Bl. Comm., App. 296; 2 *id.,* App. Note G.]. It was never intended by the Constitution that the Government should be prohibited from recognizing religion—where it might be done without drawing any invidious distinctions between different religious beliefs, organizations, or sects."[49]

III

All in all, it is fairly evident that Justice Rutledge sold his brethren a bill of goods when he persuaded them that the "establishment of religion" clause of the First Amendment was intended to rule out all governmental "aid to *all* religions." However, the First Amendment, taken by itself, is binding only on Congress; and the legislation involved in the McCollum case was state legislation. The *immediate* basis of the decision in this case was, in fact, the "due

47. *Id.* section 1879.
48. Cooley, *Constitutional Limitations* 469 (2d ed. 1871).
49. Cooley, *Principles of Constitutional Law* 224–25 (3d ed. 1898). It is perhaps worth noting that it is in Tucker's *Blackstone* (1803) that Madison's and Jefferson's Virginia and Kentucky Resolutions were first elevated to the rank of an authoritative gloss on the Constitution.

process'' clause of the Fourteenth Amendment; or more strictly speaking, the word ''liberty'' there. In other words, the theory of the case is that the Fourteenth Amendment renders the ban of the First Amendment on an establishment of religion applicable also to the states. Whence came this theory; and to what, logically, does it lead?

I shall deal with these questions in a moment. But first I wish to comment briefly on Justice Frankfurter's supplemental opinion in the McCollum case, in which he is joined by three other justices. For while the opinion throws no additional light on the meaning of the ''establishment of religion'' clause, it does have bearing on the broader subject of religion in the schools.

The opinion is a well-documented sketch of the secularization of public school education in the United States, a reform effected—so far as it has been effected—purely by the political process, unaided up to this point by the Supreme Court. An outstanding figure in the fight on *sectarianism* in the schools was Horace Mann, who lived and wrought in Massachusetts in the second quarter of the last century. Of him Justice Frankfurter writes:

> In Massachusetts, largely through the efforts of Horace Mann, all sectarian teachings were barred from the common school to save it from being rent by denominational conflict. The upshot of these controversies, often long and fierce, is fairly summarized by saying that long before the Fourteenth Amendment subjected the States to new limitations, the prohibition of furtherance by the State of religious instruction became the guiding principle, in law and feeling, of the American people.[50]

This account of things requires some amplifying. Any implication that he was totally opposed to religious instruction in the schools Mann himself would have denied vehemently. Summing the matter up, Culver writes in his authoritative work on the subject:

> It is true that Mr. Mann stood strongly for a ''type of school with instruction adapted to democratic and national ends.'' But it is not quite just to him to contrast this type of school with the school adapted to religious ends, without defining terms. Horace Mann was opposed to sectarian doctrinal instruction in the schools, but he repeatedly urged the teaching of the elements of religion common to all of the Christian sects. He took a firm stand against the idea of a purely secular education, and on one occasion said he was in favor of religious instruction ''to the extremest verge to which it can be carried without invading those rights of conscience which are established by the laws of God, and guaranteed to us by the Constitution of the State.'' At another time he said that he regarded hostility to religion in the schools as the greatest crime he could commit. Lest his name should go down in history as that of one who had attempted to drive religious instruction from the schools, he devoted several pages in his final Report—the twelfth—to a statement in which he denied the charges of his enemies.[51]

---

50. McCollum v. Board of Education, above note 5, at 215.

51. Raymond B. Culver, *Horace Mann and Religion in the Massachusetts Public Schools* 235 (1929). With this statement of Mann's position it is interesting to compare the following extract from a colloquy of Justice Frankfurter with counsel for the School Board, in the course of the argument at Washington: ''Mr. Justice Frankfurter. I put my question again: We have a school system of the

At another point, Justice Frankfurter quotes President Grant's "famous re-marks" in 1875 to a convention of the Army of Tennessee, and his message to Congress of the same year, asking for a constitutional amendment which, among other things, would forbid the use of public funds for sectarian education, and attacking the exemption of church property from taxation.[52] Acting on these suggestions James G. Blaine introduced a resolution providing that "no State shall make any law respecting an establishment of religion" and prohibiting any appropriation of public school money by any state to sectarian schools. The proposal was adopted by the House overwhelmingly, but was lost in the Sen-ate.[53] Down to 1929 it had been reintroduced some twenty times, without result. The proposal assumes, of course, that it was necessary in order to fill a gap in the Constitution. Conversely, the Court's reading of the "due process" clause of the Fourteenth Amendment in the McCollum case assumes that any such amendment would be superfluous.

That the Fourteenth Amendment would make the Bill of Rights applicable to the states was frequently asserted in the congressional debates on the former, but this circumstance lends little if any support to the holding in the McCollum case. For one thing, the Court can hardly rely on it and at the same time reject the conception of the "establishment of religion" clause which prevailed in 1868. If history is to be followed on the one point, it cannot fairly be abandoned on the other. Again, the expectations of its framers regarding the operation of the amendment rested mainly on two ideas, both of which were early discredited by the Court itself. The first of these was that the "privileges and immunities of citizens of the United States" protected by the amendment covered the whole realm of civil rights; the second was that Congress's legislative power under Section V of the amendment would be equally extensive. Thus the application of the Bill of Rights to the states would be effected by congressional action; the notion that the Court would have any hand in the business was not widely entertained.[54]

The Court itself, however, had different ideas. In the famous Slaughter House Cases[55] of 1873 it adopted a conception of "privileges and immunities of cit-

---

United States on the one hand, and the relation it has to the democratic way of life. On the other hand we have the religious beliefs of our people. The question is whether any kind of scheme which introduced religious teaching in the public school system is the kind of thing we should have in our democratic institutions." J. M. O'Neill, *op. cit.* above note 44, at 234.

52. McCollum v. Board of Education, above note 5, at 218.

53. M. A. Musmanno, *Proposed Amendments to the Constitution* 182 (1929).

54. In his dissenting opinion in Adamson v. California, 332 U.S. 46, 68ff. (1947), Justice Black argues that the Fourteenth Amendment adopts the Bill of Rights in toto and quotes from the congres-sional debates on the former to prove the point, relying especially on speeches by Representative Bingham of Ohio and Senator Howard of Michigan. He overlooks the fact that both these high authorities expected that the application of the Bill of Rights to the states would be effected by congressional legislation. See the Appendix compiled by Justice Black to his opinion, 332 U.S. 92–123, especially at pp. 93, 94, 95, 97, 98, 101, 106, 107, 110, 112, 114, 115, 117, and 118.

55. Slaughter House Cases, 16 Wall. 36 (U.S. 1873).

izens of the United States'' which extruded all "fundamental" rights from the term. In the Civil Rights Cases[56] ten years later it pared down Congress's powers under the fifth section of the amendment to the bare disallowance of state legislation violative of the first section—a function better left to the processes of judicial review. The subsequent judicial history of the Fourteenth Amendment has in the main been the history of the Court's interpretation of the due process clause; but of this history the only phase of interest in the present connection is that which involves the word "liberty" in that clause. In 1898, thirty years after the adoption of the amendment, the Court, responding to the pressure of preponderant legal opinion in the country, at last adopted a definition of "liberty" embracing "freedom of contract," and especially freedom of contract in the sphere of employer-employee relations.[57] More expansive conceptions of the term, on the other hand, it steadily repelled throughout the next quarter of a century.[58] Even as late as 1922 we find it using the following words:

> Neither the Fourteenth Amendment nor any other provision of the Constitution of the United States imposes upon the States any restrictions about "freedom of speech" or the "liberty of silence."[59]

Following the First World War, however, the Court began shifting its position; and in the notable case of Pierce v. Society of Sisters,[60] decided in 1925, it held that the word "liberty" in the Fourteenth Amendment protects the rights of parents to guide the education of their children, and hence the right to send them to parochial schools rather than the public schools, if they so choose. And on this basis, the Oregon compulsory school law, which made it impossible, practically, for children to attend parochial schools, was pronounced unconstitutional. As I shall point out in a moment, the holding in the McCollum case is logically incompatible with the decision just mentioned. Finally, in this same year, 1925, the Court, in the well-known Gitlow case,[61] tentatively adopted the thesis that the word "liberty" in the Fourteenth Amendment includes freedom of speech and press as recognized in the First Amendment; and this tentative thesis has since become a firm part of the Court's jurisprudence. In many recent cases, most of which involve Jehovah's Witnesses, the same doctrine has, moreover, been applied to religious liberty.[62]

That the Court was warranted by a considerable line of recent decisions in taking the position in the McCollum case that if the "released-time" program there involved amounted to an invasion of anybody's freedom of religion it was unconstitutional, is clear. Indeed, whether the program did this or not was,

56. Civil Rights Cases, 109 U.S. 3 (1883).

57. Holden v. Hardy, 169 U.S. 366 (1898).

58. On this and the following paragraph, see my *Liberty Against Government* 134–68 (1948).

59. Prudential Insurance Co. v. Cheek, 259 U.S. 530, 543 (1922).

60. 268 U.S. 510 (1925).

61. Gitlow v. New York, 268 U.S. 652 (1925).

62. Cantwell v. Connecticut, 310 U.S. 296 (1940); West Virginia State Board of Education v. Barnette, 319 U.S. 624 (1943), and cases there cited.

properly speaking, the only question before the Court; and talk about "an establishment of religion" was entirely beside the point *unless the "released-time"
program of the Champaign schools involved an establishment of religion of such
a nature as to deprive the plaintiff in the case of freedom of religion.* That is to
say, the Fourteenth Amendment does not authorize the Court to substitute the
word "state" for "Congress" in the ban imposed by the First Amendment on
laws "respecting an establishment of religion." *So far as the Fourteenth Amendment is concerned, states are entirely free to establish religions, provided they
do not deprive anybody of religious liberty.* It is only *liberty* that the Fourteenth
Amendment protects. And in this connection it should not be overlooked that
contemporary England manages to maintain as complete freedom of religion as
exists in this country alongside an establishment of religion, although originally
that establishment involved a ban upon all other faiths.[63]

Vital, therefore, to the Court's argument in the McCollum case is the proposition that such children in the Champaign schools as came under the program
were *coerced* to do so by virtue of the fact that they were gathered there—
"recruited" is the Court's word—in consequence of the state compulsory school
law. The answer is that no children were admitted to the program unless their
parents formally requested that they be, and the choice of the parent must be
imputed to the child. There is still, of course, the coercion exercised by the
parent, but it seems unlikely that the Court is out to emancipate children from
their parents!

This is not to say, however, that there was no question of coercion involved in
this case and involved in a very significant way, although one which appears to
have escaped entirely the careful diligence of the Court. I recur to my reference a
paragraph or two back to the decision in 1925 in Pierce v. Society of Sisters,[64] in
which an Oregon compulsory school law was set aside as impairing the right of
parents, who wished their children to attend parochial schools, to guide the
education of their children. Two observations seem called for. In the first place,
it is an inevitable implication of the case that compulsory school laws which
permit attendance at parochial schools are constitutional, notwithstanding the
compulsion which is thereby lent such schools in "recruiting" pupils. This
compulsion is, in fact, immensely more evident than that which was put upon
pupils to avail themselves of the Champaign "released-time" program. In the
second place, the parental right which was vindicated in the Pierce case, whatever else it is, must also be reckoned to be an *element of the right which the*

63. In the Cantwell case, cited above, it is stated incidentally (p. 303) that the Fourteenth
Amendment makes the "establishment of religion" clause of the First Amendment operate with the
same force on the states as it does on Congress; but this statement is based on the idea that an
establishment signifies "compulsion by law of the acceptance of . . . [a] creed or the practice of
. . . [a] form of worship." *Id.* Story, on the other hand, holds that an ecclesiastical establishment
may be perfectly compatible with full freedom of religion for all sects. Joseph Story, *Commentaries
on the Constitution* section 1872 (1833).

64. See note 60 above.

Constitution guarantees to all to "the free exercise" of their religion. The question accordingly arises whether this right is confined to parents who can afford to send their children to parochial or other private schools; whether, in other words, parents who must for financial or other reasons send their children to the public schools have no right to guide their education to the extent of demanding that the education there available shall include some religious instruction, provided nobody's freedom of religion is thereby impaired? *All in all, it seems clear that the Court, by its decision in the McCollum case, has itself promulgated a law prohibiting "the free exercise" of religion, contrary to the express prohibition of the First Amendment!*

To summarize the argument against the decision in the McCollum case: In the first place, the justification for the Court's intervention was trivial and directly violative of restrictions hitherto existing on judicial review. In the second place, the decision is based, as Justice Reed rightly contends,[65] on "a figure of speech," the concept of "a wall of separation between Church and State." Thirdly, leaving this figure of speech to one side, the decision is seen to stem from an unhistorical conception of what is meant by "an establishment of religion" in the First Amendment. The historical record shows beyond peradventure that the core idea of "an establishment of religion" comprises the idea of *preference;* and that any act of public authority favorable to religion in general cannot, without manifest falsification of history, be brought under the ban of that phrase. Undoubtedly the Court has the right to make history, as it has often done in the past; but it has no right to *remake* it. In the fourth place, the prohibition on the establishment of religion by Congress is not convertible into a similar prohibition on the states, under the authorization of the Fourteenth Amendment, unless the term "establishment of religion" be given an application which carries with it invasion of somebody's freedom of religion, that is, of "liberty." Finally, the decision is accompanied by opinions and by a mandate which together have created great uncertainty in the minds of governing bodies of all public educational institutions. And, of course, as is always the case, the Court's intervention is purely negative. It is incapable of solving the complex problem with which forty-six states and 2,200 communities have been struggling by means of the "released-time" expedient. With the utmost insouciance the Court overturns or casts under the shadow of unconstitutionality the "conscientious attempt" of hundreds of people to deal with what they have considered to be a pressing problem in a way that they have considered to be fair and just to all.

Finally, this question may be asked: Is the decision favorable to democracy? Primarily democracy is a system of ethical values, and that this system of values so far as the American people are concerned is grounded in religion will not be denied by anybody who knows the historical record. And that the agencies by which this system of values has been transmitted in the past from generation to

65. McCollum v. Board of Education, above note 5, at 247.

generation—the family, the neighborhood, the church—have today become much impaired will not be seriously questioned by anybody who knows anything about contemporary conditions. But what this all adds up to is that *the work of transmission has been put more and more upon the shoulders of the public schools.* Can they, then, do the job without the assistance of religious instruction? At least, there seems to be a widely held opinion to the contrary.

I wonder just how the shade of Justice Holmes would comment on this decision. I can imagine the late justice repeating some words which he used in a dissenting opinion in 1921:

> There is nothing that I more deprecate than the use of the Fourteenth Amendment beyond the absolute compulsion of its words to prevent the making of social experiments that an important part of the community desires, in the insulated chambers afforded by the several States, even though the experiments may seem futile or even noxious to me and to those whose judgment I most respect.[66]

Indeed, he might even feel called upon to repeat his gibe about judges being "naïf, simple-minded men"[67] one mark of naiveté being a preference for slogans over solutions.

And what would the Court answer? Perhaps it might adopt the words of Justice Jackson in a recent case:

> We [the Court] act in these matters not by the authority of our competence but by force of our commissions. We cannot, because of modest estimates of our competence in such specialties as public education, withhold the judgment that history authenticates as the function of this Court when liberty is infringed.[68]

This is a plea in confession and avoidance which can by no means be granted. It is not to be presumed that the Constitution puts burdens on the Court in the discharge of which with appropriate modesty it must still risk disaster for the country. The decision in the McCollum case, however, is not a "modest" decision. Instead it is to be grouped with those high-flying *tours de force* in which the Court has occasionally indulged, to solve "forever" some teasing problem—slavery, for example, in the Dred Scott case[69]—or to correct, as in the Pollock case,[70] "a century of error."

In my opinion the Court would act wisely to make it clear at the first opportunity that it does not aspire to become, as Justice Jackson puts it, "a super board of education for every school district in the nation."[71]

---

66. Truax v. Corrigan, 257 U.S. 312, 244 (1921). The "watchfulness of state interests against exuberant judicial restrictions," which Holmes gave expression to in the passage just quoted, is praised by Justice Frankfurter with warm enthusiasm in his *Mr. Justice Holmes and the Supreme Court* 86–88 (1938). See also his recent opinion in Adamson v. California 332 U.S. 46, 59, 62.

67. Holmes, *Collected Legal Papers* 295 (1921).

68. West Virginia State Board of Education v. Barnette, above note 62, at 640.

69. Dred Scott v. Sanford, 19 How. 393 (U.S. 1856).

70. Pollock v. Farmers Loan and Trust Co., 157 U.S. 429 (1895).

71. McCollum v. Board of Education, above note 5, at 237.

8. The Supreme Court's Construction of the Self-Incrimination Clause

THE Fourth Amendment of the Constitution reads as follows: "The right of the people to be secure in their persons, houses, papers, and effects against unreasonable searches and seizures, shall not be violated, and no warrants shall issue but upon probable cause, supported by oath or affirmation, and particularly describing the place to be searched, and the person or things to be seized."[1] The so-called "self-incrimination clause" of Amendment V reads as follows: "No person . . . shall be compelled in any criminal case to be a witness against himself."

Hard upon the centenary of the Constitution the Supreme Court informed the country that these two provisions, which had hitherto produced no cases before that tribunal, were intended to be read together, with the result that today they jointly support a highly important body of constitutional law—important especially in the field of national criminal law. Which of the two members of this jural partnership is the more important, it would be difficult to say; nor is the attempt to do so here made. The procedure of the present study in centering attention primarily on the self-incrimination clause rather than on Amendment IV merely parallels the similar procedure of the leading cases.

I

Considered in the light to be shed by grammar and the dictionary, the words of the self-incrimination clause appear to signify simply that nobody shall be compelled to give oral testimony against himself in a criminal proceeding under way

From 29 *Michigan Law Review* 1–27, 191–207 (1930). Reprinted by permission.

1. The Fourth Amendment was aimed particularly at "general warrants," which were finally overthrown in England in the cases of Wilkes and Entick. See Cooley, *Const. Lim.* (7th ed.), 426, 428; Wilkes' Case, 19 St. Trials 1405; Entick v. Carrington, *id.*, 1030. The closest analogue to the "general warrant" in the prerevolutionary history of this country is to be seen in the "writ of assistance," for the history of which see Quincy, Reports (Mass.), 51 and app. p. 395.

in which he is defendant. This reading is, moreover, strongly confirmed when we consider the clause in conjunction with similar clauses from the early state constitutions.

The earliest statement of the principle against self-incrimination to be found in an American constitution is that in section 8 of the Virginia Declaration of Rights of 1776. It reads thus: "That in all capital or criminal prosecutions a man hath a right to demand the cause and nature of his accusation . . .; nor can he be compelled to give evidence against himself." The mental picture called up is clearly that of a prosecution actually under way against the party entitled to claim the protection of the clause. In both the North Carolina and Pennsylvania Declarations of the same year the language used is closely similar, except that for the word "man" is substituted the word "person"; while in the Massachusetts Declaration of Rights of 1789, as well as the New Hampshire constitution of 1784, the term employed is "subject."

In the Pennsylvania constitution of 1790, the intention of such provisions is, if possible, made even more explicit by the use of the phrase "the accused" to designate the beneficiary of the privilege—a phraseology which also occurs in the Kentucky constitution of 1792, the Tennessee constitution of 1796, the Ohio constitution of 1802, the Louisiana constitution of 1812, the Mississippi constitution of 1817, the Connecticut constitution of 1818, the Maine constitution of 1819, the Missouri constitution of 1820, and which in fact remains today the standard form of the clause in state constitutions; and while the Fifth Amendment reverts to the term "person," the person thought of is manifestly one under formal accusation.[2]

Judicial application of the self-incrimination clause of Amendment V has, however, drawn singularly little upon the sources of illumination just mentioned. Its dependence has been upon the English common law as this stood at the time of the establishment of our government. In this, as in other instances, the formal phraseology of the Constitution has been utilized by the Court to lift certain doctrines of the common law beyond the reach of ordinary legislative power, though at the same time remoulding them itself with considerable freedom.

The self-incrimination clause of Amendment V is a particular rendition of the "maxim" "*Nemo tenetur prodere* (or *accusare*) *seipsum*—nobody is bound to accuse himself." The source of the maxim itself is more doubtful. That it owed nothing to any *text* of the canon law can be stated with confidence, though the contrary has been sometimes asserted.[3] Rather, it first came into general notice

2. The foregoing constitutional provisions can be readily located in Thorpe's *Am. Charters, Consts.*, etc. See also F. J. Stimson, *Federal and State Consts.*, section 136.

3. It is so asserted, e.g., in the solicitor general's brief in Ballmann v. Fagin, 200 U.S. 186, 190. In his article on the maxim in 5 *Harv. L. Rev.* 71, at p. 83, Professor Wigmore makes an equivalent statement: "The fact is that the maxim *nemo tenetur* was an old and established one in ecclesiastical practice." In support of this assertion, Professor Wigmore cites Strype's *Whitgift*, app., pp. 136–37, where is given an "Opinion of Nine most learned Doctors of the Civil Law," defending the oath *ex officio* procedure of the English ecclesiastical courts at that date—about 1590. The salient passage of the opinion runs as follows: "*Licet nemo seipsum prodere; tamen proditus per famam, tenetur*

in England, as we shall see in a moment, as a protest against characteristic procedures of that law. Neither, on the other hand, did it spring in the first instance from the common law. Far down into the seventeenth century the first step against an accused person in England was his forced examination, which might or might not be under oath, before a justice of the peace; and almost the first step in his subsequent trial was the reading of results of this examination, while the most important feature of the trial was the direct questioning of the accused, both by the prosecution and by the court itself. It is true that the accused was not now under oath, unless the court had chosen to concede him it as a favor; but the verdict of the jury was apt to be reached largely, if not altogether, on the

---

seipsum ostendere, utrum possit suam innocentiam ostendere et seipsum purgare.'' As given in this context, however, the maxim, it seems clear, does not purport to be a recital of a rule of canon law. Rather the passage quoted would seem to be an effort to square ecclesiastical practice with an idea which was already (see below) beginning to be urged against it with telling effect.

I am assured by Fr. Louis Motry of the Catholic University, who is a recognized authority in the field, that no *text* of canon law contains the words of the maxim and this assurance is confirmed by a careful examination of Gravina's *Institutiones Canonicae,* Pithou's *Corpus Juris Canonici,* and Cance's *Le Code De Droit Canonique* (3 vols., Paris, 1920). Modern *authors,* on the other hand, sometimes use the words of the maxim, in which connection Fr. Motry cites 4 Lega, *De Judiciis Eccl.* 295 (Rome, 1901). Moreover, the canon law has always recognized the general principle that a man should not be required to accuse himself *in the first instance.* Thus the sixth of the eleven "rules of law" attributed to Gregory IX (see the 5th book of his Decretals) provides: "*Tormenta, indiciis non praecedentibus, inferenda non sunt* (torture ought not to be resorted to until some evidence has been forthcoming)." To the same general effect, too, is the answer returned to Questio V, Decreti II Pars., Causa VI, in Pithou's *Corpus: "Si in probatione deficit accusator, an reus sit cogendus ad probationem suae innocentiae."* The question is answered "no," on the basis of the authority of Gregory, but with this important reservation: "*Hoc autem servandum est, quando reum publica fama non vexat. Tunc enim auctoritate ejusdem Gregorii propter scandalum removandum, famam suam reum purgare oportet.''* Pertinent, too, in this connection are two provisions of the *Codex Juris Canonici,* to which Fr. Motry refers, and which at first glance seem to approximate in purpose fairly closely to the constitutional clause against self-incrimination. These are canon 1743 (Par. 1), which reads as follows: "*Judici legitime interroganti partes respondere tenentur et fateri veritatem, nisi agatur de delicto ab ipsis commisso;''* and canon 1744, the words of which are "*Jusjurandum de veritate dicenda in causis criminalibus nequit judex accusato deferre.''* The date of the former canon Fr. Motry is unable to furnish; the latter, however, was established by Benedict XIII in the Provincial Council of Rome in 1725. It is therefore important to note that as late as 1749, Conset could write, with reference to the oath *ex officio* procedure, as follows: "If the fame of it [a charge] is proved or confessed, the defendant ought to answer to the positions [charges], although they be criminal, or, if he doth refuse, he is to be pronounced *pro confesso,* after being admonished to answer." *Practice of Spiritual Courts,* p. 384; Wigmore, *loc. cit.,* p. 83. The above quoted canons, were not, therefore, it seems, regarded as late as 1749 as having invalidated the oath procecure. It should be added that, in English ecclesiastical practice at least, the existence of a rumor *(fama)* was sufficiently established by the testimony of two persons. Dr. Hunt's Case, Cro. El. 262.

Summing up, we may say: (1) that the specific maxim *nemo tenetur* finds no place in any *text* of canon law; (2) that canon law recognition of the general principle that a person ought not to be forced to accuse himself was always attenuated by the qualification that one accused by a sufficiently authenticated rumor could be legitimately required to clear his reputation or have the charge taken as confessed. That some moralist or canonist may, in urging this principle, whether with or without the qualification mentioned, have coined the maxim *nemo tenetur* before Coke brought it into notice (see below) as an argument against the oath procedure of the English ecclesiastical courts, is of course quite possible.

impressions conveyed by such an examination.[4] The practice of the Star Chamber from 1487 was still more drastic. That year the Chamber, which already had a conceded jurisdiction to fine and imprison for nearly all offenses, was vested with authority to compel defendants to testify under oath; and in the exercise of the power thus given torture was employed not infrequently.[5] Nor indeed, at that date, was torture altogether unknown to the ordinary courts as a means of eliciting testimony from an accused, albeit according to Coke the practice was always contrary to the common law.[6]

The immediate occasion for the appearance of the maxim "*nemo tenetur*" was the contest which developed towards the close of the sixteenth century between the common law courts and the Court of High Commission over the penal jurisdiction claimed by the latter. From the ecclesiastical courts of the middle ages the High Commission claimed to have inherited the right to administer within the field of its jurisdiction the so-called "oath *ex officio.*" This was an oath which bishops, or those who were deputed by them, were authorized to administer to clerymen {*sic*; clergymen}, or even to laymen, whom rumor had brought under suspicion respecting some matter either of faith or morals, for the purpose of enabling them to clear themselves. Persons taking the oath were sworn to tell the whole truth in answer to the questions about to be put them, and a refusal to take the oath or to answer under it was taken as confession of the offense charged.[7] The handle which such a procedure lent to the High Commission's power to fine and imprison for "heresies . . . offenses . . . and enormities"[8] is manifest; and once the latter was challenged the former was bound to be also.

4. 1 Stephen, *History of the Criminal Law of England*, 216–25, 324–37, 345–57; the same author on "the Practice of Interrogating Persons Accused of Crime," in 1 *Juridical Soc. Papers*, 456ff. Examination of prisoners before justices of the peace was directed by 1 & 2 Ph. and M. c. 13 and 2 & 3 Ph. and M. c. 10; also by 7 Geo. IV, c. 64. In 1655 the judges directed that the examination should be without oath. *Starkie on Evidence* (2d ed.), p. 29.

5. 1 Stephen, *op. cit.* 166–83, 337–45.

6. 1 *id.*, 222: 3 *Inst.*, 35. For an instance of torture see Lyon and Block's *Edward Coke, Oracle of the Law* (1929), pp. 192–93. The victim was Edward Peacham, a Puritan clergyman. His bishop having made charges against him, Peacham was first brought before the High Commission; then later, on a charge of high treason, before the Privy Council. Bacon, then attorney general, was present at his ensuing examination upon this charge, and reported it thus: "Upon these interrogatories, Peacham was examined before torture, between torture, and after torture; nothing could be drawn from him, he still persisting in his obstinate and inexcusable denials and former answers."

7. For the oath *ex officio* and the procedure based on it, see 4 Wigmore, *Evidence in Trials at Common Law* (2d ed., 1923), section 2250; R. G. Usher, *Rise and Fall of the High Commission passim* (see index); 12 Rep. 26; 2 *Inst.* 657; Gravina, *Inst. Can.* lib. III, tit. X (*de juramento calumniae*) tit. XI (*de probationibus*). The oath procedure was devised by Innocent III to combat heresy. In a canon issued in 1199 it was provided: "*Licet contra cum nullus accusator legitimus appareret, ex officio tuo tamen fama publica deferente, voluisti plenius inquirere veritatem.*" 4 Wigmore 798 n. 23. This is the source of the *Inquisitio*; the practice of putting the party under oath to tell the truth in answer to all questions about to be put him was added in 1205, in the Decretals of that year. Wigmore, *loc cit.* For the introduction of this procedure into England see *id.*; also 12 Rep. 28, 29.

8. 1 Eliz. c. 1; cf. 4 *Inst.* 324, especially 332–34, for denial of the Commission's penal jurisdiction.

The oath first came under serious attack the last quarter of the sixteenth century, in the interest of Puritan nonconforming clergymen, who were rapidly becoming its usual victims.[9] In 1589 the same cause enlisted the important support of Sir Edward Coke. This year Coke as attorney for a client who had been haled before an ecclesiastical ordinary on a charge of incontinency obtained a prohibition from the King's Bench against the oath procedure. Coke's argument was that the oath *ex officio* could be employed only in causes testamentary and matrimonial, "because *nemo tenetur prodere seipsum.*"[10] Inasmuch as this is the earliest actual statement of the maxim known to be extant, Bentham conjectures that it was of Coke's own invention.[11] The surmise is not lacking in plausibility, as Coke delighted in nothing more than to give his ideas a Latin phrasing for the purpose of investing them with the apparent sanction of antiquity. At the same time, he rarely created out of whole cloth; nor was he necessarily doing so on this occasion, as the data furnished in note 3, above, showed. There is, in fact, pauseworthy authority for the statement that the notion that an accused should not be forced to testify against himself had found recognition and enforcement, at least in some measure, in the procedure of the ancient Roman courts.[12]

But Coke's most weighty assault upon the oath *ex officio* was delivered without reference to the maxim. This occurred in 1607, the year following his elevation to the chief justiceship of the Common Pleas, when in answering a question propounded by the House of Commons, Coke and Popham, chief justice of the King's Bench, formally laid down the doctrine that the oath could be legally exacted of laymen only in cases affecting wills and marriages, while even

9. Usher, *op. cit.*, 125–30, 141–51, 170–75, 182, 320, 328; see also Strype's *Whitgift,* 340.

10. Cullier v. Cullier, Cro. El. 201; Moor, 906. As chief justice of the King's Bench Coke repeats the maxim in his judgment in the case of Sir William Boyer, Pl. against the High Commission (1613), 2 Bulstr. 182–83: "They would have examined him upon oath; as touching this, the Rule of Law is, *Nemo tenetur seipsum prodere*; they may there examine upon oath if he be a Parson, or an Ecclesiastical man, but not a lay person." In Dighton and Holt's Case (1615), 3 Bulstr. 48; Cro. Jac. 388 he takes a similar line, but without repeating the maxim. "Because this examination is made to make them accuse themselves of the breach of a penal law, which is against the law; for they ought to proceed against them by witnesses, and not enforce them to take an oath to accuse themselves." In both these cases, as well as in his opinion in 12 Rep. 26 on the Oath *ex officio*, Coke refers to Leigh's Case, which he says was decided in the tenth year of Elizabeth's reign, and was reported by Lord Dyer, but not printed. See also Coke's *Littleton,* 158b: "If the cause of the challenge touch the dishonor or discredit of the juror he shall not be examined upon his oath," citing 49 Eliz. 3. 1, 2. Other early cases in which Coke did not participate, but which reflects {*sic*; reflect} the viewpoint of the above are Clifford v. Huntley (1610), 1 Rolle's Abr., Prohibition (J) 6, where it was held that a prohibition would lie to prevent the exaction in an ecclesiastical court of an answer on oath which might show forfeiture of an obligation; Bradston's Case (1614), *id.,* Prohibition (J), where a similar result was reached; Spendlow v. Smith (1616?), Hob, 84, of like import; and Jenner's Case (1620), Rolle's Abr., Prohibition (J) 5, also to the same general effect.

11. 5 *Rationale of Judicial Evidence,* 221–29; see also *id.,* 250–66, 455, 462.

12. "One author on Canonical Procedure (Roberti, *De Processibus*) in writing on the subject states that it was *jus commune* in the Roman law courts not to force the guilty one to give any information concerning his own crime. He refers to a practice or custom but adds no sources." Fr. Motry to the present writer.

as to ecclesiastics it could not be exacted regarding any matter punishable at common law. For said they, "it standeth not with the right order of justice nor good equity that any person should be convict and put to the loss of his life, good name, or goods, unless it were by due accusation, and witnesses, or by presentment, verdict, confession, or process, of outlawry."[13]

These words, which Coke, although citing them to a statute of Henry VIII,[14] asserts to be merely declaratory of the common law, make abundantly clear the nature of the issue between the common law judges and the court of High Commission. This issue arose, or at least drew its substance, from the conspicuous difference between, on the one hand, the *accusatorial* method of the common law, which centers in the grand jury, and on the other hand, the *inquisitorial* method of the canon law, in which accusation might be by rumor (*fama*), provided the existence of the rumor was authenticated by two witnesses. It was not, therefore, concerned primarily, if it was concerned at all, with the rights of persons under accusation by a proper mode of procedure. It dealt with the preliminary question of what were the necessary incidents of such a procedure; and the answer of Coke and his confreres to this question was naturally that of the common law itself.

First obtaining general currency in consequence of the fight of the common law courts upon the penal jurisdiction of the Court of High Commission, the phrase "*nemo tenetur*" began to assume something of its modern (which may also be its ancient) connotation in connection with Lilburne's trial before the Star Chamber in 1637.[15] Basing his claim upon the law of God as shown in Christ's and St. Paul's trials, on "the law of the land," and the Petition of Right, Lilburne refused to take an oath to be "ensnared by answering things concerning other men"; but he significantly added that if "he had been proceeded against by a bill" (that is, of indictment), he would have answered. That is to say, as a *witness* concerning the conduct of others he was protected from incriminating himself, although had he been regularly *accused* he would have had to testify. All of which is strictly harmonious with Coke's employment of the maxim.

But the rest of the story is also instructive. For his contumacy Lilburne was sentenced to be whipped, and in April, 1638, sentence was executed. Three years later, though before the Star Chamber had been abolished, the House of Commons voted the sentence illegal. Then on February 13th, 1646, the House of Lords consented to hear a petition by Lilburne's attorney Bradshaw against the sentence, wherein the unqualified doctrine was urged that it "was contrary to the laws of God, nature and this kingdom, for any man to be his own accuser." The House, thereupon, ordered the sentence to be totally vacated as "illegal and most unjust, against the liberty of the subject, and law of the land, and Magna Carta;" and some months later Lilburne was voted £3,000 reparation.

13. 12 Rep. 26–29; to the same effect, 2 *Inst.* 657.
14. 25 Hen. 8, c. 14.
15. 3 How. St. Tr. 1315; see also narrative in Wigmore, *op. cit.*, section 2250.

Lilburne's trial, together with this aftermath, has, therefore, a twofold bearing upon the development of the modern doctrine against self-incrimination: first, in the wide advertisement which it afforded the maxim as a constituent element of "law of the land," deemed to have been consecrated by Magna Carta; and secondly, in substantially obliterating the distinction which had existed, certainly in Coke's mind, between the status in relation to the maxim of a regularly *accused defendant* and that of other persons.

From this time forth judicial recognition and development of the maxim proceeded with great rapidity, so much so indeed that long before the Constitution of the United States was adopted, or even before American independence was thought of, the privilege against self-incrimination had received an extension in the English cases which in some respects is broader than its application by the United States Supreme Court today.[16]

It is requisite at this point to draw attention to the difference which exists nowadays between the privilege of an *accused* to refuse to take the stand at all in the proceedings against himself, and the privilege of a *witness* to decline to answer specific questions which "tend to incriminate" him. Of the cases just referred to the great majority were criminal proceedings in which the persons invoking the protection of the doctrine against self-incrimination were witnesses testifying under oath.[17] Protection seems to have been readily granted them upon their own claim, its pertinence being usually quite evident. The scope given the privilege of witnesses in these early cases was, moreover, very broad, extending not only to questions tending to incriminate the witness but also to questions tending to disgrace him.[18]

At first the case of accused persons not under oath, though still subject to the informal questioning of the prosecution and the court, seems to have been assimilated more or less to that of ordinary witnesses. In the trial of the regicide Scroop, in 1660, the Lord Chief Baron, having asked the defendant whether he "sat upon sentence day"—that is, the day when Charles I was condemned to die—hastened to add: "You are not bound to answer me; but if you will not, we

16. The development was aided by legislation. By 13 Car. II, c. 12 (1662), it was provided that "no one shall administer to any person whatsoever the oath usually called *ex officio*, or any other oath, whereby such persons may be charged or compelled to confess any criminal matter." This enactment explains why the question of self-incrimination did not from this time on come up in the ecclesiastical courts.

17. See especially Scroop's Trial, 5 Howell St. Tr. 1034, at p. 1039 (1660); Penn's and Mead's Trial, 6 *id*. 651, at p. 658 (1676); Reading's Trial, 7 *id*. 259, at p. 296 (1679); Whitehead's Trial, 7 *id*. 311, at p. 361 (1679); Earl of Stafford's Trial, 7 *id*. 1293, at p. 1214 (1680); Rosewell's Trial, 10 *id*. 147, at p. 169 (1680); Sir Jno. Freind's Trial, 13 *id*. 1, at pp. 16–18. Many of these references occur in 4 Wigmore, 815 n. See also, 16 How. St. Tr. 767: 17 *id*. 1342; Salk. 153; 2 Mod. 118; 3 Taunt. 424; 5 Carr. and P. 213; 3 Camp. 210; 2 Hawkins, *Pleas of the Crown*, c. 46; 1 MacNally, *Evidence*, 256–58.

18. See especially the Lord Chief Justice in 13 How. St. Tr. 1, 16–18; also Salk. 153. Priddle's Case, 1 Leach's Cr. Law (old ed.) 382; and King v. Edwards, 4 Term Rep. 440 (1792) reject this broad doctrine.

19. 5 How. St. Tr. 1034, 1039.

must prove it."[19] In the trial of Penn and Mead for riotous assembly a few years later, Mead appealed to the doctrine in the following words: "It is a maxim in your own law, '*nemo tenetur accusare seipsum,*' which if it be not true Latin, I am sure is true English, 'that no man is bound to accuse himself,'" to which his interrogator answered by denying that he had tried to "ensnare" the defendant.[20]

Following, however, the Revolution of 1688, English criminal procedure underwent a marked alteration, and the questioning of accused defendants soon ceased entirely. But while this change undoubtedly testifies to the growing influence of the maxim against self-incrimination, the manner in which it was effected was by extension from civil to criminal cases of the rule that a party is not a competent witness on account of interest (*"nemo debet esse testis in propriâ causâ"*).[21] The result was that henceforth the mouth of an accused, and his wife's as well, was closed whether *for* or against himself; and it is in this form that the immunity of accused persons passed to the American colonies balanced, that is, by the corresponding disability. Not until 1878, following a similar reform in several of the states, was the right to testify in their own behalf, under oath, accorded defendants in the national courts.[22]

But not only was an accused protected from all judicial questioning under the common law as this country inherited it, his papers which might contain incriminating matter were immune from judicial process. This principle was laid down as early as 1704, in Regina v. Mead,[23] and in 1765 it received the sanction of the two greatest legal lights of England, Lord Mansfield in Rex v. Dixon[24] and Lord Camden in Entick v. Carrington.[25] Meantime, in other cases it had been carried beyond even present-day American doctrine. In Rex v. Purnell (1748),[26] for instance, the court refused to permit the prosecution to inspect the statutes and archives of the University of Oxford, of which defendant was vice-chancellor. The doctrine of the United States Supreme Court is that an officer of a corporation is not to be shielded from the forced production of the papers

---

20. 6 *id*. 651, 657.
21. 1 Stephen, *op. cit.* 439–42; 1 *Juridical Society Papers,* 456ff.
22. 20 Stat. 30 (Act of March 16, 1878, c. 37): "That in the trial of all indictments . . . and other proceedings against persons charged with the commission of crimes, offences, and misdemeanors, in the United States courts, territorial courts, and courts-martial . . . the person so charged shall, at his own request, but not otherwise, be a competent witness. And his failure to make such request shall not create any presumption against him." The provision was construed in Wilson v. United States, 149 U.S. 60. For a general review of legislation on the same subject, see 1 Greenleaf, *Evidence* (15th ed.), 467–68; 3 *id., 54*–67. See also Cooley's *Cons'l. Lims.* (2d ed.) 317 n., 394.
23. 2 Ld. Raymond 927.
24. 3 Burr. 1687.
25. 19 How. St. Tr. 1029.
26. 1 Wils. 239. To this same effect is Rex v. Cornelius, 2 Strange 1219 (1744), where the court refused a rule asked for by the prosecutor, to inspect the books of a corporation, saying: "It is in effect obliging a defendant indicted for a misdemeanor to furnish evidence against himself." See also Rex v. Worsenham, 1 Ld. Raymond 705; Rex v. Mead, above; and Rex v. Granatelli, 7 St. Tr. (N.S.) 979, where the same principle is recognized.

thereof, inasmuch as he holds them not in a private but in a representative capacity.[27]

Finally, a series of rulings in the Court of Chancery before 1700 had clearly foreshadowed the extension of the privilege to both parties and witnesses in civil proceedings as to disclosures calculated to furnish evidence against them in possible future criminal proceedings.[28]

Comparing now the common law regarding self-incrimination with the prevalent type of constitutional provision on the same subject, at the time of the adoption of Amendment V, the question naturally arises: Why the narrow scope of the latter? The answer is simple. In the early state constitutions, as in the Fifth Amendment, immunity from self-incrimination is listed merely as *one* of a whole parcel of privileges which were in the main of interest to accused persons and to no others. That is to say, the problem being dealt with was the improvement of the lot of accused persons, a concentration of interest which was due to the tradition of the harshness of the common law in this respect, as illustrated by the trials of the Throckmortons and of Udall in the sixteenth century, the conduct of ''Bloody'' Jeffries on the Western Assizes the century following, and the terrible severity of the English penal code in the eighteenth century. At the same time, since the constitutional provisions mentioned above did not overrule the common law in excluding an accused from the witness stand, their stipulation for his immunity taken by itself became pointless. If only, therefore, to save the framers of these provisions from the charge of having loaded them with a meaningless tautology, their language had to be given other than its literal significance, and the common law was at hand to supply this in rich measure.[29]

II

Turning to the history of the clause in American constitutional law, we at once find the earlier distinction between accused persons and all others yielding in importance to that between *oral testimony* and *the evidence supplied by documents or things*. In this connection the United States Supreme Court has rendered two outstanding decisions, that in Boyd v. United States, and that in Counselman v. Hitchcock.[30] In the former it appropriated to the Constitution the safeguards which are thrown by the common law about incriminating documents, and in the

27. See below.
28. Penrice v. Parker, Finch 75 (1673); Bird v. Hardwick, 1 Vern. 109 (1682); Afr. Co. v. Parish, 2 *id.* 244 (1691). See also Boyd v. United States, 116 U.S. 616 (1886), at p. 631. One reason why the question was late in arising in the law courts was that at common law there was ordinarily no process against papers, as is pointed out by Lord Camden in his opinion in Entick v. Carrington. In Chetwind v. Marnell, Excr., 1 Bos. and P. 271 (1798), however, we find Chief Justice Eyre refusing, in an action on a bond, to order the production of the instrument on the ground that it might be a means of convicting the party of a capital felony.
29. Both Boyd v. United States, above, and Counselman v. Hitchcock, 142 U.S. 547, are replete with invocations of the common law.
30. See notes immediately preceding.

latter it definitely brought within the Constitution the protection which is afforded by the common law to witnesses giving oral testimony; and in both
instances it projected into new territory the rules which it thus assimilated to the
Constitution.

Boyd v. United States, the earlier of the two cases, was decided in 1886,
nearly one hundred years after the adoption of the Constitution. The reason for
this long interval of apparent disuse of the self-incrimination clause is to be
found, without question, in the state of the common law as just reviewed, and the
injunction which the federal courts were under from Congress to base their
procedure on that law. During the vast portion of this period accused persons on
trial in the federal courts were excluded from taking the stand at all, while the test
which was applied to the immunities claimed by witnesses—not only in the
federal courts but in the state courts as well—was the direct test of the common
law.

But in Boyd v. United States a specific provision of an act of Congress was
involved, with the result that recourse against it to the common law, unsupported
by the Constitution, would have been futile. The question presented itself, therefore, whether the Constitution afforded such support. The provision referred to
enacted that in forfeiture proceedings brought under the revenue laws, the court
might issue a notice to defendants requiring the production in court of relevant
books and papers on pain of having taken for confessed the allegations of the
government as to their contents. In the lower federal courts even more drastic
provisions had been sustained as against objections based on the self-incrimination clause of Amendment V, on the ground that forfeiture proceedings, being *in
rem,* were not "criminal prosecutions"; and that even if they were, the clause
was meant to cover only oral testimony given under oath, not evidence afforded
by books and papers.[31] In Boyd v. United States the Supreme Court overruled
both these contentions.

The question whether the self-incrimination clause applied to what was virtually forced production in court by a person of his own private papers to be used
in evidence against himself, the Court answered unanimously in the affirmative.
A majority of the Court, however, felt it requisite to go further than this and
speaking through Justice Bradley, held that a judicial order of the kind involved
in the case was also an "unreasonable search and seizure" within the sense of
the Fourth Amendment.

In support of this line of reasoning Justice Bradley relied largely upon Lord
Camden's celebrated opinion in Entick v. Carrington, in which, in condemning
"general warrants" as contrary to the common law, Lord Camden pointed out
the facility which they afforded agents of government in the search for documen-

31. See especially in re Strouse, 1 Sawy. 605 (Fed. Cas. No. 13, 548); Stockwell v. United
States, 3 Clifford 284 (Fed. Cas. 13, 466); United States v. Hughes, 12 Blatch. 553 (Fed. Cas. 15,
417); United States v. Three Tons of Coal, 6 Bliss. 379 (Fed. Cas. No. 16, 515). Some of these and
others are discussed in 116 U.S., at pp. 635–38.

tary evidence—at that moment, on account of the persecution of Wilkes, a burning issue in England. ''The great end for which men entered into society,'' said Lord Camden, ''was to secure their property. That right is preserved sacred and incommunicable in all instances where it has not been taken away or abridged by some public law for the good of the whole. . . . Papers are the owner's goods and chattels; they are his dearest property; and are so far from enduring a seizure that they will hardly bear an inspection. . . . It is urged as an argument of utility, that such a search is a means of detecting offenders by discovering evidence. I wish some cases had been shown, where the law forceth evidence out of the owner's custody by process. There is no process against papers in civil actions. . . . In the criminal law such a proceeding was never heard of. . . . It is very certain that the law obligeth no man to accuse himself; because the necessary means of compelling self-accusation, falling upon the innocent as well as the guilty, would be both cruel and unjust; and it would seem, that search for evidence is disallowed upon the same principle. Then, too, the innocent would be confounded with the guilty.''

Reciting this language, Justice Bradley found the prohibition of the Fifth Amendment against self-incrimination to be auxiliary to a broader objective common to both the Fourth and Fifth Amendments, to wit, *''the personal security of the citizen,'' in his privacy.* Acts of the national government violative of this should accordingly be brought when possible to the simultaneous test of both amendments.

For some years this opinion encountered the strongly urged criticism that the greater part of it had been gratuitous. Indeed, there was a time when the Court itself seemed inclined to repudiate the somewhat recondite doctrine of the mutuality of the two amendments and to rest the decision in the Boyd case exclusively upon Amendment V.[32]

But in Weeks v. United States,[33] decided in 1914, the Court may be seen veering back toward its earlier position. In that case, while leaving in abeyance the question whether the Fourth and Fifth Amendments ''nearly run together,'' it held that the federal courts were under a direct mandate from the former amendment, whose provisions would otherwise be without effective sanction, to prevent the use of evidence which had been seized by federal agents in violation thereof; and in such recent cases as Gouled v. United States,[34] Carroll v. United States,[35] and Agnello v. United States,[36] the Court makes it fully apparent that it today regards the Boyd case as law of the land for all of its more important implications.

32. Cf. Adams v. New York, 192 U.S. 585 (1904); Hale v. Henkel, 201 U.S. 43 (1906); Wigmore, sections 2184 and 2264; Heywood v. United States, 268 Fed. 795 (1920).
33. 232 U.S. 383 (1914).
34. 255 U.S. 298.
35. 267 U.S. 132.
36. 269 U.S. 20.

Coming then to consider what is the operation of the two amendments upon one another in current constitutional law, we can at least venture the assertion that the following propositions have today the Court's adherence: *first,* a person may not be required by a federal court to produce his own papers or effects, there to be used as evidence against himself; *secondly,* a search warrant may not validly issue from a federal court for the purpose of enabling a federal agent to search a person's premises for papers or things which are solely of evidential value against such person; *thirdly,* papers or things which have been seized by an agent of the national government in violation of a person's rights under the Fourth Amendment may not, under the Fifth Amendment, be validly received in any federal court as evidence against such person; *fourthly,* an accused may obtain the exclusion of evidence falling under the ban of any of the above rules by seasonable application to the trial court.

Except for its extension to chattels in general, the first rule is adequately supported by the self-incrimination clause alone, when interpreted in the light of the common law. The third rule, on the contrary, is the direct outgrowth of the characterization in the Boyd case of the judicial order there involved, which was the equivalent of a *subpoena duces tecum,* as "an unreasonable search and seizure." It is because such a search warrant would be, in the first place, an invasion of the privacy deemed to be protected by the Fourth Amendment that it would, in the second place, fall under the condemnation of the Fifth Amendment. But it is in connection with the second of the above rules that the reciprocity of the two amendments, as well as the direct effect of Lord Camden's opinion, appears most strikingly. Considered *separately* neither amendment would seem to forbid such a search warrant, but read *in conjunction* they are held in some undemonstrated fashion to do so. The fourth rule evidently only implements the others.

Further consideration of the first rule: Most of the cases have arisen in connection with the first and third of the above rules. The principle which is mainly restrictive of the first is the principle that the immunity conferred by the self-incrimination clause is a purely personal one, from which the Court deduces the further limitation that the papers and effects which it covers must be the private property of the person claiming its protection, or must at least be in his possession, and in a purely private capacity.[37]

It follows that the clause may not be pleaded by an officer or agent of a corporation in behalf of the corporation;[38] nor even in his own behalf as respects papers or effects of the corporation which he holds in a representative capacity.[39]

37. In addition to the cases cited in the succeeding notes, see Schenck v. United States, 249 U.S. 47.

38. Hale v. Henkel, above; Essgee Co. of China v. United States, 262 U.S. 151.

39. Wilson v. United States, 221 U.S. 361, is the leading case. "An officer of a corporation is protected by the self-incrimination provision of the Fifth Amendment against compulsory production of his private books and papers, but this privilege does not extend to books of the corporation in his

It follows also that the owner is not protected against the forced production of papers by a third party into whose hands they have passed.[40] Furthermore, the papers and effects in relation to which the protection of the clause is invoked must be *private* as regards their evidential worth, a characterization which does not apply to papers and articles already in the custody of a court of the United States in consequence of their having been there used by the owner himself as evidence in an earlier proceeding.[41] Nor does the rule apply to the surrender by a bankrupt of his books and papers even though they may contain incriminating matter. "The books and papers of a bankrupt," the Court has said, "are a part of the bankrupt's estate. . . . To permit him to retain possession because surrender might involve disclosure of a crime would destroy a property right."[42]

Further consideration of the second rule: This rule today rests immediately upon Gouled v. United States,[43] decided early in 1921. Gouled had been convicted of conspiracy to defraud the United States and of misuse of the mails in connection with his scheme. Part of the evidence against him was supplied by certain papers which were taken from his office under two search warrants issued in conformity with an act of Congress.[44] In reviewing his conviction the circuit court of appeals certified the following question to the Supreme Court: "Are papers of no pecuniary value but possessing evidential value against persons presently suspected and subsequently indicted [for an offense against the United States] . . . when taken . . . from the house or office of the person so suspected, seized and taken in violation of the Fourth Amendment?" It also asked whether the admission in evidence of such papers against such person on his subsequent trial was violative of the Fifth Amendment. The Court answered both questions in the affirmative, it being "impossible to say on the record before us

---

possession. An officer of a corporation can not refuse to produce documents of a corporation on the ground that they would incriminate simply because he himself wrote or signed them, and this even if indictments are pending against him. Physical custody of incriminating documents does not protect the custodian against their compulsory production. The privilege which exists as to private papers can not be maintained." Headnote *id*. Justice McKenna dissented on the basis of the English cases, some of which were discussed above. This marked departure from the common law as it existed in 1789 may be due in part to the connection which exists between the Fourth and Fifth Amendments. If the prohibition against self-incrimination be alone considered, the English doctrine is certainly much more logical than that of Wilson v. United States. The emphasis, on the other hand, which the Fourth Amendment lends to the security of private papers furnishes a different point of view and outlook, one from which the holding in the case at bar becomes a not illogical outcome of the mergence of the two amendments. Reiterative of the doctrine of Wilson v. United States are Wheeler v. United States 226 U.S. 478; and Essgee Co. v. United States, note 38 above.

40. Burdeau v. McDowell, 256 U.S. 465. Here was sustained the right of the United States to use as evidence papers which had been stolen from {the} defendant and then turned over to officers of the government. This also is the English rule. Reg. v. Ringlake, 11 Cox 499; Wigmore, section 2270.

41. 247 U.S. 7.

42. McCarthy v. Arndstein, 266 U.S. 34, 41.

43. Cited note 34 above.

44. 40 Stat. 217, 218 (Act of June 15, 1917, c. 30).

45. 255 U.S. at pp. 309–11.

that the government had any interest in it [them?] other than as evidence against the accused.''[45]

While under the facts of the case this particular statement of the rule limits it to papers, the Court clearly regards it as extending to chattels generally, provided the other qualifications of the rule are met; namely, first, that the things involved were seized on the premises of the persons against whom they are subsequently offered in evidence; secondly, that they were solely of evidential value to the government. The rule, therefore, does not apply to things which are legal contraband, like liquors, narcotics, gambling implements, counterfeit coin, and stolen or forfeited goods. To such things the protection of the law does not extend; they are often properly seizable by agents of the government without a search warrant, and when so seized they may be used as evidence against the persons from whom taken.[46]

The question accordingly presents itself whether there is any general criterion of contraband articles? Referring in the Gouled case to a certain executed contract, the Court concedes that it "might be an important agency or instrumentality in the bribing of a public servant and perpetrating frauds upon the government, so that it [the government], would have a legitimate and important interest in seizing such a paper in order to prevent further frauds." On the other hand, in the later case of Marron v. United States[47] the Court sustained the right of governmental agents, in making a permitted arrest under the National Prohibition Act, to seize a ledger and bills for gas, electricity, water, and telephone, and inferentially their right to offer these in evidence against the persons arrested. The ledger, said the Court, was "a part of the outfit or equipment actually used to commit the offense," and the bills "were convenient, if not in fact necessary for the keeping of accounts."[48]

The final form of the second rule would, therefore, appear to be as follows: a search warrant may not validly issue from a federal court to enable a federal agent to search a person's premises for papers or articles which are solely of evidential value against such person; but this category does not include papers and articles which were instruments of the offense charged or which are capable of other mischievous use.

It is not without interest to observe that under this statement of the rule the invoice whose forced production gave rise to the Boyd case would today be subject to seizure under a proper search warrant, as the immediate instrument of the fraud upon the revenues there alleged. In brief, the precise holding in the Boyd case is today bad law.

Further consideration of the third rule:[49] The principal question to present

---

46. So recognized in Boyd v. United States, 116 U.S. at pp. 623–24.

47. Note 45 above.

48. 275 U.S. 192, 199.

49. The Gouled, Agnello, and Marron cases contain the best statements of this rule. See notes 34, 36, and 48 above.

itself under this rule is, When may searches and seizures be validly made under the Fourth Amendment without a search warrant? While it is not in connection solely with a search for evidence that this question may arise, in point of fact it has ordinarily so arisen ever since the Boyd case, and recently it has most frequently arisen in connection with efforts to enforce national prohibition.

Two groups of cases present themselves, the first of which clusters about Adams v. New York.[50] In this case plaintiff in error contended on the basis of Boyd v. United States, that the introduction in evidence against himself of private papers which had been taken from his possession in the course of a valid search under warrant for gambling instruments forced him to incriminate himself contrary to the Fifth and Fourteenth Amendments. The Court, waiving the question whether protection against self-incrimination is a part of that "due process of law" which by the Fourteenth Amendment is required of the states, construed the Boyd decision as applying only in cases of direct testimonial compulsion upon an accused; and also ruled, in reliance on Commonwealth v. Dana,[51] a Massachusetts case decided in 1841, that a trial court is not obliged to inquire into the means whereby agents of government have obtained otherwise competent evidence.

In both these respects the Adams case must be today regarded as having been substantially overruled. The case is still, nevertheless, authority for the proposition that the implements or fruits of a suspected crime may be seized in connection with the valid arrest of the supposed criminal, and so may be subsequently introduced in evidence against him; and as we saw above, the term "implements of the crime" has been held to extend in some instances to books and papers. But private letters and diaries having no other relation to the crime than as records of it obviously would not fall within the term. If such papers may ever be validly used against the offender from whose possession they were taken they must have been found on his person at the time of his arrest.[52]

The leading case of the second group just referred to is Carroll v. United States.[53] Carroll and another had been convicted of transporting liquor contrary to the National Prohibition Act, partly through the admission in evidence against them of some of the liquor in question, which had been taken from their automobile by federal officers operating without a search warrant. To the objection that this was an "unreasonable search and seizure" the Court answered that in such a case the Fourth Amendment does not require a search warrant, but only that the officers making the search should have "probable cause," that is to say, "belief reasonably arising out of circumstances known to" them, "that the automobile or other vehicle contains that which by law is subject to seizure and

50. See note 32 above.
51. 2 Met. 329.
52. For federal and state cases bearing on the subject, see O. L. Cornelius, *The Law of Search and Seizure* (1926) section 36 and notes. Cf. the Agnello and Marron cases; also Cooley, *Const'l Lims.* (7th ed.) 432.
53. See note 35 above.

destruction." Speaking for the Court, Chief Justice Taft pointed out that Congress, while providing in the National Prohibition Act that "no search warrant shall issue to search any private dwelling occupied as such unless it is being used for the unlawful sale of intoxicating liquor, or unless it is in part used for some business purpose," had advisedly excluded a similar provision to govern searches of vehicles. He showed further that earlier congressional legislation abounded in similar provisions, "recognizing a necessary difference between a search of a store, dwelling house, or other structure, in respect of which a proper official warrant readily may be obtained, and a search of a ship, motor boat, wagon, or automobile for contraband goods, where it is not practical to secure a warrant because the vehicle can be quickly moved out of the locality or jurisdiction in which the warrant must be sought." Finally, he asserted, on the basis of an extensive review of the facts which were known to the federal officers when they searched Carroll's car, that these facts and circumstances were such as to constitute the required "probable cause."

Two clear implications of the doctrine here laid down should not be missed. In the first place, the fact upon which a "probable cause" justifying a search for contraband articles is based must be known to the officers undertaking the search *before* they commence it. In the words of a subsequent case: "A search prosecuted in violation of the Constitution is not made lawful by what it brings to light."[54] Again contraband articles may not, any more than articles in which complete property rights exist, be offered in evidence against an accused from whom they were obtained in violation of his rights under the Fourth Amendment. Thus, the third rule stated above, in contrast to the second, applies equally in the case of contraband articles and in that of "effects" to which the full protection of the law extends.[55]

An important question which the Carroll case leaves open, and one on which there has been considerable speculation, is whether a dwelling-house may ever be searched without a warrant. In the later Agnello case the Court says: "The search of a private dwelling without a warrant is, in itself unreasonable and abhorrent to our laws."[56] Yet the same case admits an exception to this statement in its recognition of the right of officials to seize the proofs or implements of a crime in connection with the arrest of an offender taken in the act.[57] A distinction should, it appears, be noted in this connection between a *search* and a *seizure*. To require an officer who saw contraband openly displayed in the window of a dwelling-house to obtain a warrant before venturing to effect a *seizure* of the same would be absurd, and would moreover be contradictory of the common law rule just alluded to as governing arrests.[58] A *search,* on the con-

54. Byars v. United States, 273 U.S. 28, 29.
55. See note 49 above. Also, Amos v. United States, 255 U.S. 313.
56. 269 U.S. at p. 32.
57. *Id.* p. 30.
58. United States v. Daison, 288 Fed. 199, and the cases there collected support this view.

trary, of itself, confesses an uncertainty still needing to be cleared up. The correct answer to our question would, therefore, seem to be this: Where search of a purely private dwelling, one not used for business purposes of any sort, is justified by "probable cause" only, this must be first passed upon by a magistrate in connection with an application for a search warrant, within the terms of the Fourth Amendment.

But does the same rule apply to all immobile structures? The language of the chief justice in the Carroll case suggests an affirmative answer; but it is contradicted by the weight of authority, by the very provision which Chief Justice Taft himself quotes from the National Prohibition Act, and indeed by the wording of the Fourth Amendment. As is pointed out by the Court in Hester v. United States,[59] where a trespass by officers upon open fields was held not to fall with the amendment, the amendment reflects the special concern of the common law for the security of the dwelling, a concern which was early summed up in the maxim that "every man's house is his castle."[60]

The following cases of seizure by United States agents operating without search warrants have been held violative of the Fourth Amendment, with the result that the things seized were not under the Fifth Amendment receivable in evidence against the party whose rights were invaded by the seizure: the obtaining by stealth of letters from the home of an accused during his absence;[61] the removal of liquors in similar circumstances;[62] the seizure of narcotics at the home of one of several conspirators, following their arrest at the home of another some distance away;[63] the procurement through stealth from the office of a suspect of a paper having evidential value only.[64] And a search warrant calling for the seizure of one thing will not authorize the seizure of something else;[65] nor is a warrant resting merely on affiant's "belief" based on the "probable cause" which is required by the Constitution.[66]

Two cases of a somewhat special type are ex parte Jackson[67] and Olmstead v. United States.[68] In the former the Court held the protection of the Fourth Amendment to extend to letters and sealed packages in the custody of the national government for the purpose of forwarding them as mail. "Whilst in the mail," said the Court, "they can only be opened and examined under like

59. 265 U.S. 57, 58.

60. The distinction made in the National Prohibition Act between private dwellings "occupied as such" and those "in part used for some business purpose" (October 28, 1919, c. 85. Title II, section 25) is to be found in substance in the statutes of most of the states. Cornelius, *op. cit.*, p. 342. See also 4 Bl. *Comm.* 223, 225, 226; Cooley, *op. cit.* (2d ed.) 22, 299; and note 56 above.

61. Weeks v. United States, above.

62. Amos v. United States, above.

63. Agnello v. Unites States, above.

64. Gouled v. United States, above.

65. Marron v. United States, above.

66. Byars v. United States, above.

67. 96 U.S. 727.

warrant . . . as is required when papers are subjected to search in one's own household.''[69]

Relying on this piece of judicial legislation, plaintiffs in error in the Olmstead case, who had been engaged in bootlegging on a large scale, protested against the use as evidence against them of information which had been obtained by agents of the national government through tapping their telephone wires off their premises and ''listening in'' on their conversations. A narrowly divided Court held that the Jackson case was distinguishable and that the Fourth Amendment did not apply.

The position of the minority on the constitutional issue is indicated in the following passage from Justice Butler's opinion. After stressing the importance nowadays of the telephone as a means of communication, often confidential, he said: ''This Court has always construed the Constitution in the light of the principles upon which it was founded. The operation or literal meaning of the words used do not measure the purpose or scope of its provisions. Under the principles established and applied by this Court, the Fourth Amendment safeguards against all evils that are like or equivalent to those embraced within the ordinary meaning of its words. That construction is consonant with sound reason and in full accord with the course of decision since McCulloch v. Maryland. That is the principle directly applied in the Boyd case.''[70]

Against Justice Butler's broad constructionism, the chief justice speaking for the majority, pitted narrow construction. ''The Amendment itself,'' said he, ''shows that the search is to be of material things . . . the person, the house, his papers or his effects. The description of the warrant necessary to make the proceeding lawful is that it must specify the place to be searched and the person or *things* to be seized.'' He added that, while ''Congress may, of course, protect the secrecy of telephone messages by making them, when intercepted, inadmissible in evidence in federal criminal trials by direct legislation, and thus depart from the common law of evidence. . . . the courts may not adopt such a policy by attributing an enlarged and unusual meaning to the Fourth Amendment.''[71]

While in view of the actual course that interpretation of the amendment has generally taken in recent decades, these words leave something to be desired in the way of candor, yet the overwhelming difficulties that today confront government in the detection of crime serve readily to vindicate them on the score of policy in a case in which the Court had a clear choice of alternatives.

The question finally presents itself, When is a search one *by the national government,* with the result that it falls within the purview of the Fourth Amend-

68. 277 U.S. 438.
69. 96 U.S. at p. 733.
70. 277 U.S. at pp. 487–88. Holmes, J., dissenting, refused to commit himself on the constitutional issue.
71. *Id.* at p. 464.

ment? In the case of Burdeau v. McDowell[72] the Court held that the United States might retain for use as evidence in the criminal prosecution of their owner, incriminating documents which had been turned over to it by private persons who had stolen them, there having been no participation or guilty knowledge of the theft on the part of government officials. In the later Byars and Gambino cases,[73] on the other hand, evidence which had been obtained through wrongful search and seizure by state officers acting in cooperation with federal officers was ruled to be inadmissible. The test, therefore, is whether there was actual participation by an officer or agent of the national government in the enterprise whereby the evidence was first obtained from the one against whom it was subsequently offered, a question of fact, but one for the Court.[74]

Nor does the Fourth Amendment regulate solely searches and seizures by the *executive* agents of the national government; it also controls, as is indicated by the Boyd case, the courts directly in their efforts to obtain evidence through the *subpoena duces tecum* or equivalent process.

In the cases illustrating this point, corporations were generally the defendant parties. For while a corporation cannot claim the immunity created by the self-incrimination clause, which confers only a personal immunity upon the agents through whom the corporation must necessarily give testimony, the corporation itself is entitled to immunity under the Fourth Amendment from unreasonable searches and seizures. Consequently it was not contempt for an officer of a corporation to refuse to produce the books and papers thereof in response to a subpoena which was based on knowledge obtained through an original illegal seizure of the books and papers in question.[75] Also, a *subpoena duces tecum* requiring the production of practically all the books and papers of a corporation was held void, no such sweeping examination of the corporation's books and papers having been definitely authorized under any act of Congress.[76] Indeed, nothing "short of the most explicit language" will induce the Court to attribute to Congress an intention to authorize a federal agency to compel a company to produce all of its books and papers in the mere hope of thus finding something against the company. Not only would such a search, say the Court, violate "the first principles of justice"; it would also transgress "the analogies of the law," which require that a party calling for documents first show some ground for believing that they contain relevant evidence.[77]

That, nevertheless, Congress possesses broad visitorial powers over all corporations engaged in interstate commerce has been repeatedly admitted, as well as

72. See note 40 above.
73. 273 U.S. 28; 275 U.S. 310.
74. The cases just cited show, too, that the Court will go into this question with some care.
75. Silverthorne Lumber Co. v. United States, 251 U.S. 385.
76. Hale v. Henkel, note 32 above.
77. Fed. Trade Com's'n v. Am. Tobac. Co., 264 U.S. 298.

that such powers may be delegated to administrative bodies, like the Interstate Commerce Commission and the Federal Trade Commission.[78]

Further consideration of the fourth rule above: In the Adams case[79] the Court, following the early Massachusetts case of Commonwealth v. Dana,[80] held that an accused was not entitled after the commencement of his trial to raise the question whether some of the evidence against him had been obtained in violation of his rights under the Fourth Amendment. In the Weeks case,[81] however, it ruled that where the accused had petitioned the trial court before his trial came on for the return of books and papers which had been taken from him contrary to the Fourth Amendment, the petition was seasonable and should have been granted, and that the admission in evidence against the accused of such books and papers constituted reversible error. Finally, in the Gouled and Amos cases[82] the ruling in the Adams case becomes confined practically to cases in which the accused has been evidently negligent in the assertion of his rights. "A rule of practice," it is said in the former case, "must not be allowed for any technical reason to prevail over a constitutional right."[83]

The Court accordingly held that "where, in the progress of a trial, it becomes probable that there has been an unconstitutional seizure of papers," it is the duty of the trial court, on objection raised by the accused, to decide the constitutional issue presented and this even though the court had earlier rejected a motion to return the papers. In the Amos case a substantially similar ruling was made with reference to liquor illegally seized.

III

The second pivotal decision of the Court in construction of the self-incrimination clause is that in Counselman v. Hitchcock,[84] decided in 1892. An advantageous approach to it is furnished by certain earlier state and federal court decisions applying the common law regarding the privilege of witnesses.

The most notable case of this nature in this early period was the trial, in 1807, of Aaron Burr for treason.[85] Willie, secretary to Burr, was asked if he understood the contents of a certain cipher letter, in his own hand, which was alleged to have been sent by Burr to an associate. By attorney Willie objected to answer on the ground that "counsel for prosecution might go on gradually from one question to another until at last he had obtained enough matter to incriminate the

78. Cases just cited; also I.C.C. v. Baird, 194 U.S. 25.
79. Note 32 above.
80. Note 51 above.
81. Note 33 above.
82. Notes 34 and 55 above.
83. 255 U.S. at p. 313.
84. 142 U.S. 547 (1892).
85. See Robertson, *Reports of the Trials of Aaron Burr,* etc. (2 vols., Phila., 1808).

witness,'' in this instance, of misprision of treason. It was agreed on both sides ''that a witness cannot be made to incriminate himself''; but it was argued on the part of the government, first, that Willie's claim of privilege rested solely on his own say-so; and secondly, that an answer to be excused under the privilege, must be incriminating in itself. Chief Justice Marshall ruled that if an answer *can*, in the judgment of the Court, incriminate a witness, the witness alone may say, ''under oath, that his answer *would* incriminate him''; also that ''if such an answer *may* disclose a fact which forms a necessary and essential link in the chain of testimony, which would be sufficient to convict him of any crime,'' the immunity must be accorded him. He held, nonetheless, that since the question related only to Willie's present knowledge of the letter, it could be safely answered.[86]

It is to be noted that, except for an unsupported allegation by Burr's attorney that the letter had ''perhaps'' been ''filched from the post office contrary to the eighth [*sic*] amendment of the Constitution, which protects every man's papers from unreasonable searches and seizures,''[87] a point which went unnoticed by the court, the discussion proceeded throughout simply on the basis of the common law and without allusion to the Constitution.

And the same situation reappears in the state courts. There, too, till shortly before the Civil War, the cases involving the privilege of witnesses seem to have been decided mainly on the basis of the common law, or even without reference to the constitutional clauses that would be today invoked. The common law rule was, on the other hand, in the general absence of unfavorable legislation, given its most liberal extension. The immunity was ordinarily held to apply not only to questions tending to incriminate the witness, but also to questions tending to degrade him. The witness's oath was, furthermore, generally conceded to be determinative of the validity of his claim unless the court could say that by no possibility could an answer to the challenged question produce the forbidden result. Finally, these cases show the extension of the privilege from criminal to civil cases taking place virtually without comment, which again testifies to the dominance of common law conceptions in discussion of the privilege.[88]

Clear and direct invocation by counsel of the constitutional provision, in the

86. 1 *id.* 193 (where authorities are cited), 218, 219, 244–45.

87. *Id.* 207. It seems to have been assumed that Burr's own papers, then in the possession of Wilkinson, would be valid evidence against him before the grand jury and on his trial. *Id.* 200.

88. In Comm. v. Gibbs, 3 Yeates (Pa.) 429 (1902), the point in issue was the right of election inspectors to put would-be voters a question bearing on their patriotism during the Revolution. While counsel invoked the state constitutional provision against self-incrimination, the court, in sustaining the objection to the question, rested its decision upon ''an established principle of law,'' quoting the maxim ''*nemo tenetur.*'' It added: the sense of these words ''is not confined to cases where the answers to the questions proposed would induce to the punishment of the party; if they would involve him in shame or reproach, he is under no obligation to answer them''; and in Galbraith et al. v. Eichelberger, 3 *id.* 515, a like ruling was laid down respecting a witness in a civil case. In People v. Herrick, 13 Johns. (N.Y.) 82 (1817), Judge Spencer held to the same effect, citing Cook's Trial, Salk. 153 (1696). In Grannis v. Branden, 5 Day (Conn.) 260 (1812), it was held, on a motion for a new trial, in an action on the case, that a certain witness need not testify whether he had conversed

form in which it usually appears in the state constitutions, occurred in cases arising in Arkansas and Georgia, in 1853;[89] while four years later a similar case arose in California,[90] to be followed in 1860 and 1861 by the case of Wilkins v. Malone in Indiana and that of People v. Kelly in New York.[91] All these cases agree in showing that the common law privilege of witnesses had been in greater or less measure recognized by the legislatures of the states concerned; while at the same time, all of them except the Wilkins case show the courts speaking to be still in considerable doubt whether the privilege rested on a constitutional basis. In the decision of the Indiana Supreme Court in the Wilkins case, these doubts disappear, and the constitutional clause is, for the first time, clearly held to protect the witness in a civil suit from giving an answer which could be produced in evidence against him in a subsequent criminal prosecution. On the other hand, it was ruled to be no objection to an answer which was not itself a link in a chain of incriminating evidence, that it might uncover other sources of such evidence—a view which was concurred in by the New York court of appeals in the Kelly case.

Then in 1871, the decision of the Massachusetts supreme judicial court was handed down in Emery's case,[92] where was involved a claim to the constitutional privilege by a witness before a joint committee of inquiry of the Massachusetts house and senate. The Massachusetts court held that the provision of the Massachusetts constitution, that no subject shall be "compelled to accuse or furnish evidence against himself," extended "to all investigations of an inquistorial nature, instituted for the purpose of discovering crime or the perpetrators of crime"; and furthermore that it protected "a person from being compelled to disclose the sources from which or the means by which evidence" against him might be obtained "without using his answers as direct admissions against him." Seven years later, in State v. Nowell, the supreme court of New Hampshire reached a like result on the basis of a similarly worded constitutional provision.[93]

---

with a juror in the original action, as this would expose him to a criminal prosecution. Said the court: "The witness alone can know what his answer will be; and he only can determine how it may affect or expose him." Cook v. Corn, 1 Overt. (Tenn.) 340 (1808) contains a reference to the state constitution, which, it is said, was intended for criminal cases; "but," the court adds, "we think the principle existed before the constitution." The case illustrates the amalgamation of the common law rule "*nemo debet esse testis in propria causa*" with the constitutional clause. A case much out of the ordinary is that of State v. Douglass, 1 Mo. 527 (1825), where it was held, in face of the usual constitutional clause protecting an "*accused*" from giving evidence against himself, that a *witness* was bound to testify, although he stood indicted for the same offense as the person on trial, and although he protested that his testimony would lead to his own conviction. These and other cases to the year 1846 can be traced through the *United States Digest* (and Supplement) (5 vols.; Boston, 1860; rev. ed.), under "Witness." Annual volumes continue the *Digest* to 1869.

89. State v. Quarles, 13 Ark. 307 (1853); Higdom v. Heard, 14 Ga. 255 (1853).

90. Ex parte Rome, 7 Cal. 184 (1857).

91. 14 Ind. 152 (1860); 24 N.Y. 74 (1861).

92. 107 Mass. 172 (1871).

93. 58 N.H. 314 (1878). Cf. Reg. v. Leatham, 3 E & E 658 (1861), for contrary doctrine.

We are thus brought to consider Counselman v. Hitchcock directly. This case arose out of a grand jury investigation which had been instituted by the then recently created Interstate Commerce Commission, into certain alleged violations by railroads of the statutes regulating interstate commerce. The inquiry was admittedly governed by section 860 of the Revised Statutes, originally enacted in 1868, which provided that no "discovery of evidence obtained from a party or a witness by means of a judicial proceeding" here or abroad "shall be given in evidence, or in any manner used against him or his property in any court of the United States, in any criminal proceeding, or for the enforcement of any penalty or forfeiture."[94] In the face of these sweeping provisions Counselman, relying on the Emery case, urged his constitutional privilege.

In the circuit court this contention fared badly. Judge Gresham was inclined to doubt whether Amendment V was intended for the protection of other than accused persons, citing the Boyd case; but if it was, then section 860 amply met the purpose of the provision, which was intended "not to shield men from the consequences of their crimes, but that they might not be obliged to furnish evidence of their own guilt." The objection therefore that the answer required of Counselman, although it could not be used as evidence against him in a subsequent proceeding, might nonetheless open up to the government other sources of evidence of his guilt was impertinent. Suppose, said the court, a man to have confessed under duress: the evidence can not be used against him; but if anyone saw him commit the crime, he may testify, even though the witness's identity was first revealed by the confession of the culprit himself.[95]

The Supreme Court, nevertheless, sustained Counselman. The deviation of phraseology in the Massachusetts constitution respecting self-incrimination from that of the usual form of the clause was found to be immaterial. It followed that section 860 was insufficient to meet the purpose of the clause as it occurs in Amendment V. "No statute," said the Court, "which leaves the party or witness subject to prosecution after he answers the incriminating question put to him can have the effect of supplanting the privilege conferred by the Constitution of the United States."[96]

But while, on the one hand, broadening the common law privilege of witnesses—and this at the moment of engrafting it on the Constitution—Counselman v. Hitchcock, on the other hand, contained an implication that might have distinctly narrowed the privilege as it exists at common law. The allusion is to the fact that in both this and the Emery case the court speaking was at pains to point out that the inquiry involved was for the purpose of discovering whether a *crime* had been committed.[97] The inference is that the privilege of witnesses, like that of accused

94. This provision was repealed by the Act of May 7, 1910, c. 216 (36 Stat. 352).

95. 44 Fed. 268 (1890).

96. 142 U.S. at pp. 585–86.

97. "The matter under investigation by the grand jury in this case was a criminal matter. . . . The case before the grand jury was, therefore, a criminal case." *Id.* 562.

persons, is confined to cases of a criminal nature actually under way. Such a theory is plainly at variance with the fundamental reason for ever conceding the privilege to witnesses as such, namely, that they may be subjected to *future* criminal proceedings directed against themselves in consequence of statements made under legal compulsion as witnesses. From this point of view it obviously makes no difference whether the proceeding in which the witness pleads his privilege is "civil" or "criminal," or what not, so long as his answer may threaten to start a "criminal case" against him.

Notwithstanding which, we find ordinarily well-read counsel arguing for the government as late as 1924 that the protection of the amendment "does not extend to examination in civil proceedings but is expressly confined to examination in criminal cases." The Court rejected the contention in these words: "The privilege is not ordinarily dependent upon the nature of the proceeding in which the testimony is sought or is to be used. It applies alike to civil and criminal proceedings wherever the answer might tend to subject to criminal responsibility him who gives it."[98] Strangely enough, Counselman v. Hitchcock is the case which the Court chose to cite in support of this statement. It is, however, amply confirmed by federal, state, and English cases, and is unquestionably the established rule.

Following the decision in the Counselman case, Congress passed its first "immunity statute," to govern investigations by the Interstate Commerce Commission. The measure provides that "no person shall be prosecuted or subjected to any penalty or forfeiture for or on account of any transaction, matter, or thing concerning which he may testify or procure evidence, documentary or otherwise, before said commission, or in obedience to its subpoena."[99]

In Brown v. Walker[100] the constitutionality of this provision was sustained by a closely divided Court. The minority argued that the immunity conferred by the Constitution upon witnesses was an immunity from testifying in certain con-

---

98. McCarthy v. Arndstein, 266 U.S. 34, 35, 40 (1924). Deportation proceedings are "civil"; but the privilege against self-incrimination is recognized in them. United States ex rel. Bilokumsky v. Tod, 263 U.S. 149; United States ex rel. Vajtauer v. Com'r of Im., 273 U.S. 103.

99. Act of February 19, 1903, c. 708, section 3 (32 Stat. 848). A like provision was adopted six days later in supplement of the Sherman Act. Act of February 25, 1903, c. 755 section 1 (32 Stat. 904). The Federal Trade Commission Act has a similar provision, limited, however, to "natural persons" (cf. Hale v. Henkel, note 32 above). Act of September 26, 1914, c. 311, section 9 (38 Stat. 722). So also of the China Trade Act of September 19, 1922, c. 346, section 15 (42 Stat. 853). Those "immunity statutes" are uniformly qualified by the proviso that the immunity they create shall not extend to punishment for perjury committed while testifying in compliance with them. The justification of this exception is the simple but conclusive one that the power to compel the giving of testimony includes the power to punish the giving of false testimony. This being so, says the Court, "The immunity afforded by the constitutional guarantee relates to the past and does not endow the person who testifies with a license to commit perjury." Glickstein v. United States, 222 U.S. 139, 141–42; Cameron v. United States, 231 U.S. 710. Only "involuntary" witnesses are covered by the immunity statutes, and they must claim their constitutional privilege; also the matters testified about must be more than remotely connected with the crimes for which immunity is granted. See generally Heike v. United States, 227 U.S. 131.

100. 161 U.S. 591.

tingencies, not an immunity from prosecution in consequence of so testifying, and that the latter was, in fact, no adequate substitute for the former. Thus, if a prosecution was instituted in the face of the act of Congress, it might be difficult or even impossible for the defendant to produce evidence showing that the act barred it, and at any rate he would have been put to expense. Again, the immunity conferred by the act was only from prosecution by the national government, not prosecution by a state or by a foreign government. And finally, Justice Field contended that it was the intention of the constitutional clause to save the witness, not merely from criminal prosecution, but from the disgrace that he might incur by his answers.

The first of these apprehensions seems not to have been realized, and this notwithstanding that the measure involved in Brown v. Walker has been succeeded by a number of similar measures to facilitate prosecutions and investigations under national authority.[101] As to Justice Field's objection, it is clear that it represented what by that date had become a generally discarded view of the scope of the testimonial privilege. The objection based on the possibility of state authorities taking advantage of testimony given in the federal courts is more pauseworthy.

The majority opinion in Brown v. Walker contended that the statutory provision under review was broad enough to control the state courts, and that it did so; but no later case appears to have repeated the suggestion.[102] The true answer to the minority's argument is clearly that the constitutional protection granted by the Fifth Amendment is solely against proceedings instituted by the national government.[103] This is today recognized to be the case so far as the double

101. Note 99 above. Cf. Sherwin v. United States, 268 U.S. 369.

102. The contention is supported by citation of Stewart v. Kahn, 11 Wall. 493, United States v. Wiley, *id.* 508, and Mayfield v. Richards, 115 U.S. 137, which, however, were based on the war powers of the national government, not on a general power to control proceedings in the state courts. 161 U.S. at pp. 606 and 622–25.

103. The leading case is, of course, Barron v. Baltimore, 7 Pet. 243, where, in dealing with the provision in the Fifth Amendment requiring just compensation for property taken for public use, Chief Justice Marshall said: "The Fifth Amendment must be understood as restraining the power of the general government, not as applicable to the states. . . . We are of opinion that the provision . . . is intended solely as a limitation on the exercise of power by the government of the United States, and is not applicable to the legislation of the states." *Id.* 247. In Ballmann v. Fagin, 200 U.S. 187, the Court, in sustaining Ballmann's claim of right to refuse to produce certain account books, on the ground that they might have shown him to be guilty of a misdemeanor under Rev. Stat. section 5209, also pointed out that he was liable to prosecution under the criminal law of Ohio, the state in which the grand jury was sitting. "According to United States v. Saline Bank, 1 Pet. 100," says Holmes, J., in his opinion, "he was exonerated from disclosures which would have exposed him to the penalties of state law." United States v. Saline Bank, however, was a bill in equity for a discovery and relief, closely analogous to Penrice v. Parker, Finch 75 (1673), mentioned in an earlier note. The prosecution was under the law of the state of Virginia, and the federal court was simply administering state law. No question regarding prosecution under another authority was involved in the remotest way. Such uncertainty as the Ballmann case momentarily created was dispersed a few months later in Hale v. Hankel {*sic*; Henkel?}, above, where, in dealing again with the objection raised in Brown v. Walker, the Court met the issue frankly, saying: "If the argument were a sound one it might be carried still further and held to apply not only to state prosecutions within the same jurisdiction, but to prosecutions under the criminal laws of other states to which the witness might

jeopardy clause of Amendment V is concerned, when the same act is an offense against both the national government and a state,[104] and there is plainly no reason why the same principle should not hold in regard to the self-incrimination clause. What bearing the Fourteenth Amendment may have on the question is discussed below.

IV

As was pointed out previously, the privilege of witnesses called to the stand is simply a privilege to refuse to answer specific questions on the ground that to do so would tend to expose the witness to a criminal prosecution. The privilege must, therefore, be claimed in each instance, and by the witness himself, and must in each instance be passed upon by the court—the witness is not the final judge.[105] Also, while the claim must relate to a past act, it must not be one that is so long past that under the statute of limitations the witness is no longer subject to prosecution on account of it.[106]

Nor does the privilege relate to an act for which the witness has been guaranteed immunity from prosecution,[107] or pardoned,[108] or, apparently, even tendered a pardon. For whereas a pardon was formerly regarded as akin to a deed, acceptance of which is necessary to validate it,[109] a recent decision proceeds on the principle that it is a public act based on considerations, not of personal leniency, but of public policy,[110] from which it would seem reasonably to follow that the court should take judicial notice of the availability of a presidential pardon, and hold its rejection by a witness to be tantamount to a voluntary waiver of his privilege.[111]

---

have subjected himself. The question has been fully considered in England, and the conclusion reached by the courts of that country that the only danger to be considered is one arising within the same jurisdiction and under the same sovereignty," citing Queen v. Boyes, 1 B. & S. 311; King of the Two Sicilies v. Willcox, 7 St. Tr. (N.S.) 1049, 1068; State v. March, 1 Jones (N.C.) 526; State v. Thomas, 98 N.C. 599. The matter is further discussed below.

104. See Lanza v. United States, 260 U.S. 377, and cases there given.

105. Brown v. United States, 276 U.S. 134. See also United States v. Burr, note 86 above; ex parte Irvine, 74 Fed. 954, 960; Brown v. Walker, 161 U.S. at p. 599, giving the English view.

106. 161 U.S. at p. 598, where English and American state cases are given. "The criminality provided against is a present, not a past criminality, which lingers only as a memory and involves no present danger of prosecution." Hale v. Henkel, 201 U.S. 43, 67.

107. See pp. —— {sic} above.

108. 161 U.S. at p. 598, discussing the English cases.

109. United States v. Wilson, 7 Pet. 150; Burdick v. United States, 236 U.S. 79.

110. Biddle v. Perovich, 274 U.S. 480.

111. The argument for the Court's recognizing the pardon involved in Burdick v. United States was strengthened by the fact that it was accompanied by a presidential proclamation. The opinion of the Court in that case approaches the limit of judicial pedantry. Preceding the Perovich case was the Gerald Chapman case, in which a notorious gunman and murderer appealed to the Court against the action of President Coolidge in "commuting" his sentence to Atlanta prison—from which Chapman had earlier affected {sic; effected?} his escape—in order to enable the state of Connecticut to hang him for crimes committed within its jurisdiction. Chapman was executed while the appeal was pending, but his argument was unanswerable on the basis of the Burdick case. The Perovich case thus enabled the Court to shape up a sort of *ex post facto* justification of Chapman's execution.

The immediate personal privilege of an accused is much more extensive—it is the privilege to refuse to take the stand at all; but again the privilege is waivable; and if the accused does take the stand to testify in his own behalf, he must submit to be cross-examined on his statement.[112]

With respect to the evidence supplied by "papers and effects," witness and accused stand more nearly on a level, since their protection is forthcoming to a great extent, as we have seen, from the Fourth Amendment. There is, nevertheless, one difference: an accused may not be required judicially to produce *any* evidence bearing on his prosecution; while a witness is at all times liable to be ordered to produce documents and other things having evidential value, and he can avoid doing so only by claiming his privilege in court and having it conceded.[113]

The important question arises whether the refusal of an accused to take the stand in his own behalf may be drawn especially to the attention of the jury by the prosecution or the court? An English statute forbids the former to comment upon the fact, but is held not to disable the latter from doing so.[114] A widely entertained view among the states is that the court also has no such right;[115] but it is highly doubtful if the Supreme Court regards this doctrine as sanctioned by the Constitution.

The most direct expression of the Court on the point is by way of a dictum in Twining v. New Jersey.[116] New Jersey is one of the two states of the Union—the other being Iowa—which has no self-incrimination clause in its constitution, although in both these states the privilege against self-incrimination exists on the basis of common law. The trial court in Twining's case instructed the jury that they were free to take account of the failure of accused to testify, and the state appeal court held this instruction not to violate Twining's privilege. Before the Supreme Court Twining's reliance was mainly on the contention that this curtailment of his privilege had violated the due process of law clause of Amendment XIV. First holding that the privilege against self-incrimination was no element of the due process of law which is required by the Fourteenth Amendment, the prevailing opinion of the Court then added: "We have assumed only for the

112. 161 U.S. at pp. 597–98, where English and state cases are collected; Reagan v. United States, 157 U.S. 301; Powers v. United States, 223 U.S. 303. There is an implication to the contrary in Cooley, *Const'l Lims.* (2d ed.), 317, but it is not sound law today.

113. Note 105 above.

114. The English Criminal Evidence Act, 1898, section 1, in making "every person charged with an offense . . . a competent witness for the defense," provides further that "a person so charged shall not be called as a witness . . . except upon his own application; the failure of any person charged with an offense . . . to give evidence shall not be made the subject of any comment by the prosecution." This was held in Queen v. Rhodes [1899] 1 Q. B. 77, not to deprive the court of the right to comment on the point. The phrase used in the act of Congress is "shall not create any presumption against him." Note 22 above.

115. See cases cited in 149 U.S. at p. 63; and in 211 U.S. at pp. 83–84, 114; Wigmore, sections 488 and 2272.

116. 211 U.S. 78.

purpose of discussion that what was done in the case at bar was an infringement of the privilege against self-incrimination. We do not intend, however, to lend any countenance to the truth of that assumption. The courts of New Jersey in adopting the rule of law which is complained of here, deemed it consistent with the privilege itself and not a denial of it. . . . The authorities upon the question are in conflict."[117] In view of this language the point should unquestionably be regarded as still an open one under the United States Constitution.

The confession of an accused may not be introduced in evidence against him if it was induced by threat or promise, or if it was obtained by compulsion, a rule which is the modern expression of the illegality of torture at the common law; and the Court has shown its intention of sifting the facts of each case with solicitude for the constitutional rights of the accused.[118] But while, in the words of the Court, "the prohibition of compelling a man in a criminal court to be a witness against himself is a prohibition of physical or moral compulsion to extort communications from him," it does not require "an exclusion of his body as evidence when it may be material,"[119] and the same view appears to have been followed in the majority of instances in the state courts.[120] Indeed, the generally accepted principle that what is seized on the person of a prisoner at the time of his arrest is valid evidence against him would seem logically to extend to the person itself. Also while testimonial evidence extorted by force would be apt to be unreliable, a physical fact, like the size of the prisoner's foot or the distinctive pattern of his fingerprints, would not be susceptible to such alteration or distortion.

It has already been pointed out that the self-incrimination clause of Amendment V, of its own independent force, reaches only evidence required under national authority. Furthermore, since the repeal in 1910 of section 860 of the Revised Statutes there has been no statutory provision forbidding the use in prosecutions instituted by the national government of evidence obtained in state or foreign courts.[121] Nor apparently does the due process clause of Amendment V stand in the way of such a result. A case in point is Jack v. Kansas,[122] in which it was held that "the fact that an immunity granted to a witness under a state

---

117. *Id.* at p. 114.
118. Bram v. United States, 168 U.S. 1; Wan v. United States, 266 U.S. 1. For a moving recital of police torture and "third degree" methods, see the latter case. *Vd.* also 1 Stephen, 447.
119. Holt v. United States, 218 U.S. 245, 252–53.
120. See an excellent article by A. L. Moffat, on "Taking Finger Prints upon Arrest," in *Am. Bar Assoc. Journal,* March 1926, pp. 175–77. I have seen quoted what purported to be a maxim, *"Confessio nominis non examinatio criminis,"* but have been unable to trace it to any authoritative source.
121. Note 94 above. The following newspaper reference to proceedings before Judge John M. Woolsey of the United States district court for the Southern District of New York, is therefore rather puzzling: "Judge Woolsey pointed out that while United States Attorney Tuttle had stated truthfully that witnesses had been compelled to answer before Federal grand juries questions bearing upon possible offenses by them against state laws, the precedents indicated that such witnesses had been protected from prosecution either by a State guarantee or by provisions of Federal law." *New York Times,* May 28, 1930.
122. 199 U.S. 372.

statute would not prevent a prosecution of such witness for a violation of a federal statute, did not invalidate such statute" under the due process clause of the Fourteenth Amendment; and it is difficult to see why the converse of this should not hold as to the due process clause of the Fifth Amendment.[123]

A broader question is whether the due process clause of Amendment XIV lays upon the states the same requirements as to self-incrimination that the self-incrimination clause of Amendment V lays upon the national government. The decision of the Court in Twining v. New Jersey[124] answers this question in the negative, but on the basis of an argument that is today partially obsolete; while in the earlier case of Adams v. New York[125] the opposite point of view was assumed tentatively. The question appears to turn on the further question whether the Court regards the protection against self-incrimination to be a "fundamental right," and on this point the dicta are by no means unequivocal.[126] In view, nevertheless, of the fact that the privilege against self-incrimination has to do immediately with procedure, that it was comparatively late in arising in the history of common law, that it has always been regarded as waivable, and finally that it has been recently held, in the case of a bankrupt, to be subordinate to his "substantive obligation" to surrender his books and papers for the benefit of his creditors, the holding in Twining v. New Jersey is presumably still good law.

V

The great creative act of the Supreme Court in its interpretation of the self-incrimination clause of Amendment V is its opinion in Boyd v. United States, in which the clause is linked up with the Fourth Amendment. The practical outcome of this feature of the Boyd case is the rule that evidence obtained in violation of a person's rights under the Fourth Amendment may not under the Fifth Amendment be validly received against him in any criminal prosecution in a federal court. This rule is a sharp departure from common law ideas,[127] and has ever since its first appearance been subjected to a constant fire of criticism, not infrequently from important sources.[128] Notwithstanding which, in recent years,

123. It is, in fact, so asserted in 210 U.S. at p. 68.

124. Note 116 above.

125. Note 32 above.

126. Cf. in this connection the Boyd and Counselman cases with McCarthy v. Arndstein, note 42 above.

127. Cf. Comm. v. Dane, note 51 above: Leggett v. Tallervey, 14 East 302; Jordan v. Lewis, id. 306 note.

128. The chief critic of the doctrine of the mutuality of the two amendments and the rule of evidence based thereupon is Professor Wigmore. See his *Evidence* (2d ed.) sections 2183, 2184, 2264. At the time of preparing this edition (1923), he believed the doctrine to have been repudiated, although it had left among its unfortunate sequelae the corollary rule of evidence still standing. 4 *id.* 869–71. This, of course, was before the decision of the Supreme Court in the Gouled and Amos cases. Judge John C. Knox of the United States district court of Southern New York is also of the opinion that Boyd v. United States, together with Weeks v. United States, and Silverthorne Lumber Co. v. United States, "should be modified, if not entirely relegated to the junk pile." 7 *Lectures on Legal Topics* (1925–26) 54. A still more recent, and carefully reasoned criticism of the "federal rule" is Judge Cardozo's opinion in People v. Defore, 242 N.Y. 13 (1926).

and especially since the addition of the Eighteenth Amendment to the Constitution, it has undergone not only decisive ratification by the Supreme Court, but also progressive acceptance in the state courts, until today it is the prevailing doctrine in the majority of jurisdictions that have had occasion to express themselves on the point in a legally binding way.[129]

The argument against the rule is that it makes an undue concession to the interest of accused persons as against the public interest in the detection and punishment of crime. The argument for it is its tendency to preserve the safeguards thrown about the security of individuals in "their persons, houses, papers and effects" by the Fourth Amendment. Justice Bradley's assertion in the Boyd case that "the 'unreasonable searches and seizures' condemned in the Fourth Amendment are almost always made" in connection with a search for evidence is, nowadays at least, not open to serious challenge. How, then, are such searches and seizures to be prevented granting they should be prevented?

The critics of the Boyd case point to the liability of officers at the common law for acts done outside the law; and also urge that officers guilty of illegal searches and seizures be made liable to fine and imprisonment.[130] Neither remedy is an effective restraint upon official zeal, and indeed would seem to be urged for that very reason; for if it were an effective restraint, the question of applying the rule established by the Boyd case would not arise.

The truth is, that the whole common law theory—Professor Dicey's boasted "rule of law"—that the citizen has a valuable remedy against official trespasses in his right to sue the authors thereof has long since been hopelessly discredited by facts; while in the matter of "unreasonable searches and seizures" it contradicts the very doctrine by which the Fourth Amendment invalidates them, namely, that they are acts of *government*. As to enacting statutory penalties against invalid searches and seizures, such legislation would be virtually a dead letter from the beginning. No government is ordinarily going to prosecute acts of its own subordinates which it otherwise encourages and of which it deliberately plans to take advantage.

A second criticism of the Supreme Court's application of the self-incrimina-

---

129. Wigmore himself had to admit that "the heretical influence of Weeks v. United States" had spread, and "evoked a contagion of sentimentality in some of the state courts, inducing them to break loose from long settled fundamentals." 4 *op. cit.* 633. The spread of "the federal rule" since 1920 has, indeed, been remarkable. That year only one state, Michigan, had adopted it. Since then the question has been reconsidered in every state except New Hampshire, New Mexico, and Vermont. "Fifteen of the courts of last resort of the remaining forty-five have adopted the federal rule and twenty have rejected it, although in only fourteen was the discussion necessary to the decision. . . . Five states have refused to apply the federal rule to contraband, leaving the general question open . . . Georgia, Maine, and New Jersey have not really reviewed the federal rule but have reaffirmed the old rule against collateral inquiry. The question remains open in Arizona and Oregon." O. K. Fraenkel, "Recent Developments in the Law of Search and Seizure," 13 *Minn. L. Rev.* 1, at pp. 2–5. It is an interesting speculation whether the Eighteenth Amendment is not, in part at least, responsible for this increasing tendency of the state courts to reconsider their earlier views and follow in the wake of the Supreme Court in this matter.

130. 4 Wigmore 639. The idea is, to a limited extent, adopted in section 25 of the National Prohibition Act.

tion clause is probably based on misapprehension. For as we have just seen, the Court has never committed itself to the proposition that a trial judge may not, consistently with the clause, call a jury's attention to the fact that accused refused to take the stand. So far, indeed, as it has expressed itself on the point the Court would seem to be distinctly inclined in favor of the opposed rule, which is also the English rule, and which perpetuates in a measure the original common law distinction between the status of duly accused persons in relation to the immunity from self-incrimination, and that of witnesses in general.[131]

The two least defensible features of the Court's system of doctrine in this field of constitutional law are the second rule under Boyd v. United States forbidding search under a warrant of a person's premises for papers or things solely of evidential value against such person, and the rule laid down in Counselman v. Hitchcock which classifies as incriminating evidence that which is not incriminating in itself but likely to lead to the discovery of such evidence.

The former, as was pointed out earlier, springs from a sort of mystical union of the Fourth and Fifth Amendments. Certainly it is difficult to see just why a search under warrant for things should be condemned where an arrest under warrant of their owner would not be. Lord Camden, to be sure, seemed to regard a person as being in a sense *embodied* in his papers and speaking through them, so that if any of these were produced in court against his will, he would by that fact be subjected to "testimonial compulsion." But if this is the explanation of the rule, then its extension to chattels in general becomes either illogical or ridiculous. Nor, as a matter of fact, is a person protected against being compelled to speak through his papers if these are obtained from a third party.[132] It was, perhaps, with the second rule in mind that Chief Justice Taft in the Olmstead case characterized the Gouled case, which is the immediate authority for the rule today, as carrying "the inhibition against unreasonable searches and seizures to the extreme limit."[133]

Still more exceptionable is the holding in Counselman v. Hitchcock.[134] It represents a departure from the common law which was originally justified by a peculiar turn of phrase in two of the early state constitutions, although this consequence of the phraseology in question went undiscovered for nearly a century. It adds a new resource to conscious guilt, and at the same time aggravates the difficulty in the way of any degree of judicial supervision of the constitutional privilege of witnesses. It does this, moreover, without ordinarily adding anything to the security of privacy, for its operation is usually confined to the giving of testimony in open court.

Commenting in Olmstead v. United States upon the purposes of the Fourth and Fifth Amendments, Justice Brandeis wrote: "The makers of our Constitution

131. Note 114 above.
132. Note 40 above.
133. 277 U.S. at p. 463.
134. Cf. Wigmore, section 2283.

undertook to secure conditions favorable to the pursuit of happiness. They recognized the significance of man's spiritual nature, of his feelings and of his intellect. They knew that only a part of the pain, pleasure, and satisfactions of life are to be found in material things. They sought to protect Americans in their beliefs, their thoughts, their emotions and their sensations. They conferred, as against the government, the right to be let alone, the most comprehensive of rights and the right most valued by civilzed men. To protect that right, every unjustifiable intrusion by the government upon the privacy of the individual, whatever the means employed, must be deemed a violation of the Fourth Amendment. And the use, as evidence in a criminal proceeding, of facts ascertained by such intrusion must be deemed a violation of the Fifth."[135]

Whatever may be said of the historical accuracy of this passage, it states as justly as it does eloquently the general intention underlying the body of doctrine which the Court has developed on the basis of the Fourth and Fifth Amendments. Unfortunately in this department of constitutional law, as in most others of daily and vital importance, the great task before the Court is not solely that of recognizing the existence of a particular set of values, but rather that of balancing these against another set.

When Boyd v. United States was decided the detection and punishment of crime had not become with us the exigent and difficult social problem that it is today; had it been, it can readily be imagined that that case might have had a very difficult {*sic*; different?} outcome. The natural expectation must be, therefore, that the system of doctrine discussed in this chapter will in the immediate future undergo curtailment rather than extension. At the same time, it might be well to bear in mind that there are other features of our constitutional organization which hamper society in its war against crime more materially than does the Supreme Court's interpretation of the Fourth and Fifth Amendments, the "federal system" itself being one of them.

135. 277 U.S. at pp. 478–79.

III.

A NATION AND THE STATES

9. National Power and State Interposition, 1787–1861

FIFTY years have elapsed since South Carolina pretended to leave the Union. Looking over recent writings of northern men on the constitutional phase of that momentous event, one will find among their authors a strong disposition to throw up the whole case on the question of the legal rightfulness of secession. For this phenomenon four reasons may be assigned: (1) sheer human indolence; (2) the fact that the apologetic zeal of the conquered is notoriously apt to overbear the conciliatory complacency of the conqueror; (3) the fact that by a species of intellectual inertia the mind of the student is apt to yield itself in the case of questions of this class to the stronger speculative current which, in 1860, was with the South; (4) finally, the fact that the historical investigator of today is prone to regard questions of this sort as academic, though in fact they may involve, as this one does, some extremely interesting considerations of institutional origins and differentiations.

The basic foundation of all theories upon which secession proceeded, as well as of that doctrine which initially paralyzed the national government in dealing with it, was the doctrine that the ''Constitution was a compact of sovereign states.'' In no sense, however, was this the doctrine of the framers of the Constitution. To their way of thinking the Constitution was indeed a compact, but a compact entered into by the people of America, acting in original and creative fashion, an act of revolution, in other words, which was designed to give legal form to the already existing American nation. Nor did the Constitution, in the thinking of the framers, leave the states ''sovereign'' in any genuine sense of the term. True, that description was often applied to the state governments, both during and after the Convention, to designate their corporate dignity, their autonomy, and finally their equality of representation in the new system. The state governments, however, were no {*sic*; not?} parties to the constitutional compact,

From 10 *Michigan Law Review* 535–51 (1912). Reprinted by permission.

which was referred to a higher authority within the states, namely the people. But the people of a state was to the men of 1787 but part and parcel of the American people, and agent of the latter in adopting the Constitution. Not till Calhoun, who denied the existence in a political sense of the American people, and elevated the people of a state to the dignity of the highest political entity in the United States, was the term "sovereign" used in connection with that agency which had ratified the Constitution.

Let us consider the attitude of the framers upon some of these topics rather more particularly. The first thing we discover is that some of the most influential members of the Convention, including King, Madison, and Gerry, deny specifically that even under the Articles of Confederation the states were genuinely sovereign. Madison was particularly emphatic upon the point. "There is," he said, "a gradation of power in all societies, from the lowest corporation to the highest sovereign. The States never possessed the essential rights of sovereignty. These were always vested in Congress. . . . The States, at present, are only great corporations, having the power of making by-laws, and these are effectual only if they are not contradictory to the general confederacy." Many years later Madison, finding himself embarrassed by this language, charged Yates, who had published it from notes taken on the floor of the Convention, with gross misrepresentation, but as Yates's testimony on the point is substantiated by that of King, and indeed by Madison's own notes, it is obviously to be preferred to that of Madison writing in 1819. The chief defender of the notion of state sovereignty on the floor of the Convention was Luther Martin of Maryland, whose main proposition, however, seems to have been not that the states were sovereign under the Articles of Confederation, but because with the assembling of the Convention the confederacy had undergone dissolution.

But even when the adjective "sovereign" is used in connection with the states by the men of 1787, it is, as I have just pointed out, only with reference to the state governments, and never with reference to the people of the states, who indeed are conceived of as political entities in only a very negative sense, a sense moreover which tended to blend them always into simply "the people" anywhere and everywhere. The matter can be put in this wise: whereas today, principally I presume because of the machinery that since 1787 has come into general use for making and revising state constitutions, the "people of a state" appears as a real organ of the body politic, in 1787 "the people" were regarded for the most part in the negative light of the ultimate source of the governing power, which, however, at least until the next revolution, had passed from them forever. True, in the language of Ellsworth a "new set of ideas" was creeping in, which tended to give the term "people" as applied to the population of a state a more positive significance. At the time, however, there can be no doubt that Dr. Johnson, who presents the converse phase of the matter, was quite accurate when he found that the "states" were considered on the floor of the Convention in two senses: first, as "political societies," in which sense the evidence is conclusive that they were identified with their governments; and secondly, "as districts of people composing *one* political society."

And to this "one political society" it is that the Constitution was submitted for ratification. On this point Hamilton's language in *Federalist* 22 is simply conclusive; while it also irradiates congenial light upon several allied topics. "It has not a little contributed," he writes, "to the infirmities of the existing federal system, that it never had a ratification by the *People*. Resting on no better foundation than the consent of the several legislatures, it has been exposed to frequent and intricate questions concerning the validity of its powers; and has in some instances given birth to the enormous doctrine {of a right} of legislative repeal. Owing its ratification to the law of a State, it has been contended, that the same authority might repeal the law by which it was ratified. However gross a heresy it may be, to maintain that a *party* to a *compact* has a right to revoke that *compact,* the doctrine itself has had respectable advocates. The possibility of a question of this nature, proves the necessity of laying the foundations of our national government deeper than in the mere sanction of developed {*sic*; delegated} authority. The fabric of American empire ought to rest on the solid basis of the *Consent of the People.* The streams of national power ought to flow immediately from that pure original fountain of legitimate authority." Confirmatory of essentially the same point of view is the language of Madison in *Federalist* 39. It is true that Madison here states that "ratification is to be given by the people, not as individuals composing one entire nation; but as composing the distinct and independent States to which they respectively belong," and will therefore be a "federal act" rather than a "national" one, but it seems obvious that what he has in mind is the character of the act of ratification itself while in process of performance rather than the character to be imparted to it by the anticipated establishment of the Constitution. For the final result is stated by Madison at the opening of the same paragraph in the following words which are as unexceptionable as those of Hamilton: "The Constitution is to be founded on the assent {and ratification} of the people of America." Already, moreover, on the floor of the Convention in urging the reference of the Constitution to state conventions, which he characterized as "agents," Madison had set forth his views of the superior binding force of such ratification. "He considered," he said, "the difference between a system founded on the legislatures only and one founded on the people to be the true difference between a *league* or *treaty* and a *constitution. . . .* The doctrine laid down by the law of nations in the case of treaties is that a breach of any one article by any of the parties frees the other parties from their engagements. In the case of a union of people under one constitution, the nature of the pact has always been understood to exclude such interpretation." In order, therefore, to avoid the idea "that the articles of union were to be considered as a treaty, only of a particular sort, among the governments of independent States," and "the doctrine . . . that a breach of any one article by any one of the parties absolved the other parties from obligation" . . . "he thought it indispensable that the new Constitution should be ratified in the most unexceptionable form and by the supreme authority of the people themselves."

But besides the necessity for the "most unexceptionable form" of ratification, Madison and others also pointed out yet another reason for the kind of ratification which ensued, namely, the necessity of establishing the paramountcy of the new Constitution to the state constitutions upon which, in many particulars, it made inroads. The paramountcy in question is of course stated in Article Six of the Constitution, but the question still remains, upon what authority it was deemed to rest, what authority was deemed competent to support it. And the answer is, of course, the authority which was conceived as establishing the Constitution, which is thus plainly designated as superior to the authority supporting a state constitution. Moreover this superior authority is named by the Constitution itself in its opening phrase: "We, the People of the United States."

The notion of the Constitution as a compact of the states was first broached in the Pennsylvania ratifying convention where it was met and disposed of by James Wilson, as follows: "The *State governments* make a bargain with one another; that is the doctrine that is endeavored to be established by gentlemen in opposition; their *State sovereignties* wish to be represented! But far other were the ideas of this convention, and far other are those conveyed in the system itself." But not only did the friends of the Constitution refuse to concede that the Constitution was a compact of the states, but the enemies of the Constitution found in the fact that it was not, one of the strongest reasons for opposition to its ratification. "It is, in its very introduction," wrote Luther Martin, the most philosophical of the opponents of the Constitution, "declared to be a compact between the people of the United States, as individuals; and it is to be ratified by the *people* at large, in their capacity as *individuals*; all which . . . would be quite right and proper if there were *no State governments,* if all the people of this continent were in a *state of nature,* and we were forming one *national government for them as individuals.*"

The significance of this passage from the *Genuine Information* is perhaps greater than is at first glance conveyed. In the first place, it brings out once more the identity that obtained in the minds of 1787, between a state in its political capacity and the government thereof. In the second place, it also brings out the correlative idea that the people of a state comprised so many individuals, merely inhabitants of a larger community, namely "America," "the American nation," or "the American Empire," according as we use one or other of the terms employed so often by the authors of the *Federalist*. But thirdly, it also brings forward the idea of the revolutionary character of the Constitution. That the Constitution comprised an act of revolution was a constant charge of the opponents of its ratification. Nor were the advocates of the Constitution able to gainsay this charge, even had they been disposed to do so. But they do not seem to have been so disposed, for on the floor of the Convention, at least, the idea of revolution was accepted in the frankest possible manner with all its implications. This fact comes out best, perhaps, in connection with the discussion as to how many ratifications should be required to set the new system in operation. The Convention "must be said in this case," Wilson declared, "to go to the original powers of society," or as King put it later, to represent "a recurrence to first principles," which, in the political terminology of 1787, meant neither more nor less than revolution. Moreover from this same idea as the obvious premise of his thought, Madison proceeded to derive the most terrific consequences, unless these should be obviated by the plain terms of the Constitution. "The Constitution as it stands," he declared, "might be put in force over the whole body of the people though less than a majority of them should ratify it." In other words, the competence of the power standing back of and ordaining the Constitution was, so far as existing institutions were concerned, absolutely unlimited and irresistible. Moreover, that competence was represented by the Convention itself, with whom alone it rested to specify how many ratifications should be required to set the new system into operation, and whether such ratifications should implicate the whole American people or only such portion of them as resided within the states rendering ratification. Wilson, it is true, dissented from Madison's view, but King, who had earlier expounded the idea that the people of the several states had been merged into one people under the Articles of Confederation, concurred with him, with the result that in the final form the Constitution stipulated specifically that its ratification by the conventions of nine states should be sufficient for its establishment "between the *States so ratifying*," that is, between those only.

To its framers, therefore, the Constitution meant what it says: it rested—to quote the language of one of its opponents, Richard Henry Lee,—upon the ordination, "not of the people of New Hampshire," etc., but upon that of "the people of America"; it was a compact among the people of the United States, to whom it gave legal form and semblance; and while the people of America acted, at one stage in the process of establishing the Constitution, through the medium of conventions chosen by the people of the states, each of these conventions,— like the general Convention which preceded them,—derived its competence, which was the transcendent competence of revolution, not from the source of its immediate appointment, which had never borne sovereignty nor indeed had ever had sovereignty attributed to it, but from its ulterior agency for the people of the United States. But let us go a step further and inquire, what qualities the framers of the Constitution intended to impart to the government thus founded upon the ordination of the people of the United States. First and most important was this quality: it was to be a government over individuals between whom and itself the states were to have no faculty whatsoever of intervening. For the framers had no other object half so much at heart as to be rid once and forever of that state intervention which had made the Confederacy a sham and a mockery. But suppose the national government should abuse its powers, would not the states then have the right to intervene to protect its citizens? No; for though it was recognized as sheer matter of fact that the state governments might on occasion become centers of resistance to the national government, the only right recognized in the case of an abuse of power by the national government was the right of the people of the United States to oppose it by the same means as those which the people of a state would have the right to use in case the government of that state abused its power. Such means would embrace, for example, a resort to the right of petition, to the ballot, and ultimately to the right of revolution. Such is plainly Madison's point of view in the *Federalist,* and the same point of view is again revealed by the Virginia ratifying convention. That body adopted the following oft-quoted and as often misinterpreted declaration: "We, the delegates of the people of Virginia . . . do in the name and in behalf of the people of Virginia, declare and make known, that the powers granted under the Constitution, being derived from the people of the United States, may be resumed by them whensoever the same shall be perverted to their injury or oppression." To cite this declaration as an assertion of the right of seccession or indeed of any kind of state intervention is simply absurd. It is a plain statement of the current doctrine of the right of revolution, which right in this particular case is conceived as belonging to the people of the United States.

But the right of revolution was never, either in 1787 or even in 1776, conceived of as an absolute right. Whether indeed it was a right at all was always contingent, in the theory of the matter, upon whether it had back of it power adequate to make it good. In other words the obverse of the right of revolution was always recognized to be the right of the authority revolted against to resist revolution. And so it was in this case; the government to be established by the Constitution would have, it was recognized, the right of self-preservation. The first consideration to be adduced in support of this proposition is the fact that the members of the Convention were constantly referring to their tasks as one to be discharged for "ages to come," or in similar phrase. True, at one stage of the Convention when the controversy between the large and small states was at its bitterest, and conflict of interests between North and South and East and West had come to light, there were some, notably Gorman of Massachusetts, who had despaired of forming a lasting union. But this very despair was index to that desire which finally furnished the Constitution with its intention. In the second place, moreover, the opponents of the ratification of the Constitution used essentially the same language, though with contrary intent, warning their fellow-citizens that once the "yoke" of the Constitution was assumed, it was assumed "forever." But thirdly, the framers of the Constitution took every precaution that was necessary from their point of view to furnish the national government with the *means* of self-preservation. In this connection three clauses of the Constitution claim our attention: first, the clause defining "treason" against the United States; secondly, the clause authorizing the president to call forth the militia to suppress "insurrection"; and thirdly, the clause authorizing Congress to "pass all laws necessary and proper for *carrying into execution* the foregoing powers."

The debate on the subject of treason occurred August 20. Article seven of the Report of the Committee on Detail contained the following clause: "Treason against the United States shall consist only in levying war against the United States or any of them. . . . The legislature of the United States shall have power to declare the punishment of treason." Gouverneur Morris was displeased with these provisions. He "was for giving the Union an exclusive right to declare what should be treason. In case of a contest between the United States and a particular state," he pointed out "the people of the latter must, under the disjunctive terms of the clause, be traitors to one or other authority." To this practical argument Dr. Johnson of Connecticut added a theoretical one: "Treason could not be both against the United and the individual States, being an offence against the sovereignty, which can be but one in the same community." Upon motion by Wilson and Johnson, accordingly, the phrase "any of them" was stricken out of Article seven without a dissenting vote. However, as Madison pointed out, the article still left it with the states to define treason against themselves. But said Johnson, "There can be no treason against a particular State; it could not even at present as the Confederacy now stands; the sovereignty being in the Union; much less can it be under the proposed system." Johnson, therefore, and King now set to work to make the constitutional definition of treason exclusive, first by striking out "against the United States" after the word "treason" in Article seven and then by inserting the word "sole" in front of the word "power." But at this stage another view of the matter, represented particularly by Ellsworth and Mason, began to find expression; the view, namely, that whereas the United States would be sovereign "on one side of the line," on the other side the states would be sovereign. By the final disposition of the matter, therefore, while the concept of treason against a state was denied any place in the Constitution by unanimous vote of the Convention, by the close vote of six states against five, the power was still left the states of defining treason against themselves individually. But the point of view from which this concession to state pride was made is plainly indicated by Ellsworth, who was primarily responsible for it: "There can be," he urged, "no danger to the general authority from this; as the laws of the United States are to be paramount."

Equally instructive in the intentions of the Convention was the failure on August 30, of an attempt of the states-rights contingent to eliminate from what is today Article four, section four, of the Constitution, the phrase "domestic violence" and to substitute therefor the term "insurrection" of the militia clause. The purpose of the attempt is of course palpable: it was to confine, at least by implication, the right of the national government to use the militia, to cases where application came from the state authorities themselves for military aid. But as Dickinson had already pointed out, the state legislatures might be the very source of the mischief; and the attempt was voted down. The deduction is obvious and indeed is stated by the Constitution itself; the Convention intended that the national government should have within the sphere of its competence all the powers "necessary and proper" for executing its mandates, a powerful executive, a complete system of courts through which it would judge finally of the scope of its own authority, the power of raising and supporting an army and navy, the power of calling forth its able-bodied citizenship to suppress insurrection, the power of suspending the writ of habeas corpus in case of insurrection, the power of reaching anywhere and everywhere within the national boundaries those who forcibly resisted its laws and punishing them as traitors. In short, it was to be vested executively with full territorial sovereignty.

And thus we are brought to consider the subject that troubled President Buchanan and his associates so greatly in early December of 1860, namely state coercion. Upon this subject the point of view of the Convention of 1787 was, for all purposes of this discussion, set forth quite adequately by Ellsworth in the Connecticut ratifying convention in the following words: "The coercive principle is necessary for the Union; the only question is, shall it be a coercion of law or a coercion of arms? There is no possible alternative. Where will those who oppose a coercion of law come out? Where will they end? . . . This constitution does not attempt to coerce sovereign bodies, States in their political capacity. No coercion is applicable to such bodies but that of an armed force. If we should attempt to execute the laws of the Union by sending an armed force against a delinquent State, it would involve the good and bad . . . in the same calamity. But legal coercion singles out the guilty individual and punishes him for breaking the laws of the Union." This passage is the most pronounced and clear-cut of any I have come upon, dealing with its subject matter. The only question is whether it is not too *much* so. Undoubtedly the Convention of 1787 designed to obviate all necessity for state coercion, which had proved ineffectual under the Articles of Confederation. Undoubtedly, too, it thought it had succeeded in its design by making the national government a government over individuals, that is, a government of laws. This the passage above quoted establishes perfectly. What it does not establish is the proposition later deduced from it and similar passages, that the Convention absolutely closed its eyes to all possibility of a collision between the states and the national authorities and therefore conferred upon the latter no power to deal with a situation arising out of unwarranted pretensions of the former. Of the falsity of this proposition, the utterances of Gouverneur Morris and Dickinson, cited above, and the votes that ensued upon them, afford completest proof. Still, making this due qualification, Ellsworth's words set forth the general point of view of the Convention both vividly and truthfully, instigating inevitably the inquiry as to how the design of the constitutional fathers had been so far overturned by 1860 that it had come to be thought necessary to raise again the question of state coercion. The answer to this inquiry is not far to seek: The states, deposed by the Constitution of 1787 from their position of mediation between their citizens and the central government, but left so strong in other respects by the Constitution as to become the natural rallying points of opposition to national policies, had by 1860 succeeded to greater or less extent in assuming once more, in the constitutional thinking of the time, that earlier position of mediation. And, by the same token, naturally, even those who saw clearly in 1860 that the states had constitutionally no such function of mediation, yet hesitated to urge upon the national government a course that would bring it into collision with state authorities, a possibility which, despite the action of Jackson in 1833, they insisted did not fall within the contemplation of the Constitution.

And so we return to our starting point, the noxious doctrine, namely, that "the constitution was a compact of sovereign States." The documentary source of this idea, at least in the history of the mischief it worked, was the Virginia Resolution of 1798, of which the author was James Madison, though the Jacob of the transaction was Thomas Jefferson. The important resolution is the third, which reads as follows: "Resolved . . . that this assembly (namely the Virginia legislature) doth explicitly and peremptorily declare that it views the powers of the federal government as resulting from the compact to which the States are parties . . . that in case of a deliberate, palpable and dangerous exercise of other powers not granted by the said compact, the States who are parties thereto have the right and are in duty bound to interpose for arresting the progress of the evil and for maintaining within their respective limits the authorities, rights and liberties appertaining to them." The essential ideas here are two: first, the idea of the Constitution as a compact of the states, and secondly, the derivative idea of the right and duty of the individual states under the Constitution to interpose the shield of their sovereignty on occasion, between their respective citizens and the national government. Years later Madison was at great pains to show that he was laying claim in 1798 only to a quasi-revolutionary right to be exercised by the whole body of states. But if interposition was a mere revolutionary right, why base it upon the alleged character of the Constitution as a compact of the states; and if it was a right to be exercised by the whole body of states, why the word "respectively" in the above passage? But there is also another circumstance equally fatal to Madison's disingenuous attempts to escape responsibility for his rash facility. While these resolutions were pending, Madison was in correspondence with Breckenridge of Kentucky who, also in association with Jefferson, was promoting similar doctrine in that commonwealth. The subject of this correspondence was whether the proper constitutional agency for the promulgation of the resolutions in question was the state legislature or a constitutional convention. Madison urged that it was the latter, because constitutional conventions in the states had originally ratified the Constitution, but Breckenridge was confident that it was the former, inasmuch as it was with its legislature that the state's sovereignty reposed. The purport of this correspondence is obvious: it shows the anxiety of its authors to present their doctrine as correct constitutional doctrine, and the difficulty in the way of their doing so because the recognized organ of the state's sovereignty, even in 1798, was other than the organ through which the Constitution had originally received ratification within the state.

On the other hand, it must be said, in justification of Madison, that as early as 1800 he had begun to reconsider his position and to seek retreat from it. For being communicated to the sister states, the resolutions from Virginia, together with resolutions of a similar character from Kentucky, had drawn forth from the northern legislatures responses which reiterated the doctrine of Madison himself, in *Federalist* 39, namely that the final interpretation of the Constitution lay with the national judiciary. In his report to the Virginia legislature in 1800, therefore, Madison is forced to confront the question of where the power to interpret the Constitution with ultimate legal authority really rests. He begins by reiterating the view set forth in the resolutions: The states are sovereign, any decision of the federal judiciary therefore, while possibly ultimate in relation to the authorities of the other departments of the federal government, cannot possibly be so "with relation to the rights of the parties to the constitutional compact, from which the judicial as well as the other departments hold their delegated trusts." Fifty pages along, however, Madison's audacity has oozed entirely away. "It has been said," he writes, restating the issue, "that it belongs to the judiciary of the United States and not the State legislatures to declare the meaning of the federal constitution. But," he urges in a far different tone to the one with which he set out, "a declaration that proceedings of the federal government are not warranted by the constitution is a novelty neither among the citizens nor among the legislatures of the States . . . nor can the declarations of either, whether affirming or denying the constitutionality of measures of the federal government, be deemed, in any point of view, an assumption of the office of judge. The declarations in such cases are expressions of opinion, unaccompanied with any other effect than what they may produce on opinion by exciting reflection. The expositions of the judiciary, on the other hand, are carried into immediate effect by force." What a tremendously lame conclusion to so much fulmination! The boasted right of the sovereign state to insert itself between its citizenship and the national government, on such occasions as it deemed the latter to be exceeding its powers dangerously, comes down to a mere right on the part of its legislature to vote resolutions expressive of opinion, resolutions which in the last analysis are no more authoritative than any ebullition of opinion on the part of a group of citizens congregated of a Saturday night in a crossroads grocery store.

But at any rate, Madison had constructed a bridge of retreat from the position in which the Resolutions of 1798 had landed him. Unfortunately, the same bridge afforded to others less timid, less scrupulous than himself, and less bent upon keeping the cake they fain would eat, an easy means of approach to the abandoned position, which—to continue the figure—now became a veritable pirates' den of destructive speculation. Between the Resolutions of 1798 and Calhoun's theorizing a generation later, three developments occurred in the field of American constitutional doctrine which were of the utmost importance: first, the theory of the social compact underwent a serious decline in reputation; second, the notion of sovereignty which Rousseau offers as the ultimate indivisible will of a community came into wide acceptance; thirdly, in consequence particularly of the rise of the state constitutional convention, the notion of the "people" as the highest political embodiment of the state and the residence of its sovereignty became common property. Of all these notions, with their novel and bright definiteness, Calhoun proceeded to make dextrous appropriation, while Madison, upon whom he endeavored to fasten the paternity of his ideas, bitterly warned his countrymen against "those errors which have their source in the innovations wrought by time upon the meaning of words and phrases." So far as Calhoun at least was concerned this warning fell upon utterly deaf ears. The Constitution, therefore, he proceeded to write down a *mere* compact and the parties to it as *absolutely* sovereign and so controlled by it only to such degree as they might in their infinite discretion at any moment individually decide. Finally, the organ of that sovereignty which *eo nomine* he found attributed to the state in 1787, but which in fact was a far different sort of sovereignty to that of his speculation, he asserted to be the state convention; and the state convention, summonable by the legislature at will, he asserted to be the identical organ which, summoned at the behest of the Convention of 1787, had originally ratified the Constitution. Little wonder that it irked Madison to be made sponsor for this ridiculous parcel of puns, pseudo-philosophy, and falsified history. Yet it is undeniable that he gave Calhoun the one essential idea to which all the latter's absurd theory-monging {*sic*; mongering?} afforded but a newly framed supporting scaffold, the idea namely of state interposition,—the idea that for some reason or other the state had the right, either in constitutional crises to be judged of by itself, or at its own sweet will, to step between citizens of the United States and the government of the United States, when such citizens happened to be, in another relationship, their own citizens too. This is the idea that lies back, not only of Calhoun's theory, but of all theories of secession; of all theories, in other words, which sought to impart to rebellion a false glamour by associating with it the states in their political capacity.

Nor even is this the full toll of Madison's responsibility. For it is to him also that were ultimately due those singular contradictions of thinking which at first threatened to paralyze the national authorities indefinitely in dealing with the situation confronting it in December, 1860. As evidence of this paralysis, though it proved only temporary, we have two famous documents: first, Attorney General Black's opinion of November 20, 1860, written in response to a series of questions by President Buchanan, as to the legal means at his disposal in executing the laws of the United States in face of forcible resistance within the states; and secondly, the presidential message of December 3, following, dealing with the question of the right of secession and the subject of state coercion. As I have just stated, the remarkable feature of these documents is the singular contradiction of thought to be found running through them, a contradiction due entirely and exclusively to an endeavor to harmonize the true concept of the national government as a government over individuals, supreme and uncontrollable within the sphere of its powers, with the Madisonian theory of 1798, which in the last analysis left the national government without territorial authority save at the sufferance of the states.

Let us consider first the attorney general's opinion. At the very outset Black reveals an equivocal attitude on the crucial question of secession, for while stating the correct doctrine that "the will of a State, whether expressed in its constitution or laws, cannot . . . absolve her people from the duty of obeying the just and constitutional requirements of the central government," he introduces after the word "cannot" the invidious qualification, "while it remains in the Confederacy." The same fatal point of view again emerges when he comes to construe the act of 1795, authorizing the president to call forth the militia, "whenever the laws of the United States shall be opposed by combinations too powerful to be suppressed by the ordinary course of judicial proceedings, or by the power vested in the marshals." His main proposition in this connection is that if the federal civil service be once expelled from a state it cannot, under "existing law," be restored by military force. "Under such circumstances, to send a military force into any State with orders to act against *the people* would be simply making war upon them." Nor apparently was this supposed defect of the national executive power due merely to "existing law": it was grounded in the Constitution itself. The language in which Black states the issue is itself significant: "Whether Congress has constitutional right to *make war against one or more States* and require the exercise of the federal government to carry it on by means of force to be drawn from other States." The fatal idea of interposition lurks in every word of this sentence, as it does also in every turn of the argument that follows upon it. For the attorney general proceeds to argue that Congress has no such power expressly given it, "nor are there any words in the constitution which imply it." It has indeed a power to declare war, but the kind of war contemplated is foreign war. It also has the power to provide for calling forth the militia, "and *using them within the limits of the State.*" But this power can be exercised only in aid of federal officers "in the performance of their regular duties," or to repel invaders from the state, or "to suppress insurrection against the State," where "the State herself shall apply for assistance against her own people." In short, he confines the power of the federal government in the use of militia to its use within the state from which it is called forth, and he translates the word "insurrection" of Article one, section eight, of the Constitution into the term "domestic violence"; of Article four, section four—substantially the very thing the Convention of 1787 had refused to do. Finally, he reveals once more his point of view, in the remarkable dictum, that "all these provisions" which he is engaged in construing "are made to protect the States." Harmoniously with this marvelous train of exegesis by interpolation, any exertion of military force by the federal government within a state, save within the limitations he prescribes, takes on in his eye the character of a "war against" such state, effecting its "expulsion" from the Union.

Not essentially different is the process of thought revealed in President Buchanan's message of December 3, 1860. In its statement of the doctrine of the permanency of the Union, this document is thoroughly admirable. It is better formulated and more effective at this point than Lincoln's later utterances upon the same topic, which indeed owe not a little to it. "That the Union was designed to be perpetual," it proceeds, "appears conclusively from the nature and extent of the powers conferred by the constitution on the federal government. These powers embrace the very highest attributes of national sovereignty. . . . This government, therefore, is a great and powerful government, invested with all the attributes of sovereignty over the special subjects to which its authority extends. Its framers never intended to implant in its bosom the seeds of its own destruction, nor were they at its creation guilty of the absurdity of providing for its own dissolution. . . . They did not fear, nor had they reason to imagine, that the constitution would ever be so interpreted as to enable any State by her own act, and without the consent of its sister States, to discharge her people from all or any part of the federal obligations. . . . In short, . . . secession is neither more nor less than revolution. It may, or it may not be, a justifiable revolution; but still it is revolution." So far, very excellent; to this language no exception need have been taken, save perhaps at one or two minor points, by the strictest nationalist.

It is only when President Buchanan proceeds to inquire into the question of power that the presence of incompatible elements in his system of constitutional doctrine appear distinctly. The president's sworn duty, he states, is of course to execute the laws, but, he continues, "this duty cannot" under existing statutes "by possibility be performed in a State where no judicial authority exists to issue process, and where there is no marshal to execute it, and where, even if there were such an officer, the entire population would constitute one solid combination to resist him." True, the same objections did not lie in the way of executing the laws for the collection of the customs. The revenue still continued to be collected, as heretofore, at the custom-house in Charleston, and should the collector unfortunately resign a successor might be appointed to perform this duty. Also, as to the property of the United States in South Carolina, "it was not believed that any attempt would be made to expel the United States from this"; "but if in this I should prove mistaken, the officer in command of the forts has received orders to act strictly in the defensive. In such a contingency, the responsibility for consequences would rightfully rest upon the heads of the assailants." Here, plainly, is Attorney General Black's main proposition over again, namely, that the national government, once expelled from a state, could not return thither with such force as might be necessary to secure its reinstitution; minus, however, Black's admission that it could *probably* recapture property unlawfully taken from it.

And when he passes to consider Congress's powers in the premises, President Buchanan still cleaves to his adviser, though translating Black's phrase, "waging war upon a State" into the phrase "coercing a State." For he asserts the question before Congress to be the question whether it possesses "the power by force of arms to compel a State to remain in the Union" or, in other words, the question whether the Constitution has "delegated to Congress the power to coerce a State into submission, which is attempting to withdraw or has actually withdrawn from the Confederacy." The most notable thing about this question is the way in which, in its assumption of the possibility of secession, it appears to contradict all that its author has just said in denial of the right of secession. But the next most notable feature of it, is its obvious intent of trapping a negative answer. On this point, Buchanan's biographer Curtis has endeavored to show that all that Buchanan had in mind in putting the question was to deny to Congress the right to intervene beforehand to prevent state authority from putting through an ordinance of secession in accordance with what they considered the due forms. This apology can scarcely pass muster, for three reasons: In the first place, the kind of coercion which it alleges Buchanan to have been discussing was never demanded by anybody, and therefore to have discussed it would have been perfectly gratuitous and indeed silly; in the second place, the distinction upon which the apology rests arose only subsequently to the message of December 3; and in the third place, the answer which Buchanan himself gives to his question precludes any such construction being put upon it. For that answer is couched in the following words: "Congress possesses many means of preserving it (the Union) by conciliation, but the power of the sword was not placed in their hands to preserve it by force,"—a statement of the matter which, at least when taken with the entire context of the message, demonstrates beyond a doubt that Buchanan was canvassing the whole question of Congress's powers in dealing with a case of pretended secession and the situation arising therefrom.

Thus, what the total doctrine of Buchanan's message amounts to is this: A state cannot constitutionally withdraw from the Union, but if it pretends to do so, its unconstitutional act has the constitutional effect of cutting off the national government from all contact with the citizens of such state,—in other words, precisely the constitutional effect that it would have had, had it been a constitutional act. Fortunately, we are not left in the dark as to the fountainhead of this muddled doctrine and halting imbecility. It is "Mr. Madison's justly celebrated report" to the Virginia legislature, and the "resolutions of the preceding legislature." Also, it is Buchanan's own construction of a "brief but powerful speech," in which "Mr. Madison opposed" a proposition before the Convention of 1787, to authorize "an exertion of the whole against a delinquent State." This speech ran as follows: "The use of force against a State would look more like a declaration of war than an infliction of punishment, and would probably be considered by the party attacked as a dissolution of all previous compacts by which it might be bound." What Buchanan forgets is, that in the face of this sentiment Madison advocated from the opening to the close of the Convention, and even after its adjournment, that the national legislature be given a power of direct veto of state legislation. True, this idea was not accepted; instead, the function of keeping state legislation within constitutional bounds was handed over to the national judiciary, whose mandates are enforceable, in the first instance, against individuals. But what was the right and duty of the national government in case a state should resist its judicial mandates was plainly indicated by Madison himself in 1809, when in response to protests by the legislature and governor of Pennsylvania against the recent decision of the Supreme Court in United States v. Peters, he gave solemn warning of ''the awful consequences'' that must ensue in the event of any attempt on the part of that commonwealth to prevent the enforcement of such decison. ''Continue to execute all the express provisions to our national constitution,'' said Lincoln in his first inaugural, ''and the Union will endure forever.'' Such plainly was the point of view of Madison, president of the United States, and such, it may be urged with confidence, was the point of view of the Convention which framed the Constitution. It was Buchanan's and Black's misfortune in December, 1860, that instead of resorting to the true and authoritative sources of constitutional construction, they pinned their faith upon the unsuccessful views of a protesting minority,—views that had been framed largely for political effect under the brilliant but irresponsible direction of an opportunist doctrinaire.

10. The "Full Faith and Credit" Clause

ARTICLE IV of the Constitution, sometimes called "the Federal Article," defines in certain particulars the relations of the state entities to one another and of the national government to the states. Its opening section reads as follows: "Full faith and credit shall be given in each state to the public acts, records, and judicial proceedings of every other state. And the Congress may by general laws prescribe the manner in which such acts, records and proceedings shall be proved, and the effect thereof." What was the intention and what has been the operation of this provision?

I

The historical background of the above section is furnished by that branch of private law which is variously termed "Private International Law," "Conflict of Laws," or "Comity." This comprises a body of rules, based largely on the writings of jurists and judicial decisions, in accordance with which the courts of one country or "jurisdiction" will ordinarily, *in the absence of a local policy to the contrary,* extend recognition and enforcement to rights claimed by individuals by virtue of the laws or judicial decisions of another country or "jurisdiction."[1]

The nature of the problem thus dealt with is indicated in the following passages from Story's classic work on the *Conflict of Laws:*

A person sometimes contracts in one country, and is domiciled in another, and is to pay in a third; and sometimes the property, which is the subject of the contract, is

From 81 *University of Pennsylvania Law Review* 371–89 (1933). Reprinted by permission. Copyright 1933, by the University of Pennsylvania.
1. Stowell, *International Law* 246–60 (1931), contains an excellent brief discussion. An outline of the subject is supplied in Holland, *Jurisprudence* ch. XVIII (13th ed. 1924), where the designation "assimilation of laws" is suggested.

situate in a fourth; and each of these countries may have different, and even opposite laws, affecting the subject-matter. What then is to be done in this conflict of laws? What law is to regulate the contract, either to determine the rights, or the remedies, or the defenses growing out of it; or the consequences following from it? What law is to interpret its terms, and ascertain the nature, character, and extent of its stipulations?[2]

And again:

> Suppose . . . a marriage celebrated in England, where marriage is indissoluble, and a divorce obtained in Scotland, *a vinculo matrimonii,* as it may be for adultery under the laws thereof, will that divorce be operative in England, so as to authorize a new marriage there by either party? Suppose a marriage in Massachusetts, where a divorce may be had for adultery, will a divorce obtained in another State, for a cause unknown to the laws of Massachusetts, be held valid there? If, in each of these cases the divorce would be held invalid in the country, where the marriage is celebrated, but would be held valid, where the divorce is obtained; what rule is to govern in other countries as to such divorce? It is to be deemed valid, or invalid there? Will a new marriage contracted there by either party be good, or be not good?[3]

Illustrative of the solutions supplied to such questions by Comity, Conflict of Laws, or Private International Law—as one chooses to call it—is the rule that a marriage which is good in the country where performed (*lex !oci*) is good elsewhere;[4] likewise the rule that contracts are to be interpreted in accordance with the laws of the country where entered into (*lex loci contractus*) unless the parties clearly intended otherwise;[5] also the rule that immovables may be disposed of only in accordance with the law of the country where situated (*lex rei sitae*[6]); also the converse rule that chattels adhere to the person of their owner and hence are disposable by him, even when located elsewhere, in accordance with the law of his domicile (*lex domicilii*[7]); also the rule that regardless of where the cause arose, the courts of any country where personal service can be got upon the defendant will take jurisdiction of certain types of personal actions, hence termed "transitory," and accord such remedy as the *lex fori* affords.[8] Still other rules of first importance in the present connection determine the recognition which the judgments of the courts of one country shall receive from those of another country.

So even had the states of the Union remained in a mutual relationship of entire independence, still private claims originating in one would often have been

---

2. Story, *Conflict of Laws* section 232 (5th ed. 1857). The first edition appeared in 1834.
3. *Id.* at 203.
4. A rather extreme case is Wall v. Williamson, 8 Ala. 48 (1845).
5. In certain circumstances this rule is fortified in the United States by the "obligations of contracts" clause. See Morley v. Lake Shore Ry., 146 U.S. 162, 13 Sup. Ct. 54 (1892).
6. Clark v. Graham, 6 Wheat. 577 (U.S. 1821), is an early case in which the Supreme Court enforced this rule.
7. 2 Kent, *Commentaries* *428–29 (14th ed. 1896). While the rule generally holds as a rule for the inheritance of property, it is today subject to many exceptions, as a rule for voluntary transfers.
8. LeForest v. Tolman, 117 Mass. 109 (1875); Machado v. Fontes, [1897] 2 Q.B. 231 (Eng.) are illustrative.

assured recognition and enforcement in the others. But even the framers of the Articles of Confederation had felt that the rules of private international law should not be left as among the states altogether on a basis of comity, and hence subject always to the overruling local policy of the *lex fori,* but ought to be in some measure at least placed on the higher plane of constitutional obligation.

The fourth of the Articles[9] is, indeed, the immediate source of the provision now under consideration. The latter, however, exhibits two developments upon its predecessor: the "acts" and "records" to which it extends full faith and credit are not confined to those of "courts and magistrates," and it endows Congress with power to enact supplementary and enforcing legislation. A motion to the latter effect, which was offered on the floor of the Convention by Gouverneur Morris, was recast in committee to confine Congress's power to that of prescribing the manner in which "such acts, records, and proceedings shall be proved, and the effect *which judgments obtained in one state shall have in another,*" whereupon Morris moved to strike out the phrase here given in italics and proposed the substitution for it of the word "thereof." Despite a warning by Johnson of Connecticut that this would authorize the new government "to declare the effect of the legislative acts of one state in another state" and the more general protest of Randolph that such loose definitions of power would enable the new government to usurp all the state powers, the amendment was carried.[10]

In point of fact, these fears have to date proved largely groundless. Congressional legislation under the "full faith and credit" clause is today embraced in sections 905 and 906 of the Revised Statutes, which consolidate the acts of May 26, 1790, and of March 27, 1801.[11] The former section lays down the rules for the authentication of the legislative acts of the several states and territories and of "any country subject to the jurisdiction of the United States," and of the records and judicial proceedings of the same. It then provides that "the said records and judicial proceedings authenticated as aforesaid shall be given such faith and credit in every court of the United States as they have by law and usage in the courts of the state from whence the said records are or shall be taken." Section 906 lays down similar provisions with reference to nonjudicial records.

Several points clearly emerge: (1) the word "effect" is construed as referring to the effect of the records when authenticated, not to the effect of the authentication; (2) the "faith and credit" which is required by the rules of private international law is superseded as to "the records and judicial proceedings" of each state by a rule of complete obligation; *as to these the local policy of the forum state can have no application.* On the other hand, (3) while the Act of 1790 lays down a rule for the authentication of the statutes of the several states, it says nothing regarding their extraterritorial operation; and (4) it is similarly silent regarding the common law of the several states. The practical effect whereof to

9. "Full faith and credit shall be given in each of these states to the records, acts and judicial proceedings of the courts and magistrates of every other state."

10. 2 Farrand, *Records* 488–89.

11. 1 Stat. 122 (1790); 2 Stat. 298, 299; 28 U.S.C.A. sections 687–88 (1928).

date has been, in the main, to leave the extrastate protection of rights, except such as have ripened into a definite judicial judgment, exactly where the Constitution found it, that is to say, on a basis of comity, and so at the mercy of the adverse local policy of the *forum* state.

In this connection it is instructive to turn to the famous case of Scott v. Sanford.[12] Said Justice Nelson, who spoke the sentiments of the Court on this point: "No State, therefore, can enact laws to operate beyond its own dominions. . . . Nations, from convenience and comity . . . recognise and administer the laws of other countries. But of the nature, extent, and utility, of them, respecting property, or the state and condition of persons within her territories, each nation judges for itself";[13] and he added that it was the same with the states of the Union in relation to one another. It followed that even though Dred had become a free man in consequence of his having resided in the "free" state of Illinois, he had nevertheless upon his return to Missouri which had the same power as Illinois to determine its local policy respecting rights acquired extraterritorially, reverted to servitude under the laws and judidical decisions of that state. It was upon this ground indeed that the Court had intended originally to dispose of the case, when the slaveholding majority of the justices fancied they saw an opportunity for the Court to settle the slavery question in the way they wanted it settled, by passing upon the validity of the Missouri Compromise. And even Justices McLean and Curtis assented to the underlying premise of the above doctrine, the subjection of extrastate acquired rights to local policy. They merely contended that Missouri's laws and judicial decisions did not evince the policy toward the kind of case before the Court that the majority of the justices imputed to her.

Since the Civil War the Thirteenth and Fourteenth Amendments have, to be sure, imposed radical restrictions upon the power of the states in the determination of the *status* and legal capacities of even their own inhabitants. Furthermore, as we shall see in a later section, the Supreme Court has in recent decades handed down a series of judgments based on the "full faith and credit" clause which attribute what is unquestionably a limited extraterritorial operation in certain situations to state laws. But this has been done apologetically and to the accompaniment of denials that it was being done; and it is still undoubtedly true in the main that "no state can legislate except with reference to its own jurisdiction."[14]

Thus the clause has not abolished the general principle of the dominance of local policy over the rules of comity. These, indeed, have always been regarded by the Court as constituting merely a part of the local common law of each state.[15] Nor has it to date been held to require the states to open their courts to

12. 19 How. 393 (U.S. 1856).

13. *Id.* at 460.

14. Bonaparte v. Tax Court, 104 U.S. 592 (1881), where it was held that a law exempting from taxation certain bonds of the enacting state did not operate extraterritorially by virtue of the "full faith and credit" clause. See also note 68 below.

15. Bank of Augusta v. Earle, 13 Pet. 519, 589–96 (U.S. 1840). See *e.g.* Kryger v. Wilson, 242 U.S. 171, 37 Sup. Ct. 34 (1916); and Bond v. Hume, 243 U.S. 15, 37 Sup. Ct. 366 (1917).

actions in cases of personal liability, the "transitory actions" above referred to. Such constitutional obligation as rests upon the states in this respect comes from section 2 of Article IV or from the Fourteenth Amendment. Neither does the section, as heretofore applied, enable state courts to send their writs across state lines. "No sovereignty," says Story, "can extend its process beyond its own territorial limits, to subject either persons or property to its judicial decisions";[16] and this principle has been followed by the Supreme Court in its application both of the "full faith and credit" clause and the "due process" clause of Amendment XIV.[17]

Article IV, section 1, has had its principal and, apart from the cases just alluded to, its sole operation in relation to *judgments*. The cases fall into two groups: first, those in which the judgment involved was offered as a basis of proceedings for its own enforcemment outside the state where rendered, as for example, when an action for debt is brought in the courts of state *B* on a judgment for money damages rendered in state *A*; secondly, those, in which the judgment involved was offered, in conformance with the principle of *res judicata*, in defense in a new or "collateral" proceeding growing out of the same facts as the original suit, as for example, when a decree of divorce granted in state *A* is offered as barring a suit for divorce by the other party to the marriage in the courts of state *B*.

The English courts and the different state courts in the United States, while recognizing "foreign judgments *in personam*" which were reducible to money terms as affording a basis for actions in debt, originally accorded them generally only the *status* of *prima facie* evidence in support thereof, so that the merits of the original controversy could always be reopened. When offered in defense, on the other hand, "foreign judgments *in personam*" were always ordinarily treated as conclusive, as between parties, of the issues they purported to determine, provided they had been rendered by a court of competent jurisdiction and were not tainted with fraud. And judgments "*in rem*" rendered under the same conditions were regarded as conclusive upon everybody on the theory that, as stated by Chief Justice Marhsall, "it is a proceeding *in rem* to which all the world are parties."[18]

II

The earliest cases to arise in which the support lent by the "full faith and credit" clause to the above principles was invoked were actions in debt brought on money judgments rendered in a sister state; and the question at issue was the

16. Story, *op. cit.* above note 2, section 539.
17. The leading case is Pennoyer v. Neff, 95 U.S. 714 (1877).
18. Mankin v. Chandler, 2 Brock. 125 at 127 (C.C.D. Va. & N.C. 1823). An English admiralty court recognized a duty to cooperate in the enforcement of a foreign judgment as early as 1607, 1 Rolle Abr. 530; and Sir Leoline Jenkins instructed the king and Privy Council to like effect in 1666, 2 Wynne, *Life of Jenkins* 762. Cf. Stowell, *op. cit.* above note 1, at 252 n., 256–57.

precise *status* of such a judgment in the courts of the *forum* state. Was it a "foreign judgment" or a "domestic judgment" or was it something approaching a national judgment?

The pioneer case was Mills v. Duryee,[19] decided in 1813. In an action brought into the circuit court of the District of Columbia—the equivalent of a state court for this purpose—on a judgment from a New York court, the defendant endeavored to reopen the whole question of the merits of the original case by a plea of "*nil debet*," his argument being that "the full faith and credit" due the judicial records and proceedings of a state under Article IV was only such as was due them as "evidence," and that therefore, from the nature of evidence they were open to rebuttal. From the other side it was answered, in the words of the Act of 1790 itself, that such records and proceedings were entitled in each state to the same faith and credit as in the state of origin; and that inasmuch as they were records of a court in the state of origin, and so conclusive of the merits of the case there, they were equally so in the *forum* state.

The Court adopted the latter view, saying that it had not been the intention of the Constitution merely to reenact the common law—that is, the principles of private international law—as to the reception of foreign judgments, but to amplify and fortify these. And in Hampton v. McConnell[20] some years later, Chief Justice Marshall went even further, using language which seems to show that he regarded the judgment of a state court as constitutionally entitled to be accorded in the courts of sister states not simply the faith and credit of conclusive evidence, but the *validity of a final judgment.*

When, however, the next important case arose, the Court had come under new influences. This was McElmoyle v. Cohen,[21] decided in 1839, in which the issue was whether a statute of limitations of the state of Georgia which applied only to judgments obtained in courts other than those of Georgia could constitutionally bar an action in Georgia on a judgment rendered by a court of record of South Carolina. On the one hand, it was contended, on the strength of the above cases that the "judgment of a state court carries with it into every state all its original attributes and incidents"; that "it goes forth armed with the powers of the court that pronounced it, and clothed with the authority of the laws under which it was pronounced." But it was answered on the other hand, that the Constitution was not intended "materially to interfere with the essential attributes of the *lex fori*"; that the Act of Congress only established a rule of evidence, of conclusive evidence to be sure, but still of evidence only; and that it was necessary, in order to carry into effect in a state the judgment of a court of a sister state, to institute a fresh action in the court of the former, in strict compliance with its laws; and that consequently, when remedies were sought in support of the rights accruing in another jurisdiction, they were governed by the *lex fori.*

19. 7 Cranch 481 (U.S. 1813). Cf. Bartlet v. Knight, 1 Mass. 401 (1805).
20. 3 Wheat. 234 (U.S. 1818).
21. 13 Pet. 312 (U.S. 1839).

The Court adopted the latter position, declining to follow Marshall's lead in Hampton v. McConnell.[22] The result is that even nowadays it is sometimes confronted with the contention that a state need not provide a *forum* for some particular type of judgment from a sister state, a claim which it has by no means met with clear-cut principles. Thus in one case it held that a New York statute forbidding foreign corporations doing a domestic business to sue on causes originating outside the state was constitutionally applicable to prevent such a corporation from suing on a judgment obtained in a sister state.[23] But in a later case it ruled that a Mississippi statute forbidding contracts in cotton futures could not validly close the courts of the state to an action on a judgment obtained in a sister state on such a contract, although the contract in question had been entered into in the *forum* state and between its citizens.[24] Subsequent cases follow the later rather than the earlier precedent.[25] Nor is there any apparent reason why Congress, acting on the implications of Marshall's word in Hampton v. McConnell, should not clothe extrastate judgments of any particular type with the full *status* of domestic judgments of the same type in the several states.[26]

III

The second great class of cases to arise under the "full faith and credit" clause embraces those raising the question whether a judgment for which extrastate operation was being sought, either as the basis of an action or as a defense in one, had been rendered with jurisdiction. The question occurs both in relation to judgments *in rem* against property or a *status* alleged not to have been within the jurisdiction of the court which handed down the original decree, and also in connection with judgments *in personam* against a nonresident defendant or defendants upon whom it is alleged personal service was not obtained in the state of the origin of the judgment.[27] We shall consider the latter type first.

The pioneer case is that of D'Arcy v. Ketchum,[28] decided in 1850. The

22. The result is undoubtedly harmonious with common law principles by which a judgment can only be executed in the jurisdiction where rendered, so that if enforcement of it in another jurisdiction is desired, a fresh action must be brought on it. In civil law countries, on the other hand, a foreign judgment, either after examination into its merits or without such examination, is executed directly as if it were in all respects a domestic judgment.

23. Anglo-American Provision Co. v. Davis Provision Co., 191 U.S. 373, 24 Sup. Ct. 92 (1903).

24. Fauntleroy v. Lum, 210 P.S. {*sic*; U.S.?} 230, 28 Sup. Ct. 641 (1908). Justice Holmes, who spoke for the Court in both cases, asserted in his opinion in the latter that the New York statute was "directed to jurisdiction," the Mississippi statute to "merits," but four justices could not grasp the distinction.

25. Kenney v. Supreme Lodge, 252 U.S. 411, 40 Sup. Ct. 371 (1920), and cases there cited. Holmes again spoke for the Court. See also Cook, "The Powers of Congress under the Full Faith and Credit Clause" 28 *Yale L. J.* 421, 434 (1919).

26. Thus why should not a judgment for alimony be made directly enforcible in sister states instead of merely furnishing the basis of an action in debt? See Thompson v. Thompson, 226 U.S. 551, 33 Sup. Ct. 129 (1913).

27. On the general subject see Cooper v. Reynolds, 10 Wall. 308 (US. 1870).

28. 11 How. 165 (U.S. 1850).

question presented was whether a judgment rendered by a New York court under a statute which provided that, when joint debtors were sued and one of them was brought into court on a process, a judgment in favor of the plaintiff would entitle him to execute against all, must be accorded full faith and credit in Louisiana when offered as the basis of an action in debt against a resident of that state who had not been served by process in the New York action.

Pressed with the argument that by "the immutable principles of justice" no man's rights should be impaired without his being given an opportunity to defend them, the Court ruled that, interpreted in the light of the principles of "international law and comity" as they existed in 1790, the Act of Congress of that year did not reach the case. The truth is that the decision virtually amended the act, for had the Louisiana defendant ventured to New York, he could, as the Constitution of the United States then stood, have been subjected to the judgment to the same extent as the New York defendant who had been personally served. The subsequent disappearance, or at least reduction, of this disparity between the operation of a personal judgment in the home state and a sister state is to be attributed to the adoption of the Fourteenth Amendment.

Thus in Pennoyer v. Neff,[29] decided in 1877, and so under the amendment, the Court held that a judgment given in a case in which the state court had endeavored to acquire jurisdiction of a nonresident defendant by an attachment upon property of his within the state and "constructive notice" to him, had not been rendered with jurisdiction and hence could not afford the basis of an action in the court of another state against such defendant, although it bound him so far as the property attached was concerned, on account of the inherent right of a state to assist its own citizens in obtaining satisfaction of their just claims. Nor would such a judgment, the Court further indicated, be due process of law in the state where rendered to any greater extent. In the words of a recent case, "An ordinary personal judgment for money, invalid for want of service amounting to due process of law, is as ineffective in the State as outside of it."[30]

Meantime, in 1855 the Court had decided Lafayette Insurance Co. v. French et

29. Note 17, above.
30. McDonald v. Mabee, 243 U.S. 90 at 92, 37 Sup. Ct. 343 at 344 (1917). See also Old Wayne Mutual Life Ass'n v. McDonough, 204 U.S. 8, 27 Sup. Ct. 236 (1907); Wetmore v. Karrick, 205 U.S. 141, 27 Sup. Ct. 434 (1907). The claim that a judgment was "non-responsive to the pleadings" raises the jurisdictional question. Reynolds v. Stockton, 140 U.S. 254, 11 Sup. Ct. 773 (1891). But the fact that a nonresident defendant was only temporarily in the state when he was served in the original action does not vitiate the judgment rendered as the basis of an action in his home state. Renaud v. Abbott, 116 U.S. 277, 6 Sup. Ct. 1194 (1886); Jaster v. Currie, 198 U.S. 144, 25 Sup. Ct. 614 (1905). Inasmuch as the principle of *res judicata* applies only to proceedings between the same parties and privies, the plea by defendant in an action based on a judgment that he was no party or privy to the original action raises the question of jurisdiction; and while a judgment against a corporation in one state may validly bind a stockholder in another state to the extent of the par value of his holdings. Hancock National Bank v. Farnum, 176 U.S. 640, 20 Sup. Ct. 506 (1900), an administrator acting under grant of administration in one state stands in no sort of relation of privity to an administrator of the same estate in another state. Stacy v. Thrasher, 6 How. 44, 58 (U.S. 1848); Brown v. Fletcher, 210 U.S. 82, 28 Sup. Ct. 702 (1908).

al.,[31] a pioneer case in its general class. Here it was held that "where a corporation chartered by the state of Indiana was allowed by a law of Ohio to transact business in the latter state upon the condition that service of process upon the agent of the corporation should be considered as service upon the corporation itself, a judgment obtained against the corporation by means of such process" ought to receive in Indiana the same faith and credit as it was entitled to in Ohio.[32]

Later cases establish under both the Fourteenth Amendment and Article IV, section 1, that the cause of action must have arisen within the state obtaining service in this way,[33] that service on an officer of a corporation, not its resident agent and not present in the state in an official capacity, will not confer jurisdiction over the corporation;[34] that the question whether the corporation was actually "doing business" in the state may be raised.[35] On the other hand, the fact that the business was interstate is no objection.[36]

Still more recently, by analogy to the above cases, it has been held that a state may require nonresident owners of motor vehicles to designate an official within the state as an agent upon whom process may be served in any legal proceedings growing out of their operation of a motor vehicle within the state;[37] and while these cases arose under the Fourteenth Amendment alone, unquestionably a judgment validly obtained upon this species of service could be enforced upon the owner of a car through the courts of his home state.

IV

In sustaining the challenge to jurisdiction in cases involving judgments "*in personam*" the Court was in the main making only a somewhat more extended application of recognized principles. In order to sustain the same kind of challenge in cases involving judgments "*in rem*" it has had to make law outright. The leading case is Thompson v. Whitman,[38] decided in 1873. Thompson, sheriff of Monmouth County, New Jersey, acting under a New Jersey statute, had seized a sloop belonging to Whitman, and by a proceeding *in rem* had obtained its condemnation and forfeiture in a local court. Later, Whitman, a citizen of New York, brought an action for trespass against Thompson in the

---

31. 18 How. 404 (U.S. 1855).

32. To the same effect is Connecticut Mt. Ins. Co. v. Spratley, 172 U.S. 602, 19 Sup. Ct. 308 (1899).

33. Simon v. Southern Ry., 236 U.S. 115, 35 Sup. Ct. 255 (1915).

34. Goldey v. Morning News, 156 U.S. 518, 15 Sup. Ct. 559 (1895); Riverside Mills v. Menefee, 237 U.S. 189, 35 Sup. Ct. 579 (1915).

35. International Harvester Co. v. Kentucky, 234 U.S. 579, 34 Sup. Ct. 944 (1914); Riverside Mills v. Menefee, above note 34.

36. International Harvester Co. v. Kentucky, above note 35.

37. Kane v. New Jersey, 242 U.S. 160, 37 Sup. Ct. 30 (1916); Hess v. Pawloski, 274 U.S. 352, 47 Sup. Ct. 632 (1927).

38. 18 Wall. 457 (U.S. 1873).

United States circuit court for the Southern District of New York, and Thompson answered by producing a record of the proceedings before the New Jersey tribunal. Whitman thereupon set up the contention that the New Jersey court had acted without jurisdiction inasmuch as the sloop which was the subject matter of the proceedings had been seized outside the county to which, by the statute under which it had acted, its jurisdiction was confined.

As previously explained, the plea of lack of privity cannot be set up in defense in a sister state against a judgment *in rem.* It is, on the other hand, required of a proceeding *in rem* that the *res* be within the Court's jurisdiction which was the point denied in Thompson v. Whitman. Yet could the Court consider this challenge with respect to a judgment which was offered not as the basis for an action for enforcement through the courts of a sister state, but merely as a defense in a collateral action? As the law stood in 1873, it most clearly could not.[39]

All difficulties, nevertheless, to its consideration of the challenge to jurisdiction in the case were brushed aside by the Court in a single sweeping gesture. Whenever, it said, the record of a judgment rendered in a state court is offered "in evidence" by either of the parties to an action in another state, it may be contradicted as to the facts necessary to sustain the former court's jurisdiction; "and if it be shown that such facts did not exist, the record will be a nullity, notwithstanding the claim that they did exist."

In other words, the challenge to jurisdiction is treated as equivalent to the plea *nul tiel record,* a plea which was recognized even in Mills v. Duryee as always available against an attempted invocation of the "full faith and credit" clause. What is not pointed out by the Court, is that it was also assumed in the earlier case that such a plea could always be rebutted by producing a transcript, properly authenticated in accordance with the Act of Congress, of the judgment in the original case. The decision in Thompson v. Whitman boils down to the proposition that it may be asserted that there is no record where palpably there is one. Nor does it help to say that the trial court had no jurisdiction to produce the record, for the very point at issue was whether this question could be raised.

This, however, is only the beginning of the Court's lawmaking in cases *in rem.* The most important class of such cases arising under Article IV, section 1, is that in which the respondent to a suit for divorce offers in defense an earlier decree from the courts of a sister state. By the almost universally accepted view prior to 1906 a proceeding in divorce was one against the marriage *status* and might be validly brought by either party in any state where he or she was *bona fide* domiciled.[40] But in the year named, the Court, under the leadership of the

---

39. See 1 Black, *Judgments* section 246 (1891).

40. Atherton v. Atherton, 181 U.S. 155, 21 Sup. Ct. 544 (1901); 2 Cooley, *Constitutional Limitations* 848 (8th ed. 1927); Cheever v. Wilson, 9 Wall. 108 (U.S. 1869); Ditson v. Ditson, 4 R.I. 87 (1856); Dunham v. Dunham, 162 Ill. 589, 44 N.E. 841 (1896). "In divorce cases, no more than in any other, can the court make a decree for the payment of money by a defendant not served with process, and not appearing in the case, which shall be binding upon him personally." 2 Cooley, *op. cit.* above at 858. See also note 49 below.

ever ingenious Justice White, discovered by a vote of five to four, a situation in which a divorce proceeding is one *in personam.*

The case referred to is Haddock v. Haddock,[41] while the earlier rule is illustrated by Atherton v. Atherton, decided five years previously. A comparison of the two cases is indeed striking. In the latter it was held, in the former denied, that a divorce granted a husband without personal service upon the wife, who at the time was residing in another state, was entitled to recognition under the "full faith and credit" clause and the acts of Congress; the difference between the cases consisting solely in the fact that in the Atherton case the husband had driven the wife from their joint home by his conduct, while in the Haddock case he had deserted her. The court which granted the divorce in Atherton v. Atherton was held to have had jurisdiction of the marriage *status,* with the result that the proceeding was one *in rem* and hence required only service by publication upon the respondent. Haddock's suit on the contrary, was held to be as to the wife *in personam,* and so to require personal service upon her, or her voluntary appearance, neither of which had been had; although, notwithstanding this, the decree in the latter case was held to be valid as to the state where obtained on account of the state's inherent power to determine the *status* of its own citizens. The upshot was a situation in which a man and a woman, when both were in Connecticut, were divorced; when both were in New York, were married; and when the one was in Connecticut and the other in New York, the former was divorced and the latter married.[42]

The practical difficulties and distresses likely to result from such anomalies were pointed out by critics of the decision at the time.[43] In point of fact, they have been largely avoided, because most of the state courts have continued to give judicial recognition and full faith and credit to one another's divorce proceedings on the basis of the older idea that a divorce proceeding is one *in rem,* and that if the applicant is *bona fide* domiciled in the state the court has jurisdiction in this respect.[44]

The Haddock case is another of these instances in which the Court—or a narrow majority of it—permitted itself to be overpersuaded that it owed society a duty superior to logic, respect for precedent, or even common sense. This is

41. 201 U.S. 562, 26 Sup. Ct. 525 (1906). See also Thompson v. Thompson, above note 26.

42. The Court had said in Atherton v. Atherton, above note 40, at 162, 21 Sup. Ct. at 547: "A husband without a wife, or a wife without a husband, is unknown to the law." In Dunham v. Dunham, above note 40, at 606, 44 N.E. at 847, Judge Carter of the Illinois Supreme Court had characterized in anticipation, as it were, the doctrine of Haddock v. Haddock by the remark that "It would seem to be as logical to say that one of the Siamese twins might have been severed from the other without that other being severed from the one."

43. See especially Beale, "Constitutional Protection of Decrees for Divorce" 19 *Harv. L. Rev.* 586 (1906). In an article published twenty years later, however, Beale, "Haddock Revisited" 39 *Harv. L. Rev.* 417 (1926), Professor Beale retracts much of his earlier criticism.

44. See Note (1903) 59 L.R.A. 135, 162, and 167; (1909) 18 *id.* (N.S.), 647, 649. No constitutional question is, of course, raised when a state gives full faith and credit to a divorce granted in another state, whether this was constitutionally required or not.

revealed by Justice White's expression of concern lest, if the implications of the Atherton case were to be followed, "the States whose laws were the most lax" in the matter of causes for divorce and in residence and procedural requirements, "would in ecect {*sic*; effect?} dominate all the other States."[45] In point of fact, the obstacle set up in the Haddock case to easy divorce is a ridiculously feeble one. On the one hand, it does not and could not prevent applicants from flocking to states with lax laws and respondents from putting in necessary appearances to validate the proceedings; on the other hand, the vast majority of divorces are granted by courts within whose jurisdictions both parties reside, and to such instances the Haddock case again has no application.

Furthermore, while a divorce granted to one not *bona fide* domiciled within a state is, as already indicated, granted without jurisdiction, and hence not entitled to extrastate recognition under the "full faith and credit" clause,[46] not the slightest disposition has appeared within recent years to challenge judicially the power of the states to determine what shall constitute domicile for divorce purposes. Thus in March, 1931, Nevada, in an effort, as we learn, "to retain for Reno its position as the nation's divorce capital against competition from Hot Springs, Arkansas, and Boisé, Idaho," enacted a law requiring only six weeks residence by an applicant for divorce in the courts of that state.[47] But why six *weeks?* Why not six days, or six hours? Haddock v. Haddock or not, suit for divorce seems to have become for those who can pay the transportation charges little more than an *ex parte* proceeding.

V

Some other aspects of judgments may be dealt with more briefly. Many of the cases involve decrees of courts of probate respecting the distribution of estates. In order that a court have jurisdiction of such a proceeding, the decedent must have been domiciled in the state, and the question whether he was so domiciled at the time of his death may be raised in the court of a sister state.[48] What is more important, however, is that the *res* in such a proceeding, that is, the estate, must, in order to entitle the judgment recognition under Article IV, section 1, have been located in the state or legally attached to the person of the decedent. Such a judgment is accordingly valid, generally speaking, to distribute the intangible property of the decedent, though the evidences thereof were actually located elsewhere.[49] This is not so, on the other hand, as to tangibles and realty. In order

45. Haddock v. Haddock, above note 41, at 574, 26 Sup. Ct. at 529.

46. Andrews v. Andrews, 188 U.S. 14, 23 Sup. Ct. 237 (1903). See also German Savings Society v. Dormitzer, 192 U.S. 125, 24 Sup. Ct. 221 (1904).

47. See *New York Times,* March 17, 1931. During the first six weeks of the new dispensation 513 cases were filed and 331 decrees granted. *Id.* May 31, 1931.

48. Tilt v. Kelsey, 207 U.S. 43, 28 Sup. Ct. 1 (1907); Burbank v. Ernst, 232 U.S. 162, 34 Sup. Ct. 299 (1914).

49. Blodgett v. Silberman, 277 U.S. 1, 48 Sup. Ct. 410 (1928).

that the judgment of a probate court distributing these be entitled to recognition under the Constitution, they must have been located in the state; as to tangibles and realty outside the state, the decree of the probate court is entirely at the mercy of the *lex rei sitae*.[50]

That a statute legitimizing children born out of wedlock does not entitle them by the aid of the "full faith and credit" clause to share in the property located in another state is not surprising, in view of the principle that statutes do not have extraterritorial operation.[51] For the same reason adoption proceedings in one state are not denied full faith and credit by the law of a sister state which excludes children adopted by proceedings in other states from the right to inherit land therein.[52]

A proceeding which combines some of the elements of both an *in rem* and an *in personam* action is the proceeding in garnishment cases. Suppose that A owes B and B owes C, and that the two former live in a different state than C. A while on a brief visit to C's state is presented with a writ attaching his debt to B and also a summons to appear in court on a named day. The result of the proceedings thus instituted is that a judgment is entered in C's favor against A to the amount of his indebtedness to B. Subsequently he is sued by B in their home state, and offers the judgment, which he has in the meantime paid, in defense. It was argued in behalf of B that A's debt to him had a *situs* in their home state, and furthermore that C could not have sued B in this same state without formally acquiring a domicile there. Both propositions were however rejected by the Court, which held that the judgment in the garnishment proceedings was entitled to full faith and credit as against C's action.[53]

Are there other challenges than the jurisdictional one to the recognition of a judgment outside the state where rendered? There are *dicta* to the effect that judgments for which extraterritorial operation is demanded under Article IV, section 1, and acts of Congress are "impeachable for manifest fraud," but unless the fraud affected the jurisdiction of the Court the vast weight of authority is against the proposition.[54] And it is universally agreed that a judgment may not be

50. Kerr v. Devisees of Moon, 9 Wheat. 565 (U.S. 1824); McCormick v. Sullivant, 10 Wheat. 192 (U.S. 1825); Robertson et. al. v. Pickrell et al., 109 U.S. 608, 3 Sup. Ct. 407 (1883); Clarke v. Clarke, 178 U.S. 186, 20 Sup. Ct. 873 (1900). The controlling principle of these cases is not confined to proceedings in probate. A court of equity "not having jurisdiction of the *res*, cannot affect it by its decree, nor by a deed made by a master in accordance with the decree." Fall v. Eastin, 215 U.S. 1 at 11, 30 Sup. Ct. 3 at 7 (1909).

51. Olmsted v. Olmsted, 216 U.S. 386, 30 Sup. Ct. 292 (1910).

52. Hood v. McGehee, 237 U.S. 611, 35 Sup. Ct. 718 (1915).

53. Harris v. Balk, 198 U.S. 215, 25 Sup. Ct. 625 (1905). See also Chicago, R.I. & Pac. Ry. v. Sturm, 174 U.S. 710, 19 Sup. Ct. 797 (1899).

54. Christmas v. Russell, 5 Wall. 290 (U.S. 1866); Maxwell v. Stewart, 21 Wall. 71 (U.S. 1874); Hanley v. Donoghue, 116 U.S. 1, 6 Sup. Ct. 242 (1885); Wisconsin v. Pelican Ins. Co., 127 U.S. 265, 8 Sup. Ct. 1370 (1888); Cole v. Cunningham, 133 U.S. 107, 10 Sup. Ct. 269 (1890); Simmons v. Saul, 138 U.S. 439, 11 Sup. Ct. 369 (1891); American Exp. Co. v. Mullins, 212 U.S. 311, 29 Sup. Ct. 381 (1909). In Cole v. Cunningham, the Court sustained the Massachusetts court in enjoining, in connection with insolvency proceedings instituted in that state, a Massachusetts creditor

impeached for alleged error or irregularity;[55] or as contrary to the public policy of the state where recognition is sought for it under the "full faith and credit" clause; although as we have seen, there are cases in which the Court has in fact permitted local policy to determine the merits of a judgment under the pretext of regulating jurisdiction.[56]

Finally, the clause has been interpreted in the light of the "incontrovertible maxim" that "the courts of no country execute the penal laws of another."[57] In the leading case of Huntington v. Attrill,[58] however, the Court so narrowly defined "penal" in this connection as to make it substantially synonymous with "criminal," and on this basis held a judgment which had been recovered under a state statute making the officers of a corporation who signed and recorded a false certificate of the amount of its capital stock liable for all of its debts, to be entitled under Article IV, section 1, to recognition and enforcement in the courts of sister states. And a recent case[59] suggests the possibility that a judgment for taxes might be sued upon in the name of the taxing state in the courts of sister states.[60]

VI

The most significant cases arising under the "full faith and credit" clause within recent years have been those, referred to in the opening section of this paper, in which the Court has invoked the clause in order to give statutes extrastate operation in certain situations. The initial effort in this direction was made in connection with transitory actions based on statute. Earlier, such actions

---

from continuing in New York courts an action which had been commenced there before the insolvency suit was brought. This was done on the theory that a party within the jurisdiction of a court may be restrained from doing something in another jurisdiction opposed to principles of equity, it having been shown that the creditor was aware of the debtor's embarrassed condition when the New York action was instituted. The injunction unquestionably denied "full faith and credit" to the New York proceedings, the jurisdiction of the New York courts being unquestioned. The decision commanded the assent of only five justices, and must be reckoned another of the numerous instances of the Court's attempting the role of special providence under this clause.

55. Cases just cited, above note 54.

56. Notes 23 and 24 above.

57. Chief Justice Marshall, in the Antelope, 10 Wheat. 66, 123 (1825); see also Wisconsin v. Pelican Ins. Co., above note 54. The importance of the maxim is chiefly felt in connection with the question of what causes of actions originating in sister states the courts of a state shall treat as transitory, and so furnish a *forum* for them. See Leflar, "Extrastate Enforcement of Penal and Governmental Claims" 46 *Harvard L. Rev.* 193–225 (1932).

58. 146 U.S. 657, 13 Sup. Ct. 224 (1892); Dennick v. R.R., 103 U.S. 11 (1880) had paved the way for the later case.

59. Moore v. Mitchell, 281 U.S. 18, 50 Sup. Ct. 175 (1930).

60. In Am. Exp. Co. v. Mullins, above note 54, it was held that a summary judgment whereby property was seized and destroyed as contraband in one state must be recognized when offered in defense in a suit brought in the courts of another state for the value of the property. Clearly this result cannot rest on the principle of *res judicata*. Perhaps the case should be classified with those dealt with in the next section.

had rested upon the common law, which was fairly uniform throughout the states, so that there was usually little discrepancy between the law under which the plaintiff from another jurisdiction claimed his action (*lex loci*) and the law under which the defendant responded (*lex fori*). In the late seventies, however, the states, abandoning the common law rule on the subject, began passing laws which authorized the representatives of a decedent whose death had resulted from injury to bring an action for damages.[61] The question at once presented itself whether, if such an action was brought in a state other than that in which the injury occurred, it was governed by the statute under which it arose or by the law of the *forum* state, which might be less favorable to the defendant. Nor was it long before the same question presented itself with respect to transitory actions *ex contractu*, where the contract involved had been made under laws peculiar to the state where made, and with those laws in view.

In Chicago and Alton R. R. v. Wiggins,[62] decided in 1887, the Court, confronted with the latter form of the question, indicated its clear opinion that in such situations it was the law under which the contract was made, not the law of the *forum* state, which should govern. Its utterance on the point was, however, not merely *obiter;* it was based on an error of the most palpable nature, namely, the false supposition that the Constitution gives "acts" the same extraterritorial operation as the Act of 1790 does "judicial records and proceedings." Notwithstanding which, this *dictum* is today the basis of "the settled rule" that the defendant in a transitory action is entitled to all the benefits resulting from whatever material restrictions the statute under which plaintiff's right of action originated sets thereto, except that courts of sister states cannot be thus prevented from taking jurisdiction in such cases.[63]

Nor is it alone to defendants in transitory actions that the "full faith and credit" clause is today a shield and a buckler. Some legal relationships are so complex, the Court holds, that the law under which they were formed ought always to govern them as long as they persist.[64] One such relationship is that of a stockholder and his corporation. Hence, notwithstanding the principle that no state need admit a "foreign" corporation to do local business except on such terms as it chooses to lay down, yet if it does so and a question later arises as to the liability of the stockholders of the corporation, the courts of the state are required by the "full faith and credit" clause to determine the question in

61. Dennick v. R.R., above note 58, was the first of the so-called "Death Act" cases to reach the Supreme Court. See also Stewart v. B. & O. R.R., 168 U.S. 445, 18 Sup. Ct. 105 (1897).

62. 119 U.S. 615, 7 Sup. Ct. 398 (1887).

63. Glenn v. Garth, 147 U.S. 360, 13 Sup. Ct. 350 (1893); Northern Pac. R.R. v. Babcock, 154 U.S. 190, 14 Sup. Ct. 978 (1894); Slater v. Atchison, T. & S. F. Ry. v. Sowers, 213 U.S. 55, 67, 28 Sup. Ct. 397, 401 (1908); Tennessee Coal Co. v. George, 233 U.S. 354, 34 Sup. Ct. 587 (1914). A state court does not violate the "full faith and credit" clause by mere error in construing the law upon which a transitory action from another state depends. Glenn v. Garth, above; Banholzer v. N.Y. Life Ins. Co., 178 U.S. 402, 20 Sup. Ct. 972 (1900).

64. See Holmes, in Modern Woodmen of Am. v. Mixer, 267 U.S. 544, 551, 45 Sup. Ct. 389 (1925).

accordance with the constitution, laws, and judicial decisions of the corporation's home state.[65]

And the same principle applies to the relationship which is formed when one takes out a policy in an insurance company. Thus in Royal Arcanum v. Green,[66] in which a fraternal insurance association chartered under the laws of Massachusetts was being sued in the courts of New York by a citizen of the latter state on a contract of insurance made in that state, the Court held that the defendant company was entitled under the "full faith and credit" clause to have the case determined in accordance with the laws of Massachusetts and its own constitution and by-laws as these had been construed by the Massachusetts courts.

Finally, by a recent case the relationship of employer and employee, so far as the obligations of the one and the rights of the other under a workmen's compensation act are concerned, is similarly classified.[67] The cause of action in the case was an injury in New Hampshire, resulting in death, to a workman who had entered the defendant company's employment in Vermont, the home state of both parties. The Court held that the case was governed under the "full faith and credit" clause by the Vermont workmen's compensation act, not that of New Hampshire. The relationship, it said, "was created by the law of Vermont, and so long as that relationship persisted its incidents were properly subject to regulation there."[68]

Thus the Court from according an extrastate operation to statutes and judicial decisions in favor of defendants in transitory actions, proceeded next to confer the same protection upon certain classes of defendants in local actions in which the plaintiff's claim was the outgrowth of a relationship formed extraterritorially. But can the Court stop at this point? If it is true, as Chief Justice Marshall once remarked, that "the Constitution was not made for the benefit of plaintiffs alone," so also it is true that it was not made for the benefit of defendants alone. The day may come when the Court will approach the question of the relation of the "full faith and credit" clause to the extrastate operation of laws from the same angle as it today views the broader question of the scope of state legislative power. When and if this day arrives, state statutes and judicial decisions will be

65. Converse v. Hamilton, 224 U.S. 243, 32 Sup. Ct. 415 (1912); Selig v. Hamilton, 234 U.S. 652, 34 Sup. Ct. 926 (1914).

66. 237 U.S. 531, 35 Sup. Ct. 724 (1915); *followed* in Aetna Life Ins. Co. v. Dunken, 266 U.S. 389, 45 Sup. Ct. 129 (1924); Modern Woodmen of Am. v. Mixer, above note 64.

67. Bradford Electric Co. v. Clapper, 286 U.S. 145, 52 Sup. Ct. 571 (1932).

68. *Id.* at 158. The Court had earlier remarked that "Workmen's Compensation legislation rests upon the idea of *status,* not upon that of implied contract." Cudahy Packing Co. v. Parramore, 263 U.S. 418 at 423, 44 Sup. Ct. 153 at 154 (1923). In contrast to the above cases, see Kryger v. Wilson, above note 15. Where it was held that the question whether the cancellation of a land contract was governed by the *lex rei sitae* or the *lex locus contractus* was purely a question of local common law; also Bond v. Hume, above note 15, where the general principle of the dominance of local policy over the rules of comity is set forth at length by Chief Justice White, only to be ignored in the decision of the case.

given such extraterritorial operation as seems reasonable to the Court to give them. In short, the rule of the dominance of local policy of the *forum* state will be superseded by that of judicial review.[69]

VII

The question arises whether the application to date, not by the Court alone but by Congress and the Court, of Article IV, section 1, can be said to have met the expectations of its framers. In the light furnished by the account given in an earlier paragraph of the framing of the clause this may be seriously doubted. The protest was raised against the clause, it will be recalled, that in vesting Congress with power to declare the effect state laws should have outside the enacting state, it enabled the new government to usurp the powers of the states; but the objection went unheeded.

The main concern of the Convention, it may be admitted, was to render the judgments of the state courts in civil cases effective throughout the Union. Yet even this objective has been by no means completely realized, owing to the doctrine of the Court that before a judgment of a state court can be enforced in a sister state, a new suit must be brought on it in the courts of the latter; and the further doctrine that with respect to such a suit, the judgment sued on is only "evidence"; the logical deduction from which proposition is that the sister state is under no constitutional compulsion to give it a *forum*.

These doctrines were first clearly stated in the McElmoyle case and flowed directly from the new states' rights premises of the Court; but they are no longer in harmony with the prevailing spirit of constitutional construction nor with the needs of the times. Also, the clause seems always to have been interpreted on the basis of the assumption that the term "judicial proceedings" refers only to final judgments and does not include intermediate processes and writs; but the assumption would seem to be groundless, and if it is, then Congress has the power under the clause to provide for the service and execution throughout the United States of the judicial processes of the several states.

Under the present system, suit has ordinarily to be brought where the defendant, the alleged wrongdoer, resides, which means generally where no part of the transaction giving rise to the action took place. What could be more irrational? "Granted that no state can of its own volition make its process run beyond its

---

69. Reviewing some of the cases treated in this section, a writer in 1925 said: "It appears, then, that the Supreme Court has quite definitely committed itself to the program of making itself, to some extent, a tribunal for bringing about uniformity in the field of conflicts . . . although the precise circumstances under which it will regard itself as having jurisdiction for this purpose are far from clear." E. M. Dodd, "The Power of the Supreme Court to Review State Decisions in the Field of Conflict of Laws" 39 *Harv. L. Rev.* 533–62 (1926). It can hardly be said that the law has been subsequently clarified on this point.

borders . . . is it unreasonable that the United States should by federal action be made a unit in the manner suggested?"[70]

Indeed, there are few clauses of the Constitution, the merely literal possibilities of which have been so little developed as the "full faith and credit" clause. Congress has the power under the clause to decree the effect that the statutes of one state shall have in other states. This being so, it does not seem extravagant to argue that Congress may under the clause describe a certain type of divorce and say that it shall be granted recognition throughout the Union, and that no other kind shall. Or to speak in more general terms, Congress has under the clause power to enact standards whereby uniformity of state legislation may be secured as to almost any matter in connection with which interstate recognition of private rights would be useful and valuable.[71]

Nor should the limited initiative taken by the Court in this matter in recent years deter Congress from action. The little that can be accomplished by "the judicial process of inclusion and exclusion" will go neither far nor fast toward meeting present-day necessities. Besides it is to *Congress* that the Constitution itself reserves the initiative in the application of the "full faith and credit" clause, not to the Court.

As was seen earlier, the legislation of Congress comprised in sections 905 and 906 of the Revised Statutes lays down a rule not merely for the recognition of the records and judicial proceedings of state courts in the courts of sister states, but for their recognition in "every court of the United States," and it further lays down a like rule for the records and proceedings of the courts "of any territory or any country subject to the jurisdiction of the United States."

These features of the acts of Congress are to be referred not to Article IV, section 1, but to Congress's power under the "necessary and proper" clause in relation to Article III, and to its powers in connection with the government of the territories and of the District of Columbia.[72] Doubtless, Congress might also by virtue of its powers in the field of foreign relations lay down a mandatory rule regarding recognition of foreign judgments in every court of the United States. At present, the duty to recognize such judgments even in the national courts rests only on comity and is qualified, in the judgment of the Supreme Court by a strict rule of reciprocity.[73]

---

70. Cook, above note 25, at 430. The entire article is important; see also the Australian Service and Execution of Process Act, given in an appendix to it, at 441–49.

71. 1 Schofield, *Essays on Constitutional Law and Equity* 211 *et seq.* (1921).

72. Embry v. Palmer, 107 U.S. 3, 2 Sup. Ct. 25 (1882); Atchison, T. & S. F. Ry. v. Sowers, above note 63.

73. Hilton v. Guyot, 159 U.S. 113, 16 Sup. Ct. 139 (1895), where a French judgment offered in defense was held not a bar to the suit. Four justices dissented on the ground that "the application of the doctrine of *res judicata* does not rest in discretion; and it is for the government, and not for its courts, to adopt the principle of retorsion, if deemed under any circumstances desirable or necessary." *Id.* at 234, 16 Sup. Ct. at 171. At the same sitting of Court, an action in a United States circuit court on a Canadian judgment was sustained on the same ground of reciprocity. Ritchie v. McMul-

len, 159 U.S. 235, 16 Sup. Ct. 171 (1895). See also Ingenohl v. Olsen, 273 U.S. 541, 47 Sup. Ct. 451 (1927), where a decision of the supreme court of the Philippine Islands was reversed for refusal to enforce a judgment of the supreme court of the British colony of Hongkong, which was rendered "after a fair trial by a court having jurisdiction of the parties." In *Foreign Relations of the United States* 7–8 (1897), will be found a three-cornered correspondence between the State Department, the Austro-Hungarian Legation, and the governor of Pennsylvania, in which the last named asserts that "under the laws of Pennsylvania the judgment of a court of competent jurisdiction in Croatia would be respected to the extent of permitting such judgment to be sued upon in the courts of Pennsylvania. . . ." Stowell, *op. cit.* note 1 above, at 254–55. Another instance of international cooperation in the judicial field is furnished by "letters rogatory." "When letters rogatory are addressed from any court of a foreign country to any district court of the United States, a commissioner of such district court designated by said court to make the examination of the witnesses mentioned in said letters, shall have power to compel the witnesses to appear and depose in the same manner as witnesses may be compelled to appear and testify in courts." 28 U.S.C.A., above note 11, section 653. Some of the states have similar laws. See 2 Moore, *Digest of International Law* 108–9 (1906).

11. National-State Cooperation—
Its Present Possibilities

In an admirable article commenting upon certain recent decisions of the Supreme Court, Professor Bunn has remarked:

Effective governmental power to regulate the main strategic factors of "ordinary private business" is non-existent in this country. To those who think that everywhere and always an unregulated economy is best, that business decisions are necessarily more wise and beneficial to the public if made by business people rather than politicians, the situation must be highly satisfactory. To those who disagree, who think that government must interfere before the oil is gone and the soil blown away into the ocean, and that at other points our economic life now or hereafter may need major regulation at the hands of government, the present status is a nightmare. For when power is lacking the wisest statesmen in the world are ineffective. The question is, what shall we do about it?[1]

Professor Bunn thereupon proceeds to answer his own question thus: "Within the Constitution, two main methods are proposed: interstate compacts and a Constitutional amendment." The former alternative he rejects outright, for the following cogent reasons:

1. Where the states concerned are scattered or their interests diverse, agreement is unlikely. In Congress a majority governs, to make a compact requires unanimity.
2. Where the states concerned are near together and their interests united, there is danger of action for sectional rather than national welfare. Congress has a veto, but it has no affirmative authority, and it can hardly be expected to be as alert to the national interests as it should be where it initiates action itself.
3. A compact once made is a contract—it is as hard to amend it as to make it in the first place.
4. States cannot by compact acquire powers which the Constitution denies them.

Reprinted by permission of the Yale Law Journal Company and Fred B. Rothman & Company from the *Yale Law Journal,* Vol. 46, pp. 599–623 (1937).
1. Bunn, "Production, Prices, Income and the Constitution" (1936) 11 *Wis. L. Rev.* 313.

The Fourteenth Amendment and the commerce clause will continue to control state action however much the states may contract to the contrary.

Compacts are clearly therefore not the main solution.[2]

Mr. Bunn then turns to the amendment method as the single remaining possibility. But this, too, I contend, is open to strong objections when the underlying reasons for the present situation are thoroughly explored. As I have elsewhere put the matter:

> Most, if not all, of the principal New Deal legislation might have been sustained had the Court chosen to given the doctrines invoked against it as liberal an application as it has sometimes done in the past; or if it had simply chosen to give the words of the Constitution itself their logical and historical meanings.
>
> But if this is so, what would be the point in adding "new" powers to Congress by Constitutional amendment? And more especially, what would be the point in doing so if these powers were to be exposed to the same principles of construction as made them necessary?
>
> How long would they, subjected to the vague, indefinite tests of constitutionality to which the New Deal legislation succumbed, remain adequate to the purposes for which they were adopted?
>
> The further question accordingly arises, whether those who urge Constitutional amendment as the best means of meeting the present situation would like to see the above mentioned tests of constitutionality abolished? It seems not.
>
> What they propose is really that the power which was originally granted in broad terms to the National Government should be regranted piece by piece, and that without any guaranty that the regrant would be more effective than the original grant has turned out to be!
>
> This may not be quite the same thing as proposing that the national legislative power be gradually transferred from Article I to Article V of the Constitution, but it is pretty nearly that.
>
> The suggestion of specific Constitutional amendments as a means of meeting the present situation may, therefore, be ruled out without more ado. If the Court does not exchange its present application of "the reserved powers of the States" concept, the "due process of law" concept, and the maxim against delegated legislation for more liberal views, such amendments would not suffice—indeed, they might prove a positive menace to admitted powers, on the well-known principle of construction that a specific power argues against a more general one.
>
> If, on the other hand, the Court does come around to the liberal views on which the New Deal legislation was justifiably predicated, then such amendments would be unnecessary.[3]

In short, *we must still trust the Court, as we have so largely in the past, to correct its own errors.* At the same time, however, we must recognize that admission of error comes hard to human nature, and especially to that indurated type of human nature which is apt to occupy high judicial office. Can we then help the Court out of its present predicament by suggesting to it a somewhat different approach to some of the problems of constitutionality which it must solve in the near future? To put the matter otherwise—Why should the Court be

2. *Id.* at 320–21.
3. See *New York Post,* December 1, 1936, p. 1, col. 2.

led back over the Serbonian bog of its past mistakes if a new path can be pointed out to it which avoids said bog? And can that way be found in the manifold possibilities of national-state cooperation?

I

The following are the salient and pertinent features of "our dual form of government": (1) as in all federations, a union of several autonomous political entities, or "states," for common purposes; (2) an apportionment of the sum total of legislative power permissible in a free commonwealth between a "national government," on the one hand, and constituent "states," on the other; (3) the direct operation for the most part of each of these centers of government, within its assigned sphere, upon all persons and property within its territorial limits; (4) the provision of each center with the complete apparatus of law enforcement, executive and judicial; (5) the supremacy of the "national government" within its assigned sphere over any conflicting assertion of "state" power; (6) dual citizenship.

The problem which I shall treat in this paper is, what species of national-state relationship do the above "fixed data" of dual federalism admit of? The question may, conceivably, be approached from either of two points of view. The two governmental centers may be envisaged as *more or less jealous rivals for power,* or they may be viewed as *mutually supplementing agencies of government.* Fortunately, except for the period immediately preceding the Civil War, when the self-defensive necessities of slavery affected constitutional interpretation unduly, the latter is the conception which has generally prevailed.

The theory of the Articles of Confederation was that the powers of the general government should be exercised through the state governments. The theory was not effectively realized in practice, with the result, pointed out by Chief Justice Marshall in McCulloch v. Maryland, that the government set up by the Constitution of 1787 was not, in general, left dependent upon the states "for the execution of the great powers assigned to it."[4] At the same time, however, this independence was very far from being regarded as utterly divorcing the two governmental centers or as making state governmental machinery unavailable for national purposes.

In point of fact, it would seem that the framers of the Constitution looked forward to something like a mixed system of *functional* and *dual* federalism— one which would permit the gradual transference of the greater part of the legislative power to the national government, while incorporating the judicial and executive organs of the states into the national administrative mechanism. In this connection the following entry in the official Journal of the Convention for July 17th becomes most instructive:

4. 4 Wheat. 316, 424 (U.S. 1819).

"It was moved and seconded to postpone the consideration of the second clause of the Sixth resolution reported from the Committee of the whole House in order to take up the following:

'To make laws binding on the People of the United States in all cases which may concern the common interests of the Union: but not to interfere with the government of the individual States in any matters of internal police which respect the government of such States only, and wherein the general welfare of the United States is not concerned' which passed in the negative (Ayes—2; noes—8). It was moved and seconded to alter the second clause of the 6th resolution so as to read as follows, namely

"and moreover to legislate in all cases for the general interests of the Union, and also in those to which the States are separately incompetent, or in which the harmony of the United States may be interrupted by the exercise of individual legislation."

"which passed in the affirmative (Ayes—6; noes—4). . . .

"It was moved and seconded to agree to the following resolution namely

"Resolved that the legislative acts of the United States made by virtue and in pursuance of the articles of Union and all Treaties made and ratified under the authority of the United States shall be the supreme law of the respective States as far as those acts or Treaties shall relate to the said States, or their Citizens and Inhabitants—and that the Judiciaries of the several States shall be bound thereby in their decisions, anything in the respective laws of the individual States to the contrary notwithstanding." Which passed unanimously in the affirmative."[5]

Two things here emerge: (1) that it was the intention of the Convention that the legislative powers subsequently to be delegated the national government should be interpreted from the point of view of making them adequate "for the general interests of the Union" and for those purposes "to which the States are separately incompetent"; (2) that it was not intended that the supremacy which the Constitution accords national legislation made in pursuance of the Constitution should be qualified or limited by the powers of the states even with respect to "matters of internal police" only. National-state relationship was at first rested squarely upon the principle of national supremacy as thus conceived; and it has continued to rest there to this day within the field of judicial power.

Turning to the Constitution itself, we find it directly incorporating the states into the new national structure at vital points—conspicuously in the choice of senators and of presidential electors. The feature of the Constitution, however, which bears most directly on the question here under investigation is its provision in Article VI, paragraph 3, that "the members of the several State legislatures and all executive and judicial officers . . . of the States shall be bound by oath or affirmation to support this Constitution."

Commenting upon this provision in the *Federalist* No. 27, Hamilton wrote:

Thus the legislatures, courts and magistrates of the respective members will be incorporated into the operations of the national government, *as far as its just and constitutional authority extends*; and will be rendered auxiliary to the enforcement of its laws.[6]

5. 2 Farrand, *Records of the Federal Convention* (1911) 21.
6. *The Federalist* (Lodge ed. 1888) 162. Madison speaks to the same effect in No. 44, *id.* at 284–85. See also Holcombe, "The States as Agents of the Nation" (1921) 1 *Southwestern Pol. {sic.; Social?}Sci. Q.* 307.

Indeed, the younger Pinckney had expressed the same idea on the floor of the Philadelphia Convention:

> They (the States) are the instruments upon which the Union must frequently depend for the force and execution of its powers.[7]

And substituting the word "may" for "must" in Pinckney's statement, we find it to be amply justified by early congressional legislation. The Judiciary Act of 1789 left the state courts in sole possession of a large part of the jurisdiction over controversies between citizens of different states and in concurrent possession of the rest. What is more important, it was provided by the famous Twenty-fifth Section of this act that a case "arising" under the Constitution and laws of the United States which was first brought into a state court, should remain there for final disposition unless the decision of the highest state court into which the case might under state law be brought, was adverse to the party claiming under national authority, in which contingency there should be an appeal on writ of error to the Supreme Court of the United States. By other sections of the same act state courts were authorized to entertain proceedings by the United States itself to enforce penalties and forfeitures under the revenue laws, while any justice of the peace or other magistrate of any of the states was authorized to cause any offender against the United States to be arrested and imprisoned or bailed under the usual mode of process.[8] Even as late as 1839, Congress authorized all pecuniary penalties and forfeitures under the laws of the United States to be sued for before any court of competent jurisdiction in the state where the cause of action arose or where the offender might be found.[9]

Pursuant also to the same idea of treating state governmental organs as available to the national government for administrative purposes, the Act of 1793 entrusted the rendition of fugitive slaves in part to national officials and in part to state officials, and the rendition of fugitives from justice from one state to another exclusively to the state executives.[10] Certain later acts empowered state courts to entertain criminal prosecutions for forging paper of the Bank of the United States and for counterfeiting coin of the United States;[11] while still others conferred on state judges authority to admit aliens to national citizenship and provided penalties in case such judges should utter false certificates of naturalization—provisions which are still on the statute books.[12]

And from the first, treaties of the United States have thrown open the state

7. 1 Farrand, *op. cit.* above note 5, at 404.
8. 1 Stat. 73 (1789).
9. 5 Stat. 322 (1839).
10. 1 Stat. 302 (1793).
11. 2 Stat. 404 (1806). For the development of opinion, especially on the part of state courts, adverse to the validity of the above discussed legislation, see 1 Kent's *Commentaries* (1826) *396–*404.
12. 2 Kent's *Commentaries* (1826) *64–*65. 34 Stat. 596 (1906), 8 U.S.C. sections 357, 379; 34 Stat. 602 (1906), 18 U.S.C. section 135 (1934). For cases recognizing the right of Congress to authorize naturalization proceedings in state courts, see Holmgren v. United States, 217 U.S. 509 (1910) and citations there given.

courts to aliens on the most-favored-nation basis and have in other ways stipulated the active aid of state authorities in certain contingencies, as in the interception and return of deserting alien seamen. Indeed, the unity of the United States in the sphere of international relationships is today an accepted feature of our dual system. In this field the national government is not a "foreign" government with respect to the states, nor are the latter "sovereign" or "independent" with respect to the former. And with the establishment of this principle the relationship between the two is not normally one of competition, but rather of cooperation and reciprocal service. The treaty-making authority is the champion of the interests of the states, safeguarding their local laws and customs, subject only to the proviso that these shall not, in general, discriminate against aliens as such. On the other hand, it is through these same local laws and authorities that the rights stipulated for on behalf of aliens, in return for similar rights to American citizens abroad, are rendered effective.[13]

Cooperation, nevertheless, between the two governmental centers, on the basis of the supremacy of the national government, came in time to be challenged, and first of all in the area in which it was most extensively employed in early legislation, namely, in the judicial field. The basis of the challenge was furnished by the notion of the equal sovereignty of the states and the national government in their respective spheres. Quite obviously this notion cannot be harmonized with the supremacy clause of the Constitution[14] so long as the two spheres of jurisdiction overlap, as they inevitably do when state organs are utilized for national purposes. If, therefore, the principle of equal sovereignty was to make good, it was incumbent upon its advocates to establish first the total independence of the two governmental centers within their respective fields. The effort initially took the form of an assault on the constitutionality of Section 25 of the Judiciary Act of 1789.

In the Philadelphia Convention the champions of states rights had urged that it was unnecessary to provide for an inferior federal judiciary. It would be sufficient, they contended, if state courts were employed as national courts of first instance, with a final appeal to the Supreme Court; and the wording of Article III, section 1, which provides that "the judicial power of the United States shall be vested in one supreme court and in such inferior courts as the Congress may from time to time ordain and establish," represents a concession to this point of view.[15] Indeed, as late as 1802 the suggestion was broached that the entire inferior federal judicial establishment ought to be abolished and its jurisdiction distributed between the state courts and the Supreme Court[16]—an idea which

13. See generally Mitchell, *State Interests in American Treaties* (1936).

14. U.S. Const. Article VI, par. 2.

15. See especially the proceedings of June 5th, 1 Farrand, *op. cit.* above note 5, at 124–25. The New Jersey Plan reverted to the idea of using state courts as national courts of first instance, with appeals to "a federal judiciary . . . to consist of a supreme Tribunal, . . ." *Id.* at 244.

16. 1 Warren, *The Supreme Court in United States History* (1922) 219–22.

was effectively spiked when the latter held in Marbury v. Madison[17] that its original jurisdiction might not be enlarged by statute.

Yet ten years later the Virginia Court of Appeals, in Hunter v. Martin,[18] held the Twenty-fifth section to be void on the ground that it was not competent for Congress to authorize appeals from the courts of another sovereignty, in this instance Virginia, to those of the United States; and this argument was renewed in 1821 in Cohens v. Virginia,[19] where the Court, speaking by Chief Justice Marshall, disposed of it in these terms:

> It (the National Government) can, in effecting its objects, legitimately control all individuals or governments in the American territory. . . . The States are constituent parts of the United States. They are parts of one great empire—for some purposes sovereign, for some purposes subordinate.[20]

Proceeding from this basis Marshall held the Twenty-fifth section to be a law "necessary and proper" to effectuate the judicial power of the United States and hence within the legislative power of Congress.

And meantime, in the case of Houston v. Moore,[21] the Court had recognized a similar relationship as existing between the power of Congress "to provide for calling forth the militia" and state executive power. Here the legislation under review was an act of Pennsylvania which provided that the officers and privates of the militia of that state, "neglecting or refusing to serve, when called into actual service, in pursuance of any order or requisition of the President of the United States, shall be liable to the penalties defined in the Act of Congress of the 28th of February, 1795, c. 277,[22] or to any penalties which may have been prescribed since the date of that act, or which may hereafter be prescribed by any law of the United States."[23] While the act was sustained by a divided Court the division was not over the question whether Congress had the power which the Pennsylvania act itself inferred, but over the exclusiveness of this power. Also, it was conceded that this power did not stop short of the chief executive of the state. In the words of Justice Johnson's concurring opinion:

> The doctrine must be admitted, that Congress might, if they thought proper, have authorized the issuing of the President's order even to the Governor. For when the constitution of Pennsylvania makes her Governor commander in chief of the militia, it must subject him in that capacity (at least when in actual service) to the orders of him who is made commander in chief of all the militia of the Union.[24]

17. 1 Cranch 137 (U.S. 1803).
18. 4 Munford 3 (Va. 1814) overturned in Martin v. Hunter's Lessee, 1 Wheat. 304 (U.S. 1816).
19. 6 Wheat. 264 (U.S. 1821).
20. *Id.* at 414.
21. 5 Wheat. 1 (U.S. 1820).
22. 1 Stat. 424 (1795).
23. It is interesting to note that nobody seems to have commented on the delegation of legislative power here involved.
24. 5 Wheat. 1, 40 (U.S. 1820).

The Court first lent definite approval to the equal sovereignty theory in Prigg v. Pennsylvania,[25] decided in 1842, in which the constitutionality of the provision of the Act of 1793, making it the duty of state magistrates to aid in the return of fugitive slaves, was challenged. Speaking for the Court, Justice Story said:

> The clause relating to fugitive slaves is found in the national Constitution, and not in that of any state. It might well be deemed an unconstitutional exercise of the power of interpretation, to insist that the states are bound to provide means to carry into effect the duties of the national government; nowhere delegated or intrusted to them by the Constitution. On the contrary, the natural, if not the necessary conclusion is, that the national government, in the absence of all positive provisions to the contrary, is bound through its own proper departments, legislative, executive, or judiciary, as the case may require, to carry into effect all the rights and duties imposed upon it by the Constitution.[26]

The Court, nevertheless, sustained the challenged provision in the sense and to the extent "that State magistrates may, if they choose, exercise the authority (conferred by the act) unless prohibited by State legislation."[27] In other words, the cooperation of the state in the enforcement of the act was purely voluntary, and the principle of national supremacy did not apply.

And in Kentucky v. Dennison,[28] decided on the eve of the Civil War, the provisions of the same act making it "the duty" of the chief executive of a state to render up a fugitive from justice upon the demand of the chief executive of the state from which the fugitive had fled, was given a similar construction. Pertinently, Chief Justice Taney remarked for the Court:

> Looking to the subject-matter of this law, and the relations which the United States and the several States bear to each other, the court is of the opinion, the words "it shall be the duty" were not used as mandatory and compulsory, but as declaratory of the moral duty which this compact created, when Congress had provided the mode of carrying it into execution. The act does not provide any means to compel the execution of this duty, nor inflict any punishment for neglect or refusal on the part of the Executive of the State; nor is there any clause or provision in the Constitution which arms the Government of the United States with this power. Indeed, such a power would place every State under the control and dominion of the General Government, even in the administration of its internal concerns and reserved rights. And we think it clear, that the Federal Government, under the Constitution, has no power to impose on a State officer, as such, any duty whatever, and compel him to perform it; for if it possessed this power, it might overload the officer with duties which would fill up all his time, and disable him from performing his obligations to the State, and might impose on him duties of a character incompatible with the rank and dignity to which he was elevated by the State.[29]

"It is true," the chief justice conceded, "that in the early days of the Government, Congress relied with confidence upon the cooperation and support of the

25. 16 Pet. 539 (U.S. 1842).
26. *Id.* at 541 (headnote), 615–16.
27. *Id.* at 542 (headnote), 622.
28. 24 How. 66 (U.S. 1861).
29. *Id.* at 107–8.

States when exercising the legitimate powers of the General Government, and were accustomed to receive it.'' But this, he explained, was ''upon principles of comity and from a sense of mutual and common interest where no such duty was imposed by the Constitution.''[30]

The holding, therefore, does not question the doctrine of the Prigg case, that the national government may invite the cooperation of the executive agencies of the states in the enforcement of national laws, so long as it leaves the state authorities, and ultimately the state legislatures, free to decline the invitation. Nor does it disturb the principle of earlier cases that state courts may be required, within their assigned jurisdiction, to enforce rights claimable under the Constitution and laws of the United States, whenever Congress chooses to employ them for the purpose.[31]

During the Civil War, President Lincoln repeatedly exercised his military functions through the state governors, especially in the early years of the war, but the cooperation accorded by the latter was regarded as strictly voluntary. Said Attorney General Bates in an official opinion dealing with the matter:

> The Governors of the loyal States have, both personally and officially, rendered most valuable and effective service to the National Government. . . . But these labors are in aid of the Government and with its approbation. They are performed not because it is a legal duty imposed by Congress, or in many instances, even by their respective States, but under the impulse of a generous humanity and patriotism.[32]

Not only does this language seem to traverse the doctrine of Houston v. Moore,[33] it also contrasts sharply with assumptions which prevailed later during the World War, when the Selective Service Act was enforced almost entirely through state officials, who were held to strict accountability to national law.

Tendencies following the Civil War were, in fact, conflicting. In Collector v. Day,[34] decided in 1870, the Court, speaking by Justice Nelson, asserted that the principle of national supremacy did not operate in the field of the ''reserved powes'' of the states—a doctrine which if literally applied would go far to repeal the supremacy clause of the Constitution. Actually the decision in the case holds only that the national government may not tax state instrumentalities, a result which could have been easily rested on the guaranty by the United States to each state of a republican form of government.

Nine years later in the Siebold case,[35] the Court sustained the right of Congress under Article I, section 4, paragraph 1, of the Constitution, to cast additional duties upon state election officials in connection with a congressional election and to prescribe additional penalties for the violation by such officials of

30. *Id.* at 108.
31. See e.g., Claflin v. Houseman, 93 U.S. 130, 136, 137 (1876); Second Employers' Liability Cases, 223 U.S. 1, 55–59 (1912).
32. *Official Records of the Union and Confederate Armies,* Ser. III, Vol. II, 151.
33. 5 Wheat. 1 (US. 1820).
34. 11 Wall. 113 (U.S. 1870).
35. 100 U.S. 371 (1879).

their duties under state law. While the doctrine of the holding is expressly confined to cases in which the national government and the states enjoy "a concurrent power over the same subject matter," no attempt is made to catalogue such cases.[36] What is more, the outlook of Justice Bradley's opinion for the Court is decidedly nationalistic rather than dualistic, as is shown by the answer made to the contention of counsel "that the nature of sovereignty is such as to preclude the joint cooperation of two sovereigns, even in a matter in which they are mutually concerned." To this Justice Bradley replied:

> As a general rule, it is no doubt expedient and wise that the operations of the State and national governments should, as far as practicable, be conducted separately, in order to avoid undue jealousies and jars and conflicts of jurisdiction and power. But there is no reason for laying this down as a rule of universal application. It should never be made to override the plain and manifest dictates of the Constitution itself. We cannot yield to such a transcendental view of State sovereignty. The Constitution and laws of the United States are the supreme law of the land, and to these every citizen of every State owes obedience, whether in his individual or official capacity.[37]

And he later added:

> We may mystify anything. . . . If we allow ourselves to regard it (the National Government) as a hostile organization, opposed to the proper sovereignty and dignity of the State governments, we shall continue to be vexed with difficulties as to its jurisdiction and authority.[38]

Obviously, these words are much more in the spirit of Cohens v. Virginia than of Kentucky v. Dennison.

Thus, the framers of the Constitution did not regard it as incompatible with the nature of our dual system that the national government should utilize the states as subordinate instruments of its powers. Nor did the later contrary principle, of the equal dignity of the states with the national government, operate to displace the idea of the availability of state powers for national purposes; it only transferred this idea to a new basis, that of state consent. Furthermore, the chief result of the earlier principle for our constitutional system, the subordination of the state judiciaries in the enforcement of the national Constitution and laws, still remains unimpaired, while as to state executive power it has been restored to an undefined extent. In short, the two governmental centers may cooperate voluntarily in matters of common interest without affront to our dual system. Such becomes even more apparent from an examination of more recent legislation and adjudication.

2

We come, therefore, to consider two forms of joint action by the national government and the states which have been developed within recent decades and

36. *Id.* at 384–86.
37. *Id.* at 392.
38. *Id.* at 393.

which call into exercise primarily the legislative powers of the two governmental centers. The two forms of joint action referred to are these: (1) the national government has brought its powers over interstate commerce and communications to the support of certain local policies of the states in the exercise of their reserved powers; (2) the national government has held out inducements, primarily of a pecuniary nature, to the states to use their reserved powers to support certain objectives of national policy in the field of expenditure. The same rationale governs both types. On the one hand, there has been a growing recognition of problems demanding to be dealt with on a national scale; on the other hand, there has been reluctance to incur the dangers of centralization. So devices have been sought which will secure both these desiderata as far as practicable.

1. The outstanding reason for federal cooperation of the first type arises from the principle that Congress's power over interstate commerce and communication is ordinarily exclusive, from which it results, usually, that a state may not obstruct the flow of commerce across its borders from its sister states even when such flow threatens to undermine local legislation.[39] In consequence Congress has come, at different times, to the aid of the state police powers in the repression of lotteries,[40] of the liquor traffic,[41] of traffic in game taken in violation of state laws,[42] of commerce in convict-made goods,[43] of various criminal activities,[44] and—though thus far ineffectively—of commerce in child-made goods.[45]

The constitutionality of congressional legislation stopping interstate commerce in lottery tickets was finally established in 1903.[46] Supplementing the state prohibition laws offered greater difficulty, inasmuch as liquor was regarded by the Court as "a legitimate article of commerce," whereas lottery tickets were not. After a thirty-year struggle, however, it was at last conceded that Congress could place liquor coming from other states unrestrictedly under the laws of the state of destination. This occurred in the case of the Clark Distilling Co. v. Western Maryland Railway,[47] in which the Webb-Kenyon Act of 1913 was sustained. Chief Justice White remolded the argument against the act into "the

39. Many of the cases are collected in the Minnesota Rate Cases, 230 U.S. 352, 398–402 (1913).
40. 28 Stat. 963 (1895), 18 U.S.C. section 387 (1934).
41. 26 Stat. 313 (1890), 27 U.S.C. section 121 (1934); 37 Stat. 699 (1913), 27 U.S.C. section 122 (1934).
42. 31 Stat. 188 (1900), 35 Stat. 1137 (1909), 18 U.S.C. section 392 (1934).
43. 45 Stat. 1084 (1929), 49 U.S.C. section 60 (1934).
44. The white slave traffic, 36 Stat. 825 (1910), 18 U.S.C. section 399 (1934); traffic in stolen motor vehicles, 41 Stat. 324 (1919), 18 U.S.C. section 408 (1934); kidnapping, 47 Stat. 326 (1932), 18 U.S.C. section 408a (1934); stolen property, 48 Stat. 794, 18 U.S.C. section 415 (1934); racketeering, 48 Stat. 979, 18 U.S.C. section 420a (1934). The leading cases are Hoke v. United States, 227 U.S. 308 (1913), sustaining the White Slave Act; and Brooks v. United States, 267 U.S. 432 (1925), sustaining the Motor Vehicles Theft Act. In Gooch v. United States, 297 U.S. 124 (1936), the Federal Kidnaping Act was broadly construed without comment on the constitutional question. For a survey of the legislative proposals of 1934, many of which were subsequently enacted, see the *New York Times*, May 24, 1934, p. 2, col. 2.
45. Hammer v. Dagenhart, 247 U.S. 251 (1918); Bailey v. Drexel Furniture Company, 259 U.S. 20 (1922).
46. Champion v. Ames, 188 U.S. 321 (1903).
47. 242 U.S. 311 (1917).

contradiction in terms that because Congress in adopting a regulation lesser in power than it was authorized to exert, therefore, its action was void for excess of power.'' He then went on:

> Or, in other words, stating the necessary result of the argument from a concrete consideration of the particular subject here involved, that because Congress in adopting a regulation had considered the nature and character of our dual system of government, State and Nation, and instead of absolutely prohibiting, had so conformed its regulation as to produce cooperation between the local and national forces of government to the end of preserving the rights of all, it had thereby transcended the complete and perfect power of regulation conferred by the Constitution.

It is true that this statement of the issue did something less than justice to the case against the act, but that is a matter of minor importance. The thing in which we are interested is the glimpse here afforded of the availability of the idea of national-state cooperation as a way of retreat in certain instances from the difficulties created by embarrassing precedents.

And meanwhile in sustaining, early in 1913, the Mann "White Slave" Act,[48] the Court had voiced the general conception of dual federalism upon which national-state cooperation rests, in these terms:

> Our dual form of government has its perplexities, State and Nation having different spheres of jurisdiction . . . , but it must be kept in mind that we are one people; and the powers reserved to the States and those conferred on the Nation are adapted to be exercised, whether independently or concurrently, to promote the general welfare, material and moral."[49]

And it is in reliance on this precedent that the national government has subsequently come to the assistance of the states in the suppression of automobile thefts, of kidnaping, and of other criminal activities involving the crossing of state lines,[50]—a somewhat striking development when set alongside the original assumption of the Constitution that the problem of the migratory offender would be dealt with by the process of interstate extradition.[51] Nor, in fact, has the national government confined its assistance to the states in the discharge of their most primitive function to the precincts of the legislation just alluded to. Notorious offenders against state laws who had previously escaped punishment were in many instances proceeded against successfully under the National Income Tax Act, the Alien Deportation Act, and the Anti-Trust Acts.[52] The Court, moreover, has distinctly countenanced national-state administrative cooperation in

48. Hoke v. United States, 227 U.S. 308 (1913).
49. *Id.* at 322.
50. Note 44 above.
51. U.S. Const. Article IV, section 2, par. 2.
52. This type of cooperation originated in joint national and state efforts to break up bootlegging in prohibition days. In this connection President Coolidge, on May 8, 1926, issued an order permitting the appointment of state and local officials as federal prohibition officers. For the controversy over validity of this order, which terminated in its vindication by the Senate Committee on the Judiciary, see *New York Times*, May 22, 1926, p. 1, col. 8; *id.* May 25, 1926, p. 1, col. 6; *id.* May 26, 1926, p. 1, col. 8; *id.* June 8, 1926, p. 1, col. 5. See also *New York Times*, October 21, 1923, p. 1, col. 4, for the Conference of Governors called by President Coolidge to consider national and state

criminal law enforcement, even when proceeding on no definite statutory basis.[53]

Yet, when Congress undertook to prohibit the transportation of child-made goods from one state to another, in the aid presumably of states maintaining a superior standard with reference to this subject, it was held, in Hammer v. Dagenhart, to have exceeded its powers, and its legislation was invalidated as an effort to coerce certain states "into compliance with Congress's regulation of State concerns."[54] Thus the Court deliberately placed itself in the same predicament in relation to antichild labor legislation as that from which it had so recently—and, as it turned out, resultlessly—extricated itself in relation to antiliquor legislation. And once again it has had to beat a retreat from an untenable position. The retreat is, to be sure, still under way, but who, with the results of the recent election in mind, can seriously doubt that it will be carried out? The starting point is Whitfield v. Ohio,[55] decided last term, where was sustained the Hawes-Cooper Act of January 29, 1929, which prohibits the sale in the original package of convict-made goods entering a state through the channels of foreign or interstate commerce.[56] The basis of the holding was a liquor case which was decided nearly half a century ago,[57] and Hammer v. Dagenhart, on which the opponents of the act had relied, is not even mentioned in the Court's opinion! Even more recently, the Court has upheld the validity of the Ashurst-Sumners Act of July 24, 1935,[58] which applies the principle of the Webb-Kenyon Act to convict-made goods.[59] Speaking for the unanimous Court, Chief Justice Hughes said:

> The subject of the prohibited traffic is different, the effects of the traffic are different, but the underlying principle is the same. The pertinent point is that where the subject of commerce is one as to which the power of the State may constitutionally be exerted by restriction or prohibition in order to prevent harmful consequences, the Congress may, if it sees fit, put forth its power to regulate interstate commerce so as to prevent that commerce from being used to impede the carrying out of the state policy. . . . The Congress in exercising the power confided to it by the Constitution is as free as the States to recognize the fundamental interests of free labor.

Can it be doubted that these words sound the doom of Hammer v. Dagenhart? It may be contended, however, that there is a genuine difference, from the

---

cooperation in prohibition enforcement. Nor has national-state cooperation in the administrative field been confined to the criminal field. Thus President Hoover authorized the opening of federal income tax returns to the inspection of officials of states with income tax laws. Under the Transportation Act of 1920, 41 Stat. 456 (1920), 49 U.S.C. sections 71–74, 76–78, 141 (1934), cooperation between the Interstate Commerce Commission and state commissions has become an established practice.

53. Ponzi v. Fessenden, 258 U.S. 254 (1922).

54. Hammer v. Dagenhart, 247 U.S. 251 (1918). The quoted words are from Chief Justice Taft's opinion in the Child Labor Tax Case of 1922, 259 U.S. 20, 39.

55. 297 U.S. 431 (1936).

56. 45 Stat. 1084 (1929), 49 U.S.C. section 60 (1934).

57. *In re* Rahrer, 140 U.S. 545 (1891).

58. 49 Stat. 494, 49 U.S.C.A. section 61 (Supp. 1935).

59. Kentucky Whip and Collar Co. v. Illinois Central R.R., U.S. Sup. Ct. (1937), 4 *U. S. L. Week* 485.

point of view of concern for our dual system, between the act disallowed in
Hammer v. Dagenhart and an antichild labor act modelled on the Webb-Kenyon
Act; that while the one was coercive of state policies, the other would be
cooperative with them. The contention derives such plausibility as it possesses
from the fact that the state policies thought of are in the one instance those of
producing states and in the other instance those of consuming states. But Congress's purpose in both cases is precisely the same, namely, to prevent a certain
type of goods from reaching the interstate market. In the one case, it relies on its
own unaided power, in the other it supplements certain legislation of the consuming states; but in both instances the producing states are, as such, "coerced."
For what is the interstate market after all except the sum total of the individual
state markets for goods coming from without?

On the other hand, we must not overlook the fact that the same bench which
decided the Whitfield case[60] also decided, practically contemporaneously, the
Ashton case,[61] the Constantine case,[62] and the Carter case,[63] in all of which it
professed to treat proffers of national cooperation with state policies as coercive
of the latter, and this in face of vigorous protests in two of these cases, by the
states most immediately concerned, that they favored the condemned legislation.[64]

What it all boils down to is this: In the instances in which the national
government has been sustained in bringing its regulatory powers to the aid of
state policies, its right to do so has been ultimately based by the Court on the
plenary nature of those powers as to the subject matter governed; and in such
instances, as the Court has not hesitated to declare, the national government may
with equal right traverse state policies.[65]

Yet even so, the final result was assisted, on one occasion at least, by a
judicial invocation of the idea of national-state cooperation, which thus served to
screen in some measure the Court's retreat from an untenable position; and what
is more, the same thing seems to be happening today all over again. In a word,
permitted national-state cooperation in a field of *regulation* is, it would seem, a
halfway house to national domination of the field, and little more. Is it of greater
significance in the field of national *expenditure?* The question brings us to the so-
called "federal grant-in-aid."

2. The earliest precursor of the present "grant-in-aid" was the act under
which, in 1802, Ohio was admitted to the Union. This measure contained provisions whereby, in return for a grant of lands to each township in the state for

60. Whitfield v. Ohio, 297 U.S. 43 (1936).
61. Ashton v. Cameron Water Imp. Dist., 298 U.S. 513 (1936).
62. United States v. Constantine, 296 U.S. 287 (1935).
63. Carter v. Carter Coal Co., 298 U.S. 238 (1936).
64. The Whitfield case was decided March 2, 1936; the Carter case, May 18th; the Ashton case,
May 25th; the Constantine case, December 9, 1935.
65. United States v. Hill, 248 U.S. 420, 425 (1919). And note the chief justice's further words in
Kentucky Whip and Collar Co. v. Illinois Central R.R., U.S. Sup. Ct. (1937) 4 *U.S.L. Week* 485,
487: "The Congress has exercised its plenary power. . . ."

public schools, and other concessions, the state pledged itself to withhold its hand in the matter of taxation for a term of years as regards land sold by the national government to settlers. Later similar compacts were entered into with other states as they were admitted into the Union.[66]

Building upon these beginnings, and animated especially by its increasing interest in agricultural development, Congress in February, 1859, passed a bill the purpose of which was announced to be "the endowment, support, and maintenance of at least one college (in each State) where the leading object shall be, without excluding other scientific or classical studies, to teach such branches of learning as are related to agriculture and the mechanic arts, as the legislatures of the States may respectively prescribe, in order to promote the liberal and practical education of the industrial classes in the several pursuits and professions of life."[67] The bill assigned to each state twenty thousand acres of land for each senator and representative in the existing Congress and an additional twenty thousand acres for each additional representative to which it might become entitled under the census of 1860. In return each state was required "to provide within five years at least not less than one college, or the grant to said state," was to cease forthwith, and the state was to pay over to the United States any amounts it had received from lands previously sold. Other conditions were also specified, and the consent of the state must be communicated to the national government within two years. Although the bill was upset by presidential veto,[68] the Morrill Act embodying substantially the same provisions became law three years later.[69]

But while grants-in-aid were made by Congress in exercise of its power to "dispose" of the property of the United States,[70] present-day federal grants-in-aid are of money appropriated from the revenues of the United States, and hence call into requisition Congress's power to lay and collect taxes and to spend the proceeds thereof for "the general welfare."

A significant grant-in-aid of this character, marking a distinct advance upon previous donations from the national Treasury, was the act of 1911 whereby the secretary of agriculture was authorized:

> On such conditions as he deems wise, to stipulate and agree with any State or group of States to cooperate in the organization and maintenance of a system of fire protection on any private or State forest lands within such State or States, and situated upon the watershed of a navigable river. No such stipulation or agreement shall be made with any State which has not provided by law for a system of forest-fire protection. In no case shall the amount expended in any State exceed in any fiscal year the amount appropriated by that State for the same purpose during the same fiscal year.[71]

66. Corwin, "The Spending Power of Congress" (1923) 36 *Harv. L. Rev.* 548, 570. On the power of Congress, when admitting a new state into the Union, to make such compacts with it, see Stearns v. Minnesota, 179 U.S. 223, 244–50 (1900).
67. 5 Richardson, *Messages and Papers of the Presidents* (1898) 543.
68. *Id.* at 547–48.
69. 12 Stat. 503 (1862), 7 U.S.C. section 301 (1934).
70. U.S. Const. Article IV, section 3, par. 2.
71. 36 Stat. 961 (1911), 16 U.S.C. section 563 (1934).

Thirteen years later the authorization was extended from timber to cut-over lands and from watersheds of navigable streams to those from which water for domestic use for irrigation was taken in the cooperating states. Also the secretary of agriculture was

Authorized and directed, in cooperation with appropriate officials of the various States or, in his discretion, with other suitable agencies, to assist the owners of farms in establishing, improving, and renewing wood lots, shelter belts, windbreaks, and other valuable forest growth, and in growing and renewing useful timber crops. Except for preliminary investigations, the amount expended by the Federal Government under this section in cooperation with any State or other cooperating agency during any fiscal year shall not exceed the amount expended by the State or other cooperating agency for the same purpose during the same fiscal year.[72]

By similar legislation since 1911 the national government has undertaken to subsidize agricultural extension work in the states,[73] the training of teachers in agriculture and industrial subjects and of home economics,[74] vocational rehabilitation and education,[75] the maintenance of nautical schools,[76] experiments in reforestation,[77] the construction of highways,[78] the equipment and training of the National Guard,[79] and other matters falling normally under the reserved powers of the states. Most of the measures referred to stipulate for financial participation by the cooperating states, usually on an equal basis, while some of them, the Federal Highway Act and the National Defense Act in especial, subject state policies and activities in the field of cooperation to national supervision in some detail. With, however, the exception of the National Defense Act, none of these measures brings pressure to bear upon the states to enter into cooperation with the national government other than the advantage to be anticipated from doing so. The National Defense Act is of a different character, since by virtue of Congress's power to withhold consent to a state's maintaining "troops" in time of peace, the states are virtually prohibited from keeping a militia except in accordance with the terms of this act.[80]

On the other hand, it should be noted, the cooperation which the grant-in-aid brings about between the national government and the states is not merely a cooperation in expenditure. Even the consideration moving from the national government to the states is not exclusively pecuniary, for the national government, in laying down standards, supplies a guidance for state policies which the

72. 43 Stat. 653 (1924), 16 U.S.C. sections 564, 565 (1934).
73. 38 Stat. 372 (1914), 7 U.S.C. sections 341–48 (1934).
74. 39 Stat. 929 (1917), 45 Stat. 1151 (1929), 48 Stat. 792 (1934), 20 U.S.C. sections 11–15d (1934).
75. 41 Stat. 735 (1920), 43 Stat. 431 (1924), 46 Stat. 524 (1930), 47 Stat. 448 (1932), 29 U.S.C. sections 31–38 (1934).
76. 36 Stat. 1353 (1911), 34 U.S.C. section 1122 (1934).
77. 45 Stat. 699 (1928), 16 U.S.C. section 581 (1934).
78. The Federal Highway Act, 42 Stat. 212 (1921), 23 U.S.C. sections 1–25 (1934).
79. The National Defense Act, 39 Stat. 197 (1916), 32 U.S.C. sections 1–4 (1934).
80. U.S. Const. Article 1, section 10; 39 Stat. 198 (1916), 32 U.S.C. section 192 (1934).

states generally welcome, rather than accept with reluctance. Nor is the consideration which prompts the national government to initiate cooperative programs solely the financial aid which the states will bring to such programs, but also the aid which they can lend through their reserved powers. Thus federal highway construction relies on the state power of eminent domain, as well as on state power to police and protect highways during and after their construction. Also, national protection of forests is supplemented by the power of the states to regulate the conduct of persons entering forests; and the Sheppard-Towner Maternity Act was implemented by the power of the cooperating states to compel birth registration, the licensing of midwives, etc.

There is, in short, a real wedding of diverse powers on the part of the two governmental centers. The greater financial strength of the national government is joined to the wider coercive powers of the states.

Various objections have been made to federal grants-in-aid, some of which may bear, indirectly at least, upon the question of their constitutionality.[81] One is that they are financially oppressive to certain states, especially to those which pay the larger share of the national income tax. The argument ignores the fact that the vast proportion of the income referred to is drawn from the country at large, and that so much of it is paid from a certain few states simply because the takers thereof—whether individuals or corporations—choose to reside or maintain their headquarters in these states. The fact is, as was pointed out by the United States Treasury Department in 1922, "there is no way of ascertaining from the income tax returns the amount of income earned in the separate States or the amount of tax paid on that basis." On the other hand, as the leading authority on the subject has pointed out, if we compare the amount of each state's wealth or its current income with the amounts received by it under federal grants-in-aid, the discrepancy made so much of by certain critics is ordinarily very greatly reduced.[82]

A more serious charge against the grant-in-aid from the point of view of concern for our dual system, is that it breaks down state initiative and devitalizes state policies. The exact contrary appears to be the case. For:

> State and county funds for extension work, vocational education, highways—in fact, for every line of activity subsidized by the federal government—have multiplied several fold as a direct result of the stimulus of federal funds. Federal aid is often referred to as the "fifty-fifty" system, but it might more accurately be called the "eighty-twenty" or "ninety-ten" system. Most of the money is coming from local sources. The people in their local communities are testifying to their interest most concretely by more than matching federal funds. Often federal funds are matched several times over. State and local expenditures for agricultural extension work are nearly twice as large as the federal subsidy. For forest fire prevention state and local funds are three times as large as the federal grant. Every subsidy except that for the National Guard is exceeded by local appropriations, and most of these local appropria-

81. See MacDonald, *Federal Aid* (1928) c. X.
82. *Id.* at 248–50.

tions would never have been made, in the judgment of state officials, without the stimulus of federal funds. The administration of all these appropriations, federal and state alike, is in the hands of state authorities. They are directly responsible for the framing and execution of state policies. How, then, is it possible to justify the assertion that local initiative is being stifled? When the records show four or five states with satisfactory, well developed programs of civilian rehabilitation or child hygiene in 1918 or 1920, and forty or forty-five with such programs in 1927, controlled by state authorities and largely supported by state funds, it is difficult to believe that local responsibility is being shirked, and that the people are sitting back in complacent indifference.[83]

Finally, it is charged that federal aid means the growth of an immense bureaucracy in Washington, which in turn will threaten our dual system. Granting, however, the inevitability of the increase in governmental services in response to the needs of modern society, it would seem that the federal grant-in-aid was well devised to obviate this very difficulty. On the basis of the grant-in-aid a most varied exchange of official services has developed in recent years between the national government and the states, with the result that, while the usefulness of the state administrative systems to their several localities has increased, the national civil service had not, prior to the depression, been enlarged to anything like the dimensions that it must have attained had the national government chosen to proceed alone in the field of national-state cooperation.[84] For example, during the war with Germany, when the national government decided to seek state cooperation in the enforcement of the Selective Service Act, there were at one time more than 192,000 persons "who functioned directly under State superiors, while the office of the Provost-Marshal General in charge of the Federal Operation of the Act had only 429 employees throughout the States."[85] This is an extreme instance, no doubt, but it serves to demonstrate the effect of national-state cooperation in diffusing bureaucracy in preference to concentrating it at the national capital.

The positive case for the grant-in-aid is that it has activated state policies with respect to certain governmental services which modern conditions make desirable from both a local and national point of view, and has at the same time enabled certain states to avail themselves of improved standards in the rendition of such services. Local government has not been broken down, but has on the contrary been endowed with increased usefulness, and therefore with the in-

83. *Id.* at 255–56.
84. See especially Clark, "Joint Activity between Federal and State Officials" (1936) 51 *Pol. Sci. Q.* 230; also Fite, *Government by Cooperation* (1932) c. III; also a series of articles, "Topical Survey of the Government," which appeared in the *United States Daily* during the summer and early autumn of 1928, each by an expert of some departmental bureau of the national government. Said Mr. Hoover, when secretary of commerce: "There is an . . . important field for cooperation by the federal government with the multitude of agencies, state, municipal, and private, in the systematic development of those processes which directly affect public health, recreation, education, and the home. We have need further to perfect the means by which government can be adapted to human service." Fite, above, at 7. See also note 52, above.
85. Clark, above note 84, at 243.

creased prospects of survival which go with usefulness. On the other hand, the expanded employment by the national government of its power to make financial provision for the "general welfare" has not resulted in a corresponding expansion in national official personnel. All these advantages go to stamp federal aid as a type of national-state relationship entirely harmonious with the spirit of dual federalism, while they illustrate also the continued capacity of the Constitution to adjust itself to modern conditions.

The question remains whether federal grants-in-aid run afoul of any decisions of the Court. Two cases are directly in point: Massachusetts v. Mellon,[86] decided in 1923, and United States v. Butler,[87] decided during the past term. In the former the Court declined to enjoin, upon the application of a state, the secretary of the treasury from paying out certain sums which had been appropriated by Congress in the furtherance, it was contended, of "non-Federal purposes." In the words of the Court:

> What, then, is the nature of the right of the State here asserted and how is it affected by this statute? Reduced to its simplest terms, it is alleged that the statute constitutes an attempt to legislate outside the powers granted to Congress by the Constitution and within the field of local powers exclusively reserved to the States. Nothing is added to the force or effect of this assertion by the further incidental allegations that the ulterior purpose of Congress thereby was to induce the States to yield a portion of their sovereign rights; that the burden of the appropriations falls unequally upon the several States; and that there is imposed upon the States an illegal and unconstitutional option either to yield to the Federal Government a part of their reserved rights or lose their share of the moneys appropriated. But what burden is imposed upon the States, unequally or otherwise? Certainly there is none, unless it be the burden of taxation, and that falls upon their inhabitants, who are within the taxing power of Congress as well as that of the States where they reside. Nor does the statute require the States to do or to yield anything. If Congress enacted it with the ulterior purpose of tempting them to yield, that purpose may be effectively frustrated by the simple expedient of not yielding.
>
> In the last analysis, the complaint of the plaintiff State is brought to the naked contention that Congress has usurped the reserved powers of the several States by the mere enactment of the statute, though nothing has been done and nothing is to be done without their consent; and it is plain that that question, as it is thus presented, is political and not judicial in character, and therefore is not a matter which admits of the exercise of the judicial power.[88]

This language, it seems clear, goes beyond rejecting the application of the state on the ground of its raising "a political question." It also meets the contention that this type of legislation is coercive with respect to the states, and rejects that contention.

The decision in United States v. Butler does not in any wise impair the authority of Massachusetts v. Mellon touching this matter. In the later case it was

86. 262 U.S. 447 (1923).
87. 297 U.S. 1 (1936).
88. 262 U.S. 447, 482–83 (1923).

held that certain payments to agriculture which were conditioned on the recipients' contractually agreeing to perform certain acts not within the power of the national government to compel, represented an effort by the national government to regulate matters which the Constitution had reserved to the states. The decision turned on the proposition that the proposed beneficiaries of federal largess were not free to reject it on account of the sharp competitive relation in which they stood to each other. Clearly this line of reasoning in no wise disturbs the statement in the Mellon case, with reference to a statute not to be differentiated in this respect from any grant-in-aid, that it did "not require the States to do or yield anything." And in another respect United States v. Butler clearly improves the standing in constitutional law of the federal grant-in-aid, inasmuch as Justice Roberts took occasion in his opinion to record the Court's acceptance of the Hamiltonian theory of the scope of the spending power of Congress.[89]

And with these results before us, let us turn for a moment to the Social Security Act, which marks the culmination to date of the federal grant-in-aid.[90] In what terms ought the constitutional case for the act be formulated? The question is asked with special reference to Titles III[91] and IX,[92] which have to do with unemployment compensation. The first and foremost task of the defenders of the act is, obviously, to show that the outlay of national funds which it authorizes is for "the general welfare of the United States"; in light of the history of public relief the last few years this ought to be a comparatively easy task. And the remission of taxes provided for in Title IX is to be justified in the same way, Florida v. Mellon[93] making this method of purchasing state compliance equally eligible with the more conventional method of an outright appropriation. Next it should be shown that the terms stipulated by the act for state cooperation are designed to make such cooperation better promotive of the main purpose of the act and are not intended to foist policies upon the cooperating states which are not relevant to this purpose. Lastly, the argument should invoke the right of the states to set up a system of unemployment compensation.[94]

89. See 297 U.S. 1, 65 (1936).

90. 49 Stat. 620, 42 U.S.C. sections 301–1305 (Supp. 1935). The act has already been held constitutional in Davis v. Boston & Maine R.R., Mass., (1936) 4 *U. S. L. Week* 416 and by Judge David J. Davis in the federal district court for Alabama in dismissing a suit by 200 Alabama concerns to enjoin collection of the tax levied by the act. *New York Times,* January 15, 1937, p. 7, col. 3. The Davis case is now on appeal and argument has already been had before the Circuit Court of Appeals. *Id.,* January 15, 1937, p. 7, col. 4. For an extended discussion of the constitutionality of the Social Security Act, see Shulman, "The Case for the Constitutionality of the Social Security Act" (1936) 3 *Law and Contemp. Prob.* 298; cf. Denby, "The Case against the Constitutionality of the Social Security Act" (1936) 3 *Law and Contemp. Prob.* 315.

91. 49 Stat. 626, 42 U.S.C. sections 501–3 (Supp. 1935).

92. 49 Stat. 639, 42 U.S.C. sections 1101–10 (Supp. 1935).

93. 273 U.S. 12 (1927).

94. See Associated Industries of New York State, Inc. v. Department of Labor of State of New York, 57 Sup. Ct. 122 (1936) wherein an equally divided Court affirmed the New York Court of Appeals which had upheld the constitutionality of the New York Unemployment Insurance Act [271 N.Y. 1, 2 N.E. (2d) 22 (1936)]. See also Gillum v. Johnson, Cal. Sup. Ct. (1936) 4 *U. S. L. Week*

Cooperating with the states in implementing this right, the national government is relieved from the necessity of vindicating, in face of the hostile dicta of the A. A. A.[95] and Alton[96] cases, its own independent right to do the same thing.

National-state cooperation has rested successively on the principle of national supremacy and that of voluntary cooperation on the part of the states constitutionally equipped to cooperate. The participation of the state courts in certain portions of the jurisdiction which is described in Article III, section 2, of the Constitution still testifies to the effectiveness of the earlier type of cooperation. But there are also cases in good standing that hold that the state executive power too may be at times laid under requisition by the national government. Nevertheless, the very extensive joint activity between national and state officialdom which has grown up within recent decades rests almost exclusively on the principle of voluntary cooperation.[97]

Cooperation between the national government and the states in the legislative field rests, likewise, upon the voluntary principle—in the main, can rest on no other. Such cooperation takes two forms: first, the national legislative power, particularly that over commerce and communications, is exerted in aid of state policies; secondly, the national power to tax and spend is used to provide financial inducements to the states to exert their reserved powers in the furtherance of the legitimate objectives of national expenditure. The validity of the former type of cooperation is dependent upon the Court's recognition of the national legislative power which is exerted as being one which is not conditioned by the reserved powers of the states. The validity of the latter depends on the Court's conception of "the general welfare of the United States," as that term is used in the first clause of Article I, section 8 of the Constitution.

It is this last type of national-state cooperation, effected by means of the federal grant-in-aid, which best realizes the ideal of cooperative federalism. By this device there is brought about a real mergence of powers and a real reciprocity of service for common ends, on the part of the two governmental centers. But the other type, too, has its value at the present moment in enabling the Court to beat a retreat from its recent out-of-date positions regarding national power, with a minimum loss of face.

419, and Haines Brothers Co. v. Unemployment Compensation Commission, Mass. Sup. Jud. Ct. (1936), upholding the constitutionality of the California Unemployment Reserves Act and the Massachusetts Unemployment Compensation Law respectively. But *cf.* Gulf States Paper Corp. v. Carmichael, N.D. Ala. (1936) 4 *U. S. L. Week* 450 in which a three-judge federal court held the Alabama Unemployment Compensation Law unconstitutional.

95. United States v. Butler, 297 U.S. 1 (1936).

96. Railroad Retirement Board v. Alton R.R., 295 U.S. 330 (1935).

97. See Clark, *loc. cit.* above note 84.

12. The Passing of Dual Federalism

Within the generation now drawing to a close this nation has been subjected to the impact of a series of events and ideological forces of a very imperative nature. We have fought two world wars, the second of which answered every definition of "total war," and have submitted to the regimentation which these great national efforts entailed. We have passed through an economic crisis which was described by the late president as "a crisis greater than war." We have become the exclusive custodian of technology's crowning gift to civilization, an invention capable of blowing it to smithereens, and we greatly hope to retain that honorable trusteeship throughout an indefinite future. Meantime we have elected ourselves the head and forefront of one of two combinations of nations which together embrace a great part of the Western world and in this capacity are at present involved in a "cold war" with the head of the opposing combination; and as one phase of this curious and baffling struggle we find ourselves driven to combat at obvious risk to certain heretofore cherished constitutional values, the menace of a hidden propaganda which is intended by its agents to work impairment of the national fiber against the time when the "cold war" may eventuate in a "shooting war." Lastly, though by no means least, the most widespread and powerfully organized political interest in the country, that of organized labor, has come to accept unreservedly a new and revolutionary conception of the role of government. Formerly we generally thought of government as primarily a policeman, with an amiable penchant for being especially helpful to those who knew how to help themselves. By the ideological revolution just alluded to, which stems from the Great Depression and the New Deal, it becomes the duty of government to guarantee economic security to all as the indispensable foundation of constitutional liberty.

Naturally, the stresses and strains to which the nation has been subjected by

From 36 *Virginia Law Review* 1–24 (1950). Reprinted by permission.

these pressures has not left our constitutional law unaffected. In general terms, our system has lost resiliency and what was once vaunted as a Constitution of rights, both state and private, has been replaced by a Constitution of powers. More specifically, the federal system has shifted base in the direction of a consolidated national power, while within the national government itself an increased flow of power in the direction of the president has ensued. In this article I shall deal with the first of these manifestations of an altered constitutional order.

I

The medium by which social forces are brought to bear upon constitutional interpretation, by which such forces are, so to speak, rendered into the idiom of constitutional law, is judicial review, or more concretely, the Supreme Court of the United States. This of course is a commonplace. The nature, on the other hand, of the materials with which the Court works is often a more recondite matter; and it is definitely so in the present instance.

Thus, for one thing, the Court has not been called upon, in adapting the federal system to the requirements of total war and other recent exigencies, to assimilate new amendments to the constitutional structure, as was the case after the Civil War. The period in question witnessed, it is true, the adoption of no fewer than four such amendments, the 18th, 19th, 20th and 21st; and the first of these, the Prohibition Amendment, contemplated a considerable augmentation of national power at the expense of the states—so much so, indeed, that some people argued that it transcended the amending power itself. Although the Supreme Court in due course rejected that contention, the controversy continued for some thirteen or fourteen years, when it was terminated in the same abrupt and drastic manner as that in which it had been precipitated, namely, by constitutional amendment. By repealing outright the 18th Amendment, the 21st Amendment restored the *status quo ante* so far as national power was concerned. Nor is the 19th Amendment establishing woman suffrage, or the 20th, changing the dates when a newly elected president and a newly elected Congress take over, relevant to our present inquiry.

Nor again has judicial translation of the power requirements of national crisis into the vocabulary of constitutional law been effected for the most part by affixing new definitions to the phraseology in which the constitutional grants of power to the national government are couched. One thinks in this connection especially of the "commerce clause." The phrase "commerce among the States" was held by the Court five years ago to embrace the making of insurance contracts across state lines,[1] but the ruling in question—negligible in itself so far

1. United States v. South-Eastern Underwriters Ass'n., 322 U.S. 533, 64 Sup. Ct. 1162, 88 L. Ed. 1441 (1944).

as our purpose goes—was presently considerably diluted in effect by act of Congress.[2] Such expansion of the commerce power as is of relevance to this inquiry has been a *secondary,* even though important, consequence of other more immediate factors of constitutional interpretation.

Finally, the structural features of our federal system still remain what they have always been, to wit: (1) a written Constitution which is regarded as "law" and "supreme law"; (2) as in all federations, the union of several autonomous political entities or "states" for common purposes; (3) the division of the sum total of legislative powers between a "general government," on the one hand, and the "states," on the other; (4) the direct operation for the most part of each center of government, acting within its assigned sphere, upon all persons and property within its territorial limits; (5) the provision of each center with the complete apparatus, both executive and judicial, for law enforcement; (6) judicial review, that is, the power and duty of all courts, and ultimately of the Supreme Court of the Union, to disallow all legislative or executive acts of either center of government which in the Court's opinion transgress the Constitution; (7) an elaborate and cumbersome method of constitutional amendment, in which the states have a deciding role.

Not only have these features of the American federal system never been altered by constitutional amendment in any way that requires our attention, none has within recent years been *directly* affected by judicial interpretation of the words of the Constitution in a way that need interest us. So far as the form and actual phraseological content of the constitutional document are concerned, Professor Dicey's dictum that federalism implies "a legally immutable Constitution," or one nearly immutable, has been fully realized in the American experience.[3]

In just what fashion then has the shift referred to above of our federal system toward consolidation registered itself in our constitutional law in response to the requirements of war, economic crisis, and a fundamentally altered outlook upon the purpose of government? The solution of the conundrum is to be sought in the changed attitude of the Court toward certain postulates or axioms of constitutional interpretation closely touching the federal system, and which in their totality comprised what I mean by dual federalism. These postulates are the following: (1) the national government is one of enumerated powers only; (2) also the purposes which it may constitutionally promote are few; (3) within their respective spheres the two centers of government are "sovereign" and hence "equal"; (4) the relation of the two centers with each other is one of tension rather than collaboration. Here I shall sketch briefly the history of each of these concepts in our constitutional law and show how today each has been superseded by a concept favorable to centralization.

2. 59 Stat. 33, 34 (1945), 15 U.S.C. sections 1011–15 (1946); see Prudential Ins. Co. v. Benjamin, 328 U.S. 408, 66 Sup. Ct. 1142, 90 L. Ed. 1342 (1946).
3. A. V. Dicey, *Introduction to the Study of the Law of the Constitution* 142 (7th ed. 1903).

II

In settling the apportionment of powers between the central and local governments of a federal system any one of several principles is conceivably available, two of them being illustrated by the great Anglo-American federations. In the United States, as in the Australian Commonwealth, the principle originally adopted was that the national government should possess only those powers which were conferred upon it in more or less definite terms by the constitutional document, while the remaining powers should, unless otherwise specified, be "reserved" to the states; or in the vocabulary of constitutional law, the national government was a government of "enumerated powers," while the states were governments of "residual powers." On the other hand, in the case of the Dominion of Canada, which was established in the near wake of our Civil War, the reverse principle was followed. For taking counsel from that event, the founders of the dominion thought to avoid yielding too much to "states rights." Yet surprisingly enough, when "New Deal" programs were being tested judicially under the two constitutions a decade and a half ago, it was the United States Constitution which proved to be, in the final upshot, the more commodious vehicle of national power, the reason being that the draughtsmen of the British North America Act, besides generally using more precise language than did the framers, designated certain of the powers which they assigned the Canadian provinces as "exclusive," with the result of rendering them logically restrictive of the powers of the dominion—or at least the Judicial Committee of the House of Lords so ruled.[4] As we shall see presently, there was a long period of approximately a hundred years when the foes of national power in this country achieved a comparable result through their interpretation of the Tenth Amendment—one which the Supreme Court has definitely discarded only within recent years.

Today the operation of the "enumerated powers" concept as a canon of constitutional interpretation has been curtailed on all sides. Nor in fact did it ever go altogether unchallenged, even from the first.

Article I, section 8, clause 1 of the Constitution reads:

> The Congress shall have power to lay and collect taxes, duties, imposts and excises, to pay the debts and provide for the common defense and general welfare of the United States. . . .

What is "the general welfare" for which Congress is thus authorized to "provide," and in what fashion is it authorized to provide it? While adoption of the Constitution was pending some of its opponents made the charge that the phrase "to provide for the general welfare" was a sort of legislative joker which was designed, in conjunction with the "necessary and proper" clause, to vest Congress with power to provide for whatever it might choose to regard as the

4. Illuminating in this connection is Professor W. P. M. Kennedy's *Essays in Constitutional Law* 105–22, 153–57 (1934).

"general welfare" by any means deemed by it to be "necessary and proper." The suggestion was promptly repudiated by advocates of the Constitution on the following grounds. In the first place, it was pointed out, the phrase stood between two other phrases, both dealing with the taxing power—an awkward syntax on the assumption under consideration. In the second place, the phrase was coordinate with the phrase "to pay the debts," that is, a purpose of money expenditure only. Finally, it was asserted, the suggested reading, by endowing Congress with practically complete legislative power, rendered the succeeding enumeration of more specific powers superfluous, thereby reducing "the Constitution to a single phrase."

In the total this argument sounds impressive, but on closer examination it becomes less so, especially today. For one thing, it is a fact that in certain early printings of the Constitution the "common defense and general welfare" clause appears separately paragraphed, while in others it is set off from the "lay and collect" clause by a semicolon and not, as modern usage would require, by the less awesome comma. To be sure, the semicolon may have been due in the first instance to the splattering of a goose quill that needed trimming, for it is notorious that the fate of nations has often turned on just such minute *points*.

Then as to the third argument—while once deemed an extremely weighty one—it cannot be so regarded in light of the decision in 1926 in the case of Myers v. United States.[5] The Court held that the opening clause of Article II of the Constitution, which says that "the executive power shall be vested in a President of the United States," is not a simple designation of office but a grant of power, which the succeeding clauses of the same article either qualify or to which they lend "appropriate emphasis." Granting the soundness of this position, however, why should not the more specific clauses of Article I be regarded as standing in a like relation to the "general welfare" clause thereof? Nor is this by any means all that may be said in favor of treating the latter clause as a grant of substantive legislative power, as anyone may convince himself who chooses to consult Mr. James Francis Lawson's minute and ingenious examination of the subject.[6]

Despite these considerations, or such of them as he was aware of, the great Chief Justice Marshall in 1819 stamped the "enumerated powers" doctrine with his approval. This was in his opinion in McCulloch v. Maryland,[7] where, in sustaining the right of the national government to establish a bank, he used the following expressions:

> This government is acknowledged by all to be one of enumerated powers. The principle, that it can exercise only the powers granted to it, would seem too apparent to

---

5. 272 U.S. 52, 47 Sup. Ct. 21, 71 L. Ed. 160 (1926).

6. The three preceding paragraphs are drawn largely from Corwin, *Twilight of the Supreme Court* 152–54 (1934).

7. 4 Wheat. 316, 4 L. Ed. 579 (U.S. 1819).

have required to be enforced by all those arguments which its enlightened friends, while it was depending before the people, found it necessary to urge. That principle is now universally admitted.[8]

At the same time, however, Marshall committed himself to certain other positions in that same opinion which in their to'al effect went far in the judgment of certain of his critics to render the national government one of "indefinite powers." One of these was the dictum that "the sword and the purse, all external relations, and no inconsiderable portion of the industry of the nation, are entrusted to its government." Another was his characterization of "the power of making war," of "levying taxes," and of "regulating commerce," as "great, substantive and independent" powers. A third was his famous and for the purposes of the case, decisive construction of the "necessary and proper" clause as embracing "all [legislative] means which are appropriate" to carry out "the legitimate ends" of the Constitution.[9]

Approaching the opinion from the angle of his quasi-parental concern for "the balance between the States and the National Government," Madison declared its central vice to be that it treated the powers of the latter as "sovereign powers," a view which must inevitably "convert a limited into an unlimited government" for, he continued, "in the great system of political economy, having for its general object the national welfare, everything is related immediately or remotely to every other thing; and, consequently, a power over any one thing, not limited by some obvious and precise affinity, may amount to a power over every other." "The very existence," he consequently urged, "of the local sovereignties" was "a control on the pleas for a constructive amplification of national power."[10]

So also did Marshall's most pertinacious critic, John Taylor of Caroline, pronounce the chief justice's doctrines as utterly destructive of the constitutional division of powers between the two centers of government.[11] A third critic was the talented Hugh Swinton Legaré of South Carolina, who in 1828 devoted a review of the first volume of Kent's *Commentaries* to a minute and immensely ingenious analysis of Marshall's most celebrated opinion. "That argument," he asserted, "cannot be sound which necessarily converts a government of enumerated into one of indefinite powers, and a confederacy of republics into a gigantic and consolidated empire." Nor did one have to rely on reasoning alone to be convinced of this; one needed only to compare the Constitution itself as expounded in the *Federalist* with the actual course of national legislation. For thus, he wrote:

---

8. *Id.* at 405, 4 L. Ed. at 601.
9. *Id.* at 421, 4 L. Ed. at 605.
10. 8 *Writings of James Madison* 447–53 (Hunt ed. 1908); 2 *Letters and Other Writings of James Madison* 143–47 (1867).
11. Taylor, *Construction Construed and Constitutions Vindicated* 9–28 *passim,* 77–89 *passim* (1820).

He will find that the government has been fundamentally altered by the progress of opinion—that instead of being any longer one of enumerated powers and a circumscribed sphere, as it was beyond all doubt intended to be, it knows absolutely no bounds but the will of a majority of Congress—that instead of confining itself in time of peace to the diplomatic and commercial relations of the country, it is seeking out employment for itself by interfering in the domestic concerns of society, and threatens in the course of a very few years, to control in the most offensive and despotic manner, all the pursuits, the interests, the opinions and the conduct of men. He will find that this extraordinary revolution has been brought about, in a good degree by the Supreme Court of the United States, which has applied to the Constitution—very innocently, no doubt, and with commanding ability in argument—and thus given authority and currency to, such canons of interpretation, as necessarily lead to these extravagant results. Above all, he will be perfectly satisfied that that high tribunal affords, by its own shewing, no barrier whatever against the usurpations of Congress—and that the rights of the weaker part of this confederacy may, to any extent, be wantonly and tyrannically violated, under colour of law, (the most grievous shape of oppression) by men neither interested in its destiny nor subject to its controul, without any means of redress being left it, except such as are inconsistent with all idea of order and government.[12]

These words purported one hundred and twenty years ago to be history; they read today much more like prophecy.

What is the standing today of the "enumerated powers" doctrine as a postulate of constitutional interpretation? Even so recently as 1939 the doctrine received the endorsement of a standard work on constitutional law in these words: "The courts in construing the scope of the grants of power to the several organs of the federal government by the federal Constitution do so on the assumption that the people of the United States intended to confer upon them only such powers as can be derived from the terms of the express grants of power made to them in that Constitution."[13]

In point of fact, the doctrine, when applied to Marshall's three "great, substantive and independent powers," that over external relations, the power to levy taxes and, *subaudi*, the power to expend the proceeds, and the power of commercial relations, had become a very shaky reliance. As to the first of these, indeed, it had been directly repudiated by the Court; and while as to the other two fields, it was still valid in a certain sense, its restrictive potentialities had, for reasons which will soon appear, become practically *nil*.

III

We turn now to the second of the above postulates. The question raised is whether it was the intention of the framers of the Constitution to apportion not only the powers but also the purposes of government between the two centers,

---

12. 2 *The Southern Review* 72–113, No. 1 (1828); 2 *Writings of Hugh Swinton Legaré* 102, 123–33 (1846).
13. Rottschaefer, *Handbook of American Constitutional Law* 11 (1939).

with the result of inhibiting the national government from attempting on a national scale the same ends as the states attempt on a local scale? In view of the latitudinarian language of the Preamble to the Constitution, an affirmative answer to this question might seem to encounter ineluctable difficulties. For all that, it has at times received countenance from the Court. Even in the pages of the *Federalist* can be discerned the beginnings of a controversy regarding the scope of Congress's taxing power which was still sufficiently vital 150 years later to claim the Court's deliberate attention, although the substance of victory had long since fallen to the pro-nationalist view.[14] In brief the question at issue was this: Was Congress entitled to levy and collect taxes to further objects not falling within its other powers to advance? Very early the question became dichotomized into two questions. First, was Congress entitled to lay and collect tariffs for any but revenue purposes; secondly, was it entitled to expend the proceeds from its taxes for any other purpose than to provision the government in the exercise of its other enumerated powers, or as Henry Clay once put the issue, was the power to spend the *cause* or merely the *consequence* of power?

The tariff aspect of the general question was, for instance, debated by Calhoun, speaking for the states rights view, and by Story in his *Commentaries* by way of answer to Calhoun.[15] Yet not until 1928 did the Court get around to affix the stamp of its approval on Story's argument, and then it did so only on historical grounds. Said Chief Justice Taft for the unanimous Court:

> It is enough to point out that the second act adopted by the Congress of the United States July 4, 1789 . . . contained the following recital:
>
> "Sec. 1. Whereas it is necessary for the support of government, for the discharge of the debts of the United States, and the encouragement and protection of manufactures, that duties be laid on goods, wares and merchandises imported:
>
> "Be it enacted, . . ."
>
> In this first Congress sat many members of the Constitutional Convention of 1787. This court has repeatedly laid down the principle that a contemporaneous legislative exposition of the Constitution when the founders of our government and framers of our Constitution were actively participating in public affairs, long acquiesced in, fixes the construction to be given its provisions. . . . The enactment and enforcement of a number of customs revenue laws drawn with a motive of maintaining a system of protection since the Revenue Law of 1789 are matters of history.[16]

In short, the constitutional case against the tariff went by default; and substantially the same is true also of the restrictive conception of the spending power. The classical statment of the broad theory of the spending power is that by Hamilton, in his Report on Manufactures in 1791. Reciting the "lay and collect taxes" clause of Article I, section 8 he says:

14. *The Federalist*, Nos. 30, 34, 41.
15. See *Commentaries* section 1090.
16. Hampton & Co. v. United States, 276 U.S. 394, 411, 48 Sup. Ct. 348, 353, 72 L. Ed. 624, 631 (1928).

The phrase is as comprehensive as any that could have been used, because it was not fit that the constitutional authority of the Union to appropriate its revenues should have been restricted within narrower limits than the "general welfare," and because this necessarily embraces a vast variety of particulars which are susceptible neither of specification nor of definition. It is therefore of necessity left to the discretion of the National Legislature to pronounce upon the objects which concern the general welfare, and for which, under that description, an appropriation of money is requisite and proper. And there seems to be no room for a doubt that whatever concerns the general interests of learning, of agriculture, of manufactures, and of commerce, are within the sphere of the national councils, *as far as regards an application of money.* [17]

Endorsed contemporaneously by Jefferson, stigmatized by him on further reflection, rebutted by Madison in his veto of the Bonus Bill in 1806, rejected by Monroe in the early years of his presidency, endorsed by him in his famous message of May 4, 1822, Hamilton's doctrine has since the Civil War pointed an ever-increasing trend in congressional fiscal policy. Yet even as recently as 1923 we find the Court industriously sidestepping the constitutional question and displaying considerable agility in doing so. I refer to a brace of suits in which Massachusetts and a citizen thereof, a Mrs. Frothingham, sought independently to challenge Congress's right to vote money in aid of expectant mothers. It was no function of a state, the Court instructed Massachusetts, to interpose in behalf of the constitutional rights of its citizens, who, being also citizens of the United States, could rely on getting adequate protection against the national government from the national courts. Thus, at long last was John C. Calhoun's doctrine of state interposition answered. Turning then to Mrs. Frothingham, the Court informed her that her interest as a taxpayer was much too trivial to entitle her to the interposition of the national courts. [18]

Twelve years later, however, in the A.A.A. case, the Court at last came to grips with the constitutional issue, which it decided in line with the Hamiltonian thesis. Said Justice Roberts for the Court:

> Since the foundation of the Nation sharp differences of opinion have persisted as to the true interpretation of the phrase, ["lay and collect taxes to . . . provide for . . . the general welfare"]. Madison asserted it amounted to no more than a reference to the other powers enumerated in the subsequent clauses of the same section; that, as the United States is a government of limited and enumerated powers, the grant of power to tax and spend for the general national welfare must be confined to the enumerated legislative fields committed to the Congress. In this view the phrase is mere tautology, for taxation and appropriation are or may be necessary incidents of the exercise of any of the enumerated legislative powers. Hamilton, on the other hand, maintained the clause confers a power separate and distinct from those later enumerated, is not restricted in meaning by the grant of them, and Congress consequently has a substantive power to tax and to appropriate, limited only by the requirement that it shall be exercised to provide for the general welfare of the United States. Each contention has had the support of those whose views are entitled to weight. This court has noticed the question, but has never found it necessary to decide which is the true

17. 4 *Works of Alexander Hamilton* 151 (Federal ed. 1904).
18. Massachusetts v. Mellon, 262 U.S. 447, 43 Sup. Ct. 597, 67 L. Ed. 1078 (1923).

construction. Mr. Justice Story, in his Commentaries, espouses the Hamiltonian position. We shall not review the writings of public men and commentators or discuss the legislative practice. Study of all these leads us to conclude that the reading advocated by Mr. Justice Story is the correct one. While, therefore, the power to tax is not unlimited, its confines are set in the clause which confers it, and not in those of § 8 which bestow and define the legislative powers of the Congress. It results that the power of Congress to authorize expenditure of public moneys for public purposes is not limited by the direct grants of legislative power found in the Constitution.[19]

In short, the Court once more ratified the history that congressional practice had made.

The theory that the enumerated powers may be validly exercised for certain limited purposes only was first passed upon in relation to the commerce power in 1808 under Jefferson's Embargo Act. The proposition offered the court—the United States District Court for Massachusetts—was that the power of Congress to regulate foreign commerce was only the power to adopt measures for its protection and advancement, whereas the embargo destroyed commerce. The court rejected the argument. Pointing to the clause of Article I, section 9, which interdicted a ban on the slave trade till 1808, the judge remarked: "It was perceived that, under the power of regulating commerce, Congress would be authorized to abridge it in favor of the great principles of humanity and justice."[20]

One hundred and ten years later the same argument was revived and revamped in opposition to the congressional embargo on interstate commerce in child-made goods, and this time it prevailed. The act, said the Court, was not a commercial regulation, but a usurpation of the reserved power of the states to protect the public health, safety, morals, and general welfare.[21] And when Congress next sought to use its taxing power against firms employing child labor, the Court, adopting the narrow purpose concept of the taxing power *ad hoc,* frustrated that attempt too.[22] We shall now see how this course of reasoning has since toppled to the gound along with other supporting canons of interpretation.

IV

Our third postulate is addressed particularly to this question: By what rule are collisions between the respective powers of the two centers of government supposed by the Constitution to be determined? In answer two texts of the Constitution itself compete for recognition, Article VI, clause 2, which reads as follows:

> This Constitution, and the laws of the United States which shall be made in pursuance thereof, and all treaties made, or which shall be made, under the authority of

19. United States v. Butler, 297 U.S. 1, 65, 56 Sup. Ct. 312, 319, 80 L. Ed. 477, 488 (1936).
20. United States v. The William, 28 Fed. Cas. No. 16, 700, at 421 (D. Mass. 1808).
21. Hammer v. Dagenhart, 247 U.S. 251, 38 Sup. Ct. 529, 62 L. Ed. 1101 (1918).
22. Bailey v. Drexel Furniture Co., 259 U.S. 20, 42 Sup. Ct. 449, 66 L. Ed. 817 (1922).

the United States, shall be the supreme law of the land; and the judges in every State shall be bound thereby, anything in the Constitution or laws of any State to the contrary notwithstanding.

and the Tenth Amendment, which says:

The powers not delegated to the United States by the Constitution, nor prohibited by it to the States, are reserved to the States respectively, or to the people.

It was quite plainly the intention of the Federal Convention that national laws, otherwise constitutional except for being in conflict with state laws, should invariably prevail over the latter;[23] or, as Madison later phrased the matter, state power should be "no ingredient of national power."[24] This was also Marshall's theory. Indeed, the principle of "national supremacy" was in his estimation the most fundamental axiom of constitutional interpretation touching the federal relationship, one even more vital to the Union and more unmistakably ordained by the constitutional document itself than the doctrine of "loose construction," loosely so-called by his critics.

"If," said he in McCulloch v. Maryland, "any one proposition could command the assent of mankind, one might expect it would be this—that the government of the Union, though limited in its powers, is supreme within its sphere of action." Nor did the Tenth Amendment affect the question. In omitting from it the word "expressly," its authors had—and apparently of deliberate purpose— left the question whether any particular power belonged to the general government "to depend on a fair construction of the whole instrument."[25] Counsel for Maryland, Luther Martin, agreed—the Tenth Amendment was "merely declaratory."[26]

Yet when, five years later the Court came to decide Gibbons v. Ogden,[27] in which the question was whether a New York created monopoly was compatible with legislation of Congress regulating the coasting trade, Marshall was confronted with a very different set of ideas by counsel for the local interest. "In argument," Marshall recites, "it had been contended that if a law, passed by a State in the exercise of its acknowledged sovereignty, comes into conflict with a law passed by Congress in pursuance of the Constitution, they affect the subject, and each other, like equal opposing powers." This contention Marshall answered as follows:

But the framers of our constitution foresaw this state of things, and provided for it, by declaring the supremacy not only of itself, but of the laws made in pursuance of it. The nullity of any act, inconsistent with the constitution is produced by the declaration

23. See 1 Farrand, *Records of the Federal Convention* 21–22 (1911).

24. 2 Annals of Congress col. 1891 (1790–91). See Corwin, *Commerce Power versus States Rights* 117–72 (1936).

25. 4 Wheat. 316, 405, 4 L. Ed. 579, 601 (U.S. 1819).

26. *Id.* at 374, 6 L. Ed. at 593.

27. 9 Wheat. 1, 6 L. Ed. 23 (U.S. 1824).

that the constitution is the supreme law. The appropriate application of that part of the clause which confers the same supremacy on laws and treaties, is to such acts of the State Legislatures as do not transcend their powers, but, though enacted in the execution of acknowledged State powers, interfere with, or are contrary to the laws of Congress made in pursuance of the constitution, or some treaty made under the authority of the United States. In every such case, the act of Congress, or the treaty, is supreme; and the law of the State, though enacted in the exercise of powers not controverted, must yield to it.[28]

Whence came the notion of national-state "equality," and what effect did it have on the Court's jurisprudence? The germ of it is to be found in the theory of the Constitution's origin developed in the Virginia and Kentucky Resolutions, that it was a compact of "sovereign" states, rather than an ordinance of "the people of America." The deduction from this premise that the national government and the states, both being "sovereign," faced each other as "equals" across the line defining their respective jurisdictions, was made by John Taylor of Caroline in his critique of the decision in McCulloch v. Maryland. But earlier, the Virginia Court of Appeals had contributed to Taylor's system of constitutional interpretation the notion that under the "supremacy" clause itself, the state judiciaries were the constitutionally designated agencies for the application of the principle of supremacy.[29] It followed that the Supreme Court no more than Congress was able to bind the "equal" states, nor could they on the other hand bind Congress or the Court.

The notion of national-state equality became in due course a part of the constitutional creed of the Taney Court, but stripped of its anarchic implications and reduced to the proportions of a single thread in a highly complicated fabric of constitutional exegesis. It was early in this period that the concept of the police power emerged. This, broadly considered, was simply what Taney termed "the power to govern men and things" defined from the point of view of the duty of the state to "promote the happiness and prosperity of the community"; more narrowly, it was a certain central core of this power, namely the power of the states to "provide for the public health, safety, and good order." Within this latter field at least, the powers reserved to the states by the Tenth Amendment were "sovereign" powers, "complete, unqualified, and exclusive." Yet this did not signify that the states, acting through either their legislatures or their courts, were the final judge of the scope of these "sovereign" powers. This was the function of the Supreme Court of the United States, which for this purpose was regarded by the Constitution as standing outside of and over both the national government and the states, and vested with authority to apportion impartially to each center its proper powers in accordance with the Constitution's intention. And the primary test whether this intention was fulfilled was whether

28. *Id.* at 210, 6 L. Ed. at 73.
29. See Hunter v. Martin, 4 Munf. 1, 11 (Va. 1814), *rev'd*, Martin v. Hunter's Lessee, 1 Wheat. 304, 4 L. Ed. 97 (U.S. 1816).

conflict between the two centers was avoided.[30] In Judge Cooley's words, "The laws of both [centers] operate within the same territory, but if in any particular case their provisions are in conflict, one or the other is void," that is, void apart from the conflict itself.[31]

Thus the principle of national supremacy came to be superseded by an unlimited discretion in the Supreme Court to designate this or that state power as comprising an independent limitation on national power. In only one area was the earlier principle recognized as still operative, and that was the field of interstate commercial regulation. This field, indeed, was not properly speaking a part of the "reserved powers" of the states at all; it belonged to Congress's enumerated powers. The states, however, might occupy it as to minor phases of commerce unless and until Congress chose to do so, in which case Article VI, paragraph 2, came into play and conflicting state legislation was superseded.[32]

While, as we have seen, the police power was defined in the first instance with the end in view of securing to the states a near monopoly of the right to realize the main *objectives* of government, the concept came later to embrace the further idea that certain *subject matters* were also segregated to the states and hence could not be reached by any valid exercise of national power. That production, and hence mining, agriculture, and manufacturing, and the employer-employee relationship in connection with these were among such subject matters was indeed one of the basic postulates of the Court's system of constitutional law in the era of laissez faire.[33] The decisions in both the first Child Labor case and the A.A.A. case were largely determined by this axiom; and as late as 1936, Justice Sutherland's opinion in the Bituminous Coal case gave it classic expression.[34] The question before the Court concerned the constitutionality of an attempt by Congress to govern hours and wages in the soft coal mines of the country. Said Justice Sutherland for the Court:

> In addition to what has just been said, the conclusive answer is that the evils are all local evils over which the federal government has no legislative control. The relation of employer and employee is a local relation. At common law, it is one of the domestic relations. The wages are paid for the doing of local work. Working conditions are obviously local conditions. The employees are not engaged in or about commerce, but exclusively in producing a commodity. And the controversies and evils, which it is the object of the act to regulate and minimize, are local controversies and evils affecting local work undertaken to accomplish that local result. Such effect as they may have upon commerce, however extensive it may be, is secondary and indirect. An increase in the greatness of the effect adds to its importance. It does not alter its character.[35]

---

30. On this system of constitutional interpretation, see especially New York v. Miln, 11 Pet. 102, 9 L. Ed. 648 (U.S. 1837); see also License Cases, 5 How. 504, 527–37, 573–74, 588, 613, 12 L. Ed. 256, 266–71, 287–88, 294, 305 (U.S. 1847) *passim.*

31. Cooley, *Principles of Constitutional Law* 152 (3d ed. 1898).

32. Cooley v. Board of Wardens, 12 How. 299, 13 L. Ed. 996 (U.S. 1851).

33. See Corwin, *Commerce Power versus States Rights* 175–209 (1936).

34. Carter v. Carter Coal Co., 298 U.S. 238, 56 Sup. Ct. 855, 80 L. Ed. 1160 (1936).

35. *Id.* at 308, 56 Sup. Ct. at 871, 80 L. Ed. at 1187.

This entire system of constitutional interpretation touching the federal system is today in ruins. It toppled in the Social Security Act cases and in N.L.R.B. v. Jones & Laughlin Steel Corporation, in which the Wagner Labor Act was sustained.[36] This was in 1937 while the "Old Court" was still in power. In 1941 in United States v. Darby,[37] the "New Court" merely performed a mopping-up operation. The Act of Congress involved was the Fair Labor Standards Act of 1938, which not only bans interstate commerce in goods produced under substandard conditions but makes their production a penal offense against the United States if they are "intended" for interstate or foreign commerce. Speaking for the unanimous Court, Chief Justice Stone went straight back to Marshall's opinions in McCulloch v. Maryland and Gibbons v. Ogden, extracting from the former his latitudinarian construction of the "necessary and proper" clause and from both cases his uncompromising application of the "supremacy" clause.[38]

Today neither the state police power nor the concept of federal equilibrium is any "ingredient of national legislative power," whether as respects subject matter to be governed, or the choice of objectives or of means for its exercise.

V

Lastly, we come to the question whether the two centers of government ought to be regarded as standing in a competitive or cooperative relation to each other. The question first emerged at the executive and judicial levels. In Article VI, paragraph 3, the requirement is laid down that members of the state legislatures, their executive and judicial officers shall take an oath, or make affirmation, to support the Constitution, thus testifying, as Hamilton points out in *Federalist* 27, to the expectation that these functionaries would be "incorporated into the operations of the national government," in the exercise of its constitutional powers. In much early legislation, furthermore, this expectation was realized. The Judiciary Act of 1789 left the state courts in exclusive possession of some categories of national jurisdiction and shared some others with it. The Act of 1793 entrusted the rendition of fugitive slaves in part to national officials and in part to state officials, and the rendition of fugitives from justice from one state to another exclusively to the state executives. Certain later acts empowered state courts to entertain criminal prosecutions for forging paper of the Bank of the United States and for counterfeiting coin of the United States; while still others conferred on state judges authority to admit aliens to national citizenship and provided penalties in case such judges should utter false certificates of naturalization—provisions which are still on the statute books.[39]

36. 301 U.S. 1, 57 Sup. Ct. 615, 81 L. Ed. 893 (1937).
37. 312 U.S. 100, 61 Sup. Ct. 451, 85 L. Ed. 609 (1941).
38. *Id.* See also United States v. Carolene Products Co., 304 U.S. 144, 58 Sup. Ct. 778, 82 L. Ed. 1234 (1938); Mulford v. Smith, 307 U.S. 38, 59 Sup. Ct. 648, 83 L. Ed. 1092 (1939).
39. For references, see Corwin, *Court over Constitution* 135–36 and notes (1938).

The subsequent rise, however, of the states rights sentiment presently overcast this point of view with heavy clouds of doubt. From the nationalist angle Marshall stigmatized the efforts of Virginia and those who thought her way to "confederatize the Union"; and asserting in McCulloch v. Maryland the administrative independence of the national government, he there laid down a sweeping rule prohibiting the states from taxing even to the slightest extent national instrumentalities on their operations. "The power to tax is the power to destroy," said he; and whatever a state may do at all it may do to the utmost extent.[40]

But when a few years later the Taney Court took over, the shoe was on the other foot. In 1842, the state of Pennsylvania was sustained by the Court, speaking by Marshall's apostle Story, in refusing to permit its magistrates to aid in enforcing the fugitive slave provisions of the Act of 1793. Said Story:

> . . . the national government, in the absence of all positive provisions to the contrary, is bound through its own proper departments, legislative, executive, or judiciary, as the case may require, to carry into effect all the rights and duties imposed upon it by the Constitution.[41]

And in Kentucky v. Dennison, decided on the eve of the Civil War, the "duty" imposed by this same act on state governors to render up fugitives from justice on the demand of the executives of sister states, was watered down to a judicially unenforcible "moral duty." Said the chief justice: ". . . we think it clear, that the Federal Government, under the Constitution, has no power to impose on a State officer, as such, any duty whatever, and compel him to perform it; . . ."[42]

Nor was even this the end, for as late as 1871 the Court laid down the converse of Marshall's doctrine in McCulloch v. Maryland, holding that, since the states enjoyed equal constitutional status with the national government, what was sauce for the one was sauce for the other too, and that therefore a national income tax could not be constitutionally applied to state official salaries.[43]

The doctrine of tax exemption was the climactic expression of the competitive theory of federalism, and is today largely moribund in consequence of the emergence of the *cooperative* conception. According to this conception, the national government and the states are mutually complementary parts of a *single* governmental mechanism all of whose powers are intended to realize the current purposes of government according to their applicability to the problem in hand. It is thus closely intertwined with the multiple-purpose conception of national power and with recent enlarged theories of the function of government generally. Here we are principally interested in two forms of joint action by the national

40. See 4 Wheat. 316, 427–31, 4 L. Ed. 579, 606–7 (U.S. 1819); Brown v. Maryland, 12 Wheat. 419, 439, 6 L. Ed. 678, 685 (U.S. 1827).

41. Prigg v. Commonwealth of Pennsylvania, 16 Peters 539, 616, 10 L. Ed. 1060, 1089 (U.S. 1842).

42. 24 How. 66, 107, 16 L. Ed. 717, 729 (U.S. 1861).

43. Collector v. Day, 11 Wall. 113, 20 L. Ed. 122 (U.S. 1871).

government and the states which have developed within recent years, primarily through the *legislative* powers of the two centers.

Thus in the first place the national government has brought its augmented powers over interstate commerce and communications to the support of local policies of the states in the exercise of their reserved powers. By the doctrine that Congress's power to regulate "commerce among the States" is "exclusive," a state is frequently unable to stop the flow of commerce from sister states even when it threatens to undermine local legislation. In consequence Congress has within recent years come to the assistance of the police powers of the states by making certain crimes against them, like theft, racketeering, kidnapping, crimes also against the national government whenever the offender extends his activities beyond state boundary lines.[44]

Justifying such legislation, the Court has said:

> Our dual form of government has its perplexities, state and Nation having different spheres of jurisdiction . . . but it must be kept in mind that we are one people; and the powers reserved to the states and those conferred on the nations {*sic*; nation} are adapted to be exercised, whether independently or concurrently, to promote the general welfare, material and moral.[45]

It is true that in the Child Labor case of 1918 this postulate of constitutional interpretation seemed to have been discarded, but the logic of United States v. Darby, restores it in full force.

Secondly, the national government has held out inducements, primarily of a pecuniary kind, to the states—the so-called "grants-in-aid"—to use their reserved powers to support certain objectives of national policy in the field of expenditure. In other words, the greater financial strength of the national government is joined to the wider coercive powers of the states. Thus since 1911, Congress has voted money to subsidize forest protection, education in agricultural and industrial subjects and in home economics, vocational rehabilitation and education, the maintenance of nautical schools, experimentation in reforestation, and highway construction in the states; in return for which cooperating states have appropriated equal sums for the same purposes, and have brought their further powers to the support thereof along lines laid down by Congress.[46]

The culmination of this type of national-state cooperation to date, however, is reached in the Social Security Act of August 14, 1935. The act brings the national tax-spending power to the support of such states as desire to cooperate in the maintenance of old-age pensions, unemployment insurance, maternal welfare work, vocational rehabilitation, and public health work, and in financial assistance to impoverished old age, dependent children, and the blind. Such legislation is, as we have seen, within the national taxing-spending power. What, however, of the objection that it "coerced" complying states into "abdicating"

---

44. For references, see Corwin, *Court over Constitution* 148–50 and notes (1938).
45. Hoke v. United States, 227 U.S. 308, 322, 33 Sup. Ct. 281, 284, 57 L. Ed. 523, 527 (1913).
46. Corwin, *op. cit.* above note 44, at 157–63.

their powers? Speaking to this point in the Social Security Act cases, the Court has said: "The . . . contention confuses motive with coercion. . . . To hold that motive or temptation is equivalent to coercion is to plunge the law in endless difficulties."[47] And again: "The United States and the state of Alabama are not alien governments. They co-exist within the same territory. Unemployment is their common concern. Together the two statutes before us [the Act of Congress and the Alabama Act] embody a cooperative legislative effort by state and national governments, for carrying out a public purpose common to both, which neither could fully achieve without the cooperation of the other. The Constitution does not prohibit such cooperation."[48]

It has been argued, to be sure, that the cooperative conception of the federal relationship, especially as it is realized in the policy of the "grants-in-aid," tends to break down state initiative and to devitalize state policies. Actually, its effect has often been the contrary, and for the reason pointed out by Justice Cardozo in Helvering v. Davis,[49] also decided in 1937; namely, that the states, competing as they do with one another to attract investors, have not been able to embark separately upon expensive programs of relief and social insurance.

The other great objection to cooperative federalism is more difficult to meet, if indeed it can be met. This is, that "cooperative federalism" spells further aggrandizement of national power. Unquestionably it does, for when two cooperate it is the stronger member of the combination who calls the tunes. Resting as it does primarily on the superior fiscal resources of the national government, cooperative federalism has been, to date, a short expression for a constantly increasing concentration of power at Washington in the instigation and supervision of local policies.

VI

But the story of American federalism may also be surveyed from the angle of the diverse interests which the federal "contrivance"—to use Dicey's apt word—has served. Federalism's first achievement was to enable the American people to secure the benefits of national union without imperilling their republican institutions. In a passage in his *Spirit of the Laws* which Hamilton quotes in *The Federalist,* Montesquieu had anticipated this possibility in general terms. He said:

It is very probable that mankind would have been obliged, at length, to live constantly under the government of a single person, had they not contrived a kind of

47. Steward Machine Co. v. Davis, 301 U.S. 548, 589, 57 Sup. Ct. 883, 892, 81 L. Ed. 1279, 1292 (1937).
48. Carmichael v. Southern Coal & Coke Co., 301 U.S. 495, 526, 57 Sup. Ct. 868, 880, 81 L. Ed. 1245, 1262 (1937).
49. 301 U.S. 619, 57 Sup. Ct. 904, 81 L. Ed. 1307 (1937).

constitution, that has all the internal advantages of a republican, together with the external force of a monarchical government. I mean a Confederate Republic.[50]

In fact, the founders of the American federal system for the first time in history ranged the power of a potentially great state on the side of institutions which had hitherto been confined to small states. Even the republicanism of Rome had stopped at the Eternal City's walls.

Then in the century following, American federalism served the great enterprise of appropriating the North American continent to Western civilization. For one of the greatest lures to the westward movement of population was the possibility which federalism held out to the advancing settlers of establishing their own undictated political institutions, and endowing them with generous powers of government for local use. Federalism thus became the instrument of a new, *a democratic, imperialism,* one extending over an "Empire of liberty," in Jefferson's striking phrase.

Then, about 1890, just as the frontier was disappearing from the map, federalism became, through judicial review, an instrument of the current laissez-faire conception of the function of government and a force promoting the rise of big business. Adopting the theory that the reason why Congress had been given the power to regulate "commerce among the several states" was to prevent the states from doing so, rather than to enable the national government to pursue social policies of its own through exerting a positive control over commerce, the Court at one time created a realm of no-power, "a twilight zone," "a no-man's land" in which corporate enterprise was free to roam largely unchecked. While the economic unification of the nation was undoubtedly aided by this type of constitutional law, the benefit was handsomely paid for in the social detriments which attended it, as became clear when the Great Depression descended on the country.

Finally, by the constitutional revolution which once went by the name of the "New Deal" but now wears the label "Fair Deal," American federalism has been converted into an instrument for the achievement of peace abroad and economic security for "the common man" at home. In the process of remolding the federal system for these purposes, however, the instrument has been overwhelmed and submerged in the objectives sought, so that today the question faces us whether the constituent states of the system can be saved for any useful purpose, and thereby saved as the vital cells that they have been heretofore of democratic sentiment, impulse, and action.

And it was probably with some such doubt in mind that Justice Frankfurter wrote a few years ago, in an opinion for the Court:

> The interpenetrations of modern society have not wiped out state lines. It is not for us to make inroads upon our federal system either by indifference to its maintenance or

50. *The Federalist,* No. 9 at 48 (Lodge ed. 1888).

excessive regard for the unifying forces of modern technology. Scholastic reasoning may prove that no activity is isolated within the boundaries of a single State, but that cannot justify absorption of legislative power by the United States over every activity.[51]

These be brave words. Are they likely to determine the course of future history any more than Madison's similar utterance—130 years ago—has done to date?

51. Polish National Alliance v. NLRB, 322 U.S. 643, 650, 64 Sup. Ct. 1196, 1200, 86 L. Ed. 1509, 1516 (1944). The following striking contrast between the United States of 1789 and the United States of 1942 is from the pen of Professor William Anderson in "Federalism—Then and Now," 16 *State Government* 107–12 (May, 1943):

Then a small area, with a small and sparse population, mainly agricultural and poor. *Now* one of the world's great nations in both area and population, largely urban and highly industrial, with tremendous national wealth.

Then largely a debtor people and an exporter of raw materials. *Now* a great creditor nation and large exporter of manufactured as well as agricultural goods.

Then meager and slow transportation facilities, and even poorer provisions for communication. *Now* an equipment of railroads, steamship lines, highways, trucks and buses, air transport, and communications of all kinds unexcelled by any nation and undreamed of in the past.

Then state citizenship, state and local loyalties, interstate suspicions and tariffs, localized business, and considerable internal disunity. *Now* a nation, with national citizenship, primarily national loyalties, a nationwide free market, and nationally organized business, agriculture, labor, professions, press, and political parties.

Then an upstart and divided people, an international weakling, threatened from north and south, with very poor defense arrangements, and looking out over the Atlantic at an essentially hostile world. *Now* a great world power, an international leader, with a powerful army and navy, and with strong friends and interests (as well as enemies) across both Atlantic and Pacific.

Then inactive, negative, laissez-faire government with very few functions, and with only business leaders favoring a national government, and they desiring only to give it enough vigor to protect commerce, provide a nationwide free home market, and a sound currency and banking system. *Now* active, positive, collectivist government, especially at the national level, rendering many services with the support of powerful labor and agricultural elements, while many business leaders have reversed their position.

Then local law enforcement with state protection of the liberties guaranteed in bills of rights. *Now* increasing national law enforcement and national protection of civil liberties even against state and local action.

Then practically no employees of the national government and very few state and local employees. *Now* a national civil service of normally over a million persons reaching into every county of the country, plus extensive state and local civil services.

Then small public budgets at all levels. *Now* public budgets and expenditures, especially for the national government, that reach astronomical figures.

Then (before 1789) no national taxes at all for decades after 1789, only customs and excise taxes on a very limited scale, with state and local governments relying almost entirely on direct property taxes. *Now* tremendously increased and diversified taxes at both national and state levels, with a national government rising swiftly to a dominating position with respect to all taxes except those directly on property.

Then (before 1788) state grants to the Congress of the United States for defense and debt purposes. *Now* grants-in-aid by the national government to the states in increasing amounts and with steadily tightening national controls over state action.

Table of Cases

Index

263

Library of Congress Cataloging-in-Publication Data
(Revised for vol. 3)

Corwin, Edward Samuel, 1878–1963.
    Corwin on the Constitution.

    Includes bibliographical references and indexes.
    Contents: v. 1. The foundations of American
constitutional and political thought, the powers of
Congress, and the President's power of removal—v. 2.
The judiciary—v. 3. On liberty against government.
        1. United States—Constitutional history—Collected
works.   2. United States—Politics and government—
Collected works.   I. Loss, Richard.   II. Title.
JA38.C67   1981   320.973   80-69823
ISBN 0-8014-1381-8 (v. l)